CISTERCIAN STUDIES SERIES: NUMBER TWO-HUNDRED NINETEEN

Witness to Holiness
Abba Daniel of Scetis

D1448848

CISTERCIAN STUDIES SERIES: NUMBER TWO-HUNDRED NINETEEN

Witness To Holiness
Abba Daniel Of Scetis

TRANSLATIONS OF THE GREEK, COPTIC, ETHIOPIC, SYRIAC,
ARMENIAN, LATIN, OLD CHURCH SLAVONIC,
AND ARABIC ACCOUNTS

Edited, with an Introduction,
by
Tim Vivian

Translations by

Sebastian P. Brock • Vitaly Dudkin • Jehanne Gheith
• Rowan A. Greer • Michael Kleiner • Maged S.A. Mikhail
• Jeffrey Burton Russell • Mark Swanson • Tim Vivian
• John Wortley

With the Assistance of

Apostolos N. Athanassakis,
Mark Moussa, and Hany N. Takla

Cistercian Publications
Kalamazoo, Michigan

The work of Cistercian Publications is made possible in part
by support from
Western Michigan University
to the Institute of Cistercian Studies

Library of Congress Cataloging-in-Publication Data

Witness to holiness : Abba Daniel of Scetis / edited, with an
introduction by Tim Vivian.
    p. cm. — (Cistercian studies series ; no. 219)
Includes bibliographical references and index.
ISBN 978-0-87907-419-7
  1. Daniel, of Sketis, Saint, 6th. cent.   2. Holiness—Christianity.
I. Vivian, Tim.   II. Title.

BX4705.D253W58 2008
270.2092—dc22
[B]   2008003589

Printed in the United States of America.

To Rozanne Elder
Editorial Director, Cistercian Publications

Nec lingua valet dicere,
Nec littera exprimere
Expertus potest credere
Quid sit Iesum diligere

Saint Bernard of Clairvaux
De nomine Iesu, 17-20

Table of Contents

Translators

Sebastian Brock, Emeritus Reader in Syriac Studies in the University of Oxford, is the author of many books, including *Syriac Fathers on Prayer and the Spiritual Life*, *Hymns on Paradise*, *Holy Women of the Syrian Orient* (with Susan Ashbrook Harvey), and *The Luminous Eye: The Spiritual World Vision of Saint Ephrem*.

Vitaly Dudkin, currently the Rector of Holy Trinity Orthodox Church in New Salem, Pennsylvania, has more than fifty publications in the field of Philosophy of Religion and has taught in various institutions in both Russia and the United States, including Moscow University and Saint Tikhon's Orthodox Seminary. He has studied over ten years at the Philosophy and Religious Studies Department, Russian Academy of Sciences.

Jehanne M. Gheith is Associate Professor and Chair of the Slavic and Eurasian Studies Department at Duke University, where she co-directs International Comparative Studies. Her current project, 'A Dog Named Stalin: Memory, Trauma, and the Gulag', is based on her interviews with Gulag survivors. An article on Gulag survivors' non-narrative responses to catastrophic loss will shortly appear in the journal *Mortality*. She also co-facilitates bereavement groups and is pursuing master's degrees in social work and divinity to explore connections between bereavement and narration.

Rowan A. Greer is a priest of the Episcopal Church and Professor of Anglican Studies Emeritus at the Yale Divinity School, where he taught from 1966 until 1997. His latest books, published by Crossroad, are *Christian Hope and Christian Life* and *Anglican Approaches to Scripture*.

Michael Kleiner studied Middle Eastern and Northeast African History at the Universities of Freiburg-im-Breisgau and Hamburg and has made Ethiopian History his field of specialization. He has been a member of the *Encyclopaedia Aethiopica* editorial team and has held academic positions at the Universities of Hamburg and Marburg.

Jeffrey Burton Russell, Emeritus Professor of History at the University of California at Santa Barbara, is the author of nineteen books on the history of Christianity, including two books on the history of christian ideas of heaven: *A History of Heaven* (1997) and *Paradise Mislaid* (2006).

Mark N. Swanson is the Harold S. Vogelaar Professor of Christian-Muslim Studies and Interfaith Relations at the Lutheran School of Theology at Chicago. With Emmanouela Grypeou and David Thomas he co-edited *The Encounter of Eastern Christianity with Early Islam* (Brill 2006); his book on *The Coptic Papacy in Islamic Egypt* is forthcoming from the American University in Cairo Press.

Tim Vivian, Assistant Professor of Religious Studies at California State University, Bakersfield, is the author of numerous books and articles on early christian monasticism, including *The Life of Antony* (with Apostolos N. Athanassakis) and *Words to Live By: Journeys in Ancient and Modern Egyptian Monasticism* (both Cistercian Publications).

John Wortley is Emeritus Professor of History at the University of Manitoba. For Cistercian Publications he has translated *The Spiritual Meadow* of John Moschus and *The Tales of Paul of Monembasia*. His translation of John Skylitzes' *Synopsis Historiarum* is in press and his edition of the text and translation of the 'Anonymous' *Apophthegmata Patrum* (alias 'Nau') is in preparation.

Saint Seraphim of Sarov, when asked what it was
that made some people remain sinners and never make progress
while others were becoming saints and living in God, answered:
'Only determination'.

Metropolitan Anthony Bloom, *Living Prayer*

It is not from ourselves that we will learn to be better than we are.

Wendell Berry, 'A Native Hill'

Preface

THIS VOLUME has been a long time gestating. I first set out to translate the greek texts pertaining to Abba Daniel of Scetis but quickly discovered that material about Daniel existed in many other languages. I then decided, perhaps a bit foolhardily, to gather together Daniel's extended and far-flung family—Greek, Coptic, Ethiopic, Syriac, Armenian, Latin, Slavonic, and Arabic—under one roof.

That decision necessitated bringing in other scholars as translators. When the project first began, John Wortley very unselfishly turned over to me his translations and notes of the greek text. I have consulted his translation throughout, using it to improve my own, and have incorporated many of his notes. I owe him great thanks for his generosity and help. I wish to thank the following additional translators for their efforts: Sebastian P. Brock (Syriac), Vitaly Dudkin (Slavonic), Jehanne Gheith (Slavonic), Rowan A. Greer (Syriac), Michael Kleiner (Ethiopic), Maged S.A. Mikhail (Coptic), Jeffrey Burton Russell (Latin), and Mark Swanson (Arabic). Michael Kleiner, in particular, was unstinting in his efforts on the long and somewhat arduous ethiopic chapter.

As I completed this volume, I became aware that Britt Dahlman was working on a doctoral dissertation on Daniel at Uppsala University in Sweden. We exchanged several e-mails about Abba Daniel and the progress of our work. I wish to thank Dr Dahlman for supplying me with the greek text from her then unpublished dissertation. That dissertation has now been published: *Saint Daniel of Sketis: A Group of Hagiographic Texts*. Acta Universitatis Upsaliensis. Studia Byzantina Upsaliensia 10. Uppsala: Uppsala University Press, 2007. I wish to thank her for sending me a copy. She and I have come to many similar independent conclusions about Abba Daniel and the Daniel dossier while, naturally, some of our emphases vary. I am especially grateful to her for corroborating or challenging many of my conclusions. I consulted her translation of the greek text: it helped me catch a couple of my mistakes and I have adopted a few of her phrasings. Dr Dahlman's work on the textual tradition has been much more extensive than my own, and she restricts herself to eight greek texts, on which she also supplies a helpful brief Commentary. This volume differs from hers in that it also offers versions of the greek stories from various *synaxaria* (Chapter One) and, more importantly, chapters on the coptic, ethiopic, syriac, armenian, latin, slavonic, and arabic versions. Wherever appropriate, I have endeavored to supply references to Dr Dahlman's book.

I wish also to thank Apostolos N. Athanassakis, Mark Moussa, and Hany N. Takla for their assistance, and Getachew Haile for his early help with matters Ethiopic.

I wish to thank Armida Byler, one of my students in Religious Studies, for her help in preparing the Index.

Finally, my deep thanks to Rozanne Elder of Cistercian Publications, to whom this volume is dedicated, for guiding a long and sometimes taxing manuscript through to publication and for her steady encouragement and support over the years in getting a number of my books through the press.

Portions of the Introduction of this volume I have given as papers: 'Abba Daniel of Scetis', at The Second Saint Shenouda Society the Archimandrite Coptic Conference, University of California at Los Angeles, 22 July 2000; 'Figures in the Carpet: Macarius the Great, Isaiah of Scetis, Daniel of Scetis, and Monastic Spirituality in the Wadi al-Natrun (Scetis) from the Fourth to the Sixth Century', at the Wadi al-Natrun Symposium, 31 January-5 February 2002, Saint Pshoi Monastery, Egypt. A revised version of these talks—a much abbreviated portion of the Introduction to this volume—appeared in *Coptica* 2.1 (2003) 69–105 and, revised again, in *American Benedictine Review* 56:2 (June 2005) 117–151. I wish to thank the editors of these journals, Maged S. A. Mikhail and Terrence Kardong, respectively, for permission to reprint.

August 2007   T.V.
California State University Bakersfield

Abbreviations

AB	*Analecta Bollandiana*
AP	Apophthegmata Patrum
Ar./Arab	Arabic
Arm	Armenian
Arm 1, *etc.*	Daniel stories in Armenian. Chapter Five
BDAG	Friedrich Blass and Albert Debrunner, rev. W. F. Arndt, F. W. Gingrich, and F. W. Danker, *A Greek-English Lexicon of the New Testament and Other Early Christian Literature*, 3rd ed. Chicago-London: University of Chicago Press, 2001
BHG	Bibliotheca Hagiographica Graeca
BHO	Bibliotheca Hagiographica Orientalis
BN	Bibliothèque Nationale, Paris
CE	*The Coptic Encyclopedia,* ed. Aziz S. Atiya. New York: Macmillan, 1991
Clugnet	Léon Clugnet, 'Vie et Récits de L'Abbé Daniel, de Scété', *Revue de l'Orient Chrétien* 5 (1900) 49-73, 254-271, 370-391; *Revue de l'Orient Chrétien* 6 (1901) 56-87
Copt	Coptic
Crum	Crum, W. E. *A Coptic Dictionary*. Oxford: Clarendon, 1979

CS	Cistercian Studies Series
CSCO	Corpus scriptorum christianorum orientalium
Dahlman	Britt Dahlman, *Saint Daniel of Sketis: A Group of Hagiographic Texts*. Acta Universitatis Upsaliensis, Studia Byzantina Upsaliensia 10. Lund: Wallin & Dalholm, 2007
Eth	Ethiopic
Evelyn White	Hugh G. Evelyn White, *The Monasteries of the Wadi 'N Natrun*, volume 2, *The History of the Monasteries of Nitria and Scetis*. Rpt New York: Arno Press, 1973
f/ff	Folio/folios
Gk	Greek
Goldschmidt–Esteves Pereira	Goldschmidt, Lazarus and F.M. Esteves Pereira. *Vida do Abba Daniel do Mosteiro de Sceté: Versão Ethiopica*. Lisbon: Imprensa Nacional, 1897
Gr	Greek
Guidi	Guidi, Ignazio. 'Corrections de quelques passages du texte éthiopien', *Revue de l'Orient Chrétien* 6: 54–56
HM	*The Lives of the Desert Fathers: The* Historia Monachorum in Aegypto, CS 34, trans. Russell Norman. Kalamazoo: Cistercian Publications, 1980
JECS	*Journal of Early Christian Studies*
Lampe	W. G. H. Lampe, *A Patristic Greek Lexicon*. Oxford: Clarendon, 1961
Lat	Latin
Lat 1, *etc.*	See Chapter Six

Leslau	Leslau, Wolf. *Comparative Dictionary of Geᶜez (Classical Ethiopic)*. Wiesbaden: Harrassowitz, 1987
LSJ	Henry George Liddell and Robert Scott, rev. by Henry Stuart Jones, *A Greek-English Lexicon*. Oxford: Clarendon, 1968
LXX	Septuagint (Greek) version of the Bible
MS /MSS	manuscript/manuscripts
n. / nn.	Note / notes
NT	New Testament
OT	Old Testament
Paris	Bibliothèque Nationale, Paris
PG	*Patrologia Graeca*
PO	*Patrologia Orientalis*
ROC	*Revue de l'Orient Chrétien*
Slav	Slavonic
Syr	Syriac
Syr 1, *etc.*	Syriac pieces, Chapter Four
Var	Variant
Vat	Vatican (library)
Ward	Benedicta Ward, trans., *The Sayings of the Desert Fathers*. CS 59. Kalamazoo: Cistercian Publications, 1975; rev. ed., 1984

Introduction

Tell all the truth, but tell it slant.

—Emily Dickinson

HOLINESS

THE AMERICAN FARMER and writer Wendell Berry has trenchantly observed that 'It is impossible to prefigure the salvation of the world in the same language by which the world has been dismembered and defaced'.[1] One defacing of the modern Western world has been the amputation of holiness from our common vocabulary and, more importantly, our lived ethic. When does one hear about holiness even from the pulpit, much less from the secular pulpits of government, education, science, and industry? It was not always so. Holiness once mattered. 'Be holy, for I am holy', says the Lord.[2] But what is holiness? More importantly, what characteristics does a holy person have? In other words, how does a holy person concretely manifest holiness in his or her life? How does such a person prefigure the world's salvation?

Jesus, we may be surprised to learn, does not explicitly define holiness (in Greek: *hagiōsunē, hosiotēs*) or its characteristics, although that great neo-Mosaic compendium 'the Sermon on the Mount' (Mt 5) might be better titled the 'Sermon on Holiness'. What does early monastic spirituality, the lineal descendant of Jesus' desert experiences, have to say about holiness? Nor do the *Apophthegmata*, or *Sayings,* of the desert fathers and mothers explicitly define holiness, although one could entitle this seminal monastic collection 'The Book of Holiness': most—perhaps all—of its sayings are concerned with what constitutes holy behavior.[3]

The early monastic mothers and fathers (fourth to sixth centuries) often spoke in terms of 'virtues'—another 'defaced' word in the modern

1

world—and these virtues, taken singly or together, can serve as lexicon, map, and lived territory of holiness.[4] Wendell Berry understands how the virtues contribute to holiness. Virtues 'are good', he says, 'not because they have been highly recommended but because they are necessary; they make for unity and harmony'.[5] Evagrius of Pontus, the first great monastic systematic theologian, is known partly for his list of Eight Evil Thoughts, the precursors to the medieval Seven Deadly Sins, which at first seem to focus on *dis*harmony. But Evagrius is less well known for the lengthier antidotes or virtues that he supplies immediately afterwards for these evil thoughts: these point towards harmony.[6] The virtues—or Virtues—were in fact so important to monks at Bawit in Middle Egypt in late antiquity that they personified them and painted them in medallions on a wall in their monastery, giving them a 'patron saint', Ama Sibylla.[7] The Virtues were variously enumerated, either 10, 11, or 12.[8] Although the names of some of the Virtues surrounding Ama Sibylla at Bawit have been effaced over the centuries, the ones that survive are Faith, Hope, Humility, Chastity, Gentleness, Grace, and Patience.

Paul of Tamma, an egyptian monk of late antiquity, offers a lively, and somewhat surprising, image of the Virtues: 'And the Holy Spirit will illumine all your members, and the twelve Virtues will dance in the midst of your soul, and the Cherubim and Seraphim will shelter you beneath their wings'.[9] Another early monk, Stephen of Thebes, with a different metaphor names eleven 'powers' or virtues:

> Sitting in your cell, do not act like it is a tomb but rather behave like it is a banquet room filled with gold that has guards protecting it night and day. The 'guards' are the powers of God that protect your spirit, that is, knowledge and faith and patience and abstinence, sincerity and innocence, purity and chastity, love, concord, and truth.[10]

In a saying attributed to John the Little and, in the coptic tradition, to Macarius the Great, the abba gives one of the longest extant lists of holy attributes as he exhorts his disciple to 'practice every virtue and every commandment of God'. John (or Macarius) makes these attributes, importantly, part of monastic *praxis*; he instructs the monk 'when you get up in the morning each day, make it the beginning of your life as a monk'. He then goes on to detail this 'beginning':

. . . fearfully practice perseverance and patience; demonstrate a love of God and a love of people with a humble heart and bodily humility, with mourning and the distress of being confined in prison, with prayers and supplications and groans, with purity of tongue while humbly guarding your eyes, without anger, in peace, without returning evil to an evildoer, without passing judgement on those in need, without thinking of yourself in anything, placing yourself below every creature; with renunciation of material things and fleshly things, with the struggle of the cross, with spiritual poverty, with good free will and bodily asceticism, with fasting and repentance and tears, with the combat war brings and, returning from imprisonment, with pure counsel and the tasting of good goodness, quietly at midday; with manual work, with vigils, with numerous prayers, with hunger and thirst, with frost and nakedness and afflictions and the acquisition of your tomb as though you had already been placed in it, placing your death near you day after day, lost in the deserts and mountains and holes of the earth' [see Heb 11:38].[11]

A vital assumption of all the monastic sayings is that holiness and the embodying of virtues are not the cordoned off sanctuary of a privileged few, but can be manifested by anyone. We should not, however, be too easily egalitarian here. Another assumption of many of the early monastic sayings is that their interlocutor is a disciple, a seeker, a person who has left 'the world'—that is, the world's disordered values—and is out in the desert, where he prompts the recorded saying by asking how he may be saved. As Arsenius bluntly puts it, the virtues are acquired by hard work.[12]

Holiness gradually came to be seen more and more in the *person* of the holy man (and, more rarely it seems, holy woman).[13] Eventually, holiness was thought to reside less in the holy person and more in his or her relics.[14] Even in the earliest period of monasticism, however, holiness was often regarded, especially by outsiders, as the special provenance of the monks; hence the onslaught of pilgrims into the desert in the fourth century, both spiritual tourists and authentic seekers.[15] Abba Daniel of Scetis, sixth-century priest and monastic superior (*hēgoumenos*) of Scetis (modern Wadi al-Natrun, northwest of Cairo),[16] was both a holy man *and* a witness to holiness.[17] The collection of tales surrounding his name offers the modern reader an important view of one perception of holiness in late antique Egypt. The understanding of holiness in this collection is neither all-encompassing nor definitive. But the dossier offers a different and unusual slant on holiness, one that may cause us to adjust our perceptions of holiness in late antiquity. It may even lead us to ponder the etiolated holiness of our own day.

THE DANIEL DOSSIER[18]

Material about Abba Daniel of Scetis, written originally in Greek, has survived in numerous manuscripts, some of which can perhaps be dated as early as the seventh century in a multitude of languages translated in this volume: Greek (Chapter One), Coptic (Chapter Two), Ethiopic (Chapter Three), Syriac (Chapter Four), Armenian (Chapter Five), Latin (Chapter Six), Old Church Slavonic (Chapter Seven), Arabic (Chapter Eight), and Georgian.[19] Paul Van Cauwenbergh characterized the collection, a bit uncharitably, as 'a heap of anecdotes without cohesion'.[20] He also called the stories the '*Gestes*' of Daniel—that is, the Abba's deeds, heroic achievements, and exploits.[21] This term, however, even if stripped of its medieval connotations of chivalric knights and fair ladies, unfairly pigeonholes Daniel because it plays to our preconceptions and prejudices about hagiography; in fact, Daniel's lack of exploits and heroic achievements actually redefines his status as holy man.[22]

Offering a typical bifurcation of hagiography and history, Gérard Garitte identified the Daniel collection as 'having all the characteristics of edifying fables', while commenting that 'it is impossible to see if they contain any historical elements'.[23] Max Bonnet, more positively, termed the stories about Abba Daniel 'certain adventures about a wide variety of personages' which make the collection 'singularly interesting and instructive'. He then went on to suggest that the dossier represents 'one of the most curious manifestations of eastern Christianity' in late antiquity. Obviously taken with the dossier, Bonnet went on to add (using language usually lacking in modern scholarship) that the collection is 'precious' and 'engaging' and 'has preserved a naiveté and sincerity that are not without their charms'.[24]

More recently, Sebastian Brock has well captured the scholarly ambivalence about these stories, in whatever language they appear: 'For the most part these narratives take the form of uplifting tales, and their historical value is probably minimal, although it is likely that at least some of the persons who feature in them existed in the flesh'.[25] I am more optimistic about the historical value of these stories and the historicity of at least some of the characters and events, and will consider these subjects below. I also wish to suggest that these tales have value beyond their historicity—or lack thereof. They reflect a certain spiritual angle of vision and point us towards the human ability to bear witness to, and perform acts of, holiness—in whatever unsuspected forms holiness takes.

Editions of many of the greek, coptic, syriac, and ethiopic texts were published late in the nineteenth or early in the twentieth century: the greek was edited by Léon Clugnet (1900–1901),[26] and Britt Dahlman offered a new text in 2007;[27] the coptic by Ignazio Guidi (1901);[28] separate syriac pieces by Ferdinand Nau (1901)[29] and Agnes Smith Lewis (1912);[30] and the ethiopic by Lazarus Goldschmidt and F. M. Esteves Pereira (1897).[31] The armenian accounts were published in 1855.[32] More recently, Sebastian Brock has edited a syriac piece and Christa Müller-Kessler and Michael Sokoloff have re-edited the syro-palestinian pieces published by Lewis.[33] The latin and old church slavonic accounts were published in the first third of the twentieth century.[34]

Clugnet, perhaps anticipating criticism of his edition of the greek text, defended the fact that he had not produced a critical edition with two curious exculpations: 1) hagiographic texts, he said, could not be treated like classical texts because they are anonymous and designed for edification, and 2) there were just too many manuscripts to deal with.[35] Withering criticism of Clugnet's work was not long in coming.[36] In 1904 Max Bonnet took Clugnet to task for his views and disparaged his work as a 'wretched' or 'sorry' work.[37] Nevertheless, in the intervening century no one has undertaken the rather daunting task of preparing a critical edition from all the languages, although Dahlman's much better edition of the greek dossier, mentioned above, is now available.[38]

This 'heap of anecdotes', surviving in numerous manuscripts and languages, has affinities with other works of Late Antiquity that present an 'agglomeration of such stories'.[39] Van Cauwenbergh maintained that the different language versions clearly divide into two distinct groups: 1) Greek-Syriac-Arabic and 2) Coptic-Ethiopic.[40] The Syriac and Arabic (group 1) depend directly on the Greek; all the stories found in Arabic and Syriac in Van Cauwenbergh's time are also found in the greek version, but the syriac and arabic versions also lack material found in Greek. A newly-published syriac text has no relation to the manuscript tradition of the greek dossier but does have connections with independent greek manuscripts;[41] in fact, there really is no syriac collection or dossier, just scattered manuscripts with two or three pieces.[42] The coptic-ethiopic versions (group 2) lack material found in the greek but each also includes an extra story and adds anti-chalcedonian material and information about Daniel's move away from Scetis and his death.[43] In addition, both the coptic and ethiopic versions use the material found in Greek to fashion a 'Life of Daniel'.[44] Other coptic material, furthermore, supplies an important *terminus ad quem* for at least the coptic portion of the dossier: two sections of the coptic *Life*, 'Abba Daniel Refuses to Accept the Tome of Leo' and 'Abba Daniel Returns to Tambôk; the Death of Abba Daniel', have close, even verbally exact, parallels with sixth- and seventh-century coptic writings: the *Life of Samuel of Kalamun*; and a homily *On Cana of Galilee* by Patriarch Benjamin I (for a full discussion, see the Introduction to Chapter Two below).

The order in which the tales appear in the greek versions (the original language) varies widely. As a result, as Bonnet observed, 'it is not possible to determine with any kind of certitude the primitive order' of the stories'.[45] Unfortunately Clugnet did not help matters by beginning his edition with the wrong story. He starts with the account of a monk in a tomb who is ignored by two demons (II.1 in this volume). This story, however, is not a narrative *about* Abba Daniel, as are all the other narratives found in the main manuscripts, but is instead an apophthegm or saying *by* Daniel (for another, see II.2). It begins in classic 'saying' fashion: 'Abba Daniel of Scetis related. . . ': Διηγήσατο ὁ ἀββᾶς Δανιήλ ὁ σκητιώτης.

Two manuscripts open with this monk-in-the-tomb story by Daniel (Coislin 232 and 283), and Clugnet, choosing 283 to represent the order of the texts he published, apparently did not see that the account of Mark the Fool (I.1), which he has as the third story, works much better as the first piece of the collection; one manuscript that Clugnet used indeed begins with this tale:[46] 'There was an old man in Scetis by the name of Daniel': ἦν τις γέρων ἐν τῇ Σκήτει, ὀνόματι Δανιήλ.[47] The identification of Daniel and his disciple at the beginning of this story is redundant if the story is placed third (as Clugnet has it). This story is clearly designed to be the first 'chapter' in the collection.[48] Other than this clear beginning, however, the stories do not appear to have a set order or to develop systematically any kind of theme, and the attempt by the ancient coptic editor to form a *Vita* or *Life* from the material is superficial. The stories about Abba Daniel, then, should be read as independent pericopes (except for I.5 and I.6, which belong together) that someone gathered together and wrote down. Below I hope to show that this someone may well have been an eyewitness—Daniel's disciple.

Table I offers a synoptic view of the stories as gathered in various languages and collections.

SYNOPTIC TABLE I[49]

Greek	Copt	Eth	Syr	Arab	Arm	Lat	Slav
I.1 [3] Mark the Fool	X	X			X		
I.2 [8] Daniel Atones							
I.3 [4] A Holy Mendicant		X			X		
I.4 [7] A Drunken Monastic		X	X		X	X	X
I.5 [10] Andronicus & Athanasia		X	X		X	X	
I.6 [5] Thomaïs		X				X	X
I.7 [6] The Tempted Monk		X		X	X		
I.8 [2] Anastasia		X	X	X	X	X	X
I.9 [9] Eulogius	X	X	X	X	X	X	
II.1 [1] A Monk and Demons						X	
II.2 [11] A Monk Accused of Theft					X	X	
III.1 A Monk and His Sister				X			
IV.1 Daniel Refutes Charges			X				
IV.2 A Possessed Female Monastic							
V.1 A Licentious Monk							
V.2 Monastic Stability							
V.3 Abba Longinus & Abba Daniel							
Stories Not Found in Greek							
1. The Thief who Repented	X	X					
2. Anti-Chalcedonian Material	X	X					
3. Removal to Tambōk	X	X					
4. Daniel's Death	X	X					
5. The Female Hermit		X					
6. About a Young Man							X

ABBA DANIEL OF SCETIS[50]

In his monumental history of the monasteries of the Wadi al-Natrun (ancient Scetis), Hugh G. Evelyn White remarked that 'the history of

Scetis in the Byzantine period can show but one individual figure worthy of remark'—Abba Daniel, priest and superior.[51] Evelyn White construed the term 'byzantine' more narrowly than most historians would today, excluding the fourth and fifth centuries with their great figures of Arsenius, Evagrius, Isaiah, John the Little, Macarius the Great, Moses the Ethiopian, and Poemen, to name only a few. But his comment does point to a certain paucity of information about the monastic leaders of subsequent periods. The monks themselves in later centuries looked back nostalgically and isotropically on the fourth and fifth centuries as a golden age of monasticism when spiritual giants (or angels) inhabited the desert places.

But Evelyn White's comment raises the question: Who was this Abba Daniel, priest and superior (*hēgoumenos*) of Scetis? He is not the Daniel who appears in the *Apophthegmata*, nor is he the disciple of Arsenius.[52] This answer, however, in turn raises other questions. We have a number of stories about and sayings attributed to a certain Abba Daniel. Do all of these refer to the same person? What historical information, if any, do the stories contain? And when did he live? One thing is clear: Abba Daniel remained a popular figure. Stories about him survive in greek, coptic, ethiopic, syriac, armenian, latin, arabic, and slavonic manuscripts which were copied from the seventh through the eighteenth centuries. The main greek manuscripts, which must be given priority, gather to-gether—somewhat haphazardly and precariously—eleven stories related to Abba Daniel of Scetis. These may be supplemented by other stories of even less secure attribution from John Moschus and elsewhere.[53] The shorter arabic version offers no additional tales while the syriac adds a story not extant in the main greek collection but attested elsewhere; the coptic and ethiopic convert the stories into a *Vita* or *Life* given as a homily, undoubtedly intended for the saint's feast day:[54] each adds a tale and at the end appends important material, whether historical or hagio-graphical, or both, on Daniel's opposition to the Council of Chalcedon, his flight from Scetis and return, his final departure to Tambōk, and his death there.[55]

Faced with the wide ranging appearance (or appearances) of *a* Daniel in the ancient sources, scholars have disagreed as to whether all of the stories refer to a single person.[56] Some, noting that the greek manu-scripts—at least those that include all the major accounts—gather them under the same title referring to Abba Daniel, argue for one Daniel and say that the fact that the coptic and ethiopic versions bring together several accounts to form a biography of Daniel constitutes a presumption in favor of there being a single person.[57] Others, pointing to discrepancies in the ethiopic version, suggest that there are two or more Daniels.[58] Daniel's decidedly peripatetic nature—he travels from Scetis north to Alexandria, south to the Thebaid, and (in the ethiopic version) far east to the Red Sea—may suggest more than one person,[59] but travel is an important motif in these stories and may well be a historical reminiscence about Daniel.[60] Monks of an earlier generation—Antony and Macarius of Egypt, for example—also traveled extensively, so the mere fact that Daniel journeyed far and wide does not automatically justify splitting him into two or more persons.

The coptic and ethiopic traditions, however, seem to distinguish two Daniels, one the superior of Scetis and the other the head of the Monastery of Saint Macarius, one of the four ancient monasteries in the Wadi al-Natrun. Whether or not these two Daniels are the result of *later* confusion in the tradition is not clear.[61] The greek sources always refer to Daniel as being generally from Scetis and do not once mention the Monastery of Saint Macarius. The *Coptic Life of Daniel* resolutely follows the greek dossier in locating Daniel in Scetis, and not at the Monastery of Saint Macarius, while the coptic *Synaxary* affirms this by calling him 'Saint Daniel the archpriest of the wilderness [of Scetis]' and 'the Archpriest of Sheahat [Scetis]'.[62] The synaxary entry for 19 Kihak (15 December) on John, Bishop of El-Borollos, says that John 'went into the wilderness of Shiheet' [Scetis]. He became a monk under the guidance of Saint Daniel the archpriest of the wilderness'. One scholar has suggested that John became a monk in the Monastery of Saint Macarius 'under the hegoumenos Daniel', but the coptic Synaxary does not make this connection.[63]

The ethiopic *Synaxary* clearly bears witness to Daniel of Scetis, but it does so with some confusion.[64] In the entry on Andronicus and Athanasia, Andronicus is said to go to Abba Daniel in the desert of Scetis, while in another entry, Beyoka and Benyamin go to 'the desert of Scetis', where Benyamin meets 'Saint Abba Daniel, superior of the monastery of Scetis'. Nothing in this latter story resembles material from the greek, so this Daniel does not appear to be the Daniel *of Scetis* of the dossier. There also appears in the ethiopic *Synaxary* the commemoration of 'Abba Daniel the monk and the Emperor Honorius. This Abba Daniel was a combatant in the desert of Scetis in the Monastery of Saint Macarius'. This Synaxary entry, in which nothing corresponds to material in the Daniel dossier, locates Daniel in the time of Emperor Honorius, who reigned from 393–423. If this association is historically accurate, then the Daniel of Saint Macarius must be located early in the fifth century. But John of El-Borollos was born about 540; if he went to Scetis as a relatively young man, he would have gone while Abba Daniel was still alive, before 570 or 580 (on Daniel's chronology, see below); thus John should be associated with the Daniel of the sixth century, that is, Abba Daniel, hēgoumenos of Scetis.

ABBA DANIEL: A LOCATIVE AND CHRONOLOGICAL SEARCH

Before discussing the time frame and possible historical setting of Abba Daniel, we need first to sort out the stories about Abba Daniel locatively and chronologically:

1) Those that locate him in or from Scetis [I.1, I.2, I.3, I.4, I.5, I.6, I.7, I.8, I.9, II.1, Coptic],
2) those that associate him with Alexandria and/or its nearby monasteries [1.1, I.2, I.3, I.5, I.6, I.7, Coptic],[65]
3) those that place him in other locations [I.4, I.9, I.10, Coptic],
4) those that place him in the time of Justinian [I.8, I.9, Coptic],
5) those that otherwise situate him chronologically [I.2, Coptic], and
6) those that do none of the above [II.1, II.2].

A synoptic table of these categories follows.

SYNOPTIC TABLE II

	Scetis	Other Locations	Chronological Information
I.1 [3]	yes	Alexandria & Environs	------
I.2 [8]	yes	Alexandria & Environs	Archbishop Timothy(517-535)
I.3 [4]	yes	Alexandria & Environs	------
I.4 [7]	yes	Upper Thebaid, Hermopolis	------
I.5 [10]	yes	Alexandria & Environs	------[66]
I.6 [5]	yes	Alexandria & Environs	------
I.7 [6]	yes	Alexandria & Environs	------
I.8 [2]	yes	------	Justinian & Theodora
I.9 [9]	yes	Thebaid	Justin & Justinian
II.1 [1]	yes	------	------
II.2 [11]	----	------	------
III.1[67]	yes	Alexandria	------
IV.1	----	Terenuthis	------
IV.2	----	------	------
V.1	yes	Alexandria	------
V.2	yes	Alexandria	------
V.3	yes	Alexandria	------
Copt	yes	Tambōk	Justinian
Eth	yes	Alexandria & Environs	Justinian
Lat	yes	Alexandria & Environs	Justinian
Syriac	yes	Alexandria & Environs	Justinian
Arm	yes	Alexandria & Environs	
Slav	yes		Justinian

Several things are consistent and clear from these accounts: 1) All the sources indisputably associate Daniel with Scetis; one story (I.2) says that he lived in Scetis from childhood,[68] while several others, with more probability, refer to him as 'priest' and 'superior' (*hēgoumenos*) of Scetis. He may have been Greek, but was undoubtedly bilingual.[69] 2) Daniel traveled extensively, especially to Alexandria. 3) He lived in the sixth century.[70] The chronology of his life is worth examining in some detail.[71] In I.2, on account of a 'murder' he has committed, Daniel goes to see Archbishop Timothy of Alexandria, who was patriarch from 517–535.[72] While this story goes on to say, quite improbably, that Daniel then went on to see the Pope of Rome and 'all the patriarchs', including those of Jerusalem and Antioch, it is not inherently unlikely that Daniel went to see Timothy.[73] The first story in the dossier (I.1 in the collection here), in fact, begins with Abba Daniel going to visit the patriarch: 'One day, then, the old man took his disciple and went up to Alexandria, because it is customary for the superior of Scetis to go up to see the pope for the Great Feast [of Easter]'. A story from outside the Daniel dossier (V.3 in the present collection) also links Daniel with Timothy III:[74]

> Abba Silvanos said: 'When I was with Abba Longinos the wonder-worker I went to Alexandria with him. Abba Daniel of Scetis met us; we took him with us, and we were received by Abba Isidore the guestmaster. When Archbishop Timothy heard of the arrival of Abba Longinos and Abba Daniel, he sent his *syncellos* to them and received them as his guests'.[75]

The visit, or visits, to Timothy by themselves constitute slim grounds on which to date Daniel, but the time period they give (early sixth century) finds corroboration in the story of Anastasia, the patrician lady who fled Constantinople and became a 'eunuch' in the desert near Abba Daniel (I.8), and that of Eulogius the stonecutter (I.9), both of which place Daniel quite specifically in the reign of Emperor Justinian I (518–527).

According to the Daniel dossier, Anastasia

> was a patrician lady of the highest rank, connected with the royal court, and Emperor Justinian wanted to take her into the imperial residence on account of her great intelligence. But [Empress] Theodora found out, became angry, and wanted to exile her. When Anastasia was apprised of this, she hired a boat at night, loaded some of her things in it, came to Alexandria, and settled at the fifth milestone. Here she also founded a monastery which up to today is called the Monastery of the Patrician Lady.

Daniel tells his disciple that 'after Theodora died', Anastasia

> learned once again that the emperor wanted to send for her.
> She, however, fled Alexandria by night and came here to me,
> told me everything that had happened, and begged me to give
> her a cell outside Scetis. So I gave her this cave and she changed
> her apparel for men's clothing. See, today makes twenty-eight
> years she has lived in Scetis.

Theodora died in 548, which means Anastasia *floruit* in Scetis from 548
to 576. If Daniel is narrating her story twenty-eight years after she came
to Scetis, then he lived to at least 576.[76] He may have left Scetis during
imperial persecution, survived Justinian (who died in 565), returned to
Scetis after the emperor's death, and fled the destruction of Scetis that
took place sometime between 570 to 580.[77]

Can Anastasia be placed historically? Hippolyte Delehaye, the god-
father of the modern study of hagiography, dismissed her story as one
'created by the imagination of greek hagiographers'.[78] Letters, however,
survive in Syriac and Coptic from Severus of Antioch (*c.* 465–540) to a
Deaconess Anastasia, and the syriac 'Life of Anastasia' refers to her as a
deaconess and explicitly connects her with Severus:

> This Anastasia, the patrician lady, is the deaconess who lived
> in the days of the patriarch Severus, holy to God. He wrote
> many letters to her in answer to the questions she asked him
> when she was in the monastery with the sisters before she went
> to the desert of Scetis.[79]

She also seems to have been the wife of a counsel.[80] Severus became
patriarch of Antioch in 512 and was deposed in 518 for his opposition
to the Council of Chalcedon. He was in Constantinople in 514 and
again in 534–536.[81] The story of Anastasia in the Daniel dossier does
not say when she fled Byzantium for Alexandria, but she was in Egypt
before 548, the year of Theodora's death. It is certainly reasonable to
suggest that she was in Constantinople during Severus' exile. The *History
of the Patriarchs of Alexandria* reports that at the time of Severus numbers
of bishops and monastics were driven out of Constantinople, and it is
possible that Anastasia was a monastic who was driven from her monastery on account of her anti-Chalcedonian views.[82] If this was the case,

Egypt, with its strong opposition to Chalcedon and that council's infamous Tome of Leo, would have been a natural place for her to go.

Coptic sources in fact identify Anastasia as a refugee. A coptic panegyric, 'The Forty-nine Elders of Scetis', connects her with Hilaria, the daughter of Emperor Zeno (450–491), Justinian, and Severus, and brings her to Alexandria and thence to Scetis:

> And because of their desire for these saints, the emperors' daughters gave up their glory and their palace and secretly went to Scetis, the capital of the monks. . . . One of them was Hilaria, the daughter of the pious Emperor Zeno of blessed memory, with Anastasia, the servant of God, to whom the holy Patriarch Severus had written: when the impious Justinian— who persecuted the holy Patriarch Severus up to the time that he went to Egypt and fell asleep there so that this country came to enjoy all his benedictions—wanted to arrange a royal marriage for her, she fled from the tyrant, that bloody emperor. She went to the great city of Alexandria and from Alexandria she went to Scetis, and she prayed over the bodies of the saints whose feast day we celebrate today. . . . One of them said to her, 'Go to the holy priest Daniel the Younger who will instruct you as to what you should do'. And so she went to find Abba Daniel, who was father of Scetis and who made her an anchorite. She became a solitary in the desert and became accomplished in the love of suffering.[83]

This story adds the detail of Justinian arranging a marriage for Anastasia, a detail incompatible with her being a deaconess or monastic or the wife of a consul, but in every other way agrees with the other accounts about Anastasia. That does not prove the historicity of the details, of course, but at the very least it shows that Anastasia had fully entered coptic hagiography and mythmaking—and even, perhaps, history.

The story of Eulogius the stonecutter places Daniel even more securely in the time of Justinian. In this story Daniel tells his disciple that when he 'was younger, about forty years ago', he went to an estate to sell his handiwork; while there he was befriended by Eulogius, who made it his ministry to provide food and shelter for foreigners. After Daniel entreats God's aid for this ministry, Eulogius finds a cache of

money. Contrary to the monk's intentions, however, Eulogius runs off
to Constantinople ('Byzantium' in the text) instead of using the money
to provide hospitality. This happened when 'Justin, the uncle of Justinian',
was emperor. Eulogius ingratiates himself at court, becomes 'procurator
of the Praetorian guard', and buys 'a large house' which, interestingly,
'to this day . . . is called "the house of the Egyptian"'.[84] The text clearly
indicates that Justin dies two years and four months later, and Justinian
assumes the throne. Thus Eulogius—historically or as a fictional character—must have gone to Byzantium in 525. After Justinian's accession,
Eulogius gets involved in a conspiracy against the emperor and has to
flee for his life.

So much of the story of Eulogius is either hagiographical or folkloric
that it is difficult at first to give credence to its facts and implicit dates.[85]
The story does, however, indicate a reasonably accurate grasp of historical events that can be corroborated from other sources. After Justinian
became emperor, the text tells us, 'Hypatius and Dexikratius and Pompeius and Eulogius the procurator rose up against him. The first three
were seized and beheaded and all their possessions were confiscated, as
was Eulogius' estate'. Eulogius fled Constantinople at night, having exchanged his fine clothing for that of 'the country folk', and returned
home. Emperor Justin, historical sources inform us, had adopted his
nephew Justinian and on 1 April 527 made him co-emperor, and then
died on August first of that year.

Historically, we know that early in 532, Hypatius and Pompeius,
nephews of Emperor Anastasius, who had died in 518, rebelled against
Justinian (in what is called the Nika riot) and a number of senators
proclaimed Hypatius emperor. After the riot was suppressed, Hypatius
and Pompeius were arrested; on 19 January they were executed and
their bodies cast into the sea. According to one scholar who has studied
this period, 'Their property, and that of those senators who had supported them [as the story in the Daniel dossier asserts], was confiscated.
The patricians who had been with them, people whose identity we
unfortunately do not know, fled'.[86] Is it just possible that Eulogius, even
in his rags-to-riches-to-rags story, was indeed one of those unnamed
patrician conspirators? If he was, then this story places Daniel squarely
within the time of Justinian I (483–565). If Eulogius went to Constantinople in the early 520s, then Daniel is telling his disciple the story
some forty years later, in the 560s. This sequence of events squares with

other dates in Daniel's chronology.[87] Daniel's visits to Archbishop Timothy (I.2) around 520 and his first encounter with Eulogius around 525 (I.9) occurred when he was 'younger' and seem to have taken place before he became superior of Scetis. Evelyn White suggests that Daniel was born in 485.[88]

The coptic *Life of Abba Daniel*, based in part on stories from the greek collection, also connects Daniel to Justinian. The events in the Coptic *Life* are more problematic but are still plausible (for a full discussion of this material, see the Introduction to the Coptic *Life of Daniel* in Chapter Two). According to the *Life*, Daniel opposed the Tome of Leo, which to Egyptians most fully represented the detested decisions of the Council of Chalcedon (451 CE). For his efforts in opposition to Chalcedon Daniel, like other monastic leaders in Egypt, had to flee his monastery. He went to Tambōk, a small village in the eastern Delta. After Justinian's death, in 565, the coptic *Life* reports, Daniel returned to Scetis. Not long afterwards, 'barbarians came to the holy monastic settlement, laying it waste and killing the old men and taking some of them as prisoners to their country'. After this destruction of Scetis, which probably occurred between 570 and 580, Daniel went back to Tambōk, where he died.[89] Thus it may be possible to date Daniel's life from 485 to 570–580.[90] These dates may at first seem to suggest that he lived an uncommonly long life, but such a life span was apparently not uncommon among the early monks: Antony and Shenoute lived longer.[91] According to the coptic *Life*, Daniel 'went to God' at Tambōk on the eighth of Pashons (8 Bashans = 3 May [Julian] and 16 May [Gregorian]). He is commemorated in the coptic orthodox calendar on that date.[92]

THE NARRATOR AS DISCIPLE AND EYEWITNESS:
HAGIOGRAPHY AND HISTORY[93]

The collection of stories about Abba Daniel should begin, as was suggested above, with the story of Mark the Fool (I.1): 'There was an old man in Scetis by the name of Daniel'. This tale then continues with a number of pieces of important information:

> and he had a disciple, and a brother by the name of Sergius lived for a short time with the aforesaid disciple and then went to sleep in Christ. After the perfection of Abba Sergius, Abba Daniel gave his disciple the freedom to speak freely, for he

loved him. One day, then, the old man took his disciple and
went up to Alexandria, because it is customary for the superior of Scetis to go up to see the pope for the Great Feast [of
Easter].

The narrative unassumingly slips in the information that Daniel had a
disciple. Actually, he had two disciples who lived together. When one of
them, Sergius, died, Daniel conferred *parrēsia*, 'freedom of speech', on
the other, unnamed, disciple.[94] Then, in a *topos* that repeats itself throughout the collection, Daniel and his disciple go off to Alexandria, the setting of many of the events in the dossier. The narrative then adds the
reason for their journey: it was 'customary for the superior of Scetis to
go up to see the pope for the Great Feast [of Easter]'.

Just as it is important to distinguish the stories about Daniel chronologically and locatively, it is equally important to divide these tales between those in which Daniel's disciple appears and those in which he
does not. First, those in which he does *not* figure (II.1 and II.2) are not
narratives *about* Daniel; they are apophthegms spoken *by* the old man.
III.1, though presumably by or about Daniel, does not include the narrator, and shows confusion in the manuscripts.[95] IV.1 and IV.2 are stories
told, respectively, by John Moschus and Abba Peter, the disciple of Abba
Isaiah, and do not appear in the Daniel dossier; they come from material
related to Moschus, and may in fact not be about Abba Daniel of Scetis.
These stories have different narrators. An Abba Palladius narrates events
in V.1, the disciples of an Abba Eulogius tell about their *abba* and Daniel
in V.2, and Abba Silvanus narrates V.3. The unnamed narrator of the
greek dossier appears in none of these stories.

The story of Andronicus and Athanasia (I.5), then, is the only third-
person narrative in the main collection in which Daniel's disciple does
not figure.[96] In fact, Daniel himself makes only a cameo appearance in
this tale. All of the other stories in the primary Daniel collection (Part
I, that is, the original dossier) are third-person narratives in which Daniel's unnamed disciple figures prominently. One notes also that in some
of the manuscripts the narrator, like the narrator of Acts in the New
Testament, occasionally slips into the first person plural (I.4); thus the
Daniel collection, like the biblical book, has its own 'we' section. Max
Bonnet long ago observed that the Daniel dossier is 'quite clearly the
work of one of [Daniel's] disciples'.[97] This hypothesis has important

implications for any historical assessment of the collection and for our understanding of sixth-century monasticism in Egypt.

In the story about Mark the Fool, Abba Daniel and his disciple 'arrived at the city at about four in the afternoon' and, the narrator observes:

> as they were walking in the street, they saw a brother who was naked, wearing a cloth around his loins. That brother was pretending that he was half-witted and there were other imbeciles with him. The brother would go around like a half-wit and babble nonsensically and he would snatch things from the stalls in the marketplace and give them to the other imbeciles. His name was 'Mark of the Horse'. 'The Horse' is a public bath; there Mark the Fool worked.

Mark is a 'holy fool', a character well-known in antiquity.[98] Did Daniel's disciple take over and adapt older material about such late antique characters as holy fools (I.3, I.4) and monastic 'transvestites' (I.8), that is, women who dressed as men in order to live the monastic life in the desert?[99] Or did he and Daniel actually encounter such persons?[100] The idea of being a 'fool for Christ', 'holy foolery',[101] goes back to Paul (1 Cor 1:20, 27; 2 Cor 11:21). It also has roots in early monastic tradition, a tradition that Daniel would have known. Abba Or told his disciples, 'In fleeing, either flee from people or mock the world and people by making yourself for the most part foolish'.[102] In a sense, becoming a monk made one *ipso facto* a fool for Christ, at least initially. Routine and security could blunt the edge of foolishness; the irony, and lesson, in the story of Mark the Fool is that Abba Daniel has to go to the city—commonly seen as the antithesis to monasticism—to find a whetstone.[103]

Modern scholars usually assume a suspicious stance towards such ancient figures as holy fools and transvestite monks.[104] But such characters (I use the term advisedly but deliberately, and refer the reader to several meanings in being 'a character') did in fact exist. The difficulty—perhaps impossibility—moderns have with the idea lies in the effort to distinguish the historical person from hagiographical overlay (or inlay).[105] Daniel, intrigued by the half-wit he encounters in the story, tells his disciple to find out where he is living; after Mark's death, Daniel sends his disciple to Scetis to inform the fathers there and to summon them to Alexandria to be blessed by the deceased saint. These sorts of instruction occur frequently in the dossier (here, I.3, I.4, I.6, I.8, I.9) and demonstrate both

the disciple's privileged status and the perspective his position gives him
in observing the goings-on surrounding the old man.

What is striking in this particular story is both the specificity of
Mark's dress, actions, and setting—things an eyewitness certainly could
have reported. 'The Horse', Mark's place of employment, in fact, is
known from other ancient sources as a *dēmosion* or public building,
perhaps a bath, in Alexandria.[106] Such specific, localized details recur
throughout the collection: in I.3 Daniel and his disciple go to Saint
Mark's Outside-the-City, the church associated with the martyrium of
Saint Mark the Evangelist in Boukolou (Baucalis). By the third century
the city had shrunk, and the church had become a suburban one, outside
the city, as the story accurately reports. In I.4 *abba* and disciple journey
south from Scetis into the Upper Thebaid for the feast day of Abba
Apollo, a monastic figure from Middle Egypt well known in antiquity;[107]
they then go on to Hermopolis and visit a 'monastery for women' associated with the Monastery of Abba Jeremiah.[108]

Such geographical details as these would seem to lend credence to
the narrator's accounts, especially when they are coupled with vividness
of narration, a strong characteristic of the Daniel dossier. But the situation is not that simple. These two criteria—environmental and narrative—are among ten that John P. Meier fruitfully discusses in his
exhaustive study of the historical Jesus.[109] That discussion is also relevant
here. 'Liveliness and concrete details', Meier observes, 'are sometimes
taken to be indicators of an eyewitness report',[110] but such an assumption is not without historical difficulties. Although the tradition behind
the Daniel dossier is undoubtedly not as 'convoluted' (Meier's term) as
that of the Synoptic Gospels, a similar historical hesitancy with regard
to the material is warranted, especially when one figures in the dis-
ciple/narrator's 'agenda' (discussed immediately below). As several New
Testament scholars have concluded, 'the burden of proof is simply on
anyone who tries to prove anything'.[111] This burden, of course, is a
weight that all scholarly lawyers must bear: for someone who wishes to
argue that the Daniel dossier is the work of Daniel's disciple and reflects
eyewitness, historical, reports, as well as for someone who wishes to
deny such attestation and who sees the dossier as largely ahistorical hagiography. Meier wisely reminds us that modern historical efforts have
much in common with other activities of everyday life, concluding that
the use of historical criteria:

is more an art than a science, requiring sensitivity to the individual case rather than mechanical implementation. It can
never be said too many times that such an art usually yields
only varying degrees of probability, not absolute certitude . . . .
Since moral certitude is nothing but a very high degree of
probability, and since we run most of our lives and make many
of our theoretical and practical judgments on the basis of moral
certitude, we must not feel that the results of our quest will be
unusually fragile or uncertain. They are no more fragile or
uncertain than many other parts of our lives.[112]

Daniel's story (or stories) is narrated by his unnamed disciple, who
thereby becomes the spokesman or amanuensis for the entire monastic
community gathered around Abba Daniel. Just as the Gospels are post-
Easter narratives based on the writers' belief in a resurrected and living
Christ, so too is the Daniel dossier the subjective reporting of a disciple
or community that remembered Abba Daniel and valued that living
memory.[113] There is no such thing as objective history; as Philip Rousseau has observed, 'we have to accept that the role of the holy man was
being promoted as much as it was [being] recorded'.[114] The modern
historian's take on Abba Daniel, however, influenced as it is by modern
presuppositions and prejudices, is not automatically more objective than
was that of Daniel's disciple (or community). One needs to consider
that disciple's views, what understanding he brought to his material that
helped him shape—or caused him to shape—his narrative. In the second
story of the dossier—in the order followed in this volume—Daniel
atones for a murder he committed by taking care of lepers one at a time.
The disciple-narrator does not figure in the early portions of this tale
but then appears suddenly:

One day, then, about noon, the old man summoned his disciple
to serve him something to eat. Through God's divine agency
it happened that the old man had forgotten that the door to
his cell had been left open. He was sitting in the sun, treating
the leper. The leper was completely eaten up by his many
wounds. The old man's disciple returned from his duties and,
finding the door open, observed how the old man was treating
the leper.[115]

The narrator seems to be saying that it was only by accident that the disciple saw his *abba*'s ministrations to the leper. What he describes, however, is both gruesome and touching and leaves a powerful impression:

> Because the leper had so completely rotted away, Abba Daniel kneaded the food and put it in the leper's mouth. When the disciple saw the amazing work that the old man was doing, he was astonished and glorified God who was supplying such great patience to the old man to serve the leper like this.

This is not dispassionate, disinterested reporting. What the disciple inadvertently observes has come about 'through God's divine agency'.[116] What he sees causes him astonishment and he glorifies God who gives the old man the incredible patience to treat someone horribly deformed. Deformation, as Susan R. Holman has observed, is not just physical but can be spiritual as well, and the spiritually deformed (like the 'murderer' Abba Daniel) may, through their contact with lepers, be healed:

> From its identification as the prototype of all religious pollution, physical leprosy is reformed into sanctity, and its identification with pollution reserved for 'spiritual' leprosy, the diseased soul. Physical lepers become the essential means by which spiritual lepers may find a mediator to wipe away their own polluting spots of greed and passion.[117]

Abba Daniel had committed the 'passion' of murder (*pathos* in Greek meant both 'disease' or 'illness' and a 'passion' or disfigurement of the soul) and the lepers he consequently cared for became for him mediators of forgiveness, just as Abba Daniel would become the mediator of holiness for his community.

Such demonstrations of faith that the narrator reports remind us that his interest does not lie in reporting facts *per se* but in getting at the spiritual truths that, for him, underlie the events he is recording. As William Harmless has observed, 'we cannot let modern questions about historicity divert us from understanding how memory worked' in early monastic communities. Those communities,

> from all indications, did take great pains to remember accurately. But it was not accuracy for accuracy's sake. It was not the accuracy that might move a modern historian, or one that

might have moved an ancient historian. *It was accuracy for the sake of spirituality* [my emphasis] . . . . Its concern was not past facts, but past wisdom that might serve the present quest.[118]

Two examples well illustrate how the narrator of the Daniel dossier uses past facts for the sake of spirituality and the present spiritual quest. After the death of Mark the Fool, Abba Daniel sends his disciple to Scetis to summon the monks to Alexandria:

And all of Scetis came wearing white and bearing olive branches and palms, and the Enaton and Kellia did likewise, and those in the monastic settlement of Nitria and all the lavras around Alexandria. As a result, the corpse was not buried for five days and they were forced to embalm blessed Mark's corpse. And so the whole city and the monks, with lighted candles and incense and tears, purified the center of the city and buried the precious corpse of blessed Mark the imbecile, glorifying and praising God, the lover of humanity, who gives such grace and glory to those who love him, both now and in the age to come.

In I.5, similar events occur after the death of 'blessed Athanasia': 'The old man sent and brought all of Scetis and the inner desert and all the lavras of Alexandria came and the whole city [of Alexandria] came out with them and the monks of Scetis were dressed in white, for this is their custom in Scetis'. Now, one may reasonably doubt that essentially all the inhabitants of Lower Egypt, monastic and non-monastic, came for the funerals of these recently deceased holy ones—these details are undoubtedly hagiographic, intended to heighten the temporal and spiritual importance of the occasions. What is striking, though, are precisely the details: for example, the narrator testifies that the wearing of white on such occasions was the custom in Scetis. Similar ceremonial details occur in I.4. When Daniel goes to the Thebaid,

all the fathers for about seven miles around went out to greet him; there were about five thousand of them. They could be seen lying face down on the sand like a rank of angels welcoming Christ with fearful reverence: some were spreading their clothing before him while others were laying down their cowls, raining tears upon the earth.

When Daniel and his disciple travel on to the women's monastery, the superior 'opened the two gates and came running out, as did the whole community, and they spread their veils from the gate out to where the old man was, rolling themselves at his feet and licking the soles of his feet.' Then the narrator vividly describes a striking act of obeisance:

> After they went inside the monastery, the mother superior brought a pan and filled it with warm water and herbs and stood the sisters in two choirs and they washed the old man's feet and those of his disciple in the water. She took a cup and, taking water from the pan, poured it over the brothers' heads and afterwards she poured it over her breast and over her head.

In the coptic account of the thief who repented—not found in the greek collection—the same ritual foot washing and sanctifying ablutions occur, but in a striking twist of events they take place not in the presence of Abba Daniel but before a thief masquerading as the venerable old man. Despite this deception, the water *ex opera operato* still has sanctifying effects:

> When one of the sisters, who had been blind from childhood, heard the sisters' rejoicing, she said to them, 'Give me some of the old man's water too', and they took hold of her and stood her over the basin. She cried out, 'Blessed are you, my holy father Abba Daniel! May God and your name have mercy on me!' And she filled her hand with water and rubbed it on her face. Immediately she was able to see. How great were the shouts and the rejoicing of all the sisters at that moment! They ran and kissed the thief's feet. She who could now see cried out all the more, 'Blessed are you, my holy father! With the water from your feet, you have given the light back to me'.

When the thief saw this wonder,

> he was seized with fear and trembling. After all the sisters had gone to sleep, the thief did not go to sleep at all but instead sat weeping until his tears drenched the earth, saying, 'God help me! I am a weak and sinful person. I have wasted all my time doing incredibly vain and foolish things as if by taking his name

I could actually be this man. *He* caused the water that was used
to wash my feet to give light to the blind. What sort of a person
is this man? God help me! I am a weak and sinful person. I
have neglected my salvation'.

In the coptic story, holy water leads both to the recovery of eyesight
and to the thief's repentance. Undoubtedly historical detail—the ritual
of washing and ablution—is coupled with hagiographic miracle and
moral. In the story of Eulogius the stonecutter (I.9), authentic historical
knowledge (details about the plot against Justinian) rubs shoulders with
fairytale-like material. Such combinations confront us with intractable
questions: If we accept the ritual or the history, can miracle and conversion be *ipso facto* ruled non-historical? If so, on what grounds?[119] What
criteria do we use to accept, say, the custom of the water and exclude
its results? As I have noted elsewhere, modern Copts do not readily
distinguish between history and hagiography; this was undoubtedly even
truer in late antiquity.[120] These stories about Abba Daniel show how
history and hagiography intertwine, each at the service of the other.
Those of us in the West may feel compelled to disentangle such ancient
branches as these that have grown together;[121] such separating, in fact,
has value for historians. One can, with difficulty, untangle branches, but
it is virtually impossible to disentangle roots without doing irreparable
harm. With our scientific-historical predispositions and presuppositions,
we moderns would do well to use caution if we are not to kill these
ancient plants with their spiritual roots deep in the desert soil.

DISCIPLE AND ABBA: PORTRAYING THE HOLY MAN

Classical greek and roman historians, from Herodotus to Ammianus
Marcellinus, emphasized eyewitness (autopsy) and inquiry as the foundation of the historian's or narrator's craft, and most ancient historians
included a profession of autopsy and inquiry in their narratives.[122] Luke
the Evangelist did the same (see Lk 1:2). Early monastic 'historians' followed their example. In the Prologue to the *Lausiac History*, Palladius
declares that he will set forth 'an account of my entire experience' and
will relate the 'stories of the fathers, of both male and female anchorites,
those I had seen and others I had heard about, and of those I had lived
with in the Egyptian desert and Libya, in the Thebaid and Syene'.[123]

An historian of a holy person or saint (*hagios*) is, by definition, a hagiographer. As Palladius demonstrates, late antique christian writers, whether we call them historians or hagiographers, often followed classical examples by proudly displaying their credentials as eyewitnesses. Unlike his classical predecessors, however, the hagiographer is often a disciple of the person he is portraying, thereby claiming for himself additional 'status and authority' as 'an eyewitness of the events he describes'.[124] Such discipleship, in the eyes of many modern historians, compromises the hagiographer's credentials for credibility or at least throws them into serious question. But this is to confuse our concerns with the hagiographer's. As Claudia Rapp has observed, the hagiographer goes further than the historian and either directly or indirectly 'presents himself as the prototype of the saint's clientele, and hence as a model for the ideal audience of his own text. As a recipient of benefits from the saint, the author also assumes for himself the role of witness of the saint's miraculous abilities'.[125]

Because the Daniel dossier, at least in its original greek incarnation, is, as it were, a collection of snapshots and not an extended film or documentary, its narrator does not, like Palladius, offer a standard profession of credentials. Nor does he present the hagiographical *topos* of the saint's miraculous abilities and, connected with them, the invocation of the saint in the preface to a *vita*.[126] As Robin Lane Fox has observed, 'hagiographers, especially in the sixth century and later, call their saint "thaumatourgos" ["wonder-worker"]'.[127] The holy man is often presented 'as almost literally a fountain of divinity that others can tap into if they wish, and if they know how'.[128]

Daniel's hagiographer/biographer does not portray the saint in this manner. What he does offer, though indirectly and symbiotically, is himself. Through his narrative he is the creator of the benefactor, the saint. As disciple, he benefitted and still benefits from the holy man and offers those benefits to his readers. Ancient historians like Polybius recognized 'that a fundamental element in an historical narrative is the narrator himself'.[129] The ancients, like modern philosophers, historians, and literary theorists, worried about this very question: how narrators shape their narratives. Polybius saw 'the great complexity in any attempt to find out what actually happened'.[130] The unnamed disciple who gathered together and wrote down the stories about Abba Daniel of Scetis was not a dispassionate and disinterested observer but was, rather, a very interested participant: in writing about his spiritual father, he firmly believed that Abba Daniel *was* a holy man (I assume that the disciple wrote after the old man's death). Everything that this disciple wrote, whether we categorize it as history or hagiography, was written with that conviction. Separating the two *genres* would have made no sense to him. As Claudia Rapp comments, 'these works [of hagiography] do not make a distinction between truth and verisimilitude or like-truth. Their *raison d'être* is not the accurate representation of historical events, but the direct involvement of the audience in the narrative'.[131]

What kind of portrait, then, did this disciple leave us? Surprisingly, perhaps, a very *un*hagiographical one. Before we look at the disciple/narrator's portrait of Abba Daniel, it would be good first to observe the two of them, abba and disciple, together. Such a course will allow us to see the concrete setting in which the two lived and their interactions, and will provide a first glimpse at the way the disciple portrayed his *abba*. The stories of Anastasia (I.8) and Eulogius (I.9) provide excellent avenues for such a study.

The story of Anastasia begins simply enough: 'A eunuch was living in the inner desert of Scetis'.[132] In the next sentence we discover that the disciple will have an important role in this story: 'Once a week, then, he would visit Abba Daniel at night without anyone knowing about it except Abba Daniel and his disciple'. This sentence illustrates the disciple's privileged position (his *parrēsia;* see I.1). Then, like a good mystery, the text introduces an element of suspense. The mystery, along with the disciple's role, deepens in the next few sentences:

> The old man ordered his disciple to fill a wine jar with water for the eunuch once a week and to place it at the door and knock and go away without speaking with him at all. 'But if', he said, you ever find an ostracon with writing on it at the entrance to the cave, bring it.' And so Abba Daniel's disciple would do this.

One day the disciple does discover an ostracon written to Abba Daniel with the cryptic instructions 'Bring your tools and come alone with the brother'. When the disciple takes this message to Daniel, the old man weeps and wails and the two hurry off to see the eunuch, who is dying. After the eunuch's death, Abba Daniel instructs his disciple to clothe

the eunuch for burial. Now the reason for the mystery becomes clear: 'While the brother was dressing the eunuch, he looked and realized that the eunuch was a woman[133] but he did not say anything'. The two bury the 'eunuch', then head for home. On the way the disciple tells the old man of his discovery and the old man says, 'Do you want me to tell you about her? Listen.' Daniel then tells his disciple the story of Anastasia, the patrician lady who left the court of Emperor Justinian and became Anastasius, a 'eunuch' (more properly a monastic 'transvestite') living as a solitary in the desert. In this story the disciple's *parrēsia* puts him in the position 1) to discover the true nature of the 'eunuch', and 2) to be the first audience (the reader is the second) to hear Daniel's account of Anastasia.

A similar two-fold structure informs the next story in the collection, that of Eulogius the stonecutter, although here the lesson is more hard-won and the winning comes not without some irony and even self-deprecating humor. Once again the tale begins innocently: Daniel and his disciple are sailing down the Nile, going back to Scetis from a trip to the Thebaid. Daniel orders the sailors to stop at a certain village and tells everyone that they will remain there that day. His disciple, however, 'began to grumble, saying, "How long are we going to waste our time here? Let's go on to Scetis"'. The old man replies, 'No, we'll stay here today'. They settle down with some foreigners who appear to be camping out there and the disciple continues his bellyaching: 'Does it please God for us to sit here like brothers with them? Let's at least go to the martyrion'. The old man firmly replies, 'No, we're staying here', and they remain there, 'staying until late in the evening'. The brother, now thoroughly petulant, begins 'to fight with the old man', exclaiming rather hysterically, 'On account of you I'm going to die'.

While this melodramatic conversation is occurring, an old man appears. When he sees Abba Daniel, he grabs hold of him, weeps, and kisses his feet. Once again there is the element of mystery: who on earth is this fellow, and what is his relationship with Abba Daniel? The mystery man takes Daniel, his disciple, and the other foreigners home with him and feeds and houses them. He and the old man talk privately until dawn 'about the things that lead to salvation'. Then early in the morning Daniel and his disciple leave. Now on the road (instead of travelling by boat), the disciple, undoubtedly a bit chastened, begs his abba's forgiveness and—standing in for us and our curiosity—asks who the hospitable old man was. Daniel, understandably, refuses to speak to him. Again the brother apologizes and tries to manipulate Daniel into talking to him: 'You've confided many other things to me, and now you won't confide in me about this old man?' Daniel still refuses and the brother then tries the silent treatment, not speaking to the old man the rest of the way.

When Daniel and his disciple arrive in Scetis, the brother huffs off alone to his cell and 'did not bring the old man a small meal as was the custom'. (The narrator then adds the inside information, possibly because Daniel's custom was not the norm, that 'the old man always observed this practice at five PM').[134] When evening comes, the old man goes to the brother's cell and, now with his own hyperbole—mocking his disciple's earlier protest that he was about to die?—asks, 'Why, child, have you allowed your father to die of hunger?' The disciple angrily retorts, '*I* don't have a father! If I had a father, he would love his own child!' The old man strikes back, 'If you don't have a father, serve yourself'.

When the old man takes hold of the door to leave, the brother can no longer stand it; he comes up, grabs the old man, and begins to kiss him, saying, 'As the Lord lives, I will not let you go if you do not tell me who that old man was!' The brother, the narrator informs us, 'could not ever bear to see the old man distressed for any reason' for, he adds, 'he dearly loved him'. The old man gives in: 'Make me a little something to eat and then I will tell you'. After the old man eats, he says to the brother, 'Do not be stiff-necked. I did not tell you because you argued with me in the village and were grumbling'. The old man then rather mysteriously tells his disciple not to repeat what he hears and proceeds to tell him the remarkable and edifying story of Eulogius the stonecutter.

In both of these stories the narrator skillfully uses the disciple as the intermediary who brings the tales to us. The disciple serves firstly as a witness to events that prompt him to become a listener to things that have taken place in the past. Just as skillfully, the narrator uses self-deprecating irony—the disciple comes off as a real whiner—and mystery to add humor and build suspense: In the story of Anastasia, who is this eunuch? Why does he visit Abba Daniel at night? What is this mysterious ostracon about? In the story of Eulogius: Why does Abba Daniel want to stay in this—to the disciple—god-forsaken place? Who is the hospitality-giving old man? And how does he know Abba Daniel? These devices build up our interest for the stories of Anastasia and Eulogius that the old man then narrates.

Each of these stories-within-a-story has a moral lesson to impart which justifies its telling and is the main reason for its existence. Paul Evergetinos preserved a like-minded story-with-a-moral about an Abba Daniel that has not come down within the basic Daniel dossier (see V.1). In this tale, narrated by an Abba Palladius, Daniel travels to Alexandria with Palladius and there encounters a dissolute monk who frequents the city's baths. Daniel sighs and tells his disciple, 'You see that brother? The name of God is about to be blasphemed on account of him'. He then (see I.1, I.3, and I.4) characteristically adds, 'but let us follow and see where he is staying'. So they follow the dissolute monk. When they catch up with him, Daniel tries to correct the monk but is rebuffed; Daniel then declares that he sees swarms of demons around the licentious monk. The two return to Scetis and a few days later Palladius comes to tell Daniel that the monk has been caught *in flagrante delicto* with an official's wife and has been castrated. Daniel quietly—and callously—concludes: 'Calamity is the correction of the arrogant'.

This story, though a bit more moralistic than the others, does not seem out of place or character with the stories in the main collection. This tale becomes intriguing because it gives a name—Palladius—to the hitherto anonymous disciple/narrator.[135] Even more intriguing is the longer ending of the story attested by one manuscript.[136] In this version, Palladius goes to Abba Daniel in tears when he hears about the dissolute monk's fate and finds him with Abba Isaac, the superior of Scetis.[137] When Palladius informs Daniel, the latter weeps and gives the same quiet judgement as above. But the story does not end here. Palladius then adds, 'I privately conveyed to the superior the things the elder had seen and had said to me, whereupon, deeming them worthy to be recorded, Abba Isaac ordered them to be written and set down in the book of the wonderworking fathers for the edification and benefit of those who come upon them'. We have here nothing less than the *raison d'être* of the Daniel dossier, both the reason for its existence—edification—and the means by which it came into being: Palladius wrote it as an act of obedience. Could Isaac's order have prompted Palladius to gather other stories about Daniel? And, in doing so, did Palladius quietly and humbly remove his name from the accounts, becoming the anonymous disciple-narrator of the dossier? Once again, we cannot know for sure, but it certainly seems possible.

In the Daniel dossier itself (Part I in Chapter One in this volume) the disciple/narrator remains resolutely anonymous and thus the messenger does not get in the way of the message. As Claudia Rapp has astutely put it:

> Far from being a mere conveyor of a message, the hagiographical account . . . is thus the message itself. What is more, it is something like an event that with its own spiritual force links the saint, the eyewitness/ hagiographer, and the audience, and transports them to a level of timeless existence where the drama of the saint is played out perpetually and in eternity.[138]

But what is this timeless drama? Nothing less than the evocation of holiness on the human stage. The dramatization in the Daniel dossier has a wide variety of locales and supporting actors. The focus at first appears to be typically on the chief character and hero, Abba Daniel of Scetis, but if we look more closely through the hagiographical lens we can see that Daniel is really in the background, offering benediction, while holiness comes more sharply into focus in the foreground.

WITNESS TO HOLINESS[139]

'Life, like holiness, can be known only by being experienced'.

—Wendell Berry[140]

Douglas Burton Christie, like most scholars and readers of early christian monasticism, has linked 'the monks' pursuit of holiness' with a 'dramatic act of withdrawal', the 'separation and removal from the mainstream of society'.[141] Antoine Guillaumont has urged further that 'this movement of withdrawal, of "anachoresis", marks the movement from pre-monastic asceticism to monasticism properly called'.[142] There can be no doubt that these scholars—properly understood—are right. Monastic separation does not necessarily have to be spatial, deep into Antony's literal desert,[143] but some sort of withdrawal or distancing is necessary for the monk—and us—to gain perspective on the world and its dominions.[144] After his baptism, Jesus withdrew into the wilderness and found the Devil (Mt 4:1-11). Antony, as he is famously portrayed, confronted hordes of the Devil's disciples—demons—in the desert. So did later monks. In commenting on this phenomenon, so curious, even repellent, to moderns, Vincent Desprez has observed that

> these famous acts of the demons [*diableries*] reveal fundamen-
> tally the hard and difficult aspects [*dura et aspera*] of the mo-
> nastic experience: the monk who has renounced certain of
> life's amenities must fight against 'thoughts,' against the attrac-
> tion that these objects continue to exercise over him. The
> complete solitude of the desert exacerbates that formidable
> confrontation between a person and himself.[145]

Withdrawal, then, does not mean flight and evasion but making the hard and difficult journey that brings one closer to one's true self, which is where God is.[146] Once one reaches this harbor, to use a favorite meta-phor of the early monks, one has a secure and stable place from which to onload supplies and foodstuffs in order, like Eulogius (I.9), to sally forth in search of those shipwrecked in the world.

Abba Daniel, although certainly practicing separation or withdrawal in the desert of Scetis, is also very much engaged in the world, especially with travel from the desert *back into* 'the world'. This, in fact, is where the Daniel dossier most often pictures him, and this is where we, the audience-in-the-world, most often meet him: by our side—or up ahead, calling and beckoning to us to hurry to look. Thus withdrawal is cer-tainly an important and vital part of early monastic spirituality but, as the Daniel dossier shows, the monks balanced it with *reaching out*. Mo-nasticism, then, is as much centripetal as it is centrifugal. The monk flees one center—'the world'—in search of his (or her) true center—God. Once there, he can leave his monastic center (or, more accurately, em-body it, take it with him) and seek out the world in a gesture of healing and salvation.

This tidal action offers at least one explanation for the numerous monastic tales recognizing holiness in the world. Just as the monk knows—or should know; that is why the stories exist—that he will not reach perfection in this world, he also comes to understand that holiness and goodness do not reside solely in the desert; the belief that they do would be spiritual *hubris*. The world has multiple spiritual centers radiat-ing out from the one God; *topos* (locale) is not *tropos* (way of life):[147] 'It was revealed to Abba Antony', the classic exemplar of withdrawal, 'that there was one who was his equal in the city. He was a doctor by profession and whatever he had beyond his needs he gave to the poor, and every day he sang the *Sanctus* with the angels'.[148] In another saying, Antony, like Daniel, goes to Alexandria and there observes the virtue of a townsperson who surpasses him and learns the nature of that person's virtue: each day this person affirms that the entire city will enter heaven because of their good works while he will suffer punishment for his sins.[149]

One of the most striking examples of this genre of 'the momentary return to the world' involves Abba Macarius the Great. One time 'when he was praying in his cell', 'a voice came to him, saying, "Macarius, you have not yet reached the level of two women who live in such-and-such a village"', so Macarius decided to search out the women. When he found them he asked for their way of life and they told him that they had left their husbands and lived together for fifteen years. 'We drew up a covenant', they said, 'between ourselves and God that to the day of our death our mouths would not speak a worldly utterance but that we would direct our thoughts to God and his saints at all times and would devote ourselves unceasingly to prayers and fastings and acts of charity'. When Abba Macarius heard these things he said, 'Truly, it is not the name of "monk" or "lay person" or "virgin" or "wife and husband" but an upright disposition that God seeks, and he gives his Holy Spirit to all of these people'. This realization causes Macarius not to sulk in self-retribution but to exult.

The story seems to understand an 'upright disposition' as 'prayers and fastings and acts of charity'. The two women have indeed withdrawn, in this case from their husbands, but it is not their withdrawal *per se* that matters; it is the fruits of their *anachorēsis*. Edified, Macarius then returns to his cell, 'clapping his hands and saying, "I have not been at peace with my brothers like these lay women have with one another"'.[150] There are striking parallels between what Macarius says here and what Peter proclaims in Acts 10:34-35; these women are 'gentiles', like Cornelius, and Macarius is a 'Jew', like Peter, who learns that God's bounty is not exclusive: 'Thus Peter begins to speak to them: "I truly understand that God shows no partiality, but in every nation anyone who fears him and does what is right is acceptable to him"'.

We see here being expanded right before us the boundaries of what defined—defines—the holy man or woman. Holiness, the monks saw, almost in spite of themselves, was not the exclusive possession of *men* domiciled in the desert.[151] As Claudia Rapp has noted, 'Hagiographical texts play a significant and very particular role in the process that joins the author and his audience in their participation in the sanctity of the holy man or woman'. Rapp calls this process 'spiritual communication'.[152] In the Daniel dossier, this 'communication' is of persons *other than* the eponymous holy man. If the audience is monastic, then they are learning an important lesson in humility and equality; 'the fact that it is possible for non-monastic persons living amid the pressures of the world to attain such virtue heightens the sense of obligation which rests upon monks to rise to the same level'.[153] If the audience is non-monastic, then they are learning the equally important lesson that holiness resides in their midst and not exclusively among the monastically garbed and gifted out in the desert.

The greatest confirmation of these understandings comes in the early monastic stories where the monks learn (and they, like us, do have to learn this) that the path to heaven is not as narrow as they might have imagined. In fact, sometimes the path seems to be a broad thoroughfare, with the double gates of heaven thrown wide open:

> As Abba Silvanus sat one time with the brothers, he had a mystical experience (*en ekstasei*) and fell flat on his face. After a long time he got up and wept. The brothers entreated him, 'What's wrong, father?' but he remained silent and continued weeping. When they forced him to speak, he said, 'I was carried off to judgement and I saw numbers of people dressed like us in monastic habits going away to punishment and I saw numbers of people who were not monks going away into the kingdom'.[154]

In our own day Flannery O'Connor vividly uses this image to bulldoze the narrowly self-constructed gates of heaven that some Christians, in imitation of gated communities so popular now in suburbia, build for themselves and against others. In O'Connor's story 'Revelation', the self-righteous Mrs Turpin sees

> a vast swinging bridge extending upward from the earth through a field of living fire. Upon it a vast horde of souls were rumbling toward heaven. There were whole companies of white-trash, clean for the first time in their lives, and bands of

black niggers in white robes, and battalions of freaks and lu-
natics shouting and clapping and leaping like frogs.[155]

In another early monastic story, an old man (that is, a monastic elder)
'who served God for many years' learns from an angel that he does not
please God as does a certain gardener. The old man seeks out the gardener, and, like Eulogius the Stonecutter, the gardener shows the monk
great hospitality. Like Macarius, the old man questions the gardener
about his way of life. The gardener tells the old man that he eats late in
the evening and gives everything beyond his needs to the poor. In the
morning before he goes to work and in the evening before going to
bed he says, 'This city, from the least to the greatest, will enter the kingdom because of their righteousness, but I alone will inherit punishment
on account of my sins'.

When he hears this, the old man responds (rather smugly, we may
imagine) that these practices are good but they do not surpass all his
efforts in the desert. While the two are getting ready to eat, the old man
hears people out in the street singing songs. He asks the gardener if he's
not bothered by this and the gardener says no. 'Brother', the old man
responds, 'wanting as you do to live according to God, how do you remain in this place and not be troubled when you hear them singing
these [scandalous] songs'. The gardener replies, 'I tell you, abba, I have
never been troubled or scandalized'. When the old man hears this, he
asks the gardener what he conceives in his heart when he hears such
songs. The gardener replies, 'That they are all going to the kingdom'.
When the monk hears this he marvels and says, 'This is the practice
which surpasses my labor of all these years'.[156] Amma Syncletica seems
to have had such a person as this gardener in mind when she memorably
said, 'Many of those living in a monastic community act like those living
in cities and are lost while many of those living in cities do the works
of the desert and are saved. Indeed, it is possible to live with a multitude
and still be solitary in spirit just as it is possible to live as a solitary while
one's thoughts are with the crowd'.[157]

If the stories in the Daniel dossier, like the sayings cited above, expand
the definition of holiness, they also contract it—or, in contracting it,
kenotically empty part of it, leaving room for even greater expansion.
One of the pronounced traits of monastic hagiography is the wonder-
working of the saints, the miracles in the desert.[158] The earliest strata of

the monastic tradition, the *Apophthegmata*, do not, however, give much emphasis to miracles and wonderworking. Holiness resides in simple, quotidian, activities like prayer and basket-making and living in community.

The most noticeable—even astounding—thing about Abba Daniel, contrary to expectations, is that *he does not perform a single miracle*. It is true that in the coptic *Life's* story of the repentant thief, a blind woman is healed by water that she believes has been used to wash Daniel's feet. Both she and the thief attribute this wonder to Daniel, but the miracle appears to have taken place because of the blind woman's faith in God and Abba Daniel. (In a striking parallel in I.4, Daniel orders similar water to be thrown on a nun who appears dead-drunk and it has no effect on her. Apparently Daniel thought that the efficaciousness of the water lay in waking her up, not healing her.)

Often in ancient story-telling, John Marincola has observed, 'the author steps out of the mimetic narrative to guarantee . . . that what will seem unbelievable to the reader actually took place'.[159] There is no 'stepping out' in the Daniel dossier because there are, really, no miracles, no steps, to take. Daniel, therefore, by the standards both of hagiography and classical historiography, is an unusual holy man: he is not a thauma-turge.[160] Neither is he patron, exemplar, or intercessor—roles of the holy man identified by modern scholars.[161] His charism, at least as understood by his disciple, the narrator of the tales, lies in discerning holiness, bear-ing witness to it, and summoning others to bear witness *and* to benefit from it.

In I.1 Daniel tells the people and clergy of Alexandria that Mark, the holy fool, is a chosen vessel and that there is no one in the city (includ-ing, presumably, himself) as righteous as he. Daniel's declaration prompts the alexandrian pope to beg Mark to tell them who he is, which in turn causes Mark to tell his story. After Mark's death, Daniel summons all the monks of Scetis to come to receive the old man's blessing. In I.3 Daniel, in similar fashion, sees that a blind beggar is in truth doing great things. He and his disciple follow the beggar home and become the recipients of his generosity and hospitality. In I.4 Daniel discerns that the drunken nun is, like Mark, really a holy fool, and so he devises a plan to discover her hidden sanctity. After her holiness becomes evident to the nuns, bringing about their repentance for their ill-treatment of her, Daniel declares that it was 'for this reason' that he came there, 'for God loves such drunkards as these'. The syriac version of this story makes Daniel's point even more explicit: 'You have seen this mad girl. In truth God loves mad people such as these, who are drunkenly mad with ardent love for him.'

One scholar has commented that 'the people always were eager to see sanctity in the eccentric'.[162] But perhaps that is to put the emphasis in the wrong place—and to put down 'the people'. Yes, there are 'eccentrics' aplenty in the Daniel dossier, but the emphasis is not on eccentricities of madness and feigned drunkenness but rather on holiness. Madness sometimes points to holiness, but it is not the only indicator. Andronicus, Athanasia, and Eulogius, in their acts of charity, are far from mad (except, of course, that 'the world' may regard them as mad for giving away all their money).[163] 'Eccentricity', however, is a signal: the stories in the Daniel collection, like the parables in the Gospels (e.g., the Good Samaritan), do demonstrate that holiness may reside where we least suspect it. Daniel's role as monastic authority is to lend weight to this gospel witness. As priest and superior of Scetis, he has the power, apparently, to summon the monks of Scetis to come to Alexandria (I.1, I.5). His authority, according to the stories in the collection, was widely recognized: when Daniel went to the Upper Thebaid, 'all the fathers for about seven miles around went out to greet him; there were about five thousand of them. They could be seen lying face down on the sand like a rank of angels welcoming Christ with fearful reverence: some were spreading their clothing before him while others were laying down their cowls, raining tears upon the earth'. When he goes on to the women's monastery, the whole community comes running out 'and they spread their veils from the gate out to where the old man was' (I.4).

Although Daniel has great authority, as these stories indicate, the narrator takes quiet pains to show his readers that Daniel's power really lies elsewhere. In the stories of Anastasia (I.8) and Eulogius (I.9) Daniel appears to be holy precisely because he has the humility and discernment to see holiness *in others*. He recognizes the saintliness of the 'eunuch' Anastasia, finds a cell for her, protects her identity, and counsels her. When she is dying, Daniel asks for her blessing and prayers for himself and his disciple. In the story of Eulogius, Daniel recognizes the grace-filled charism of Eulogius' hospitality and care for strangers.[164] Thus Daniel confirms the spiritual truth that monks had long known and that the *Apophthegmata* affirm: holy persons do not reside only in the desert; they live also, and perhaps with even more difficulty and sanctity, in the towns, villages, and cities of this fallen world:'The qualities for which these non-monastic people are commended are the same qualities that the monks themselves wished to cultivate: not only charity, hospitality, and chastity, but humility, detachment, freedom from anger, and the possession of a "good will" in whatever state of life, lay or secular, married or unmarried, someone lives'.[165]

AN EXPANSIVE PERVERSITY

As part of its expansive nature, the Daniel dossier presented the ancient monk with a number of different models of asceticism, not just withdrawal into the desert, which became the norm in the fourth century.[166] The pauline ideal of celibacy in the New Testament was the first form of *anachorēsis* in the Church and 'was already a manifestation of separation from the world'.[167] Eulogius in his ministry is presumably celibate (I.9) and Andronicus and Athanasia, although married, live celibately (I.5). Despite the later identification of *anachorēsis* or separation almost solely with withdrawal into the desert, the Daniel dossier shows that separation from the world continued to take diverse forms: in the 'fool for Christ',[168] in *xeniteia* or loss of one's homeland,[169] and in monastic transvestism[170]—all forms of withdrawal from the norms of society. The fool forsook his rational self; the expatriate pulled up deeply set roots; the monastic transvestite gave up sexual and social identity. These different *anchorites* (in the original sense of *anachorēsis*), with their different ascetic disciplines and renunciations of the world's priorities, illustrate monasticism's deep and abiding need to return to its roots and sources, thus reforming itself.

Precisely because they stand *outside* the main monastic tradition, as later configured, while remaining part of the ascetic critique, the fool, expatriate, and transvestite confront and challenge the tradition, which is what they do in the Daniel dossier. Later figures like Saints Benedict, Francis, and Bernard are commonly seen as the great monastic reformers, but already in the fifth century Isaiah of Scetis, in his withdrawal from Egypt to Sinai, represents the spirit of renewal, both individual and corporate, that monasticism—and Christianity—needs:

> After many years spent in a monastery, the monk can feel resurfacing that which he had wanted to flee by leaving the

world, that is, the weight of habits, comforts, the considerations of his circle of friends, and he then feels the need—in order to remain loyal to his ideal—for a new break, which he will realise through the anchoretic life, through *xeniteia*, and by leading a reclusive life.[171]

By the sixth century monasticism had become a generally accepted perversion. Monasticism became ecclesiastically sanctioned and politically regulated, but in the process it lost some of its counterintuitive nature and countercultural reason for being. Many of the figures in the Daniel dossier, by contrast, retain monasticism's—and Christianity's—original jaggedness: the holy mendicant, anticipating the monastic fervor of Saint Francis, lives out true self-giving poverty (I.3); Andronicus and Athanasia abandon home, property, and country (I.5), as Jesus commands; Anastasia not only renounces great wealth but also completely gives up her social identity (I.8). In the Daniel dossier, holy monastic fools are sometimes the subject of abuse and vilification by their fellow monastics (I.4, II.2). Since compassion is—or should be—a cardinal monastic, and christian, virtue, such vilified holy fools indicate and indict the ease with which human beings resort to cruelty. Spiritually speaking, the Daniel dossier reminds us, we are all susceptible to becoming taunting children on the playground of abuse and where abuse is augmented with arms, tragedy ensues.

The foolishness of someone like Mark (I.1) or the drunken nun (I.4), whose madness, as Antoine Guillaumont acutely points out, is 'essentially a form of separation from the world', might just knock the ascetic reader back against the original sharp corners of his or her monastic vocation.[172] At a time when monasticism had pretty much settled down into basilian, pachomian, or antonian patterns, the main figures of the Daniel dossier are barbarians clambering at the monastery gates—or barbarians settled *within* the gates. Daniel, as it were, instead of merely performing his abbatial duties inside the monastery, goes outside the enclosure to welcome these atypical ascetics inside. He knows full well that their presence within will initially provoke consternation and resistance (see I.6) but that such friction will eventually wear at the accumulated rusts of lazy habits and comfortable traditions.

In post-modern terms, Daniel's greatest authority may be precisely that of witness and storyteller, communicator of holiness, for it is he who tells his disciple the stories of Anastasia and Eulogius (I.8 and I.9). It is he who causes Mark to tell his story (I.1) and it is he who discovers the blind man's story (I.3) and that of the 'drunken' female monastic (I.4). In a sense, this narrative strategy only confirms Daniel's humility: it points the reader's attention *away* from the holy man and *towards* the virtues and holiness of the saints whose stories he tells—that is, it creates a hermeneutic loop that encircles the reader himself. Daniel becomes a narrator within the narrative, and his position as monastic superior and his status as holy man lend weight and credence to the disciple's tales. Unlike most hagiographical narratives, these stories allow Daniel to disappear from the narrative. This disappearance seems to happen in spite of the narrator's intentions. Or does it? Himself humbly anonymous, perhaps he saw that Daniel's greatness lay precisely in his humility and that both Daniel's holiness and his humility could best be shown by having him act as narrator for others rather than be the chief actor in these small, saving, sometimes radical, dramas. It is as though he had Daniel saying, in the words of Saint Macarius the Great, 'That is why I said that I have not yet become a monk, but I have seen monks'.[173]

CHAPTER ONE

The Greek Accounts

WITH WITNESSES FROM THE GREEK SYNAXARY

Translated by Tim Vivian
with the assistance of John Wortley

A NOTE ON THE GREEK TEXTS[1]

The textual transmission of the greek texts about Abba Daniel
of Scetis, as with so many other hagiographic texts, is very
complicated. There are many different redactions of the texts
and almost every manuscript contains a unique Daniel dossier with its
own combination of stories and its own ordering of different redactions
of the texts. It is impossible, or at least very difficult, to reconstruct the
original texts.[2]

Léon Clugnet first edited the greek redactions and, with some exceptions, followed the sequence of stories in the Daniel dossier of MS Paris
Coislinianus 283. He edited tales missing from this dossier with the help
of other manuscripts and inserted these redactions among the others
(e.g. he used MS Paris gr 914 for his No. 8 [I.2 in the present volume]).[3]
He also, in an inconsistent and careless way, supplied redactions from
other manuscripts as variants.[4]

Most recently, Britt Dahlman has chosen to edit the redactions and
follow the sequence of stories as they appear in four related MSS.: **E** =
El Escorial R.II.1 (Revilla 21); **P** = Paris gr 919; **M** = Moscow 345
(Vladimir 342); and **V** = Vat. Gr 858. These four manuscripts can be di-
vided into two groups containing two Daniel dossiers: **E** (ff. 9–13v) and
P (ff.12v-22) on the one hand and **M** (ff. 39–53v) and **V** (ff. 40v-59)

on the other. These two dossiers are very similar and may derive from a common source.[5] The main differences are that I.4 (in the numbering used in this volume) is absent in **E** and **P** and I.6 is represented as two different redactions in the two groups of manuscripts. Dahlman therefore edited the material as if it were a single dossier, with the exception of I.6, whose two redactions she edited as No. 4A and 4B.[6] (I have followed 4A for my translation.) The most important manuscript is **E**, but unfortunately it has lost several folios (e.g. I.3 and I.6 are missing) and it is difficult to read because of damage from a fire.

I completed my translations of the greek dossier, using Clugnet's texts, before I knew of Dahlman's work. Dr Dahlman later graciously supplied me with unpublished copies of her texts. Subsequently I compared her texts with Clugnet's and found hers almost invariably superior, and modified my translations by using her edition as my primary text. In 2007 Dr Dahlman sent me a copy of her newly published book on Abba Daniel, which I then used to revise this chapter on the greek text. Originally, I placed variants from Clugnet's published texts in a kind of *apparatus criticus* at the end of Chapter One. This decision mandated a rather cumbersome double-note system, one explanatory, marked with arabic numerals; and one textual, indicated with roman numerals.

I came to realize—a bit belatedly, alas, especially after seeing Dahlman's work—that this set up was, at best, a quasi-critical edition with little value either to general readers or to scholars: general readers probably would have little interest in textual minutiae, and textual scholars would rightly criticize my naïve apparatus as incomplete and unsystematic. Therefore, for the purposes of this volume, I have dropped the textual notes and apparatus;[7] some day, someone will publish a complete critical edition of the Daniel dossier. For the present, my main desire, and that of my many co-translators, is to present the Daniel dossier in english translation to what is apparently an increasing audience for early monastic writings. I have, however, saved the original notes and anyone who would like them may request a digital copy by contacting me at tvivian@csub.edu.

GREEK ACCOUNTS[8]

I. STORIES ABOUT ABBA DANIEL
FROM THE DANIEL DOSSIER

I.1 (2) [3] *Mark the Fool*[9]

(121) [60] There was an old man in Scetis by the name of Daniel[10] and he had a disciple, and a brother by the name of Sergius lived for a short time with the aforesaid disciple and then went to sleep in the Lord.[11] After the perfection[12] of Abba Sergius, Abba Daniel[13] gave his disciple the freedom to speak freely,[14] for he loved him.

One day, then, the old man[15] took his disciple and went up to Alexandria, because it is customary for the superior[16] of Scetis to go up to see the pope[17] for the Great Feast.[18] When they arrived at the city about five in the afternoon and as they were walking in the street, they saw a brother[19] who was naked, wearing a loincloth[20] around his loins.[21] That brother was pretending to be half-witted[22] and there were other imbeciles with him. The brother would go around like a half-wit, babbling nonsensically,[23] snatching things from the stalls in the marketplace, and giving them to the other imbeciles.[24] His name was 'Mark of the Horse' ('The Horse' is a public bath).[25] There Mark the Fool worked, earning a hundred *noumia*[26] a day, and there he would sleep on the benches.[27] From the hundred *noumia*, he would buy provisions for himself with twelve *noumia*[28] and give the rest to the other imbeciles. The whole city knew Mark of the Horse on account of his mad babbling.

The old man said to his disciple, 'Go and see where that half-wit is living', and he left and made inquiries and they told him, 'At The Horse; he's an imbecile'. After the old man took leave of the pope the next day, in accordance with God's divine purpose he found Mark the Fool at the Great Tetrapylon,[29] and the old man ran and took hold of him and began to cry out, saying, 'Men of Alexandria, help!'[30] The half-wit was mocking the old man and a large crowd gathered around them. The disciple, fearful, stood at a distance and everyone was saying to the old man, 'Do not take his insolence seriously; he's an imbecile!' (121) The old man said to them, '*You* are [61] the imbeciles, for today I have not found a person in this city except for this fellow'.[31]

Some clergy from the church, who knew the old man, also arrived and said to him, 'What has this half-wit ever done to you?' The old man said to them, 'Take him to the pope for me', and they did so, and the old man said to the pope, 'Today in this city there is not such a vessel as this one'.[32] The pope, knowing that the old man had been given confidence by God to speak about this fellow, threw himself at the imbecile's feet and began to adjure him to reveal to them who he was.

The imbecile came to himself and confessed, saying, 'I was a monk and was ruled by the demon of sexual sin for fifteen years.[33] Coming to my senses, I said, "Mark, for fifteen years you've been a slave to the Enemy.[34] Go and likewise be a slave to Christ". So I went to the Pempton[35] and remained there eight years, and after eight years I said to myself, "Come on, go to the City and make yourself into a fool in order to be released from your sins". Today I have completed another eight years as an imbecile'.[36] Those who heard wept and gave glory to God.

Mark slept in the episcopal residence along with the old man, and when dawn came the old man said to his disciple, 'Call Abba Mark for me to offer a prayer for us so we may leave for our cell'. So the disciple left and found Mark asleep in the Lord and he went and told the old man that Abba Mark had died. The old man told the pope and the pope told the general[37] and he ordered everything to come to a stop in the city. The old man sent his disciple to Scetis,[38] saying, 'Sound the signal and gather the fathers together and say to them, "Come to be blessed by the old man"'.[39]

All of Scetis came wearing white[40] and bearing olive branches and palms,[41] and the Enaton and Kellia did likewise, and those in the monastic settlement of Nitria and all the lavras around Alexandria.[42] As a result, (122) the corpse was not buried for five days and they were forced to embalm blessed Mark's remains.[43] And so the whole city and the monks, with lighted candles and incense and tears, purified the main street of the city[44] and buried the precious corpse of blessed Mark the imbecile,[45] glorifying and praising God, the lover of humanity, [62] who gives such grace and glory to those who love him, both now and in the age to come.

I.2 (1) [8] *Abba Daniel Atones for a Murder He Committed*[46]

(114) [71] This Abba Daniel[47] from childhood renounced[48] the world by living in Scetis.[49]

He lived first in a cenobium for forty years and afterwards practiced asceticism alone. The barbarians attacked and took him prisoner and he lived with them for two years, when a certain Christ-loving man rescued him from the barbarians.[50] A short time later the barbarians again came and carried him off and he lived with them six months and escaped from them. A third time they attacked and took him prisoner.[51] Mistreating him, they mercilessly tortured him. One day, then, Abba Daniel had the good fortune to find a rock;[52] picking it up, he hit the foreigner, who happened to die from being struck with the rock. Fleeing, Abba Daniel was saved.

He repented the murder he had committed and went to Alexandria and conferred with Archbishop Timothy[53] about what had happened. When the archbishop understood what had taken place, he blamed him, saying, 'Would not he who twice delivered you from the barbarians also have been able to deliver you again? Nevertheless, you did not commit murder, for you killed a wild beast'. So Abba Daniel sailed to Rome and once again related the details of the murder, this time to the pope of Rome,[54] and the pope told him the same thing. So Abba Daniel went to Constantinople and Ephesus and Jerusalem and Antioch and explained to the patriarchs the details of the murder and all of them, in agreement, said the same thing to him.

He returned once again to Alexandria and said to himself, 'Daniel, Daniel, the person who murders will be murdered',[55] and he went to the praetorium and turned himself in to the officials of the magistrate's court, saying to them, 'I fought with someone and, overcome by (116) anger, hit him with a rock and killed him. I beg you, therefore, to hand me over [72] to the magistrate so I may die in return for the murder I committed, in order to escape future punishment'. When the magistrate's officials heard these things, they put him in jail and thirty days later reported to the magistrate the details of his case. The magistrate brought him from prison and questioned him about the murder, and Abba Daniel told him the whole truth. Marvelling at Abba Daniel's scrupulousness,[56] the magistrate released him, saying to him, 'Go, pray for me, abba. If only you had "murdered" seven more of them!'

The old man said to himself, 'I have hope, in God's merciful love for humankind, that His Goodness will not hold me responsible for this murder hereafter. From now on I pledge to Christ all the days of my life to serve a single leper in return for the murder I committed'.[57] So he took one leper to his cell and said to himself, 'If this leper dies, I will go up to Egypt and get another in his place'.[58] All the monks of Scetis knew that the old man had a leper, but no one was able to see his face except the old man, and he alone.

One day, then, about noon,[59] the old man summoned his disciple to serve him something to eat.[60] Through God's divine agency it happened that the old man had forgotten that the door to his cell had been left open. He was sitting in the sun, caring for the leper. The leper was completely eaten up by his many sores. The old man's disciple returned from his duties and, finding the door open, observed how the old man was caring for the leper.[61] [73] Because the leper had so completely rotted away, Abba Daniel kneaded the food and put it in the leper's mouth.[62]

(118) When the disciple saw the amazing work that the old man was doing, he was astonished and glorified God who was supplying such great patience to the old man to serve the leper like this.

I.3 (3) [4] *The Holy Mendicant*[63]

(126) [62] Another time Abba Daniel once again went up to Alexandria with his disciple and he saw a blind person sitting in his underclothes[64] in the square[65] and he was saying 'Give me something; have pity'. The old man said to his disciple, 'Do you see this blind man? I tell you he is a great person. Do you want me to show you what sort of person he is? Wait here'. The old man[66] went and said to the blind man, 'Please do me a favor, brother. I don't have the means to buy myself palm branches so I can work and feed myself',[67] and the blind man said to him, 'Why are you looking at *me*, abba? You see me naked and begging and you tell *me* to buy palm branches for *you*? Wait here, however'.

The old man motioned to his disciple to follow him and they went to Saint Mark's Outside-the-City,[68] for the blind man had a cell there. The blind man said to the old man, 'Wait here for me, abba', and he went inside and brought the old man a small basket containing raisins, pomegranates, and dried figs and he took from the fold of his garment[69] a *tremissis*[70] and gave it to the old man, saying, 'Pray for me, abba', The old man went to his disciple and wept, saying, 'Look! How many hidden servants God has![71] As the Lord lives, I will never turn my back on alms-giving because that is what love is'.

After they left him, a few days later they heard that the Great Steward[72] was suffering terribly with a liver ailment and was lying in Saint Mark's, and Saint Mark the apostle appeared to him and said to him, 'Send for the blind man and bring him here and he will place his hand on the [63] spot where you are suffering and you will be well again'.[73] So the Great Steward quickly sent his servants and brought the blind man by force. After the blind man prayed and placed his hands on the Steward, the suffering immediately went away and news of what had happened spread throughout the city.[74]

(128) When the pope heard about it, he went to see the blind man and found him perfected[75] in the Lord, and news of his death spread throughout Scetis. The old man went up with his disciple and other fathers and they received a blessing from their blessed fellow-brother.[76] Almost the whole city turned out also and, receiving a blessing from him, with hymns and celebration they bore his precious corpse out for burial and placed him atop Abba Mark the fool for God.[77] Such was his life: if he received any kind of alms, he would use them to buy apples, raisins, and pomegranates and would distribute them through someone else among the foreigners to the sick every Sunday.[78] He kept up this virtuous service for forty-eight years, to the glory of God.

I.4 (5) [7] *The Sister Who Pretended to be Drunk*[79]

(140) [67] Abba Daniel went up from Scetis one time with his disciple into the Upper Thebaid[80] for the feast day of Abba Apollo[81] and all the fathers for about seven miles around went out to greet him. There were about five thousand of them.[82] They could be seen lying face down on the sand like a rank of angels welcoming Christ with fearful reverence: some were spreading their clothing before him[83] while others were laying down their cowls, raining tears upon the earth. The archimandrite[84] came

out and prostrated himself seven times in front of the old man. After they
greeted one another with a kiss, [68] they sat down and the archimandrite
and monks asked to hear a word from the old man, for the latter would
not readily speak to anyone.[85] So they sat outside the cenobium on the
sand, for the church would not hold them all, and Abba Daniel said to
his disciple, 'Write "If you want to be saved, pursue poverty and silence:
the whole monastic life depends on these two virtues"'.[86] His disciple
gave what he had written to one of the brothers and he translated it into
Coptic and when it was read to the fathers all of them wept and escorted
the old man on his way, for no one dared to say to him 'Please stay'.

So he went to Hermopolis[87] and there said to his disciple, 'Go and
knock at that monastery and tell them I am here'. There was a monastery
for women there called the Monastery of Abba Jeremiah,[88] where about
three hundred sisters were living.[89] So his disciple went and knocked and
the doorkeeper said to him in a faint voice, 'May you be saved. (142) We
are pleased that you have come. Why are you calling?'

He said to her, 'Call for me the mother archimandrite;[90] I wish to
speak with her'.

She said, 'She never meets anyone, but tell me why you are calling
and I will tell her'.

He said, 'Tell her "A certain monk wishes to speak with you"', and
she left and told her. The abbess came and spoke to him, 'Why are you
calling?'

The brother said, 'I'm calling to ask you please to do me a favor and
allow me to sleep here, along with an old man; it's getting dark and we're
afraid the wild beasts will eat us'.

The mother superior[91] said to him, 'No man ever enters here. It
would be better for you to be devoured by wild beasts outside rather
than by those inside'.[92]

The brother said to her, 'Abba Daniel, from Scetis, is outside'.

When she heard this, she opened the two gates and came running
out, as did the whole community, and they spread their veils from the
gate out to where the old man was, rolling themselves at his feet and
licking the soles of his feet.

After they went inside the monastery, the mother superior brought
a basin and filled it with warm water and herbs and stood the sisters in
two choirs and they washed the old man's feet and those of his disciple
in the water. She took a cup and, taking water from the basin, [69]

poured it over the sisters' heads and afterwards she poured it over her
breast and over her head.[93] One could see all of them standing there
like stones upon stones, not moving or speaking. They moved only when
the signal[94] was given. So the old man said to the abbess, 'Do they honor
us or are the sisters always like this?' She said, 'Your servants are always
like this, master. Pray for them'. The old man said, 'Speak to my disciple,
for he assaults me like a barbarian'.[95]

One of the sisters lay sleeping in the forecourt of the church, wearing
rags that were in shreds. The old man said, 'Who is this sleeping?'

The mother superior said to him, 'She's one of the sisters, and she's
a drunk,[96] and we don't know what to do with her: we're afraid to take
the responsibility[97] of throwing her out of the monastery, and if we let
her stay, she demoralizes the (144) sisters'.[98]

The old man said to his disciple, 'Take the pan of water and throw
it on her'. When he did as the old man had commanded, she stood up
as though from a drunken stupor. The mother superior said, 'Master, this
is how she always is'.

The superior took the old man and they went to the refectory and
after she prepared dinner with the sisters she said, 'Bless your servants
so they may eat in your presence', and he blessed them. Only she and
her second-in-command sat with them. They set before the old man a
small bowl containing some soaked lentils and raw vegetables and dates
and water, while to his disciple they served boiled lentils and a small
loaf of bread and wine mixed with water.[99] To the sisters they served a
number of foods, fish and wine in abundance, and they ate very well
and no one spoke. After they got up from dinner, the old man said to
the abbess, 'What is this you've done? *We* ought to have eaten well, but
it was you and the sisters who had the good food.'

The superior said to him, 'You are a monk, and I served you a monk's
food; your disciple is a monk's disciple and I served him a disciple's food.
We, however, are novices and we ate novices' food'.

The old man said to her, 'May your charity be remembered. We have
truly profited from what you have done'.

As they were leaving the refectory to rest, the old man said to [70]
his disciple, 'Go see whether the drunken sister sleeps where she was
lying in the forecourt of the church', and he went and looked and returned and said to the old man, 'She's sleeping by the exit to the toilets'.
The old man said, 'Keep watch with me this night', and when all the

sisters had gone to sleep, the old man took his disciple and went down behind the lattice and they saw that the drunken sister was standing up and was stretching her hands to heaven; her tears were like a river and she was offering acts of contrition[100] on the ground. Whenever she perceived a sister coming to use the toilet, she would throw herself to the ground and snore. She spent all her days this way.

The old man said to his disciple, 'Call the superior[101] for me (146) without anyone noticing'. He went and called her and her second-in-command and all night they watched what the sister was doing. The superior began to weep, saying, 'I don't know how many times I've treated her badly!'

When the signal sounded,[102] a rumor concerning her spread through the sisterhood and she perceived it and went without anyone noticing to where the old man slept. She stole his staff and cowl and opened the gate of the monastery, wrote a short note, and put it between the bolt and the gate, saying, 'Pray, and forgive me whatever sins I have committed against you', and she disappeared.[103]

When day came they looked for her but did not find her. They went to the entrance and found the gate opened and the note behind it, and the monastery erupted into weeping. The old man said, 'This was the very reason I came here, for God loves drunkards such as these'.[104] All the sisters confessed to the old man what they had done to her, and the old man offered prayer for the sisters and they withdrew to their cells, glorifying and giving thanks to God, who alone knows how many hidden servants he has.[105]

I.5A (7) [10] *Andronicus the Money-Changer and His Wife Athanasia*[106]

(166) [370] There was a money-changer by the name of Andronicus in the great city of Antioch. He took as wife Athanasia, a daughter of a certain money-changer named John. She truly proved to be immortal[107] in works and in thought. Andronicus, too, was very devout, full of good works. They were very wealthy. This was their way of life: they divided the business of money-changing and their abundant wealth into three parts—one part for the poor, another [371] for the monks, and the third part for themselves.[108] The whole city loved Lord Andronicus on account

of his virtuous acts. He had intercourse with[109] his wife and she conceived and bore a son and named him John. She had already conceived and borne a daughter and named her Mary. After that Andronicus no longer approached his wife for intercourse;[110] instead, all of their time and attention was with the other lovers of Christ. Every Sunday, Monday, Wednesday, and Friday, from evening until dawn, Andronicus devoted himself to washing the men while his wife, because of her love of the poor, would devote herself to washing the women.[111]

One day, then, Lady Athanasia returned home at dawn from her church-appointed duties[112] of washing and found her two children moaning and groaning. She got into bed and placed them on her breast. When blessed Andronicus came home, he began to upbraid her for sleeping too much, but she said to him, 'Don't get angry, my lord; the children are sick'. Touching them, (168) he found them burning up with fever. He groaned and said, 'Your will be done, Lord',[113] and left the city to pray at Saint Julian's, for their parents were laid to rest there.[114] He prayed until noon; when he returned, he heard lamentation and uproar in his house. Upset, he ran and found almost the whole city in his house and the children dead. He saw the two children lying together in the bed so he went to his family's oratory and, weeping, threw himself down before the altar[115] and said, 'Naked I came from my mother's womb and naked shall I return there. The Lord gave; the Lord has taken away. Let it be as has seemed best to the Lord. May the Lord's name be praised', now and forevermore!'[116] But his wife was trying to drown herself,[117] saying, 'I will die with my children!'

The whole city turned out for the children's funeral, so that as a result even the patriarch came with all the clergy and they placed the children in the martyrion of Saint Julian on top of their grandparents. Taking blessed Andronicus, the patriarch left for the episcopal residence. His wife, however, refused to go home but instead slept in the martyrion. In the middle of the night [372] the martyr appeared to her, dressed in a monk's habit, and said to her, 'Why do you not leave in peace those who are here?'

She said, 'My lord, do not be angry with me. I am suffering. I had only two children and today I buried both of them'.

He said to her, 'How old were your children?'

She said to him, 'One was twelve years old and the other was ten', and he said to her, 'Why, then, are you weeping over them? You should be weeping for your own sins! I tell you, woman, (170) just as a person, by nature, demands food and it is impossible for that person not to give himself something to eat, so too on that day[118] the little ones will also demand of Christ the good things to come, saying, "Righteous judge, you deprived us of earthly things; do not deprive us also of heavenly things"'.

When she heard these things, she was stung to the quick and exchanged sorrow for joy, saying, 'If my children really are alive in heaven, why am I weeping?' And she turned and looked for the *abba* who had spoken to her, but did not find him, and she knocked on the doorkeeper's door and said, 'Where is the *abba* who came in here just now?'

The doorkeeper said to her, 'You see that all the doors are secured and yet you say "Where is the *abba* who came in here just now"?' Then the observant attendant realized that she had had a vision.

Confused and fearful, she begged the doorkeeper to take her home. She related to her husband what she had seen. Then blessed Athanasia said to him, 'Truly, my lord, while the children were alive I wanted to speak to you and was embarassed to do so but now, after their death, I will now say to you: "If you will heed what I say, you will put me in a monastery and I will weep for my sins"'.

He said to her, 'Go, think for a week about what you have said, and if you still want to pursue what you have proposed, we will talk'.

When she came back and said the same thing, blessed Andronicus summoned his father-in-law and handed over to him all his property, saying to him, 'We are going to the Holy Land to pray. If something befalls us as mortal human beings, therefore, you will attend to God's will in doing what you are supposed to do with this property. I implore you to establish here both a hospital and a guest-house for monks'. Freeing his slaves[119] he gave them (172) bequests and, taking a small amount of blessed bread[120] and two horses, he and his wife left the city by themselves at night.

When blessed Athanasia [373] saw her home from a distance, she looked up to heaven and said, 'God, who said to Abraham and Sarah, "Leave your land and your kindred and go to the land that I will show you",[121] be our guide also in our fear of you. Look! For your name's sake, we have left the doors to our house open; do not close the door to your kingdom on us!' And they left, both of them weeping. When they reached the Holy Land, they worshipped there and, joining the company of many fathers, went to the Shrine of Saint Menas near Alexandria and had the benefit of the martyr.[122]

[123]About three in the afternoon Andronicus happened to see a monk having an argument with a lay person and said to the lay person, 'Why are you insulting the *abba*?'

The lay person said to him, 'Master, he has hired my animal as far as Scetis and I keep saying to him, "Let's go now so we can travel all night and tomorrow until noon so we can reach our destination before it gets hot", but he doesn't want us to leave now'.

Lord Andronicus said to him, 'Do you have another animal?'

He said to him, 'Yes'.

'Go, and bring it to me and go. I will take one animal and the *abba* will take one, because I too want to go down to Scetis'. Andronicus said to his wife, 'Stay here at the shrine of Saint Menas until I go to Scetis and receive a blessing from the fathers and come back'.

She said to him, 'Take me with you'.

He said to her, 'A woman cannot go to Scetis'.

Weeping, she said to him, 'You owe it to Saint Menas to stay here and not leave until you have put me in a monastery'.

After kissing one another goodbye, (174) they separated, and Andronicus went down to Scetis. Offering obeisance to the fathers at each lavra, he heard about Abba Daniel so he went and with great difficulty was able to meet him and so told the old man[124] everything. The old man said to him, 'Go and bring your wife and I will write a letter for you and you can take her to the Thebaid to the monastery of the Tabennisiotes'.[125]

Andronicus did just as the old man had told him. He left and brought her to the old man and he spoke to them the word of salvation. He wrote a letter and sent them to the monastery of the Tabennisiotes. When Andronicus returned, the old man gave him the monastic habit and taught him about the monastic life, and Andronicus remained at his side for twelve years. After twelve years, Lord Andronicus begged the old man to release [374] him so he could go to the Holy Land. Abba Daniel offered a prayer and released him.

Abba Andronicus, traveling through Egypt,[126] sat beneath a thorny broom tree in order to get some relief from the heat[127] when suddenly, through the dispensation of God, his wife came, dressed in men's clothing; she too was leaving for the Holy Land. They greeted one another; the dove recognized her mate. But how could he have recognized such beauty as hers, withered away as it was, and when she looked like an Ethiopian?[128] So she said to him, 'Where are you going, abba, sir?'

He said to her, 'To the Holy Land'.

She said to him, 'I too want to go there. If you wish, let the two of us travel together, but let us travel in silence as though we were traveling alone'.

Andronicus said, 'As you request'.

She said to him, 'Are you not in fact the disciple of Abba Daniel?'

He said to her, 'Yes', and she said to him, 'The prayers of the old man will travel with us'.

Andronicus replied, 'Amen'.

So after they had travelled together and worshipped at the holy places, they returned to Alexandria and Abba Athanasius said to (176) Abba Andronicus, 'Do you want us to live together in a cell?'

Andronicus said, 'Yes, as you wish, but first I want to go and get the old man's blessing'.

Abba Athanasius said to him, 'Go, and I will wait for you at the Ok-tokaidekaton[129] and, if you come, let us remain in silence just as we traveled together in silence. If you do not want to do things this way, do not come. I will remain here'.

Andronicus left and greeted the old man and reported to him about the brother. The old man said to him, 'Go and devote yourself to si-lence[130] and remain with the brother, for he is a good person'. After Abba Andronicus returned and found Abba Athanasius, they remained together in the fear of God another twelve years and Abba Andronicus did not recognize that she was a woman.

The old man would often go up to visit them,[131] instructing them in things for their profit. One time, then, after the old man had gone up to see them and had said goodbye, before he reached the shrine of Saint Menas, Abba Andronicus overtook him and said to him, 'Abba Athanasius is going to the Lord', and the old man turned around and found him in pain. Abba Athanasius began to weep. The old man said to him, 'You're weeping instead of rejoicing that you are going to meet Christ?'

Abba Athanasius said to the old man, 'I am not weeping for myself but for Abba Andronicus. Please do me a favor: after you bury me you will find a note under my pillow. Read it and give it to Abba Andronicus'.

After they prayed together, she received Communion and went to sleep in the Lord. They went to bury her and a marvellous thing happened—she was found to be a woman, and the news spread throughout the lavra.[132] [375] The old man sent and brought all of Scetis and the inner desert and all the lavras of Alexandria came; the whole city came out with them and the monks of Scetis were dressed in white,[133] for this is their custom in Scetis.

THE SHORTER CONCLUSION[134]

With olive branches and palm branches, they carried out the precious corpse of Athanasia, giving glory to God, who had provided the woman with such great endurance. And the old man remained during the week of mourning for Athanasia. Afterwards, the old man wanted to take Abba Andronicus with him, but he refused, saying, 'I will die with my lady', for the old man had told him that he had learned from the note that she was Andronicus' wife. Abba Andronicus stayed there and a little later he too went to sleep[135] and Abba Daniel once again went up and, after gathering together all the fathers, he carried out the corpse with psalms and hymns[136] and placed it near Abba Athanasius.

To the glory of Father and Son and Holy Spirit, now and always and for ever and ever. Amen.

THE LONGER CONCLUSION[137]

(176 l. 170) With olive branches and palm branches, they carried out the precious corpse of Athanasia, giving glory to God, who had provided the woman with such great endurance. (178) And the old man remained during the week of mourning for Athanasia. Afterwards, the old man wanted to take Abba Andronicus with him, but he refused, saying, 'I will die with my lady'.

So the old man once again said goodbye but before he could reach the shrine of Saint Menas a brother said, 'Abba Andronicus follows Abba Athanasius'. Hearing this, the old man sent word to Scetis, saying, 'Abba Andronicus is following Brother Athanasius'. When they heard, they went up and found him alive and after they received his blessing he went to sleep in the Lord.

Then war broke out between the fathers of Oktokaidekaton and those of Scetis. The latter were saying, 'The brother is ours and we are going to take him to Scetis and keep him there so his prayers may help us'. Those from Oktokaidekaton were saying, 'We are going to bury him with his sister'. Abba Daniel as well was also saying that the brother should be buried there. Those from Scetis did not listen to him and said, 'The old man belongs to heaven and no longer fears bodily conflict; we, however, are younger and want the brother so his prayers may help us'.[138]

When the old man saw that a great disturbance was taking place, he said to the brothers, 'Truly, if you do not listen to me, I too will remain here and will be buried with my children'. Then they were at peace and they brought out the corpse of brother Andronicus. They said to the old man, 'Let us go to Scetis'. The old man said to them, 'Allow me to observe the week of mourning for the brother', but they did not allow him to remain there.

Let us also pray, therefore, to attain the stature of Abba Andronicus and of Abba Athanasius through the prayers of all the saints. Amen.

I.5B [10] [B] *Life of Saint Andronicus and of His Wife Athanasia*[139]

[375] There was a money-changer by the name of Andronicus in the great city of Antioch and he took a wife by the name of Athanasia, for, as her name indicates, she was truly deathless in the works she did.[140] Andronicus too was very devout, and was filled with good works. They were also very wealthy and they divided all their possessions into two portions, one for the poor and for the monks, and the other part for taxes and for themselves. They produced two children, the one a male, whom they called John, and the other a girl, whom they named Mary. After that they no longer came near each other, [376] but instead gave themselves to the care of the poor and to doing good works.

One day blessed Athanasia went home to look in on her children and found them gravely ill. Upset, she lay down with them in bed and placed them beside her. When Andronicus came home and found her like that, he began to shout at her, thinking she was sleeping, but she said, 'Do not be angry, my lord; our children are very sick'. When he touched them, he found them burning up with fever. He groaned and left them, saying, 'May the Lord's will be done'[141] and went outside the city to pray in the church of Saint Julian. At midday he heard lamentation and weeping in his house and he ran and found that his two children had gone to their rest. He went to the oratory in his house and threw himself down before the icon of the Saviour and said, '"Naked I came from my mother's womb, naked shall I also return there. The Lord gave; the Lord has taken away. Let it be as has seemed best to the Lord. May the Lord's name be praised", now and forevermore!'[142] His wife, however, was trying to die with her children. A large crowd gathered for the children's funeral and brought them out and placed them with Andronicus' parents in the church of the holy martyr Julian.[143]

In the middle of the night, the martyr, dressed in a monk's habit, appeared in a dream to blessed Athanasia as she slept in the martyrion of Saint Julian and said to her, 'Why do you not leave in peace those who are here?'

She said, 'Lord, do not be angry with me since I am suffering. I buried both of my children here today'.

He said to her, 'How old were they?'

She said, 'One was twelve years old and the other was ten', and he said to her, 'Why, then, are you weeping over them? You should be weeping for your own sins! I tell you that just as a person, in accordance with human nature, demands food, in the same way the children will also demand of Christ on the day of judgement the good things to come and will say, "Righteous judge, you deprived us of earthly things; do not deprive us also of heavenly things"'.

When she heard these things, she was stung to the quick and exchanged sorrow for joy, saying, 'If my children really are alive in heaven, [377] why am I weeping?' She turned and looked for the monk who had appeared to her, but did not find him, and she called the doorkeeper and said to him, 'Where is the *abba* who just came in here?'

He said to her, 'You see that the doors are secured and yet you say "Where is the man who just came in here"?' and he concluded that she had had a vision. Confused and fearful, she went home and related to Andronicus what she had seen and said to him, 'Truly, my lord, while our children were alive I wanted to speak to you and was embarrassed to do so but now I will speak to you if you will heed me: put me in a monastery so I may weep for my sins'.

He said to her, 'Go, think for a week about what you have said and if you still want to pursue this intention we will talk'.

She returned and said the same thing and blessed Andronicus summoned his brother-in-law and handed over to him all their property, saying, 'We are going to the Holy Land[144] to pray. If something befalls us as mortal human beings, therefore, attend to God's will in doing what you are supposed to do with this property. I implore you therefore to do your soul good and establish a hospital and a guest-house for monks'. Freeing his male and female slaves, he gave them a bequest, and taking a small amount of blessed bread and two mules, he left at night with his wife.

When blessed Athanasia saw her home from a distance, she looked up to heaven and said, 'God, who said to Abraham and Sarah, "Leave your land and your kindred",[145] be our guide also in our fear of you. Look! For your name's sake, we have left our house open; do not close the doors to your kingdom on us!' And they left, both of them weeping. When they reached the Holy Land, they worshipped there and, joining the company of many fathers, went to the church of Saint Menas in Alexandria.[146]

About three in the afternoon blessed Andronicus saw a lay person fighting with a monk, and he said to the lay person, 'Why are you insulting the *abba*?'

He said, 'Master, he has hired my animal as far as Scetis and I keep saying to him, "Let's go now so we can travel all night and tomorrow until noon so we can reach Scetis", but he doesn't want to'.

Blessed Andronicus said to him, 'Do you have another animal, too?'

He said to him, 'Yes'.

Blessed Andronicus said to him, [378] 'Go and bring it to me and I will hire it because I too want to leave for Scetis'. Andronicus said to his wife, 'Stay here at the shrine of Saint Menas until I go to Scetis and receive a blessing from the fathers and come back'.

Blessed Athanasia said to him, 'Take me with you'.

He said to her, 'A woman cannot go to Scetis'.

Weeping, she said to him, 'Are you being attentive to Saint Menas? Will you stay there until you place me in a monastery?'

After saying goodbye to each other, he went down to Scetis. Offering obeisance to the fathers, he heard about Abba Daniel and he left and with great effort was able to meet him and so told the old man everything. The old man said, 'Go and bring your wife and I will write a letter for you and you can take her to the Thebaid to a monastery of the Tabennisiotes'.[147]

He did so and brought her to the old man and he spoke to them the word of salvation. Having written a note, he dismissed them. When Andronicus returned, Abba Daniel gave him the monastic habit and taught him about the monastic way of life and Andronicus remained at his side for twelve years. Afterwards, he begged the old man to release him so he could go to the Holy Land. He offered a prayer for him and released him.

While Abba Andronicus was traveling through Egypt,[148] he sat beneath a thorny broom tree in order to get some relief from the heat[149] when suddenly, through the dispensation of God, his wife came, dressed in men's clothing; she too was leaving for the Holy Land. They greeted one another. The dove recognized her mate, but how could he have recognized such beauty as hers, withered away as it was, and when she looked like an Ethiopian?[150] So she said to him, 'Where are you going, abba?'

He said to her, 'To the Holy Land'.

She said to him, 'I too wish to go there; let the two of us travel together but let us travel in silence as though we were traveling alone'.

He said, 'As you wish'.

She said to him, 'Are you not in fact the disciple of Abba Daniel?'

He said, 'Yes'.

[She said,] 'Isn't your name Andronicus?'

He said, 'Yes'.

She said to him, 'The prayers of the old man will travel with us'.

He said, 'Amen'.

So after they had worshipped at the holy places, they returned to Alexandria and Abba Athanasius said to Abba Andronicus, 'Do you want us to live together in a cell?'

He said, 'Yes, but first I want [379] to get the old man's blessing'.

Athanasius said to him, 'Go and I will wait for you at the Oktokaidekaton, and if you come, let us remain in silence just as we traveled together in silence. If he does not keep you, come. I will remain at the Oktokaidekaton'.[151]

He left and [returned and] remained with him in the fear of God another twelve years and she was not recognized by him. The old man would often go up to visit them, instructing them in things for their salvation. One time, then, after he had gone up to see them and had said goodbye and returned, before he reached the shrine of Saint Menas, Abba Andronicus overtook him and said, 'Abba Athanasius is going to the Lord', and the old man returned and found him in pain. Abba Athanasius began to weep and the old man said to him, 'You're weeping instead of rejoicing that you are going to meet the Lord?'

He said to him, 'I would not be weeping except for Abba Andronicus. But please do me a favor: after you bury me you will find a note under my pillow. Read it and give it to Abba Andronicus'.

Prayer was offered and she received Communion and went to sleep in the Lord. They went to bury him and found that she was a woman, and the news spread throughout the lavra. The old man sent and called the fathers in Scetis and those of the inner desert and all the lavras of Alexandria came and the whole city came out with them and the monks of Scetis were dressed in white (for this is their custom in Scetis), with olive branches. And they brought out the precious corpse of blessed Athanasia, giving glory to God who graced the woman with such great patient endurance. The old man remained there to fulfill the week of mourning for blessed Athanasia and after the week was over he wanted to take Abba Andronicus but he refused, saying, 'I will die with my wife'.

So the old man once again said goodbye and left but before he could reach the shrine of Saint Menas a brother overtook him and said, 'Abba Andronicus is in pain', and the old man once again sent word and summoned the Scetiotes, saying, 'Come and follow Abba Andronicus'. They went up and found him alive and were blessed by him and he went to sleep in peace. Much contentious dispute broke out between the fathers of Oktokaidekaton [380] and those of Scetis; the latter were saying, 'The brother is ours and we are going to take him to Scetis so that his prayers may help us'. Those from Oktokaidekaton were likewise saying, 'We are going to place him with his sister'.

Those from Scetis were superior in number and the archimandrite of Oktokaidekaton said, 'We will do what the old man says'. The old man said he was to be buried there. Those from Scetis did not listen to him and said, 'The old man belongs to heaven and no longer fears warfare; we, however, are younger and want the brother. It should be enough for those of you from Oktokaidekaton that we have left you Abba Athanasius'.

When the old man saw that a great disturbance was taking place, he said to the brothers, 'Truly, if you do not listen to me, I too will remain here and will be buried with my children'. Then they were at peace and they brought out the brother for burial and said to the old man, 'Let us go to Scetis', and he said, 'Allow me to observe the week of mourning for the brother', but they did not allow him to do this.

Let us also pray, therefore, to reach the stature of Abba Athanasius and of Abba Andronicus, through the prayers of the saints. Amen.

I.5C [10] *Andronicus and Athanasia*[152]

[380] This holy Andronicus was from the great city of Antioch, a money-changer by profession, very devout, wealthy, and full of good works. He married Athanasia, who also was holy and God-loving and was his companion in goodness. They always divided their substance into thirds: they would ungrudgingly share one part with the poor; another part

they would lend to those in need, without expectation of repayment; with the third part they managed their money-changing business and took care of the necessities of life. They produced two children, a male and a female, and after these two children were born to them they no longer came near each other;[153] instead, both of them devoted themselves to chastity and to their prayers, zealously and tirelessly giving themselves to good works for the poor and sick.

After twelve years of living together, when their children [381] had reached that age where they would bring glory to their parents, one day both of the children died. Blessed Andronicus, not demonstrating any unworthy reaction to what had happened, instead cried out with Job's blessed voice, "'Naked I came from my mother's womb'", and so on,[154] but his wife, Athanasia, in her grief, could not be consoled. As a result, when her children were buried in the martyrion of Saint Julian,[155] she refused to leave, saying, 'I too will die and be buried with my children!'

Although the patriarch took blessed Andronicus to the episcopal residence in order to console him, his wife refused to leave the martyrion but remained there, mourning in lamentation. In the middle of the night the martyr Julian appeared to her, dressed in a monk's habit, and said to her, 'What's wrong, woman? Why do you not leave in peace those who are here?'

She replied, 'Do not harden your heart, my lord, against my sorrow, for I am filled with grief. I had only two children and today I buried both of them'.

He said to her, 'Do not weep over them, for I tell you, woman, that just as a person, in accordance with human nature, demands food and it is impossible for that person not to give himself something to eat, in the same way on that day[156] the children will also demand of God the good things to come, saying, "Righteous judge, for the sake of the earthly things that you deprived us of, do not deprive us of heavenly things"'.

When she heard these things, she was stung to the quick and exchanged sorrow for joy, saying, 'If my children really are alive in heaven, why am I weeping?' And she turned and looked for the *abba* who had spoken to her; going through the whole church, she did not find him, and she said to the doorkeeper, 'Where is the *abba* who just came in here?'

The doorkeeper said to her, 'You see that all the doors are secured and yet you say "Where is the person who was just here"?' The doorkeeper knew that she had had a vision. Confused and fearful, she went home and related to her husband what she had seen and asked him to put her in a monastery. He gladly heard what she said, for he had this same desire, and he gave the majority of his possessions to the poor and freed the slaves he had bought; the rest of his property he gave to his brother-in-law, imploring him to establish a hospital and a guest-house for monks. Taking a few supplies for the journey, he and his wife left the city at night, alone.

[382] When blessed Athanasia saw her home from a distance, she looked up to heaven and said, 'God, who said to Abraham and Sarah, "Leave your land and your kindred and go to the land that I will show you",[157] be our guide now in our fear of you. Look! For your name's sake, we have left our house open; do not close the door to your kingdom on us!' And they left, both of them weeping. When they reached the Holy Land, they worshipped there and joined the company of many fathers. When they returned from there,[158] the two of them went to see Abba Daniel and when they asked him to place Athanasia in a monastery, he sent her to the monastery of the Tabennisiotes.[159] Andronicus, receiving the angelic habit from the old man, remained by his side for twelve years.

After twelve years had elapsed, Andronicus begged Abba Daniel to allow him to go back to worship in the Holy Land. He offered a prayer and released him. Saint Andronicus, traveling through Egypt, sat beneath a tree in order to get some relief from the heat.[160] Suddenly, through the dispensation of God, his wife, who was also leaving for the Holy Land, came along, dressed in men's clothing, and met her husband, Andronicus. They greeted one another; she recognized him, but he did not recognize her because her beauty had withered due to her severe asceticism and because she looked like an Ethiopian.[161] She said to him, 'Where are you going, abba, sir?'

He said to her, 'To the Holy Land'.

She said to him, 'I too wish to go there'.

He said to her, 'Do you want to travel there together?'

She said to him, 'As you wish, but let us travel in silence as though we were traveling alone'.

Andronicus said, 'As you wish'.

She said to him, 'Are you not in fact the disciple of Abba Daniel?'

He said, 'Yes'.

She said to him, 'Isn't your name Andronicus?'

He said to her, 'Yes'.

She said to him, 'The prayers of the old man will travel with us'.

Andronicus said, 'Amen', and they traveled together.

So after they had worshipped at the holy places, they returned in silence to Alexandria. Abba Athanasius (for Athanasia had changed her name to this) said to Andronicus, 'Do you want us to live together in a cell?'

Andronicus said, 'As you wish, but first I want to go and [383] get the old man's blessing'.

Abba Athanasius said to him, 'Go and I will wait for you at the Okto-kaidekaton,[162] and if you can submit to living with me in silence just as we traveled together in silence, come back, but if not, do not return.

He left and reported to the old man about the matter, and the old man said to him, 'Go and love silence and remain with the brother, for he is a monk just as one ought to be'.

After he returned, they remained together, Andronicus and his wife, another twelve years and he did not recognize that she was a woman. The old man would often go up to visit them, instructing them in things for their profit. One time, then, after the old man had gone up to see them and had said goodbye, as he was returning Abba Andronicus ran after him, overtook him, and said, 'Abba Athanasius is going to the Lord', and the old man returned and found him burning up with fever. Abba Athanasius began to weep and the old man said to him, 'You're weeping instead of rejoicing that you are going to meet the Lord?'

He said, 'I would not be weeping except for Abba Andronicus. But please do me a favor: after you bury me you will find a note under my pillow. Read it and give it to Abba Andronicus'. They offered a prayer and she received Communion and went to sleep in the Lord.

They went to bury her and a marvellous thing happened—she was found to be a woman, and the news spread throughout the lavra. The old man sent and brought all of Scetis and the brothers dwelling in the inner desert and all the lavras of Alexandria came and the whole city came out with them and the monks of Scetis were dressed in white, for this is their custom in Scetis. With olive branches and palm branches, they carried out the precious corpse of Athanasia, giving glory to God, who had provided the woman with such great endurance. And the old man remained to finish the week of mourning for blessed Athanasia and afterwards wanted to take Abba Andronicus with him, but he refused, saying, 'I will die with my lady'.

So the old man once again said goodbye and while he was returning a brother approached him and said, 'Abba Andronicus is burning up with fever', and the old man once again sent word to Scetis, saying, 'Hurry and come, because Abba Andronicus is following his brother Athanasius'. They went up and found him alive and were blessed by him and he went to sleep in the Lord. [384] Hostile words broke out between the monks of Oktokaidekaton and those of Scetis concerning his corpse and which of the two places should have it. The old man could scarcely persuade them to allow it to be buried there with his fellow athlete Athanasia, and so both sides stopped their contentiousness and gave glory to God for everything.

I.6**A** (4A) [5] *Concerning Thomaïs, the Chaste and Holy Young Woman*

(134) [63] The same Abba Daniel another time once again went up with his disciple to Alexandria and while they were staying there, the following occurred: An *abba* of the Oktokaidekaton outside Alexandria had a son and his son had a wife, a young woman about eighteen years of age, and the *abba* lived with his son.[163] His son was a fisherman. The enemy of our souls, the Devil, was waging carnal warfare [64] against the *abba* with regard to his daughter-in-law and the *abba* was looking for an opportunity to have sexual intercourse with her but did not succeed. Therefore he began to kiss her constantly and the young woman accepted that, as from a father.

One day, then, fishermen came at night and took the young man in order to go out and fish. After the young man had left, his father got up and went over to his son's wife and the young woman said to him, 'What are you doing, father? Leave and cross yourself, for what you are doing is the work of the Devil'. He hit her numerous times but the young woman, vigorously fighting him off, refused his advances.

The young man's sword hung over the bed and, wanting to frighten her, the *abba* brandished the naked sword, saying, 'If you don't obey me, you will die!'

But she said, 'If I have to be torn limb from limb, so be it; I will never obey you!'

He suddenly lashed out with the sword and pulled the young woman down by her hips[164] and cut her in two. God immediately struck him blind and he went around groping for the door but was not able to find it.

Some other fishermen came looking for the young man at dawn, and his father told them, (136) 'He's gone fishing. Where's the door? I don't see it!'

They said to him, 'Here it is', and when they went inside they saw what had happened, and said, 'What's going on here?'

He said to them, 'Seize me; I've committed murder!'

When they heard what the father said, they seized him and handed him over to the magistrate. The magistrate interrogated him and, when he found out what he had done, punished him.

Afterwards, Abba Daniel said to his disciple, 'Let us go and view the young woman's corpse'. When they came to the Oktokaidekaton outside Alexandria, the fathers heard and came out to greet him. [65] The old man said to them, 'As the Lord my God lives, her corpse shall not be buried except with the fathers'.

Many began to grumble. The old man[165] said to them, 'This young woman is my *amma*, and she is yours: she died to protect her chastity, but our fellow monk[166] has passed away because of the sufferings he inflicted'. No one opposed the old man, and they buried the young woman with the fathers. The old man returned with his disciple to Scetis.

I.6**B** [5] *On the Same Day, the Feast of Holy Mother Thomaïs*[167]

[65] This holy Thomaïs was born in Alexandria and, having been well brought up and educated by her parents, was married to a man. She was well taken care of in her husband's home and managed everything soberly and in an orderly manner.[168] Her husband's natural father, who by marriage was also the young woman's father-in-law, also lived with the young man. When his son was not at home, the destroyer of souls, the Devil, planted shameful thoughts in the old man for his daughter-in-law and he resolved to have sexual intercourse with the young woman, plotting by every possible means to fulfill his intentions.

When blessed Thomaïs was unable to accomplish anything by severely admonishing and entreating the old man, he only became more enflamed and blinded by the demon. Taking his son's sword and dealing the young woman a mortal blow, he cut her in two and she gave up [66] her spirit to the Lord and became a martyr for chastity. The old man immediately lost his sight and went around the house blind.

Some men came by, seeking his son, and found the young woman lying dead on the ground. When they saw this and saw the old man staggering around blind and wandering to and fro, they inquired, 'What is this we see?' When the old man revealed the truth of what had happened and convicted himself of having committed the murder with his own hand, he handed himself over and, shamefaced, was detained by them for the magistrate. They took his statement and, convinced of his guilt, themselves handed the old man over to the magistrate. When the truth was ascertained, by the magistrate's command the old man had his head cut off.

When Abba Daniel, the head of Scetis,[169] learned about these events, he brought Thomaïs to Scetis and placed her in the cemetery there, since on behalf of chastity she had contended and shed her own blood. Whenever one of the monks in Scetis, thrown down by love of sexual sin, went to the tomb of the blessed one and anointed himself with oil from the window,[170] he would receive while asleep a blessing from the young woman, who would reveal herself to him. When he awakened from sleep, he would find himself set free from the passion. From that time, therefore, and up to today, the brothers of this same monastery, in their battles with the flesh, have blessed Thomaïs[171] as a great helper.

I.6C *Concerning Saint Thomaïs, Alexandrian Martyr*[172]

On the same day of April 14 occurs the feast day of the martyr Saint Thomaïs. This Saint Thomaïs was born in Alexandria and, having been brought up in all virtue and instructed in literature by her parents, was soon afterwards given in marriage to a man. She lived in the married estate with great praise for her virtue and modesty, discretely and properly conducting herself in all things. Her husband's father, who had accepted Thomaïs as his daughter-in-law, also lived in the same house.

When the old man's son, Thomaïs' husband, was not at home, the destroyer of souls, the Devil, planted shameful thoughts in the old man for his daughter-in-law so that he resolved to have sinful sexual intercourse with the young woman and to consummate the impious intentions of his wicked soul.

Blessed Thomaïs thereupon opposed the evil old man and with many words dissuaded him from acting wickedly and entreated him not to snatch away her chastity from her but he only became more and more frustrated. Driven on—or, rather, held captive by the demon in mental blindness—and goaded by burning sexual desire, he took his son's sword and, striking his daughter-in-law and son's wife, he cut her in two with the iron. As a result, she poured out her spirit and took up the martyr's crown, having been killed for protecting her chastity.

The old man and father-in-law was struck blind and wandered around the house. In the meantime it so happened that some men came by seeking his son and they found Thomaïs his wife lying dead on the ground. When they saw this and saw the old father-in-law staggering around blind and wandering to and fro, they inquired, 'What is this we see?' The old man confessed what had happened and convicted himself of murdering his daughter-in-law. He handed himself over and begged that he be taken to the magistrate, from whom he would accept judgement for the crime he had committed. They did what the old man asked and handed him over to the magistrate's bench. When the magistrate understood the situation, he ordered the old man's head cut off with the sword.

When Abba Daniel of Scetis learned about these events, he ordered Thomaïs to be brought to Scetis and buried in the cemetery there, since she had shed her own blood on behalf of chastity. Whenever one of the monks in that same Scetis was violently aroused by the spirit of fornication, he would go to the tomb and to the remains of the blessed martyr and anoint himself with oil from a light hanging there, having spent a quiet night there, during which time the martyr would appear to him. Having awakened from his heavenly prayer, the monk would find himself completely freed from all sexual desire. From that time, therefore, and up to today, each of the brothers of this same monastery, in their battles with the flesh, receives confidence through blessed Thomaïs.

I.7 (4A) [6] *A Monk, Tempted by Sexual Sin, Receives a Blessing from Thomaïs*[173]

(132 l. 43) [66] One day, then, a brother was besieged in Scetis by sexual sin. He went and told the old man[174] about it. The old man said to him, 'Go to the Oktokaidekaton[175] and stay on top of the tomb[176] of the fathers and say, "God of Thomaïs, help me!" I have faith in God that [67] he will free you from this warfare'.

The brother did as the old man had ordered and, returning three days later, said to the old man, 'Through God and your prayers[177] I have been freed from my warfare'.

The old man said to him, 'How?'

The brother said, 'I just did twelve acts of contrition[178] and placed myself on top of the tomb of the fathers and a young woman came and said to me, "Take this blessing[179] and go to your cell". She gave me three blessings', he continued, 'and, as soon as I received them, I was immediately relieved of the warfare.'

Those who do battle on behalf of God have such great freedom of speech and those who die for chastity's sake receive a crown through Christ Jesus our Lord. Amen.

I.8A (8) [2] *The Patrician Lady Anastasia*[180]

(180) [51] A eunuch[181] was living in the inner desert[182] of Scetis.[183] Once a week he would visit Abba Daniel at night without anyone knowing about it except Abba Daniel and his disciple. The old man[184] ordered his disciple to fill a wine jar with water for the eunuch once a week and [take it to him][185] and place it at the door and knock and go away without speaking with him at all. 'But if', he said, 'you ever find a potsherd with writing on it at the entrance to the cave, bring it'.[186] And so Abba Daniel's disciple did as he was told.

One day he found a potsherd with this written on it: 'Bring your tools and come alone with the brother.' When the old man read what was written, he wept and wailed and said, 'What woe there is in the inner desert! What great pillar is going to fall today!' And he said to his disciple, 'Take the implements. Let's go immediately so we reach the old man while he's still alive, for he is going to the Lord'.

Weeping, the two of them left and they found the eunuch burning up with fever. The old man threw himself on the eunuch's breast and wept, saying, 'Blessed are you because you have focused your attention on this hour[187] and have looked with contempt on an earthly kingdom!'

The eunuch said, 'Blessed are *you*, a second Abraham, because God receives so much fruit from these hands!'[188]

The old man said to him, [52] 'Offer a prayer for us.'

The eunuch replied, 'It is I who need many prayers at this hour', and the old man said to him, 'If I had preceded you, I would have been able to pray for you and bring you comfort'.

The eunuch sat up from the mat on which he was lying, took (182) the old man's head, and kissed it, saying, 'God, who guided me here, will himself bring to fulfillment your old age, just as he did with Abraham'.[189]

The old man, taking hold of his disciple, placed him at the eunuch's feet, saying, 'Bless my child, father', and the eunuch tenderly kissed him and said to him, 'God, you who are standing by me at this hour to remove me from this temporary habitation, you who know how many steps he has taken to this cell for your name's sake, cause the spirit of this brother's fathers to rest upon him just as you caused the spirit of Elijah to rest upon Elisha,[190] and may the name of this brother's fathers be invoked upon him'.

Then he said to the old man, 'For the sake of the Lord, do not take off the clothes I am wearing but rather send me to the Lord just as I am, and let no one besides yourselves know anything about me', and he said to the old man, 'Give me Communion'. After receiving Communion he said, 'Please give me the kiss of peace in Christ and pray for me', and he looked to his right to the east and said, 'It is good that you have come. Let us go.' His face shone like fire[191] and he made the sign of the cross on his mouth and said, 'Into your hands, God, I shall commend my spirit',[192] and in this way he offered up his soul to Christ.

The two of them wept. After they had dug a grave in front of the cave, the old man stripped off the clothes he was wearing and said to his disciple, 'Clothe him with more than what he is wearing'. (The eunuch was wearing a loincloth made from palm fiber and a patched cloak.)[193] While the brother was dressing the eunuch, he looked and realized that the eunuch was a woman[194] but he did not say anything.[195] After they buried him and offered a prayer, the old man said to his disciple, 'Let us break our fast here today and let us celebrate an *agapē*[196] for the old man'. After celebrating Communion, they found that the eunuch had a few (184) dried loaves of bread and some soaked lentils. They celebrated the *agapē* for the eunuch and, picking up the rope that the eunuch had made by his labor, they carried it off and left, giving thanks to God.

While they were walking on their way, the brother said to the old man, 'Do you know, father, that that eunuch was a woman?' [53]

The old man said, 'I know, my child, that he is a woman. Do you want me to tell you about her? Listen. She was a patrician lady of the highest rank, connected with the royal court, and Emperor Justinian wanted to take her into the imperial residence on account of her great intelligence. But Theodora[197] found out, became angry, and wanted to exile her. When Anastasia was apprised of this, she hired a boat at night, loaded some of her things in it, came to Alexandria, and settled at the Pempton.[198] Here she also founded a monastery, which up to today is called the Monastery of the Patrician Lady.[199]

'After Theodora died, she learned once again that the emperor wanted to send for her. She, however, fled Alexandria by night and came here to me, told me everything that had happened, and begged me to give her a cell outside Scetis. So I gave her this cave and she changed her apparel for men's clothing. See, today makes twenty-eight years that she has lived in Scetis and no one knows about her except you and one other person. How many court officials the emperor sent, searching for her—and not only the emperor but also the pope and all of Alexandria! And not a single person discovered where she was until today.

'Those raised in imperial courts contend[200] against the Devil and afflict their bodies while we, who could scarcely find a way of being filled with bread while we were in the world, have entered the monastic life and live in excessive luxury and are unable to acquire virtue! Therefore let us also pray that the Lord may think us fit to run his race[201] with the saints and find mercy with our fathers (186) and with Abba Anastasius the eunuch—for she used to be called "Anastasia"'.[202]

I.8**B** [2] *From the Same Abba Daniel:*
Concerning the Patrician Lady Who Received a New Identity as a Eunuch

[54] A eunuch was living in the inner desert of Scetis and had his cell eighteen miles from Scetis. Once a week he would visit Abba Daniel at night without anyone knowing about it except the old man's disciple and him alone. The old man ordered his disciple to fill a wine jar with water for the eunuch once a week: 'Carry the jar and put it outside the door, then just knock and go away without saying anything. Only take a look, and if you ever find an ostracon near the cave with writing on it, bring it back with you.' One day his disciple found an ostracon that had been written on: 'Bring your tools and come'. When the old man read what was written on the ostracon, he wept and wailed and said, 'What woe there is in the inner desert! What great pillar is going to fall today!' And he said to his disciple, 'Take these implements and come and follow me. Ah, but let's hurry and make our way to the old man lest we be deprived of his prayers, for he journeys to the Lord'.

And the two of them spoke and left and found the eunuch burning up with fever. The old man threw himself on the eunuch's breast and wept profusely and said, 'Blessed are you because you have made this hour your concern and have looked with contempt on an earthly kingdom and all persons!' The eunuch said to him, 'Blessed are *you*, second Abraham and one who receives Christ,[203] because God receives such a large quantity of fruit on account of these hands!' And the old man said to him, 'Offer a prayer for us, father'. The eunuch said to him, 'It is rather I who need many prayers at this hour', and the old man said to him, 'If I'd known about this hour, I would have comforted you'. The eunuch sat up from the mat on which he was lying, [55] took the old man's head, and kissed him, saying, 'God, who has been my guide in this place, will himself bring to fulfillment your old age, just as he did with Abraham'.[204]

The old man, taking hold of his disciple, placed him at the eunuch's knees, saying, 'Bless my child, father', and the eunuch tenderly kissed him and said, 'God, you who are standing by me at this hour to remove me from my corpse and who knows how many steps this brother has taken to this cell for your holy name's sake, cause the spirit of his fathers to rest upon him just as you caused the spirit of Elijah to rest upon Elisha,[205] and may the name of his fathers be invoked upon him'. And the eunuch said to the old man, 'For the sake of the Lord, do not take off the clothes I am wearing but rather send me to the Lord just as I am, and let no one besides yourselves ever know anything about me', and he said to the old man, 'Give me Communion', and after receiving Communion he said, 'Celebrate an *agape* for me in Christ and pray for me', and he looked to the east and to the right and said, 'It's good that you have come. Let us go.' His face became like fire and he made the sign of the cross on his forehead, saying, 'Into your hands, God, I will commend my spirit',[206] and in this way he offered up his soul to the Lord.

The two of them wept and dug a grave in front of the cave and the old man stripped off what he was wearing and said to his disciple, 'Clothe him with more than what he is wearing (the eunuch was wearing a loincloth made from palm fiber and a patched cloak). While the brother was dressing the eunuch, he looked at him and saw that his breasts were those of a woman and were like two withered leaves and he did not say anything.[207] After they buried him and offered prayer, the old man said to his disciple, 'Let us break our fast today and let us celebrate an *agape*[208] for the old man', and after celebrating Communion they found that the eunuch had a few loaves of dried bread and some soaked pulse and they celebrated an *agape* for him and, carrying the rope that the eunuch had made with his labor, they left for their own cell, giving thanks to God.

While they were walking on their way, the disciple said to the old man, 'Did you know, father, that that eunuch was a woman? When I was dressing him I saw his breasts, and they were a woman's, like [56] withered leaves'. The old man said to him, 'I know, child. I know he was a woman. Do you want me to tell you about her? Listen now. She was originally a patrician lady at the court of Emperor Justinian and the emperor wanted to take her into the imperial residence on account of her great intelligence. But Theodora learned about it and got angry with her and wanted to banish her. When the patrician lady found out what had happened, she hired a boat, laid in some of her possessions at night and, taking flight, came to Alexandria and took up residence at the fifth milestone outside Alexandria. At that time she also founded there a monastery and to this day it is called "The Monastery of the Patrician Lady".

'After Theodora died, she again learned that the emperor wanted to send for her and once again she fled by night from Alexandria and came here alone and entreated me to give her a cell outside Scetis and she turned over to me all of her remaining possessions. I gave her this cave and she exchanged her clothing for that of a man. Today makes twenty-eight years that she has spent in Scetis and no one knows that she is here except you and another brother and I, the old man. How many court officials Emperor Justinian sent, searching for her—and not only he but also the pope of Alexandria! And not a single person discovered where she was until today'.

[209]See, therefore, how many of those raised in royal circumstances contend against the Devil and afflict their bodies! Therefore let us pray that the Lord may think us also fit to run his race[210] and to take our place with Anastasius the eunuch—for she used to be called 'Anastasia'—with the prayers and entreaties of our Queen, the Mother of God and ever-virgin Mary, and of all the saints, and of Abba Daniel, before the fearful judgement seat of our Lord Jesus Christ, because to him it is right to give glory for ever and ever. Amen.

I.8C [2] *On the Same Day.*
The Feast of Our Holy Mother the Patrician Anastasia[211]

[57] In the days of Emperor Justinian[212] there was a woman in Byzantium by the name of Anastasia who feared God and who was born to noble and wealthy parents. She, being a high-ranking patrician at the emperor's court and having the fear of God in her, walked in accordance with God's commandments. She possessed a natural serenity and great gentleness so that everyone rejoiced at her virtues, and especially the emperor himself. And since he who is always sowing weeds[213] is accustomed to envy what is good and calumniate it and never gives up or desists, Anastasia was also envied by the empress. When Anastasia learned about the envy from someone, she whose faith was firmly established in God said to herself, 'Anastasia, a timely and genuine opportunity has arisen for you: act now and save your soul and you will free the empress of her irrational envy and you will secure for yourself the heavenly kingdom'. When she had pondered these thoughts to herself, she hired a boat and gathered together a small portion of her wealth, leaving all the rest behind, and came to Alexandria. Having founded a monastery at the fifth milestone (thus is the place named), she wove together godly threads and remained there, earnestly striving to please God. There to this very day her monastery is preserved, bearing the name 'The Monastery of the Patrician Lady'.

Some time later, after the empress had passed away from this life, the emperor remembered the patrician lady and sent people everywhere, making every effort to find her. When the lamb of God discovered that he was searching for her, she gave up her monastery at night and left to find protection with Abba Daniel. She told the most blessed old man the details of her life and he dressed her in a man's robe and called her 'Anastasius the eunuch'. He led her to a cave far from his lavra and enclosed her, giving her also [58] a monastic rule, and he ordered her never to leave the cell, not even for someone who came to see her. He appointed one of the brothers to carry to her once a week a wine jar filled with water, place it outside the cave, receive a prayer, and return.

There her brave and adamantine spirit completed eight years in addition to twenty, without going out, steadfastly keeping the monastic rule that the old man had given her. What mind or tongue could conceive of the virtues that she cultivated in God's presence for twenty-eight years or could narrate or put into writing the virtues that she, a solitary, evinced all alone for God each day? The weeping, the groanings, the lamentations; vigil, prayer, reading of Scripture, standing, kneeling, fasting, but above and beyond all of these, the attacks of the demons and the hand-to-hand combat with them, the pleasures of the flesh and evil desires and things equivalent to these? The fact that without exception she never left the cave, spending all her days like this, year after year, a woman of senatorial class, who had always been accustomed to associating with large numbers of men and women at court, boggles the mind and understanding. Battling mightily in all these ways, she became a vessel of the Holy Spirit.[214]

Knowing in advance of her departure to be with the Lord, she inscribed an ostracon to the old man, saying, 'Honorable father, bring with you as quickly as possible the disciple who brings me water and bring implements suitable for doing a burial and come close the eyes of Anastasius the eunuch'. After writing these things, she placed the ostracon outside the entrance of the cave. The old man, instructed about these things in a nocturnal vision, said to the disciple, 'Hurry, brother, to the cave where lives the brother Anastasius the eunuch, and, looking outside the entrance to the cave, you will find a potsherd with writing on it. Take it and return to me as fast as you can'. After the disciple left and returned with the potsherd, the old man read what was written on it and wept. Hurriedly taking the brother and the things they needed for a burial, he left.

When they opened the cave, they found the eunuch burning up with fever, and the old man fell on the eunuch's breast and, weeping, said, 'Blessed are you, brother Anastasius, because by always concerning yourself with this hour you looked with contempt on an earthly kingdom! Therefore pray to the Lord on my behalf!' But she said, 'It is rather I, father, who need many prayers [59] at this hour'; and the old man said, 'Had I known, I would have interceded with God!' She sat up from the mat on which she was lying, kissed the old man's head, and prayed for him. The old man, taking hold of his disciple, placed him at her feet, saying, 'Bless my disciple, your child', and she said, 'God of my fathers, you who are standing by me in this hour to remove me from this body, you who know how many steps I have taken in this cave for your name's sake, and know my weakness and suffering, cause the spirit of the fathers to rest upon him just as you caused the spirit of Elijah to rest upon Elisha'.[215] Then the eunuch turned to the old man and said, 'For the sake of the Lord, father, do not take off the clothes I am wearing, and let no one know anything about me', and partaking of the divine Mysteries[216] she said, 'Make the sign of the cross over me in Christ and pray for me'. And she raised her eyes to the east and shone as though she were holding a flaming torch before her face in the cave and she made the sign of the precious cross and said, 'Lord, into your hands I will commend my spirit',[217] and after saying this she offered up her spirit.

After a grave had been dug in front of the cave, the old man stripped off the cloak he was wearing and said to his disciple, 'Child, put this on the brother over what he is wearing'. While the brother was dressing the blessed woman, her breasts became visible to him, like withered leaves, but he did not say anything to the old man. After they had finished burying the eunuch, as they were returning the disciple said, 'Did you know, father, that the eunuch was a woman?' The old replied, 'Yes, I knew, child, but in order that word of this not be spread everywhere, I gave her a man's clothing to wear and gave her the name "Anastasius the eunuch" so she would not be suspected. I did this because the emperor was sending out people looking for her everywhere and especially in these parts. But now, by the grace of God, her secret has been kept by us'. And then the old man told the disciple in detail the story of her life.[218]

I.9 (6) [9] *Eulogius the Stonecutter*

(148) [254] Abba Daniel, the priest of Scetis, was across from the Thebaid, having with him also his disciple.[219] On their return, sailing down the river, they came to a farming village[220] to which the old[221] man had directed the sailors and the old man said, 'We will stay here today'.

His disciple began to grumble, saying, 'How long are we going to waste our time here? Let's go on to Scetis'.

The old man said, 'No, we'll stay here today'.

They stayed in the middle of the village[222] as foreigners and the brother said to the old man, 'Does it please God for us to sit here like brothers with them? Let's at least go [255] to the martyrion'.

The old man said, 'No, we're staying here', and they remained there, staying until late in the evening. The brother began to fight with the old man, saying, 'On account of you I'm going to die a miserable death'.

While they were talking, an elderly lay person came, a large man, completely gray-headed.[223] When he saw Abba Daniel, he began to kiss his feet and weep. He also greeted his disciple and said to them, 'Please come home with me'. He raised his torch and was going through the streets of the village, looking for foreigners. Taking the old man and his disciple and whatever other foreigners he found, he went home, and putting water into the basin, he washed the feet of the brothers and of the old man.[224] He had no one else in his house, or anywhere else, only God alone. He set the table for them and after they ate he took the leftovers and threw them to the village dogs. It was his custom to do this, and from evening until morning he would not allow a single crumb to remain in the house.[225] The old man took him aside (150) and sat until dawn, with many tears talking with him about the things that lead to salvation. Early in the morning, they kissed one another and the old man and his disciple departed.

While they were on the road, the disciple asked the old man's forgiveness, saying, 'Please, father, tell me who that old man was and where you know him from', but the old man refused to speak to him. Again the brother asked his forgiveness, saying, 'You've confided many other things to me, and now you won't confide in me about the old man?' (Abba Daniel had confided in him the virtues of many holy men.) But the old man refused to talk to the brother about this old man; as a result, the brother got angry and did not speak to the old man until they reached Scetis.

After the brother went to his cell, he did not bring the old man a small meal as was the custom (the old man always observed this practice at five PM).[226] When evening fell, the old man went to the brother's cell and said to him, 'Why, child, have you allowed your father [256] to die of hunger?'

The disciple said to him, 'I don't have a father! If I had a father, he would love his own child!'

The old man said, 'If you don't have a father, provide for yourself'. He was taking hold of the door in order to open it and leave when the brother came up to him and grabbed him and began to kiss him, saying, 'As the Lord lives, I will not let you go unless you tell me who that old man was!' (The brother could not bear to see the old man ever distressed, for he dearly loved him.)

Then the old man said to him, 'Make me a little something to eat first and then I will tell you'. After he had eaten, he said to the brother, 'Do not be stiff-necked. I did not tell you about the old man because you argued with me in the village and were grumbling. And now see that you repeat to no one what you hear.[227]

(152) 'This old man is called "Eulogius";[228] by trade he is a stonecutter. He earns a *keration*[229] a day from his manual labor, eating nothing until evening. When evening comes he goes out to the village and takes home whatever foreigners he finds and feeds them, and the leftover fragments he throws to the dogs, as you saw. He's been a stonecutter by trade since he was a young man up to today; today makes it more than a hundred years. Christ provides him with strength, and each day he earns the one *keration*.

'When I was younger, about forty years ago,[230] I went up to sell my handiwork in that village and at evening he came and took me and other brothers with me, as was his custom, and gave us lodging. When I went there and saw the man's virtue, I began to fast for weeks at a time and entreat God to provide him with greater wages so he might have more money and do good for even more people. After fasting for three weeks, I was half dead on account of my ascetic regimen, and I saw a certain person dressed in a holy manner coming near me and he said to me, "What's the matter with you, Daniel?"

'I said to him, "I've given my word to Christ, master, not to eat bread until he hears my request concerning Eulogius the stonecutter and bestows a blessing[231] on him so he may do good for even more people".

'He said to me, "No, he's doing fine". [257]

'I said to him, "Give him more, Lord, in order that everyone, on account of him, may praise your holy name".

'He said to me, "I myself am telling you he is fine. If you want me to provide him with more, act as guarantor[232] for his soul, that he will find salvation through benefitting many, and then I will provide for him."

'Then I said to him: "I do so guarantee it. His life is in my hands."

'I saw that it was as though we were standing in the Church of the Holy Resurrection[233] and a young man was sitting upon the holy stone[234] and Eulogius (154) was standing at his right. The young man sent to me one of those standing beside him and he said to me, "Is this the one who has pledged himself for Eulogius?" and all of them said, "Yes, master". Again he spoke: "Tell him that I will demand the pledge", and I said to him, "Yes, master, with me as the pledge. Only, give him more money". I then saw them emptying a very large amount of money into Eulogius' lap and Eulogius' lap was able to hold it, however much they kept pouring. When I woke up I knew that I had been heard and I gave glory to God.

'When Eulogius went out to do his work, he struck rock and heard a hollow-sounding thunk, so he struck again and found a small hole; again he struck the rock and found a cave filled with money. Amazed, Eulogius said to himself, "This money belongs to the Israelites! What should I do with it? If I take it to the village, the owner will hear about it and will come and take it and I'll be in danger. It would be better if I go to a foreign country where no one knows me". Hiring animals as though he were using them to haul stones, at night he hauled the money to the riverside. Having abandoned the good work he had been doing, he put the money in a boat and sailed to Byzantium. Justin the Elder was emperor at that time.[235] Eulogius gave a large amount of money to him and the emperor made him prefect of the holy praetorian guard. He also bought a large house and to this day it is called "the house of the Egyptian".

'Two years later I saw that young man again in a dream in the Church of the Holy Resurrection, as before, [258] and, a little later, I saw Eulogius being dragged away by his hair from the young man by an Ethiopian.[236]

Waking up, I said to myself, "God help me, a sinner! I have forfeited my life!" Taking my sheepskin cloak, I left for the village in order to sell my handiwork, expecting (156) to find Eulogius. Late evening came and no one invited me home, so I got up and made inquiries of an old woman, saying to her, "Surely you, mother,[237] will give me three dried loaves of bread[238] so I may eat; I haven't eaten today". She went and brought me a little boiled food. Sitting down beside me, she began to instruct me for my benefit, saying, "*Abba*, sir, don't you know that you are a young man and that you shouldn't be in town after dark? Don't you know that the monastic life requires contemplative quiet?"[239]

'I said to her, "What, then, are you telling me to do? I came to sell my handwork".

She said, "Even if you want to sell your handwork, you should not be in the village after dark like this".

'I said to her, "Really, spare me these homilies. But tell me, isn't there in this village a God-fearing person who goes out and gets the foreigners?" and she said to me, "Ah, what are you saying, *abba*, sir? We used to have a certain stonecutter here and he used to do many good things for the foreigners. When God saw his works, he gave him grace, and today, so we hear, he is a patrician".

'When I heard these things, I said to myself, "I committed this murder!" and I boarded ship and sailed to Byzantium. Diligently seeking the house of Eulogius the Egyptian, I sat in front of his gate until he came out. I saw him coming with great ostentation and I called out to him, "Have mercy on me! I wish to speak with you in private about some matter!" But he turned away from me and his escort beat me instead. I persisted and cried out once again and once again they beat me. I spent four weeks suffering like this but was not able to meet with him. Then, a little later, discouraged, I went and threw myself in front of the icon of the supremely-holy Mother of God and wept and said to the Saviour, "Lord, either release me from me the pledge I made on behalf of this person or I too will go away into the world!"[240]

(158) [259] 'While I was trying to understand these events, I fell asleep and saw a great commotion and they were saying, "The Augusta[241] is coming!" and there came before her thousands and tens of thousand ranks, and I cried out and said, "Have mercy on me, my Queen!" She stopped and said to me, "What is the matter with you?" and I said to her, "I pledged myself as surety for Eulogius the procurator. Order him

to release me from this pledge". She said to me, "I do not have authority in this matter. Fulfill the pledge as you wish".

'When I woke up I said to myself, "Even if I have to die, I am not leaving his gate unless I meet with him!" So once again I went and sat in front of the gate. When Eulogius came out, I cried out and the door-keeper attacked me and beat me with rods until he had broken every bone in my body. Then, discouraged, I said to myself, "It's time for me to go to Scetis. If God wishes, he will save both me and Eulogius."

'I went in search of a ship and, finding one bound for Alexandria, I boarded ship alone and sat by myself, feeling discouraged. I fell asleep and saw myself once again in the Church of the Holy Resurrection and that young man was sitting on the holy stone. Turning towards me in a threatening manner, he said to me, "In pledging yourself for Eulogius, have you not gotten in over your head?" I stood there trembling, unable to speak out of fear. Then he gave orders to two beings standing beside him and they hung me up with my arms tied behind my back and said to me, "Do not make pledges beyond your ability, and do not gainsay God". Hanging there like that, I was unable to open my mouth.

'Suddenly there was a voice, saying, "The Augusta is coming!" and when I saw her I felt a little encouraged and said to her in a subdued voice, "Have mercy on me, mistress of the world!"

'She said to me, "What do you want now?"

'I said to her, "I am hanging here because I pledged myself for Eulogius", and she said to me, "I am making entreaties on your behalf". I saw her leave and kiss the young man's feet and that holy young man said to me, (160) "Go away! Do not pledge yourself for Eulogius any longer".

'I said, "I have sinned. Master, forgive me. I had asked to be of service, not a hindrance".

He gave the order and they released me, and he said to me, "Return to your cell. Do not concern yourself with how I [260] will return Eulogius to his former way of life." When I awoke from sleep, I was deliriously happy, having been set free from such an onerous pledge, and I set sail, giving thanks to God.

'Three months later, I heard that Justin had died and Justinian was now emperor in his place. Then a little later Hypatius, Dexikratius, Pompeius, and Eulogius the procurator rose up against him. The first three were seized and beheaded and all their possessions were confiscated, as was Eulogius' estate.[242] Eulogius fled Constantinople at night and the emperor ordered that he was to be killed wherever he was found. Then he fled and came to his own village and exchanged his clothing for that of the country folk who lived there. The whole village gathered to see Eulogius and they said to him, "It's good to have you back. We heard that you had become a patrician." He said to them, "Indeed it is. If I had become a patrician, you would be coming to me with petitions. No, that was another Eulogius, who is also from here. I was in the Holy Land."

'So Eulogius came to his senses and said, "Eulogius, you wretch, get up, take your stonecutting tools and go before you too lose your head. There is no royal court here!" Taking his stonecutting tools, he went out to the rock where he had found the money, thinking that he would find the rest but, striking it until noon, did not find anything. He began to remember the retinues and the ostentation and the foods and once again said to himself, "Get up, Eulogius, you wretch, and get to work. You're in Egypt now." Little by little the holy young man and our Queen, the Mother of God, restored him to his (162) former way of life, for it would have been unjust of God to forget his previous labors.

'A little later I went up to that village in order to sell my handiwork and when evening fell he came and took me as he had earlier, as was his custom. When I saw him come out of a cloud of dust,[243] I groaned and, weeping, said, "How exalted your deeds are, Lord! You have done everything with wisdom.[244] What god is as great as our God? You are God, who alone does wonders. The Lord impoverishes and enriches, he humbles and exalts.[245] Who can search out your marvellous deeds and your judgements, Lord?[246] When I, a sinner, attempted to do so, my soul dwelt for a while in Hades."[247]

[261] 'Taking me, along with the others he had found, he washed our feet, as was his custom, and set a table for us. After we had eaten I said to him, "How are you, Abba Eulogius?"

'He said to me, "*Abba*, pray for me, sir. I am a wretch, having nothing to my name".

'I said to him, "I wish that you had not even had what you had!"

'He said to me, "Why, *abba,* sir? What have I ever done to offend you?"

'I said to him, "What haven't you done to offend me!" Then I laid out for him everything that had happened. Both of us wept and he said to me, "Pray, *abba*, that God sends me what I need and from now on I will follow the right track".

'I said to him, "Truly, brother, do not expect Christ to ever entrust you with anything else as long as you are in this world except for this *keration*, the fruit of your labor".

'You see? God has now seen to it all these years that each day he has the strength to earn the *keration* from his manual labor.'[248]

(164) These things Abba Daniel confided to his disciple after they had sailed up from the Thebaid. Marvellous is God's goodness, how he raised up Eulogius from nothing and humbled such a person again for his benefit! Therefore let us pray that we too may be humbled in Christ, in order that we may find mercy before his fearful judgement seat as we stand before his glory.

II. STORIES ATTRIBUTED TO ABBA DANIEL IN THE DANIEL DOSSIER

II.1 *A Monk in a Tomb is Ignored by Two Demons*[249]

[50] Abba Daniel of Scetis related that a brother who was living in Egypt[250] was walking along the road one time and, when evening overtook him, on account of the cold, went inside a tomb to sleep. Two demons were passing by and the one said to the other, 'Do you see how courageous this monk is, sleeping in a tomb?[251] Come on, let's harass him', and the other one replied, 'Why should we harass him? This guy is doing exactly what we want, eating and drinking and slandering and disregarding the monastic assembly.[252] Let's ignore this [51] guy and instead go afflict those who afflict us and who night and day wage war against us with their prayers'.

II.2 *The Monk Falsely Accused of Theft*[253]

[387] Abba Daniel related that there was a monk by the name of Doulas who was counted among the greatest of the fathers: 'This Doulas took his seat among the leaders in the cenobium for forty years and used to

say, "On different occasions I have checked and found that monks who live in cenobia make progress in a virtuous way of life much more fully and rapidly if their way of life in the monastery proceeds from a truthful heart. There was", he said, "a brother in the cenobium who wore poor and despicable clothing but whose understanding of things was great and highly honored. This fellow rejoiced and was glad when everyone despised and slighted him, when the brothers were embittered towards him because the Estranged One[254] put thoughts into their heads, and when some beat him while others spat on him and still others heaped abuse on him.

[388] "'At that time the Enemy,[255] unable to bear the vitality of this fellow's patient endurance, insinuated himself to one of the brothers who were living as hermits; going into the church, the brother stripped it of all the priestly vessels[256] and left the cenobium without being noticed. When it came time for the celebration of the synaxis, the precentor[257] came in to cense the church and found everything stolen. He left and reported it to the abbot and struck the signal and all the brothers assembled and began to get agitated, saying, 'No one could have taken them except brother you-know-who, and that is why he has not come to the synaxis. If he had not done it he would have been the first one here, as always'. They sent for him and found him standing in prayer and, knocking on the door, they went inside and violently dragged him out. He entreated them, saying, 'What's the matter, fathers?' They, however, heaped abuse and reproaches on him as they dragged him out: 'You sacrilegious thief, you don't deserve to live! Hasn't it been enough for you that you've bothered us all these years? Now you've even gone and struck at our very souls!' He said, 'Forgive me. I've done wrong', and they took him to the abbot and said to him, 'Abba, this is the person who from the beginning has been turning the cenobium upside down!' and one by one they began to say 'I know that he secretly ate vegetables!' 'He stole bread and gave it to those outside!' 'I found him drinking the best wine!'

"'All of them lied and were believed, while he told the truth and was not listened to. So the abbot took off the monk's habit, saying, 'These are not things that a Christian does!' Clapping him into irons, they handed him over to the steward of the lavra and he stripped him and beat him with an ox-hide whip to find out if what they were saying about him was true. But he laughed and said, 'Forgive me. I've done wrong.' Enraged at what he said, the steward ordered him to be thrown into the jail cell; securing his feet in the stocks, he wrote the duke with details about the matter. Immediately civil servants came, and they took him and put him on an unsaddled beast, with heavy irons clapped around his neck, and dragged him through the middle of the city.

"'Led before the magistrate, he was asked who he was and where he was from and why he had become a monk, [389] but he said nothing more than 'I have sinned. Forgive me'. Enraged, the duke ordered him to be stretched out on the rack and to have his back flayed to pieces with rawhide whips. With all four limbs stretched out, and flogged unmercifully by the cords, with a smile on his face he said to the duke, 'Beat me, beat me, you are making my money shine even more brightly!' The duke said, 'I'll show you that your idiotic behavior will melt faster than snow!' and he ordered fiery coals spread out under the monk's belly and dazzling white salt to be mixed and poured on his wounds. Those standing there were marveling at his incredible endurance and were saying to him, 'Tell us where you put the priestly vessels and you can go', but he kept saying, 'I don't know anything about it'.

"'Scarcely had the duke ordered him to be removed from the torture when he commanded the monk to be led away to prison and held without food and with complete neglect and the next day he sent someone to the lavra and ordered the monks of the cenobium and the abbot to be brought and when they came the duke said to them, 'After making every effort and subjecting him to numerous punishments, I have been unable to find out anything more than you did'. The brothers said to him, 'Master, he has done many other wicked things and for God's sake we put up with him, expecting to reform him, and look what's happened! He's gone from bad to worse!' He said to them, 'So what shall I do with him?' They said to him, 'Whatever seems legally best'. He said to them, 'The law calls for executing those who commit acts of sacrilege'. They said, 'Let him be put to death'. The duke dismissed them and brought the brother in and, sitting on the judgement seat, said to him, 'Confess, you wretch, and escape death'. The brother said, 'If you order me to say what isn't true, I'll say it'. The duke said, 'I don't want you to bear false witness against yourself'. The brother said, 'I didn't do any of the things I'm being questioned about'. When the duke saw that the monk had nothing to say, he ordered him to be beheaded.

"'Filled with compunction, the hermit who had taken the sacred vessels came [to himself] and said, 'Sooner or later this matter is going to be found out. Even if you escape detection here, what will you do on that day?[258] [390] How will you defend yourself with regard to these wicked acts?' So he went to the abbot and said to him, 'Hurry, send word so the brother doesn't die; the sacred vessels have been found!' So the abbot sent someone who reported to the duke and the brother was set free and they brought him to the cenobium. Everyone began to fall at his feet in supplication, saying, 'We have sinned against you. Forgive us'.[259] He began to weep and said, 'Forgive *me*! I owe all of you a great debt of thanks: on account of these great sufferings I am considered worthy of so many good things! I was always very happy when I heard outrageous things said about me by you because through these small humiliations I was going to be deemed worthy of great honors on that fearful day.[260] I was now rejoicing even more because you did this to me. I looked upon the affliction you brought upon me as a price to be paid in return for the repose that awaits me in the kingdom of heaven'.

"'The brother lived for three days, then went to the Lord. When one of the brothers came to see how he was doing, he found him on his knees lying on the ground, for he had been praying and making an act of prostration[261] and in this way gave up his spirit while his body remained lying in an act of prostration. The brother went and told the abbot and he ordered the brother's body to be carried into the church in order to be buried there. When, therefore, they had placed him in front of the altar, the abbot ordered the signal to be given in order that the entire lavra might be assembled, and the body was interred with many honors. When they were gathered together, each monk wished to receive a blessing from him.[262] When the abbot saw this, therefore, he placed the brother's body in the sanctuary and, having secured the bolts, awaited the *abba* of the lavra[263] in order to inter the brother together. When, therefore, the father of the lavra came with the clergy and offered prayer, they said to the abbot, 'Open the door and bring out the body so it may be buried, for indeed it is time to say the prayers appointed for the ninth hour'. When they opened the doors, they found nothing except his clothes and sandals[264] and everyone was amazed and began to glorify God with tears, saying, 'Look, brothers, at what sort of things forbearance and humility procure for us, as you can see with your own eyes!' [391]

"'Thus you too: patiently strive for humiliation and tribulation, because these know how to procure the kingdom of heaven, through the grace of our Lord Jesus Christ, to whom be the glory for ever and ever!'"

III. A STORY ATTRIBUTED TO DANIEL ELSEWHERE[265]

III.1 [A] *Concerning a Monk and His Sister*[266]

There was a man who abandoned his sister in Alexandria, left the town, and embraced the monastic way of life on the Mountain.[267] Deprived of his support, she abandoned herself to a profligate life of promiscuity, becoming the agent for the destruction of many souls. He was displeased when he heard about this and, for many years, disowned her but, later on, he was accused by some acquaintances of being himself the cause of her ruin and of those who were being destroyed with her. Praying to God to help him, he went into Alexandria and, coming to his sister's gate, sent someone to tell her, 'Your brother has come from the desert and is calling for you'.

She, who was disporting herself with her lovers with her head and her feet bare, desisted completely the moment she heard her brother's name. Out she came to meet him and embraced him, but when he saw what a state she was in he struck himself on the forehead and said to her, 'My lady sister, what has happened to you to make you look with contempt upon God and to hate your wretched soul? Why have you destroyed yourself and many others? Why have you afflicted my old age with grief?'[268] With tears in her eyes she declared, 'Ah, what a wretch I am, for I am utterly ruined! But I beg of you, holy one of God, if you know that God will receive me as a penitent, me the prostitute, the polluted one, do not leave me here. For I will be subject to you for ever, serving the Lord with all my heart'.

He rejoiced on hearing this and said to her, 'Go back and get the veil for your head and shoes for your feet, for the way is rough by which we are about to travel'.

'As the Lord lives, I shall go with you just as God delivered me into your hands', she replied. 'I shall take nothing with me that I gained by my involvement with the Devil. Let us be gone, my lord brother; it is better for me to suffer the disgrace of an uncovered head rather than to [re-]enter the Devil's place of work'.

Rejoicing even more at these words, he took her with him and set out on the long road into the desert. Here her feet were torn by the rough track and streams of blood flowed from them, but she followed her brother, sprinkling the track all the way with her tears, striking her breast and saying, 'Lord, receive my repentance as you accepted the prostitute's'.

As they were walking along the track her brother saw some people coming. He said to her, 'My lady sister, since these strangers are unaware that you are my sister, go aside a little and hide yourself until they have gone by'.

She went aside and concealed herself but, as soon as she sat down, she surrendered her spirit to the Lord. When the people they had encountered had passed by, her brother called to her saying, 'Get up, sister; come on, let us continue our journey'. But when she did not answer, he turned aside and, following her bloodstains, found her lying dead. 'Alas, I was altogether unworthy to save her', he sighed.[269]

In utter despondency he now lay down to sleep on her grave. He dreamt that he saw a person sitting in judgement on high, with many guardsmen standing around him. He heard that ruler saying, 'Bring that prostitute here to me' (meaning the *abba*'s sister) and in she was led. Now, behold: a black-looking man[270] was standing there, accusing her. With a paper in his hand, he was rehearsing her promiscuities and impurities; the place was suffused with a totally disgusting stench.[271] As for her, she just stood there, a miserable sight, with her eyes cast down. Then the ruler ordered the angel of repentance to be brought in; there entered a pleasant looking man holding a paper in his hand. To him the ruler said: 'Read out what you witnessed concerning this prostitute', whereupon he began to make known her obedience to her brother, that she followed him in repentance, her head uncovered and her feet unshod, stained with their bleeding.

The Black One retaliated, saying, 'Do you mean to deprive me of her who was with me, doing my will, for so long, just because she followed you for a tiny part of one day?' At this four men (the ones who were about to bear her off for punishment) put out their hands, grasped her hair, and began to afflict her. The ruler said, 'Do not come near to her until her repentance arrives', whereupon there entered a pleasant-looking man with a golden container in his hand; within it were her tears and the blood from her feet. 'Bring me a pair of scales and weigh her impurity against her repentance', said the ruler, whereupon her repentance was found to be the heavier. God's love for humankind[272] had triumphed. Then the ruler ordered her to be stripped of the garment she was wearing, after which they put a linen robe on her and handed her over to the angel of repentance, who then put her in a place suffused with light.

III.1 [B] *Concerning a Monk and His Sister*[273]

A brother who was eminent for his great humility was living in a cell in Egypt. He had a sister who was working as a prostitute in the city and was leading many souls to perdition. As a result, the old men[274] gave the brother grief and were able to persuade him to go down to visit her to see whether by rebuking her he could do away with the sin that she was causing.

When he was near the city, one of his acquaintances saw him and ran ahead to tell her, saying, 'Your brother is at the city gates!' Filled with emotion, she leapt up, left the lovers she was serving and, with her head uncovered, ran to see her brother. When she attempted to embrace him, he said to her, 'My dear sister, look out for your soul: many men have gone to perdition because of you. How will you be able to endure eternal and bitter punishment?'

Trembling, she said to him, 'Are you sure there is salvation for me if I repent?'

He said to her, 'If you want, there is salvation'.

She threw herself at her brother's feet, begging him to take her to the desert with him, and he said to her, 'Put your cloak over your head and follow me'.

She said to him, 'Let's go. It's better for me to be put to shame by going with my head uncovered than to go back to the brothel again'.[275]

While they were walking on the road he was admonishing her to repent. He saw some people coming their way and said to her, 'Since none of them know that you're my sister, leave the road a little until they pass'.

After they passed by he said to her, 'Let's resume our journey, sister'. When she did not answer him he turned aside and found her dead. He also saw her bloody footprints, for she had been barefoot.[276]

When the brother told the old men what had happened, they were talking to one another about it and God gave this revelation to one of the old men about her: 'Since she showed no concern at all for the things of the flesh but even paid no attention to her own body, not even moaning in pain with her bloodied feet, I have accepted her repentance'.

IV. A STORY ABOUT ABBA DANIEL
FROM MATERIAL ASSOCIATED WITH JOHN MOSCHUS

IV.1 *Through a Miracle Abba Daniel Refutes Slanderous Charges*[277]

On another occasion the same old man[278] told us about Abba Daniel the Egyptian, saying, 'One day the old man went up to Terenuthis to sell his handiwork.[279] A young man entreated the old man, saying, "For God's sake, venerable sir, come home with me and offer a prayer over my wife, for she is sterile". Compelled by the young man, he went home with him and offered a prayer for his wife and, because God had willed it, she became pregnant.

'Some men who did not fear God began to slander the old man, saying, "The truth of the matter is that the young man is sterile; his wife has become pregnant by Abba Daniel".[280] This rumor reached the old man and he ordered the woman's husband, "Let me know when your wife gives birth". So when his wife gave birth, the young man let him know, saying, "Through God and your prayers, Father, she has given birth". Then Abba Daniel went and said to the young man, "Prepare a meal and invite your relatives and friends". While he was eating, the old man picked up the baby and, in front of everyone, said to it, "Who is your father?" The child said, "This man", and with his finger the infant pointed to the young man. The child was twenty-two days old! Everyone praised God who safeguards the truth for those who seek him with their whole hearts'.

IV. 2 *The Female Monastic Possessed by a Demon*[281]

[92] Abba Peter, the disciple of Abba Isaiah, told us this story:
'Once while I was sitting with my father Abba Isaiah in Abba Macarius' cell,[282] some monks came from the Monastery of the Oktokaidekaton

[93] outside Alexandria,[283] bringing with them a consecrated virgin who was severely possessed by a demon, and they were begging the old man to have compassion and heal her, for the nun was horribly devouring her own flesh. When the old man saw her being so terribly tortured and torn apart, he made the sign of the cross and rebuked the demon. In response the demon said to the old man, "I'm not coming out of her! I went into her unwillingly and without wanting to! Your associate and aider and abettor Daniel called on God and sent me into her".

'The old man said, "How did you enter her?"'

'He said, "She was a tool I used; I taught her to make herself up without any sense of shame or decency and to go to the baths[284] all the time and I shot and wounded a lot of people with her and her with them, ensnaring not only lay people but also clergy. By titillating them with her, I caused them to have shameful intercourse with her and by their acquiescence to shameful thoughts and by means of nocturnal fantasies I overwhelmed them and deceived them into ejaculating. Now it just so happened that that old glutton Daniel met her after she had washed herself at the baths and was returning to her cell and he groaned aloud to God and prayed for him to send her something to chastise and correct her, both so she might be saved and so the other nuns who lived chaste lives might remain completely cloistered. This was the reason I came to dwell in her".

'When the old man heard this, he said, "The person who handed you over to her can also free you",[285] and the old man sent them to Abba Daniel'.

V. STORIES ABOUT ABBA DANIEL FROM OTHER SOURCES

V. 1 *Daniel Predicts the Fall of a Monk Who Frequents the Baths*[286]

[1] Abba Palladius told us: 'Once', he said, 'on account of some business, when I was going into Alexandria with Abba Daniel, we met a young man coming out of the baths; he had been bathing. When Abba Daniel saw him, the elder heaved a sigh and said to me: "You see that brother?

The name of God is about to be blasphemed on account of him. But let's follow him and see where he's living".

[2] 'So we followed him home and went in behind him and the old man took him aside and said, "Brother, you are young and in good health. You shouldn't be bathing.[287] Believe me, child, you're offending many people, not only lay persons, but monks too".[288] The young man replied to the old man, "If I were still in the business of pleasing people I would not be the servant of Christ.[289] It is written: 'Judge not so that you will not be judged'".[290] Then the old man begged his pardon, saying, "Forgive me for the Lord's sake. Being only human, I have made a mistake".

'We left him, and I said to the old man, "Maybe the brother is sick, and should not be condemned".[291] [3] The old man sighed and broke into tears, saying: "The truth will convince you, brother. I saw more than fifty demons swarming around him and pouring filth on him and an Ethiopian woman[292] sitting on his shoulders and kissing him, and another Ethiopian woman in front of him, teasing him and teaching him to be indecent and there were demons standing around him and rejoicing over him. But I did not see his holy angel, either close by or far away from him. From this I conclude that he performs every kind of obscene act. [4] Even his clothes bear witness to what I say, for they are made of goat hair and are soft and thickly woven; and so does the fact that he parades around so shamelessly in the center of this city.[293] Those who are advanced in the ascetic life come here on account of unavoidable necessities and hurry to leave on account of his behavior before they suffer any damage to their souls. [5] Moreover, if this fellow were not self-centered, self-indulgent, and lecherous, he would not shamelessly strip naked in the baths, or look at others as naked as himself.

"Our holy fathers Antony and Pachomius, Amoun, Serapion, and the rest of the God-bearing fathers inspired by God decree that no monk should ever strip naked other than for reasons of severe illness and necessity. Once, for some unavoidable reason, they wished to cross a river, and there was no ferry. They refused to take their clothes off because they were ashamed to do so in the presence of the holy angel who was watching over them and in the presence of the sun which was giving them its light. So, unseen by human eye, they interceded with God—and passed over through the air![294] Thus did God, the lover of humanity, the all-powerful one, willingly grant their just request, made with complete piety; thus did he miraculously fulfill their request and bring about what they had asked". When the old man had said these things to me, he fell silent.

[6] 'We returned to Scetis and, before many days had passed, brothers came from Alexandria and told us that that brother, the priest (for he was also ordained), who lived at the Church of Saint Isidore[295] and had recently come from Constantinople[296] (it was he of whom the elder had spoken), had been caught committing adultery with the wife of the *silentiarius;*[297] seized by the servants and neighbors of the silentiarius, his testicles were cut off along with his member. He survived this castration three days and then died, a shame and disgrace to all the monks. [7] When I heard this, I got up and went to Abba Daniel and told him what had happened. When the old man heard it, he wept and said: "Because of his arrogance, he was already dead when he got his comeuppance".[298] The old man explained that if that man had not been sick with arrogant pride, and had taken the old man's advice, no such disaster would have befallen him. So let all other arrogant persons be corrected and taught by his calamitous end to avoid such a precipice'.

[BN graec. 1596 p. 652 gives a different ending:]
'Having heard this, I rose up and, making off at a run, I went to Abba Daniel in tears. I found him with Abba Isaac, the hegoumen of Scētē,[299] and I said to him: "Such-and-such has befallen the brother whom we encountered coming out of the baths, he who shrugged off your advice". With tears in his eyes, the father said: "Calamity is the correction of the arrogant"'.

'I privately conveyed to the hegoumen the things the elder had seen and had said to me, whereupon, deeming them worthy to be recorded, Abba Isaac ordered them to be written and set down in the book of the wonderworking[300] fathers for the edification and benefit of those who come upon them'.

V. 2 *The Importance of Monastic Stability*[301]

The disciples of Abba Eulogios told this story: 'When the elder sent us into Alexandria to sell the product of our manual labor, he recommended that we not spend more than three days there: "If you spend more than three days there, I cannot be responsible for your trespasses". We asked him how it was that the monks in the towns and villages, who live night and day with people of the world, suffer no harm.

'The elder replied: "Believe me, my children, after I became a monk I spent thirty-eight years without leaving Scetis, and then I set off for Alexandria, together with Abba Daniel, to visit the Patriarch Eusebius on account of certain necessities. When we entered the town we saw many monks. I could see some of them being struck by crows, others being hugged by naked women who whispered in their ears; others were naked under young boys whom they were abusing and coating with human excrement. I saw some of them equipped with swords who were cutting up human flesh and giving it to the monks to eat. And I understood that every monk who is prey to that kind of passion[302] has demons like those to spy on him and to speak to his soul. And that, brothers, is why I do not want you ever to hang around in town, for fear you may be tormented by such thoughts, or, rather, by such demons"'.

V. 3 *Abba Silvanus Speaks of Abba Longinus and Abba Daniel*[303]

Abba Silvanus said: 'When I was with Abba Longinus the wonder-worker,[304] I went with that elder to Alexandria where we were met by Abba Daniel of Scetis. We took him into our company and were then received by Abba Isidore, noted for his hospitality. When Pope Timothy[305] heard about Abba Longinus and Abba Daniel, he sent his *syncellus*[306] and had the elders brought to him.

'It so happened that at that time some of the monks of the Okto-kaidekaton Monastery[307] had a confrontation in a paroxysm of rage, hitting and striking each other, exchanging insults and unbecoming remarks. This disturbance caused laypersons, priests, women and children to come running.

'The officers of the governor met us as we were returning to Abba Isidore's from the Patriarchate and they began upbraiding and insulting us with bitter remarks against monks. Some of the priests recognized Daniel but they did not know Abba Longinus, who was dressed in rags, black-faced and down-at-the-heel.[308] Some of the laypersons began to accuse and condemn the monks. The priests said to Abba Daniel: "As you are aware, worthy father, a servant of God must not fight but be gentle with everybody". Abba Longinus said to the priests: "Let me tell you, children, the servants of God have to fight and wrestle and struggle, not only with demons, but also with the less diligent of the brethren. Just as God saves human beings by means of a human being, so the Devil destroys a human being by means of a human being and the deformity of one spreads to the many.[309] For it is written: 'Condemn the sinners in the presence of all to strike fear into the rest'".[310]

'When the elder had said this, three non-monastics said as though with one voice: "In truth, the Devil comes out of monks". Abba Longinus said: "It is true that [the Devil] comes out of monks, my children, but he then enters those who are not monks". At these words the unclean spirit burst upon them; they began to act like demons and to foam at the mouth. The priests and the rest of the laity fell down at the feet of the monks and, with tears in their eyes, begged them to heal and be merciful to the ones who were being wretchedly chastised by the unclean spirits.

'Heaving a sigh, Abba Longinus said: "My conscience is my witness before God that what I am about to say gives me no pleasure; it is truly not said in judgement or in condemnation, but as a compassionate exhortation and counsel for improvement. You who are not monks should concern yourselves only with yourselves and not insult, criticize, and condemn the monks.[311] Most persons who aren't monks are very quick to anger and easily take offence. You get into fights and lose your tempers at the drop of a hat, meticulously carrying grudges. You are slow to engage in good works but quick to do evil. You are given to envy, jealousy, and altercations, to say nothing of what some of you have committed and perpetrated by way of fornication, adultery, bloodshed, burglary, and swindling, swearing and perjury, impurity and obscenity, gluttony, drunkenness, and prodigality."

"'How then can you who have so many and such wicked vices, how can you condemn irreproachable and innocent monks of liking to stir up trouble? The monk's confrontation and struggle is with prayer, fasting, and almsgiving by means of purity, self-discipline, endurance, and fear of God; by vigils, lying on the ground, reading, and humility. The confrontation and struggle of secular persons on the other hand is with gluttony, greed and avarice. For this reason the Devil has no need to wage war against those who are always lying on the ground, doing his will, for a friend does not fight his friend. Monks struggle, wage war, and wrestle in order to overcome the enemy of virtue and vindicator of evil: the Devil. Hence their conflict is a sweet-smelling savor, acceptable to God, because their conflict is for the deliverance and benefit of the soul. For everything that is done for God is advantageous and beneficent."

"'I am not saying this, you know, to cut fine phrases, to speak big words, or merely to sound off, but to affirm the truth. Look, this I tell you before God: If with all your heart you wish these brothers (whom God has permitted to be disciplined by demons on account of their undisciplined tongues) to be healed, take them to the monks (whom you call trouble-makers and stirrers up of discord) at the Oktokaidekaton Monastery so they can be healed by their prayers. If these brothers do not go down to minister to those monks, they will remain under Satan's yoke, led astray until their last breath."

'The clergy and the rest of the people took them and brought them to the monks; a prayer having been offered on their behalf, God healed them. For my own part, together with Abba Longinus, I returned to my cell while Abba Daniel for his part set out for Scetis'.

CHAPTER TWO

The Coptic Life of Daniel

WITH APPENDIX: COPTIC-ARABIC SYNAXARY ENTRIES

Translated by Tim Vivian and Maged S. A. Mikhail[1]

Introduction by Tim Vivian

THE COPTIC *LIFE* of *Daniel* is not really a 'Life', but is rather a homily or encomium pronounced on the saint's feast day, as the superscription makes clear. Such works are common in coptic literature; later editors or homilists took earlier 'biographical' material (sayings by and stories about the saint) and transformed it for homiletic and paraenetic purposes.[2] Surviving in just a single coptic manuscript, the coptic *Life*, unlike the ethiopic version (see Chapter Three), really has few points of contact with the greek dossier. After a brief *proemium*, the speaker tells only two stories from the greek collection—those of Mark the Fool (I.1) and Eulogius the Stonecutter (I.9)[3] —before adding a story not found in Greek (but extant in Ethiopic), that of the Thief who Repented. He then goes on to give material found only in Coptic and Ethiopic: Daniel's opposition to the Tome of Leo, his departure from Scetis to Tambōk and his return, and his final flight from Scetis to Tambōk, where he dies.

The story of the Thief who Repented begins with a common hagiographical theme: 'After these events the fame of our father Abba Daniel spread everywhere and large numbers of people desired to obtain his holy blessing, especially saints from the monasteries'. But then the narrative rather abruptly speaks of 'a monastery in which a large number of virgins lived'. Most of the greek stories are specifically localized, but this monastery is only vaguely situated 'in the fertile borderland'.[4] The narrator—who, conspicuously, is not identified as Daniel's disciple, as he is in the greek tales—then tells the story of poor but charitable virgins: the Devil cannot abide their virtuousness so he 'entered the heart of a ringleader of thieves in that region and caused him to take with him his whole band of thieves who would go with him by night to that monastery and plunder it'. The thief, thanks to a miracle brought about by the sanctity of Abba Daniel, repents of his crimes, 'and immediately headed for Scetis to our holy father Abba Daniel. He gave up everything he had and became a chosen monk until the day he died.' Abba Daniel does not even make an appearance in this account. This fact, the fact that the story does not exist in Greek, the disciple/narrator's absence, and the thaumaturgical nature of the story—Daniel is decidedly *not* a wonderworker in the greek dossier—make one suspect that it comes from later coptic tradition about Daniel of Scetis.

The rest of the *Life* is even more problematic. After the three edifying stories, the *Life* suddenly declares that 'at that time the impious and defiled Justinian . . . created disturbances throughout the world and the Catholic Church everywhere' by attempting 'to impose the accursed faith of the defiled Council of Chalcedon everywhere'. He promulgated 'the impious Tome of Leo' and 'when it was brought down to Egypt, a great disturbance broke out among all the orthodox faithful. . . . When the emperor's soldiers brought the Tome, filled with every impiety of the lawbreaking Leo, to the holy monastic settlement of Scetis, our holy father Abba Daniel came out', opposed them, and anathematized the Tome and its adherents. Evelyn White believed that this account was added later by a coptic redactor; Leslie MacCoull, however, suggests that the episode was instead dropped 'in the Greek Chalcedonian tradition of the *vita*'.[5]

Such opposition to Chalcedon as the *Life* depicts taking place at Scetis certainly would have been possible because it did in fact take place elsewhere, in both the fifth and the sixth centuries.[6] Evelyn White believed that the story of Daniel's opposition to the Tome of Leo 'must be regarded as of extremely doubtful authenticity' because 'there is no clear evidence' that Justinian inaugurated 'any policy of coercion and intimidation' in Egypt. He also pointed out that 'indirect evidence' 'shows fairly clearly' that Apollinarius, pro-chalcedonian patriarch of Alexandria, did not interfere with anti-chalcedonians at the monasteries of the Enaton outside Alexandria or of Saint Macarius in Scetis. Thus, Evelyn White concluded, 'the story of the *Tome of Leo* is apocryphal'.[7]

More recent research, however, has shown that Justinian did in fact act to force Egyptians to subscribe to the Council of Chalcedon. As one scholar has forcefully put it, 'Both Justin [Justinian's predecessor] and Justinian were convinced that Monophysitism [*sic*] must be destroyed and the empire placed upon a strong base of Chalcedonian orthodoxy'.[8] It is doubtful that Justinian's efforts resulted in anything approaching a pogrom, but there can equally be little doubt that they did result in concerted efforts of persuasion which all too easily, at least in the eyes of those affected and afflicted, turned into persecution. Such a policy joined theological concerns with political and ecclesiastical reorganization.[9] According to John of Nikiu, an anti-chalcedonian, the emperor 'commanded the Orientals to inscribe the names of the [bishops of the] Council of Chalcedon on the diptyches of the church . . . a custom which had hitherto not existed and which is not mentioned in the Apostolic Canons nor in the Councils of the Fathers'.[10] Justinian promulgated his first law concerning the organization of the monastic life in 535, and his crackdown against those opposed to Chalcedon—many of them monks in Egypt and Syria—began about the same time. In 533 a syrian stylite named Z'ura went to Constantinople to protest, in the words of his biographer: 'I will not rest until I go up to him who holds the royal authority and testify to him before Our Lord Jesus Christ concerning the persecution of the whole church, and concerning the distress and mockery of the saints in every place'.[11] Z'ura's lament was to echo down through the rest of the sixth century and find voice in a number of coptic documents.

The first attested casualty in Egypt of Justinian's pro-chalcedonian policy was Theodosius, Archbishop of Alexandria from 536 to 567.[12] In 536 he was asked to accept the emperor's Chalcedonianism, refused, and was ordered to Constantinople.[13] There he still declined to accept Chalcedon. Like other bishops and abbots after him, he was banished for his refusal, and a pro-chalcedonian was appointed in his place.[14] Justinian's policy was not, it seems, systematically applied, but nevertheless had serious and widespread repercussions: the struggle between Chalcedonians and anti-Chalcedonians in Egypt during the middle of Justinian's reign effectively destroyed the famous Pachomian Koinonia in Upper Egypt.[15] According to a *Life* and two encomia on Apa Abraham, abbot of the chief pachomian monastery of Pbow, Justinian ordered 'the bishops everywhere' and 'the leaders of the monasteries' to come to Constantinople.[16] He most likely did this, one source says, because the monastery of Pbow, and most of Egypt, had opposed the Council of Chalcedon from the beginning.[17] Abraham either went willingly or was arrested and forced to go to the imperial city.[18]

The sources (admittedly anti-chalcedonian) all agree that Abraham rejected Justinian's invitation of communion and somehow made his way back to Pbow.[19] The alexandrian *Synaxary* reports that Abraham wrote a letter from Constantinople to the monks of his monastery, telling them of Justinian's efforts. If he acceded to the emperor's wishes, he would be allowed to return to Egypt. But Abraham refused and instead renounced his abbacy and left the monastery.[20] Justinian then sent soldiers to enforce Chalcedon at Pbow; those who resisted were dispersed and many of the monks fled into the deserts and mountains.[21] One source reports that Abraham went first to the Monastery of Saint Shenoute at Atripe and later founded his own monastery at Farshut, across the river from Pbow, while the emperor sent a chalcedonian replacement to Pbow.[22]

The confrontation between Justinian and Abraham took place sometime between 537 and 548. James Goehring concludes, 'It is clear from the sources that the Pachomian movement as represented by Abraham of Pbow had been opposed to Chalcedon from the beginning. Justinian, in his desire to restore Chalcedonian obedience in Egypt, sought to establish a Chalcedonian presence in Upper Egypt at the Pachomian monastery of Pbow'.[23] Justinian undoubtedly picked Pbow because of its size and importance,[24] perhaps because the twice annual meetings of the entire Pachomian Koinonia took place there.[25] The dates for Abraham's ill-fated meeting with Justinian certainly fit within what we know of Daniel's chronology (see the general Introduction to this volume). If Justinian singled out Pbow because of its size and importance, he certainly could have done the same at Scetis, and for the same reasons: Scetis was undoubtedly the most important monastic center in Lower Egypt. And, as at Pbow, the emperor could have decided on force.[26]

As Leslie MacCoull has observed, 'With the growth of late fourth- and fifth-century imperial legislation that defined religious heresy as harm to the state, naturally the state's armed force became more involved in such damage control'.[27] Papyrus documents in fact show that troops of the *Scythae Justiniani* were quartered at the monastery of Pbow in the 540s.[28] If soldiers were similarly sent to Scetis, they would have come from the nearest camp at Terenuthis.[29] The situation is complicated by the fact that such units as the *Justiniani* in Egypt were not made up of outsiders but were composed of local citizen-soldiers who would likely, have been sympathetic to the anti-chalcedonian sentiments of most Egyptians living outside Alexandria.[30] Their 'attack' on Scetis may be the tendentious imaginings of Daniel's coptic hagiographer, the result of 'a very small number of actual incidents, perhaps not in fact directed from Constantinople'.[31] But lest we dismiss such tendentiousness, Mac-Coull reminds us of the very important fact that what 'we see reflected in the story of Daniel of Sketis and the soldiers is the degree to which *the use of armed coercion became imprinted upon the common memory of the Egyptian church*'.[32] She concludes 'that something like' the 'dramatic story' of Abba Daniel's resistance 'might indeed have happened'.[33]

The coptic *Life of Daniel* reports that 'when the emperor's soldiers brought the Tome, filled with every impiety of the lawbreaking Leo, to the holy monastic settlement of Scetis, our holy father Abba Daniel came out and stood before them . . . along with large numbers of old men among the saints'. When the soldiers tell the monks that the emperor has commanded all of them to subscribe 'to the formula of faith', Daniel 'became filled with the grace of the Holy Spirit; he leapt forward and seized that Tome filled with every kind of sacrilege. He tore it apart and cried out to the soldiers, "Anathema upon the defiled Council of Chalcedon!"' The *Life* goes on to report that the emperor's soldiers 'subjected the old men to many different kinds of suffering and numerous humiliations so that as a result they scattered throughout the land of Egypt'. When Daniel 'saw the upheaval', he left the monastic community. The *Life* says that Daniel voluntarily left Scetis but, given Abraham's deposition, it is perhaps more likely that he was forced to leave.[34]

A ninth-century coptic source, the *Life of Samuel of Kalamun*, also reports that soldiers and imperial magistrates attempted to force Leo's Tome down the throats of recalcitrant monks at Scetis. When they did so, Samuel, like Daniel, anathematized the Tome and was forced to flee.[35] The coptic *Life of Daniel*, then, adds credible information, consonant with other coptic sources, about Justinian's efforts to force obedience to the Council of Chalcedon on at least some of the monasteries of Egypt.[36] Justinian's 'imperial Chalcedonianism' produced 'vivid lamentations in later popular Coptic writing'.[37]

These sources, as David Johnson has concluded, 'were written in reaction to the new offensive launched by the emperor Justinian to force a Chalcedonian settlement throughout the empire'.[38] Johnson has observed that anti-chalcedonian polemic falls into three major periods: 1) the first quarter of the sixth century, where the main focus is on the Council of Chalcedon and its aftermath;[39] 2) the mid- to late-sixth century, where the sources are 'written in reaction to Justinian's religious policies'; and 3) after the arab conquest, when sources are 'written in reaction to the religious policies of Heraclius (d. 641)'. The anti-chalcedonian material in the coptic *Life of Daniel* falls into the second period, when coptic documents, Johnson suggests, perhaps mark 'the initial reaction to the incipient neo-Chalcedonian offensive begun by Justin I and Justinian after the death of the tolerant Anastasius in 518'.[40]

These anti-chalcedonian writings generally share six traits: 1) they focus not on conciliar decrees but on the Tome of Leo; 2) Egyptians are ordered to subscribe to the Tome; 3) confessors refuse to submit; 4) the confessors give short speeches detailing the Tome's errors and defending the orthodoxy of those who oppose the Council; 5) the confessors appeal to the Council of Nicaea, 'the faith of our fathers'; 6) the confessors give a 'short rudimentary confession of faith'.[41] The *Life of Daniel* follows the first three of these rubrics but not the last three. Instead of giving a short speech (4), Daniel pronounces a series of anathemas on the Tome and those who believe in it. Daniel neither appeals to Nicaea (5) nor offers a confession of faith (6). As Paul van Cauwenbergh long ago concluded, Daniel's opposition to the Tome of Leo is hardly surprising in a monk of Scetis during Justinian's reign.[42] If the encounter that the Coptic *Life* details did not literally take place, then it nevertheless imaginatively portrays the monks' strong opposition to the emperor and his hated tome.

Because of Daniel's opposition, the *Life* says, he was cruelly tortured and almost died. The *Life* adds that 'the soldiers also subjected the old men to many different kinds of suffering and numerous humiliations so that as a result they scattered throughout the land of Egypt'. As a result, Daniel 'arose and went to Egypt [that is, away from Scetis] with his young disciple. He went to Tambōk, a small village in Egypt, and built a small cell to the west of the village.' Tambōk may have been north-northeast of Babylon (Cairo), in the eastern Delta, possibly the present-day at-Tambuq.[43] Evelyn White doubted that Daniel could flee to Tambōk and yet care for Anastasia and the leper (I.8 and I.2, respectively, in the Greek dossier but the leper could have gone with him and he could have assigned someone else to care for Anastasia.[44] Nor do we know at what point Anastasia and the leper—if they are historical persons—figure chronologically in Daniel's life. Daniel's flight from Scetis, given Apa Abraham and Apa Samuel's forced departures, hardly seems unlikely. And Tambōk, an insignificant place, is enticingly particular; it is hardly a name that one would just make up.

After Justinian's death, in 565, Daniel returned to Scetis. Not long afterwards, 'barbarians came to the holy monastic settlement, laying it waste and killing the old men and taking some of them as prisoners to their country. Simply put, they destroyed our fathers' way of life.' After the destruction of Scetis, Daniel went back to Tambōk where he died.[45] Scetis over the years had been subjected to numerous depredations by barbarians: in 407-408, 434, and 444.[46] It is certainly possible that it was attacked and pillaged again after 565, possibly sometime between 570 and 580.[47] Some fifty to sixty years later, when Patriarch Benjamin I (623-662) visited Scetis, the monasteries were still in disrepair.[48] John Moschus travelled to Egypt after 578 and, although he visited near-by Terenuthis (to which Abba Daniel had traveled) and Kellia, he never mentions Scetis, possibly because it had been destroyed or perhaps because it was too dangerous to travel there.[49] It is possible, however, that John did hear a story about Daniel (see III.1 in Chapter One). If one accepts the historicity of the anti-chalcedonian material in the *Life*, then Daniel fled Scetis sometime in the 530s or 540s and returned after 565. The chronology of the story of Anastasia in the greek collection (I.8) suggests that he was alive in 576. If a late date is given for the sacking of Scetis, say 580, then Daniel died sometime, probably shortly, after that. If Daniel died soon after the destruction of Scetis, he would have lived during much of the sixth century, from about 485 to around 580. Such longevity was not uncommon among the desert fathers.

SYNOPTIC TABLE
The Coptic *Life of Abba Daniel*

Coptic	*Greek*
Proemium	----------
Mark the Fool	[I.1] Mark the Fool
Eulogius the Stonecutter	[I.9] Eulogius the Stonecutter
The Thief who Repented	----------[50]
Abba Daniel and Tome of Leo	----------[51]
Abba Daniel Goes to Tambōk	----------[52]
Abba Daniel Returns to Scetis	----------[53]
The Death of Abba Daniel	----------[54]
Concluding Doxology	----------

THE COPTIC LIFE OF ABBA DANIEL

The Life of Our Holy Father Abba Daniel, the Superior of
Scetis, and the Way of Life of the Saints Whom He Benefitted.
The Day that He Went to His Rest was the Eighth of Pa-
shons.[55] In the Peace of God.[56]

PROEMIUM

/535/ Truly, my beloved, as the holy prophet the psalmist David said in
his precious Psalter, 'Marvellous is God in his saints'.[57] The life and way
of life of all the saints who fully did God's will, /536/ especially that of
our father, the superior of Scetis, Abba Daniel, who was perfect in all
the virtues of the Holy Spirit, is truly a paradise filled with all sorts of
trees full of sweet fruit.[58]

MARK THE FOOL [I.1]

While our father Abba Daniel the priest lived in Scetis, his young disciple named Apa Sergius was at his side. After a while Apa Sergius departed the body. After the brother went to his rest, the old man, Abba
Daniel, arose and took his disciple with him and went to Alexandria. It
was the custom for the Great Father of Scetis to go to Alexandria for
the great feast [of Easter][59] in order to meet with the archbishop. When
they reached Alexandria at five o'clock in the afternoon, they saw a
brother girded with a linen cloth around his loins and the brother was
acting like a half-wit, with other imbeciles walking along with him, and
the brother was wandering about[60] in such a way that he appeared to
have lost his wits. He would snatch things in the marketplace and eat
them and give them to those with him. His name was Mark. He lived
in the public baths called 'The Horse'[61] and as an imbecile would work
there and earn a hundred *arkiōn*[62] a day and he would sleep there. From
the one hundred *arkiōn* that he earned each day he would spend twelve
on bread and the rest he would give to his fellow imbeciles. The whole
city knew him on account of his madness.

Abba Daniel said to his disciple, 'Go, my son, and find out where this
half-wit lives'. So he went and found out and told the old man, 'He lives
in the public bath called "The Horse"'. So after the old man had met with
the archbishop, he went the next day, /537/ in accordance with God's

divine purpose, and found Mark the Fool beside the Great Tetrapylon. Immediately the old man ran and grabbed him and cried out with a loud voice, 'Come and see, people of Alexandria!' Then the imbecile threw the old man down and made obeisance to him[63] and a large crowd gathered around him. The disciple, very afraid, stood at a distance and the crowd said to the old man, 'He's an imbecile; don't talk to him or he'll heap contempt on you'. The old man in response said to them, 'You are the imbeciles, for there is no one in this city, including me, like this fellow!'

A crowd of clergy gathered. Since they knew the old man, they said to him, 'What evil has this imbecile done to you?' The old man said to them, 'Take him to the archbishop for me', and the old man said to the archbishop, 'Truly, my holy father, there is not a righteous person in this city today like this fellow'. At this point the archbishop realized that this matter had been revealed to the old man by God. Then the archbishop arose with the old man and made obeisance before the imbecile, adjuring him at length to tell them what was going on.

Confronted by them, he wished to flee[64] but revealed to them what was going on, saying, 'I was a monk and was ruled by the passion of sexual sin for fifteen years. After so long a time, I had a heart-to-heart talk with myself, "Mark, look, for fifteen years you've been mastered by sexual sin and have become a slave to the Enemy. Get hold of yourself and enslave yourself instead to Christ. Get up now and go to the city of Alexandria. Play the half-wit there for God's sake for ten years". Today I have completed ten years as an imbecile'.[65] When the old men heard this, they wept together.

When evening came, Abba Daniel went to sleep and when morning came he said to his disciple, /538/ 'Go and call Abba Mark so he may pray for us before we return to Scetis'. When the brother went to get Apa Mark,[66] he found that he had gone to sleep in the Lord[67] so he returned and told his father. The old man told the archbishop and the archbishop told the general. Immediately the old man sent his disciple to the Enaton,[68] saying, 'Let them gather at the sound of the signal and bring all of our fathers on up to us, saying to them, "Come, all of you, that you may receive a blessing from this saint."' Thus the old men of the Enaton came up with great rejoicing, with palm branches and olive branches, and they buried him with appropriate ceremony. They offered incense in his honor while multitudes from the city walked with him, with branches in their hands and lighted candles, taking away the body of the slave of God, weeping over our father Apa Mark, glorifying God who gives these great gifts to those who love him.

CONCERNING EULOGIUS THE STONECUTTER [I.9]

Our holy father Abba Daniel was in Egypt another time with his disciple on their way back to Scetis, for they were sailing down the Nile.[69] When they arrived at a village, the old man said to the sailors, 'Let's put to shore here'. His disciple, however, was grumbling and saying, 'How long are we going to waste our time here? Let's go on to Scetis.' The old man said to him, 'No, let's put ashore here for the time being'.

When they went on up, they sat in the middle of the village like foreigners. The disciple once again spoke to the old man: 'If we sit here like this, aren't we like beggars extorting money? /539/ Since that's the case, let's go to the church until tomorrow'. The old man said, 'No, let's stay right here. It's getting dark.' The disciple became angry with the old man. While we were sitting there, an old man suddenly came up to us.[70] When he saw Abba Daniel, he kissed his feet, weeping bitterly. He also greeted the disciple and said to them, 'Please, get up, let's go to my house'. We followed him, for he was holding a flaming torch, going through the streets looking for foreigners. He would take with him everyone he found each day. When he brought the old man to his home, along with the foreigners he had found, he poured water in a basin and washed everyone's feet, for he lived alone in the house. Right away he set the table for them and they ate. After they ate he took the leftovers and gave them to the dogs in the village, for this was his custom. He would not allow anyone in his house until morning.[71] Afterwards, when Abba Daniel got up, he took him aside and spent the whole night[72] with many tears talking with him about the things that lead to salvation. Early in the morning, they kissed one another and the old man and his disciple departed.

While they were on the road, the disciple asked the old man's forgiveness, saying, 'Please, father, tell me who that old man was and where you know him from', but the old man refused to speak to him. Again the brother asked his forgiveness, saying, 'You've confided many other things to me, and now you won't confide in me about the old man?' [Abba Daniel had confided in him the virtues of many holy men.] But the old man refused to talk to the brother about this old man; as a result, the brother got angry and did not speak to the old man until they reached Scetis.

After the brother went to his cell, he did not bring the old man a small meal as was the custom (the old man always observed this practice at five pm).[73] When evening fell, the old man went to the brother's cell and said to him, 'Why, child, have you allowed your father to die of hunger?'

The disciple said to him, 'I don't have a father! If I had a father, he would love his own child!'

The old man said, 'If you don't have a father, serve yourself'. He was taking hold of the door in order to open it and leave when the brother came up to him and grabbed him and began to kiss him, saying, 'As the Lord lives, I will not let you go if you do not tell me who that old man was!' The brother could not bear to see the old man ever distressed, for he dearly loved him.

Then the old man said to him, 'Make me a little something to eat first and then I will tell you'. After he had eaten, he said to the brother, 'Do not be stiff-necked. I did not tell you about the old man because you argued with me in the village and were grumbling. Do not tell anyone what I have told you.

'Now then, my child, that old man's name is Eulogius; by trade he is a stonecutter, earning a *kas* a day by his labor.[74] When evening comes each day, he takes home any foreigners whom he finds in the village and serves them, and he takes and gives whatever he has as leftovers to the dogs of the village, as you have seen. Indeed, he has done this since he was a young man; it has been a hundred years and more. Moreover, the Lord gives him the strength to do this and he earns the one *kas* each day. When I was a young man, forty years ago, I went to that village in order to sell some of my [540] handiwork. When evening came, he took me home with him. I saw what he was doing and was completely amazed.

'When I once again returned here I remembered this man's virtue and so I fasted and continued to fast the whole week, entreating God to provide Eulogius with plenty so he might serve even more foreigners. When I had fasted three weeks I was exhausted and was asleep on account of my ascetic regimen. Suddenly a man of light[75] appeared to me and said to me, "What is wrong with you, Daniel?" I said to him, "My lord, I, Daniel, have given my promise to the Lord: if he does not listen

to me I will not eat again on account of Eulogius the stonecutter; I am
asking the Lord to bestow his blessing upon him so he may serve foreigners and not have to work". But he said to me, "You should not be
pleading like this; the Lord will make everything all right". I said to him,
"No, no, my lord. Give him what he needs to do good for foreigners so
everyone will praise the Lord". He again said to me, "I am telling you
that the Lord will make everything all right. If you want him to be
provided for, offer yourself as a pledge for his life, so he will find salvation through benefiting many,[76] then I will provide for him". I said to
him, "My lord, seek the salvation of his soul from my hands".

'I said these things in a vision. It was as though I found myself standing in the Church of the Holy Resurrection.[77] I saw a young man of
light and the person walking with me said to him, "Look! Here is the
person who is pledging himself for Eulogius". He said to me, "Be as-
sured that I will surely seek his life from your hands". I said to him, "Yes,
my lord". After I said this I saw two men pouring a large quantity of
money into Eulogius' lap. I immediately woke up and I knew that my
prayer had been heard and I gave glory to God.

/541/ 'Now Eulogius prayed to God that day, as it was his custom
to do each day. He went out and worked the rock and as soon as he
struck a rock he found that it was hollow;[78] when he struck it again, he
found a cave filled with money. He was immediately filled with amaze-
ment and said to himself, "This money belongs to the Ishmaelites![79]
What should I do? If I take it home and the landlord hears about it, he
will take it from me. No, I'll take it out of the country, someplace where
no one will know about it". He immediately found a boat, boarded it
with the money, went to Constantinople, and forgot all about the acts
of charity that he used to do. He went to the emperor Justinian[80] and
gave him a great deal of money. The emperor made him a procurator
and bestowed on him great possessions, and as a result he became vain
and pitiless.

'Two years later I once again saw in a dream that I was as it were
standing in the Church of the Resurrection. I saw the young man of
light and I said to myself, "I wonder what Eulogius is doing now?"
Afterwards I saw Eulogius being dragged to where the young man of
light was, as though he were being brought to judgement. Immediately
I awoke from the vision and my heart was greatly troubled; I said, "God
help me for what I have done! I have lost my own life!" I got up, took

my palm staff, and went to the village in order to sell my handiwork. I stayed there, looking for Eulogius, as was the custom, to come get me. When evening came, however, I had not seen him, nor had anyone spoken to me.

'When an old woman passed by, I said to her, "My mother, please go and bring me three loaves of bread so I may eat. The truth is, I haven't eaten today".[81] She did what I had told her and replied and said to me, "Don't you know that you are a young man? /542/ It's not appropriate for you to go down to the village. Don't you know that the monk requires quiet seclusion at all times?" I said to her, "Forgive me. I've come to sell a few things I've made". But she then said to me, "Sell your handiwork first and don't stay until evening comes, like you're doing. If you want to be a monk, go to Scetis". I again spoke to her, "Really,[82] spare me these instructions. Is the God-fearing man who takes in foreigners here still alive, or not?" She said to me, "O my Lord God, indeed there was a stonecutter here; he did a lot of good things for foreigners. When the Lord found out about his good deeds, he gave him grace and today he's a procurator!"

'When I heard these things I said to myself,[83] "I am [responsible for] this murder!" and I boarded ship and sailed to Byzantium. Diligently seeking the house of Eulogius the Egyptian, I sat in front of his gate until he came out. I saw him coming with great ostentation and I called out to him, "Have mercy on me! I wish to speak with you in private about some matter!" but he turned away from me and his escort beat me instead. I persisted and cried out once again and once again they beat me. I spent four weeks distressed this way but was not able to meet with him. Then, a little later, I went and threw myself in front of the icon of the supremely-holy Mother of God and wept and said to the Saviour, "Lord, either release me from me the pledge I made on behalf of this person or I will go away into the world!"[84]

'While I was trying to understand these events, I fell asleep and saw a great commotion and they were saying, "The Augusta is coming!" and there came before her thousands and tens of thousand ranks, and I cried out and said, "Have mercy on me, my Queen!" She stopped and said to me, "What is the matter with you?" and I said to her, "I pledged myself as surety for Eulogius the procurator. Order him to release me from this pledge". She said to me, "I do not have authority in this matter. Fulfill the pledge as you wish."

'When I woke up I said to myself, "Even if I have to die, I am not leaving his gate unless I meet with him!" So once again I went in front of the gate. When Eulogius came out, I cried out and the doorkeeper attacked me and beat me with rods until he had broken every bone in my body. Then I was troubled and said, "I will go to Scetis. If God wishes to save Eulogius' soul, he will save it".

'I looked for a ship and found one that was sailing for Alexandria. I boarded it in order to return to my cell. After I had boarded, I fell asleep on account of my grief and once again I saw myself in the Church of the Holy Resurrection. I again saw the young man of light sitting in the holy place. He angrily looked into my soul so that, afraid of him, I was trembling like a leaf that the wind shakes and out of fear of him I was unable to open my mouth at all, for my heart <had turned to stone> within me.[85] He said to me, "Will you not go and fulfill what you promised?" and he ordered the two who were standing beside him to hang me up and they hung me upside down and he said to me, "See that you do not try to do what is beyond your abilities, nor repeat a word of what you have heard", and, [543] hanging up high like that, I was unable to open my mouth.[86]

'Then suddenly there was a voice saying "The Empress has come!" When I saw her, I summoned up my courage and said to her, "Have mercy on me, my lady!" She said to me, "What do you want now?" and I said to her, "I am hanging up here because I pledged myself for Eulogius", and she said to me, "I am making entreaties on your behalf". I saw her take hold of the young man's feet and kiss them and he said to me, "See that you do not do anything like this again". I said, "Yes, lord. I have sinned. Forgive me". Then they loosened the ropes and let me down. He said to me, "Go to your cell. I will return Eulogius to his former way of life". When I woke up I was very happy and said, "I have been released from the pledge I made for Eulogius", and I gave glory to God and returned to my cell.

'Three months later I heard that Emperor Justinian had died and another was appointed in his place[87] and charges were brought to him concerning three consuls, and these were their names: Doxikrates, Psimpius, and Eulogius. The emperor ordered all their possessions seized and afterwards they were to be beheaded with the sword.[88] When Eulogius heard about this, he left everything behind and fled Constantinople at night, but the emperor ordered that wherever he was found he was to be killed with the sword. Immediately he went to his village and changed his clothes and clothed himself as he was before. When the people of the village saw him, all of them came to him and said to him, "We heard that you had become a procurator". He said, "To tell you the truth, that wasn't me; I was away from the village working and I went to the holy desert and prayed there. Perhaps that was some other Eulogius and not me."

'Then he remained by himself. He said, "Get up, you wretch! Take your stonecutting tools and go to work! This isn't the imperial residence! Don't go looking for one or you too will get your head cut off!" Then /544/ he took his stonecutting tools and went to the quarry where he had found the money. He looked for it once more, sure that he would find another cache, but he dug there for six hours and did not find anything. Then he sat down and recalled the money he had lost and the servants and all the pomps he had enjoyed and he said to himself, "Get up and get to work! There's nothing like this in Egypt!" So, little by little he returned to his senses through the encouragements given by our Lady Mary, the holy Mother of God, and he returned to his former way of life. Indeed, the Lord would not be so negligent as to overlook his previous labors.

'A few days later I went to that village in order to sell a few things I had made. When evening came he took me home with him, according to custom, and I saw that a large crowd of people was boasting about him. I groaned and said, "How great are your works, Lord! You have made all things with wisdom! What God is as great as our God, who raises up the poor from the earth and the weak from the dung heap?[89] The judgements of the Lord are countless. I, a sinner, exalted myself above your works, delivering[90] my soul down to Amente".[91] Afterwards, he took me home, washed my feet, according to his custom, and set the table for us. After we ate I said to him, "What is your news, Eulogius, my brother?" He said to me, "I have received your prayers on my behalf, my holy father, for I am a weak person with nothing to my name". I said to him, "It's good that you have even less than you had before". He said to me, "Why, lord father, do you take offense?" Then I told him everything and we wept together. Then he spoke to me again, "Pray for me, my lord father, that the Lord may forgive me my sins and I will walk correctly for ever".

'Look, my son, I have told you everything; moreover, the Lord gives him the strength to earn the *kas* each day. /545/ See that you do not speak a word of this to anyone until the Lord comes to get me. Let us also give glory to our Lord Jesus Christ: he gave Eulogius back his soul and did not allow his efforts to be destroyed. Glory and honor are his, now and forever. Amen.'

THE THIEF WHO REPENTED[92]

After these events, the fame of our father Abba Daniel spread everywhere and large numbers of people desired to obtain his holy blessing, especially saints from the monasteries. In the fertile borderland there was a monastery in which a large number of virgins lived. They had a few possessions that they shared[93] with the poor and with foreigners. The Devil could not stand to see the great good that these virgins were doing for everyone so he entered the heart of a ringleader of thieves in that region and caused him to take with him his whole band of thieves, who would go with him by night to that monastery and plunder it.[94] When he told his men about the plan, they gave a loud cheer and immediately went to the monastery. They were thinking about how they were going to take it but things did not turn out as they had expected, for the walls of the monastery were very strong. When the robbers saw that they were powerless to enter, they were upset and the ringleader of the thieves said to them, 'If you don't do what I tell you, you won't be able to take anything from the monastery'.

They said to him, 'We will do what you tell us'.

He said to them, 'Go find me some monastic clothing: a black head-covering[95] and a hood covered with crosses, like those that Abba Daniel of Scetis wears. Later, I will dress in his clothing and will take a palm staff in my hand and knock on the door of the monastery. When they see me they will open the door for me because they think it is Abba Daniel, and I will tell you to hurry in and you can rob the monastery at your leisure'.

When they heard these things, they gave a loud cheer and quickly went [546] and brought him clothes like [those] he had told them about and when the time came the ringleader of the thieves got up and dressed himself in the clothes. He took a palm staff in his hand and went and stood in front of the door to the monastery. When he knocked, the door-keeper answered him, 'Who are you, my father? What do you require?'

He said to her, 'Go and tell the abbess that Abba Daniel, the priest of Scetis, stands at your door: I am going to stay with you until morning.'

The doorkeeper went to the abbess and told her, 'Our father Abba Daniel, the priest of Scetis, is standing at the door and he told me to tell you'.

When she heard that Abba Daniel was standing at the door, she immediately got up, with all the sisters, and they ran to the door. They kissed the man's feet and brought him inside with honor. The abbess, along with the sisters, put water in a basin and washed his feet and when they wanted to spread a bed for him on the roof of the monastery,[96] he prevented them, saying, 'As the Lord lives, I will not leave this spot until morning'. When they had finished washing his feet, the abbess took some of the water and poured it over her head and face; likewise, all the sisters took some water from the basin and in faith poured it over their heads and faces.[97]

When one of the sisters, who had been blind from childhood, heard the sisters' rejoicing, she said to them, 'Give me some of the old man's water too', and they took hold of her and stood her over the basin. She cried out, 'Blessed are you, my holy father Abba Daniel! May God and your name have mercy on me!' And she filled her hand with water and rubbed it on her face. Immediately she was able to see. How great were the shouts and the rejoicing of all the sisters at that moment! They ran and kissed the thief's feet. /547/ She who could now see cried out all the more, 'Blessed are you my holy father! With the water from your feet, you have given the light back to me.'

When the ringleader saw these things, he was seized with trembling and fear.[98] After all the sisters had gone to sleep, the thief did not go to sleep at all but instead sat weeping until his tears drenched the earth, saying, 'God help me! I am a weak and sinful person. I have wasted all my time doing incredibly vain and foolish things as if by taking his name I could actually be this man. *He* caused the water that was used to wash my feet to give light to the blind. What sort of a person is this man? God help me! I am a weak and sinful person. I have neglected my salvation.' While the thief was weeping and saying these things, his evil men spent the whole night in front of the door, swords drawn, waiting for him to open the door for them. He was listening to them in silence, keeping his words to himself. When dawn came, still standing in front of the door like dogs, they shamefacedly turned away and went someplace else.

The next day the thief got up and left the sisters in peace. While he was walking along the road, the robbers surrounded him and said to him, 'What were you doing all night?'

He said to them, 'I'm not having anything to do with you any more'.

They said to him, 'Why?'

He related to them everything that had happened to him and immediately headed for Scetis to our holy father Abba Daniel. He said goodbye to them[99] and became a chosen monk until the day he died.

ABBA DANIEL REFUSES TO ACCEPT THE TOME OF LEO[100]

At that time the impious and defiled Justinian[101] became emperor. He created disturbances /548/ throughout the world and the Catholic Church everywhere. He attempted to impose the accursed faith of the defiled Council of Chalcedon everywhere and scattered the beautiful flocks of Christ. He ran the orthodox bishops and archbishops off their thrones, and the impious Justinian was not satisfied with this but promulgated the impious Tome of Leo, which the impious Council of Chalcedon had accepted. He promulgated it everywhere that lay under his rule in order to make everyone subscribe to it. When it was brought down to Egypt, a great disturbance broke out among all the orthodox faithful who lived in the land of Egypt, and it was brought down to the holy monastic settlement of Scetis in order that our holy fathers might subscribe to it. Since our holy father Daniel was father of Scetis at that time, the Lord revealed the matter to him before the Tome was brought to Scetis. The saint gathered together all the old men and told them what the Lord had revealed to him and he taught them everything in order to strengthen them in the orthodox faith so they would not deny the faith, even unto death.

When the emperor's soldiers brought the Tome—filled with every impiety of the lawbreaking Leo—to the holy monastic settlement of Scetis, our holy father Abba Daniel came out and stood before them. Following his example, the superior came out to meet them, along with large numbers of old men among the saints. When the old men met the soldiers, the latter produced the Tome filled with impiety and offered it to the old men, saying, 'The emperor has commanded all of you to subscribe to the formula of faith'.

Our holy father Abba Daniel, the blessed superior, in response said to the soldiers, 'What /549/ formula of faith is this?'

They said to him, 'That of the great council of Chalcedon at which six-hundred thirty-four bishops gathered'.

Our father Abba Daniel became filled with the grace of the Holy Spirit; he leapt forward and seized that Tome filled with every kind of sacrilege.[102] He tore it apart and cried out to the soldiers, 'Anathema upon the defiled Council of Chalcedon! Anathema upon everyone who is in communion with it! Anathema upon everyone who believes in it! Anathema upon everyone who denies the saving passion of Christ! As for us, we will never accept this defiled and godless decree but will anathematize everyone who accepts it and believes in it.[103] With our last breath we will believe in the Father and the Son and the Holy Spirit, consubstantial Trinity in a single Godhead'.

ABBA DANIEL GOES TO TAMBŌK

When the soldiers saw the great courage of our Abba Daniel and the way he demonstrated it, they were filled with rage and seized him and subjected him to cruel tortures so that for a few days he was near death on account of the many wounds they had inflicted on him. The soldiers also subjected the old men to many different kinds of suffering and numerous humiliations so that as a result they scattered throughout the land of Egypt. When our holy father Abba Daniel saw the upheaval, he arose and went to Egypt[104] with his young disciple. He went to Tambōk, a small village in Egypt, and built a small cell to the west of the village.[105] He lived there in quiet solitude for a few days, giving glory to our Lord Jesus Christ. He performed countless numbers of ascetic practices so that his fame spread everywhere and everyone gave glory to God who was with him.

ABBA DANIEL RETURNS TO SCETIS; ITS DESTRUCTION

He lived there a long time until the Lord struck down the impious emperor Justinian and he died. The holy old man Abba Daniel arose and went /550/ with great rejoicing to the holy monastic settlement of Scetis, wearing always the crown of confession.[106] When all the brothers saw that he had come, they arose and went out to meet him and all of them offered him obeisance, with great rejoicing, and he went inside his cave, giving glory to our Lord Jesus Christ. Not many days after our father Abba Daniel had returned to Scetis, barbarians came to the holy monastic settlement, laying waste to it and killing the old men and taking some of them as prisoners to their country. Simply put, they destroyed our fathers' way of life by hateful means, inflicting terrible sufferings on them and numerous afflictions.

ABBA DANIEL RETURNS TO TAMBŌK;
THE DEATH OF ABBA DANIEL

After these events, our father Abba Daniel said to his disciple, 'Get up; let us go to the dwelling where we lived earlier. I mean the cell in Tambōk.' And our holy father Abba Daniel got up and went there with his disciple and again undertook great ascetic practices. While he was living there it was revealed to him by an angel of the Lord, 'The days when you are going to pass away from the world are approaching and you will go to Christ, whom you have loved'. That day was the first of Pashons.[107] The holy old man got up and gathered together the brothers who were in the keep and said to them, 'The days of my death are approaching'. Immediately, on the second of Pashons, he lay down. His disciple later returned and offered his greeting[108] but the old man was unable to respond to him.[109] The disciple said to him, 'My holy father, what is wrong with you today?'

He replied and said to him, 'My son, I am having difficulty speaking today. The sinews of my body are withered and my joints are about to /551/ give out. What is earth will return to the earth again'.[110] (It was God who knew where the suffering soul would go.)

His disciple said to him, 'My father, perfect as you are, are even you afraid?'

He said to him, 'My son, if Abraham, Isaac, and Jacob come up to me and say to me, "You are righteous", I will not believe it.[111] God help everyone who sins like this! I say to you, my son, Moses—who spoke with God five-hundred seventy times—and the prophets and all the saints, were afraid when faced with this moment.[112] Even the righteous are troubled at this moment; everyone is who lives on the earth, my son. Look at the children who drink milk, that is, those who are suckling,[113] [if God comes looking for them, how they will suffer! They have not even committed any sin!][114] My dear son, I have never travelled the road that I will travel; I have never seen greater messengers than those who are coming for me; [the faces of] the ministers who are coming for me [are distorted. What will I say to them?][115] They have not accepted a gift and also have not released [me], nor, moreover, have they shown deference for my gray hair, for their duties have been determined for them'.

After blessed Daniel, the second prophet of his generation,[116] had said these things to the young man, he turned his face to the east[117] and said to his disciple, 'Come here beside me, my son. My time has come, weak old man that I am'. He took hold of the disciple's hands and laid them on his eyes and said, 'My Lord Jesus Christ, my soul's beloved, into your hands I commend my spirit'.[118] After he said this, he immediately gave his spirit into the Lord's hands on the eighth of Pashons.[119] His young disciple prepared his holy body for burial and those who were with him placed him in the cell at Tambōk with honor and due respect.

CONCLUDING DOXOLOGY

Blessed are all those who in any way show charity /552/ in his name on the day of his holy dormition, for <they>[120] will have a place with him in the kingdom of heaven, which our holy father Abba Daniel, the honored superior of Scetis, has prepared for <them>.[121] May all of us be worthy of this through the grace and love for humanity of our Lord and our God and our Savior Jesus Christ. Through him all honor and glory and adoration are due to the Father, with him and the Holy Spirit, who with him is life-giving and consubstantial, now and always and forever and ever. Amen.

May the Lord have mercy on this work that Chaēl has written [. . .]. Amen.

May the Lord give understanding to our father lectors the deacon Sarapiōn and the deacon Mēna.[122] Amen.

May God have pity on Isaac,[123] the most unworthy lector, and forgive him. Amen.

God who will say 'Amen'. God forgive him. Amen.[124]

May God have mercy on the sinner Severus.[125] Amen.

RELEVANT PASSAGES FROM THE
COPTIC-ARABIC SYNAXARY

Translated by Maged S. A. Mikhail
Introduction by Tim Vivian

THE COPTIC SYNAXARY has three entries that are certainly about
Abba Daniel of Scetis, and two others that may possibly refer to him.
The entries for Mark the Fool [above, section I] 10 Hatur (6 November);
Anastasia [III] 26 Tubah (21 January) and Daniel (and Anastas and Eu-
logius: IV, 8 Bashons (3 May) > I, 10 Hatur (6 November) Mark the
Fool; III, 26 Tubah (21 January), Anastasia; and IV, 8 Bashons (3 May),
Daniel [and Anastasia and Eulogius] correspond to the stories about
Abba Daniel in the greek dossier. Two other Synaxary entries—II, 19
Kihak (15 December), John, Bishop of El-Borollos; and V, 1 Abib (25
June), Saints Bioukha and Tayaban [Banayen]—have only the slimmest
connection with Abba Daniel. In the former, John places himself 'under
the guidance of Saint Daniel, the archpriest of the wilderness', and in
the latter, Saint Banayen goes to 'Saint Daniel, the priest of the wilderness of Sheheet [Scetis]'. Neither entry identifies Daniel more fully so
it is impossible to connect this Daniel with confidence to the Daniel of
the dossier. The ethiopic Synaxary also contains the account of Bioukha
and Tayaban [Banayen].[126] The story of Mark (I) is reasonably close in
length and content to the greek while the stories of Anastasia (III) and
Eulogius (V) are considerably abbreviated: the former has about thirty
percent of the greek version while the latter contains only about ten
percent.

I. 10 Hatur (6 November): [*Mark the Fool*][127]

Brethren, know that on this day Saint Mark[128] was reposed. This blessed man was from a district of the city of Alexandria. He went out to the wilderness and remained there for a long time, practicing asceticism with great austerities and continuous vigils. But the deceitful Enemy[129]— may God shame him—assailed him with the lust of adultery for fifteen years. Because of this Saint Mark thought in his heart, 'Mark, it has been fifteen years and you have been oppressed because of the Enemy. Rise now and enter the city of Alexandria and act as an imbecile. For the sake of God, make yourself as an imbecile'. He rose and entered the city and acted as an imbecile and walked throughout the city and he became known by all the inhabitants of the city. Each day he would earn a great deal of money. He would give it as alms, and pray and fast. All who saw him thought he was an imbecile. And many crazy people followed him over the years.

It happened that as Anba[130] Daniel headed toward Alexandria to meet with the patriarch on Easter, as is customary, this saint went to the market naked and a number of crazy people followed him throughout the city—he used to live in the Dimas in Alexandria.[131] When Anba Daniel saw him, he said to his disciple, 'Hurry, my son, find out where this imbecile lives'. The disciple inquired and found out that he lived in the Dimas. After Anba Daniel went to the patriarch and they spoke concerning the great things of God, he went out and encountered Mark the imbecile. /p. 293/ The elder immediately grabbed him and called out, 'Come, people of the City! See the servant of God'. Immediately the inhabitants of the city gathered and said to him, 'Our father, let go of this man lest he shame you, for he is an imbecile'.

Anba Daniel said to them, 'It is you who are the imbeciles; neither in the wilderness[132] nor in the city does anyone resemble this saint, and the whole world does not deserve him'. Immediately he seized him and took him to the father, the patriarch, and said to him, 'Our father, there is no one in this age who resembles this righteous man'. Immediately he informed the patriarch that Christ had revealed this to him about Mark. Immediately they brought him and made him swear by the faith, so that he would reveal his story,[133] by which he was oppressed. He tried to conceal it [his way of life] from them, but was unable. He said, 'I am a monk. The lust of adultery ruled over me, so I rose, came to this city, and acted as an imbecile for the sake of God. I have been here for eight years, while I have persisted in my prayers and my asceticism. I maintain the vigils and always keep the fasts'. Immediately, when the elders heard this, they wept. As for the saint, Anba Daniel, he spent the night in the cell of the Patriarch and in the morning said to his disciple, 'Go, my son, and summon Mark so that he may pray for us so we may return to the desert'. When the disciple went to the keep of Dimas, where [the saint] lives, he found that he was reposed in the Lord. He returned and informed his father.

Anba Daniel informed the patriarch of [Mark's] repose. Immediately, he sent to the monasteries and gathered the monks. They came from Scetis wearing beautiful clothes and in their hands [carried] olive branches and palm fronds. The monks of the Enaton came, and a large crowd beyond number gathered, and they celebrated for him with great honor. They were not able to bury him for five days. They raised sweet incense and the people of the city walked with him while holding in their hands lighted candles and incense. And they shrouded the servant of God as they wept. Many wonders appeared from his body: the healing of the sick, the exorcising of demons, and the curing of illnesses.[134] They buried him with great honor as they praised God who gives such glory to those who love him and do his will at all times. He glorifies them on earth and grants them[135] the good things of the kingdom of heaven which do not cease or parish—what no eye has seen nor ear has heard nor the human heart conceived.[136]

May the Lord God have mercy upon us
until the last breath through his prayers. Amen.

II. 19 Kihak (15 December): *John*
The Departure of Saint John, Bishop of El-Borollos,
Who Gathered the Biographies of the Saints (The Synaxarium)[137]

On this day Saint John, Bishop of El-Borollos,[138] departed. He came from a wealthy family and from priestly ancestors. His parents were charitable and gave generously to the poor. When they died, Saint John took the money they left and built a hostel for strangers. He gathered the sick, served them himself, and offered them what they needed. Once a monk visited him and saw his good deeds; the monk praised him and praised monasticism in his presence, showing him its honor. The saint was attracted to the monastic life and had a deep love in his heart for it. After the monk departed, the saint distributed his wealth among the poor and went into the wilderness of Shiheet [Scetis].

He became a monk under the guidance of Saint Daniel, the archpriest of the wilderness. Saint John was known for his zeal for worship and for his great asceticism. He lived alone in a secluded building. Satan and his soldiers envied his good deeds, and they massed against him and painfully beat him. He was sick for many days, after which the Lord Christ healed him. He regained his strength and overcame the Devil.

God then called him to become bishop of Borollos. At this time, there were some heresies and he made a great effort to eradicate them, and converted the heretics to the orthodox faith. Also in his time, a monk from upper Egypt claimed that he could reveal certain things imparted to him by the Archangel Michael, and he misled many by his deception. Saint John saw that the monk's deeds were from the Devil. He commanded the monk to be beaten until he confessed his sins and he drove him out of the country. Another claimed that Habakkuk, the prophet, appeared and revealed hidden things to him, and as a result he was followed by many. Saint John drove him out of the country after he had exposed his deception. He also put an end to the use of several bad books.

Every time this saint went up to the sanctuary to serve the Divine Liturgy, his face and all his body were flushed red, as though he had come out of a fiery furnace, and his tears poured heavily down his cheeks, for he was beholding the heavenly hosts on the altar. Three times when he placed his finger in the chalice to make the sign of the cross during the fraction prayer, he found that the cup was as hot as fire. Furthermore, in his days some infidels were partaking of the Holy Mysteries without having fasted. The saint rebuked them, but since they did not hearken to him, he excommunicated them and forbade them from the fellowship of the Church. When they disobeyed his order, he entreated God, so fire came down from heaven, and the fire burned their leader. Fear fell upon the rest and they repented.

When the Lord wanted to give him rest from the toil of this world, he sent to him Saint Antony and Saint Macarius to tell him of the day of his departure. Saint John called his people and commended them [to God], then departed in peace.

May his prayers be with us and glory be to our God forever. Amen.

III. 26 Tubah (21 January): *Anastasia*[139]

On this day also, Saint Anastasia departed. She was from a noble family in the city of Constantinople. She was very beautiful and had great moral character. Emperor Justin,[140] who was married, wanted to marry her. She refused and went and told his wife. The empress sent her to Alexandria on a private ship. She built her a monastery outside the city of Alexandria and named it after her. When the emperor knew where she was, he sent for her, but Anastasia escaped and hid herself in the wilderness of Sheheat [Scetis], disguised as a prince.

She met with Anba Daniel, the archpriest of the wilderness, and revealed her story to him. He brought her to a cave, and asked one of the elders to fill a water pot for her once every week and to place the pot at the door of the cave and leave. She remained in this place for twenty-eight years, without anyone knowing that she was a woman. She used to write her thoughts on pieces of pottery, and leave them at the door of her cave. The elder who brought her the water used to take the pieces of pottery without knowing what was written on them and give them to Saint Daniel. One day he brought a piece of pottery to Saint Daniel who wept when he read it and said to his disciple, 'Come with me now to bury the body of the saint in that cave'.

When they entered her cave, they received blessings from each other. Saint Anastasia said to Anba Daniel, 'For the sake of God, bury me with what I have on my body'. Then she prayed and bade them farewell and departed in peace. They wept and buried her. When the disciple was preparing her for burial, he found out that she was a woman, and he marveled in silence. After they buried her and returned home, the disciple knelt before Saint Daniel and said, 'For the sake of God, tell me her story, for I have seen that she was a woman'. The elder told him her story, that she was from one of the noble families of Constantinople, and how she surrendered herself to Christ, forsaking the vain glory of this world.

May her prayers be with us
and glory be to our God forever. Amen.

IV. 8 Bashons (3 May): *Daniel [and Anastasia and Eulogius]*[141]

On this day also the holy father Anba Daniel the Archpriest of Sheahat [Scetis], departed. He was a perfect and pure father.

When his fame was noised abroad, many came to him; among them was Saint Anastasia disguised in a man's apparel. She became a nun, and lived in a cell near him for twenty-eight years and no one knew who she was.

One day, the saint saw a person whose name was Olagi [Eulogius], who worked as a stonecutter for a *karat* of gold each day. With a very small portion of this he lived and with the remainder he fed the poor, without saving anything. When Abba Daniel saw his good fight and the excellence of his deeds, he asked God to give Olagi more money to increase his deeds of mercy. God answered his prayer, and Olagi found a treasure when he was cutting the stones, which he took, and went to Constantinople. With the newly found money he became a minister to the emperor, and forsook the deeds of mercy. When Saint Daniel heard about this, he went to Constantinople and found what had become of Olagi, that he had abandoned his deeds of mercy. Then in a vision the saint saw the Lord Christ sitting and judging the people. He commanded Saint Daniel to be crucified and demanded from him the lost soul of Olagi. When the saint rose up from his sleep, he went back to his monastery and entreated God to bring Olagi back to his former state. The angel of the Lord appeared to him and rebuked him for rejecting God's judgement concerning his creation. Afterwards, the Emperor of Constantinople died and there reigned another who dismissed Olagi and took his money and wanted to kill him. He fled in order to save his life and returned to his town to cut stones as before. Anba Daniel met Olagi and told him everything that had happened to him because of him.

Many hardships befell Saint Daniel because of the faith, and God manifested many miracles through him. He knew in advance the time of his departure from this world. He gathered all the monks around him, commanded, strengthened, and comforted them, and then departed in peace.

May his prayers be with us
and glory be to God forever. Amen.

V. 1 Abib (25 June):
The Departure of Saints Bioukha and Tayaban [Banayen][142]

On this day also, the fighters Saints Bioukha and Banayen departed. They were priests in the church of Tunah in the diocese of Tanda.[143] Their father was the steward of this church. When the priest Banayen was celebrating the Divine Liturgy, someone came calling him to see his father, who was dying at that moment. The priest Banayen answered him, saying, 'I cannot take off my priestly vestment before the end of the service. If God is willing, I shall see him before he dies, otherwise it will be the will of God.' His father asked for him three times, and he responded with the same answer. When he finished the Liturgy, he found his father had departed. The church vessels were stored in a place known only by his father. Banayen the priest went to Saint Daniel, the priest of the wilderness of Shiheet [Scetis], who guided him by divine inspiration to the place where the vessels were stored. These two saints lived a virtuous life until they departed in peace.

May their prayers be with us,
and glory be to God forever. Amen.

A Note on Nomenclature in Chapter Three

Although in other chapters personal names are given in the Latin form, the use of the Ethiopic forms of personal names in the following Chapter is intended to convey the diversity that these names had in the several linguistic traditions in which the Daniel narratives survive. Latin equivalents are provided in the notes.

CHAPTER THREE

The Ethiopic Life of Daniel

WITH APPENDICES: ETHIOPIC SYNAXARY ENTRIES AND ETHIOPIC APOPHTHEGMS

Translation and Notes by Michael Kleiner[1]
Introduction by Tim Vivian

T HE ETHIOPIC[2] 'Life of Daniel', like the coptic version, is not a *Vita* or 'Life' but rather a homily on Daniel for the saint's feast day.[3] The ethiopic version contains six stories from the greek dossier: Mark the Fool (Gk I.1), A Drunken Monastic (I.4), Thomaïs (I.6), The Tempted Monk (I.7), Anastasia (I.8), and Eulogius (I.9).[4] The proemium to the homily closely follows the coptic text but then the sequence of stories differs radically. The coptic account begins with Mark (I.1), whereas the ethiopic commences with Anastasia (I.8) and then proceeds to Mark (I.1), Eulogius (I.9), Thomaïs (I.6), The Tempted Monk (I.7), and The Drunken Monastic (I.4). (The coptic version contains only the stories of Mark and Eulogius.) The ethiopic version, like the coptic, follows the stories from the greek dossier with The Thief Who Repented (attested only in Coptic and Ethiopic), but then adds the account of The Female Hermit, not attested in Coptic, or any other language.[5]

The ethiopic texts are reasonably close to the coptic and greek accounts. They differ from those anterior versions precisely where the ethiopic Synaxary differs: in placing Abba Daniel—or *an* Abba Daniel—at the Monastery of Saint Macarius in Scetis. The ethiopic version of the story of The Thief who Repented places Daniel at Saint Macarius whereas the coptic version situates him more generally in Scetis. Within the anti–chalcedonian material that Ethiopic shares with Coptic, the story about the Tome of Leo makes Daniel 'bishop of the monastery of Abba Macarius' whereas the coptic version more circumspectly calls him 'father of Scetis at that time'. Either the ethiopic tradition preserves an accurate historical memory locating Daniel at Saint Macarius or, more likely, has substituted the most famous monastery in Scetis for the monastic settlement as a whole. Given the priority of the greek text, the fact that none of the greek accounts places Daniel at a specific monastery must be decisive here, although it should be pointed out that Daniel, as *hēgoumen* (monastic superior) of Scetis, like the coptic pope today, would undoubtedly have made one of the four monasteries his principal residence.[6]

The story of The Female Hermit, not found in any other language, does not place Daniel in Scetis or at Saint Macarius but the style of the story fits the general tenor of the Daniel dossier and, more importantly, embodies its main theme: that Daniel, rather than being a typical holy man or thaumaturge, is, as in the greek dossier, a witness to holiness. Here he witnesses the holiness of the female hermit. Daniel narrates his visit with this hermit, just as he narrates the stories of Eulogius and Anastasia to his disciple in the greek texts. Here, however, there is no disciple. The fact that the story of The Female Hermit does not exist in Greek would seem to weigh heavily against its being part of the original dossier. We should remember, however, that the Greek is precisely that— a dossier, a collection. It is not a cohesive whole, and it is possible that this story may have fallen out early on in some manuscript traditions of the dossier.

The ethiopic Synaxary entries about Abba Daniel, translated below in Appendix I, clearly bear witness to Daniel of Scetis, but they do so with some confusion. In the entry on Andronicus and Athanasia, 28 Hamlē, which offers a shortened version of the greek account (I.5), the two grieving parents abandon the world after the deaths of their children and go to Alexandria, from where Andronicus goes to Abba Daniel in the desert of Scetis.[7] In another entry, Beyoka and Benyamin, 'holy ascetics', priests, and brothers, go to 'the desert of Scetis', where Benyamin meets 'Saint Abba Daniel, superior of the monastery of Scetis'.[8] The version of this story in the coptic Synaxary identifies Daniel as 'the priest of the wilderness of Shiheet [Scetis]'. Nothing in the story resembles material from the Daniel dossier, so this Daniel does not appear to be

the sixth-century Daniel of Scetis. On 16 Hedar appears the commemoration of 'Abba Daniel the monk and the Emperor Honorius.
This Abba Daniel was a combatant in the desert of Scetis in the Monastery of Saint Macarius'.[9] Honorius was emperor from 393-423 and
nothing in this entry corresponds to material in the Daniel dossier, so
this Daniel—of the Monastery of Saint Macarius—must be distinguished
from Daniel of Scetis.

Ethiopic tradition clearly recognizes two Daniels but it also confuses
them. On 8 Genbot, Daniel, 'superior of the desert of Scetis', died and
is commemorated.[10] Since this entry speaks of Anastasia (I.8) and Eulogius (I.9), this Daniel is to be identified with the sixth-century Daniel
of Scetis of the Daniel dossier. That the Daniel associated with Anastasia
and Eulogius was superior of Scetis and not associated specifically with
the Monastery of Saint Macarius is important to note. Another entry,
however, this one from the 'vulgate' version,[11] remembers 'Abba Daniel
of Däbrä-Sihat,[12] of the Monastery of Saint Macarius', who died on 7
Takhsas.[13] The Synaxary entry for that date, translated below (II), also
identifies Daniel with Saint Macarius Monastery: 'On this day passed
away Abba Daniel of the Monastery of Sihat, that is, the Monastery of
Abba Macarius'. After an *incipit*, this passage gives very short epitomes
of events from the Daniel dossier that correspond, not with the greek
dossier, but rather with the ethiopic and coptic versions. Thus, although
this Synaxary entry confuses the sixth-century Daniel of Scetis with the
Daniel of Saint Macarius, there can be no doubt that this Daniel is he
of the Daniel dossier.[14]

As we have seen, the ethiopic tradition tends to conflate Scetis and
the Monastery of Saint Macarius. The Synaxary entry for 7 Takhsas
demonstrates this when it says that Daniel was from the 'Monastery of
Sihat, that is, the Monastery of Abba Macarius'. Thus it is not even certain that there are two Daniels in the ethiopic tradition, just two places
which ought to be identified as one: Scetis.

SYNOPTIC TABLE

Ethiopic	Greek	Coptic
Proemium	-------	Proemium
Bästasiyos the Eunuch	Anastasia (I.8)	-------
Marka the Madman	Mark the Fool (I.1)	Mark the Fool
Awlogiyos	Eulogius (I.9)	Eulogius
Dontiris	Thomaïs (I.6)	-------
The Tempted Monk	The Tempted Monk (I.7)	-------
The Mad Monastic	The Drunken Monastic (I.4)	-------
The Thief who Repented	-------	-------
The Female Hermit	-------	-------
The Tome of Leo	-------	The Tome of Leo
Tambōk	-------	Tambōk
Return to Scetis	-------	Return to Scetis
Death of Abba Daniel	-------	Death of Abba Daniel

THE LIFE OF ABBA DANIEL OF SCETIS[15]

Treatise on Abba Daniel[16] from the monastery of Sännayt.[17] [To be read] on the 7th of Takhsas.[18]

Treatise on Abba Daniel, about how the saints revealed themselves to him. On this day[19] he passed away in the peace of God. Amen.

[PROEMIUM][20]

Truly, O beloved ones, God works wonders through his saints, as David says in the psalter.[21] Moreover, the story of the saints is like a garden filled with trees of all good fruits for those who do God's will. And this Abba Daniel was perfect in all good works, and in the Holy Spirit.

[ANASTASIA: I.8][22]

While he lived in the monastery of Sännayt [Scetis] together with his disciples, there was a castrated man by the name of Bästasiyos[23] who lived in a cave quite some distance away from them. Nobody from among the brothers knew about him except for Abba Daniel alone. Each week he secretly came to him, and went away again without the disciples knowing about him.[24] /4/ Abba Daniel then ordered [one of] his disciple[s][25] to take to him a pitcher of water and to deposit it at the entrance of his cave. He would then go out at night and take the water, without anybody seeing him. When he wanted to inquire about anything, he would write on a potsherd and deposit it together with the pitcher. The disciple would then take it to the Elder.[26]

One day now, having gone out, the disciple found a potsherd with something written on it and took it to his master. Upon reading it, Abba Daniel found that the inscription said: 'My lord, do a work of mercy for the sake of [the] love [of God]. Take something to dig with, and come with that disciple, only the two of you'. When the Elder read[27] this message, he wept very much and said: 'Woe is me, because today a great pillar of this monastery has collapsed!' He then said to his disciple: 'Get a shovel and a basket, and then let us go to the Elder and win his blessing before he goes to his eternal dwelling place according to God's just judgement'.

When they arrived, they found that man with a fever. When Abba Daniel saw this, he exclaimed in tears: 'Blessed are you on account of this day, because you have looked forward to this day and to this hour. In anticipation of this [moment] you have pondered what eternal life means for you'.

But he answered and said: 'Blessed are you, rather, Abba Daniel, like Abraham, because through your teaching many have attained fulfillment. I for my part am in need of the prayer of many at this hour'.

Abba Daniel responded: 'If I die first, I will pray for you'.[28]

Immediately the Elder rose, took Daniel's head and said: 'May God the Lord, who gave fulfillment to the old age of Abraham and who also led me to this place, /5/ give fulfillment to your old age in honor'.

Thereupon Abba Daniel presented his disciple to him and said: 'Bless him, Father!' and he blessed him, saying: 'May God, the Lord Almighty, bless him, and let the spirit of his [spiritual] father[29] rest upon him, as the spirit of Elijah rested on Elisha.[30] As for this one, may the glory of his [spiritual] father dwell in him'. Moreover, he said to them: 'For the sake of God, do not strip me of my clothes [after my death], but send me to my Lord as I am, and nobody shall know about me except you'.[31] He further said: 'Pray over me', turned his face eastwards, made the sign of the cross upon himself and said: 'My Lord Jesus Christ, into your hand I now commit my soul'.[32] Then his spirit left him, on the 26th of the month of Tirr.[33]

Abba Daniel and the disciple wept over him and dug a grave at the entrance of the cave. Abba Daniel then said to his disciple: 'Shroud him on top of his own clothes with the clothes you have brought, because his own clothes are from goat-hair'. While he put the shrouds in place, he saw her breasts, and thereby learned that she was a woman. Her breasts were like fig-leaves, dried up from much fasting. Yet he did not speak about it until after they had said their prayers and buried her. On their way home, however, the disciple said to Abba Daniel: 'Father, did you know that she was a woman and not a castrate? In fact, when I shrouded her I saw her breasts, which were as dry as leaves from much fasting'.

Thereupon the Elder said to him: 'My son, I know[34] that she was a woman, and if you wish, I will tell you her whole story'.[35]

The disciple said to him: 'Tell me, Father'.

So the Elder told him: This woman [once] was the highest-ranking patrician lady of the city of Constantinople. The emperor Bästiyanos[36] then fell passionately in love with her and wanted to marry her, because she was very beautiful. But /6/ she did not want it. Instead, she sent messengers to the queen to tell her that her husband desired her. Thereupon the queen took her to Alexandria and built [her] a big monastery; they called it 'The Monastery of the Patrician Lady'. When the emperor heard that she was there, he sent people to her to fetch her. At night, however, she fled from Alexandria and came to this place. She asked me to give her an abode, so I gave her that cave. She then told me everything that had happened; she was twenty-eight years old at the time.

The Emperor of Constantinople and the Patriarch of Alexandria then sent out many people to search for her, but until today nobody found out about her whereabouts. Do you see, my son, how royalty, especially that queen, have to struggle with the Enemy? We, my son, by contrast have taken up monastic life, but do not [therefore necessarily] do what pleases God, or keep his commandments, nor have we rid ourselves of evil thoughts. But we implore our Lord Jesus Christ that he may help us to do good, as did Bästasiya, who changed her name and called herself Bästasiyos the Castrate until she finished her life's struggle in peace. May God grant that we find mercy before him on the day of the Just Judgement. To him be praise and glory in eternity. Amen.

[*Mark the Fool* (I.1)]

With Abba Daniel there lived a brother whose name was Särgis.[37] After a short while, he passed away and went to his Lord. Some time after that brother had fallen asleep, Abba Daniel set out with his disciple and went to Alexandria, because it is their custom to pay a visit to the patriarch every year. As he approached the city around dusk, he suddenly saw a brother[38] whose loins were girded with a linen cloth. He had /7/ the appearance of a madman, and many other people who were [equally] out of their senses followed him. He grabbed foodstuffs from the market stalls, ate, and gave to those who were with him. His name was Marka,[39] and he was a craftsman. People gave him one hundred coins every day; with ten coins he then bought bread, and what remained he gave to his companions, the other madmen. The people of the town knew him well on account of his insanity.

When Abba Daniel saw him, he said to his disciple: 'Go and find out where this madman lives', and people told him about him. The next day, emerging from [his audience with] the patriarch,[40] Abba Daniel, following God's command, found Marka, seized him, and cried out: 'Come, people of Alexandria, in order to see God's servant!' Immediately that madman prostrated himself before the Elder, in front of all the people. They marvelled at this and said to the Elder: 'Don't speak with him, so that he doesn't abuse you. Don't forget, he is out of his mind'.

The Elder responded: 'You yourselves are out of your minds, for there is nobody in this town, including myself, who is equal to this one'.

Thereupon the priests who knew Abba Daniel said to him: 'What has this madman done to you?'

He said to them: 'Raise him up, and then let us take him to the patriarch'.

So they took him, and Abba Daniel said to the patriarch: 'Truly, Master, there is no righteous one in this city who is equal to this one in his [pious] achievements'.

The patriarch understood that God had granted Abba Daniel a revelation. Therefore both of them prostrated themselves before that madman and implored him to tell them his story.[41] He, however, wanted to keep his story[42] hidden and not bring it out into the open. Yet he [eventually] told them: 'I am a monk. I was once plagued by the illness of the desire for fornication[43] for fifteen years, and tormented by the Enemy. So I said in my heart: /8/ "I am obviously given over to the desire for fornication. Therefore I will now go and become a madman in the service of Christ instead of my [original] madness". It is eight years now since I have taken on the appearance of a madman'.

After hearing this story, they wept. Then everybody returned to their respective dwelling places.

The next morning Abba Daniel sent out his disciple, after having instructed him: 'Go and call upon Marka, that he may pray for us. Thereafter we will return home'. So he went and found that Marka had passed away. Having come back, he told this to his Father, and he [in turn] told this to the patriarch, and the patriarch told the governor of Alexandria. They then convened all the elders and a great mass of people, and said: 'Let us win the blessing of this saint'. People assembled from the convents and monasteries, dressed in their finest clothes, with olive and palm branches in their hands. On account of the multitude of people, they could not bury him for five days. During this period they burned sweet-smelling incense of the finest quality and wept over him. They then took out the servant of God [to his grave], holding in their hands candles and lamps and incense [burners], on account of Father Marka. All the while they praised God, saying: 'Great is God, who gives such great glory to those who love him with all their heart'.

[*Eulogius the Stonecutter* (I.9)]

Once, when Abba Daniel, together with his disciple, was in the City of Egypt,[44] he wanted to return home. He boarded a ship, and when they had arrived at a certain village[45] he told the sailors: 'Put me ashore here'.

His disciple muttered discontentedly about this and said: 'We shouldn't remain here, like people looking for alms. Let's therefore go to the church and stay there overnight, until tomorrow'.

But the Elder refused his wish, as a result of which the disciple became annoyed at him, and like this they remained. Then suddenly an old man passed by, and when he saw /9/ Abba Daniel he kissed his feet and cried bitterly, then also embraced[46] the disciple, and said to them: 'I pray you, come into my house!' They went with him. He held a lamp in his hand,[47] walked around the village's marketplace looking for strangers, and gathered all those he met. When Abba Daniel and the others came to his home, he poured water into a basin and washed their feet. He then offered them a meal, and all of them ate. What remained he threw before the dogs. He did this so nothing would remain in his house until the next day.

They spent the evening in conversation about God. When morning came they kissed each other goodbye and left. On the way the disciple fell to the feet of his master and said to him: 'I pray you, tell me how you knew about this man and what he does', but he did not want to tell him. When they arrived home, the disciple went into a cave and did not return [to the monastery] with Abba Daniel as he usually did. Abba Daniel did not eat before the eleventh hour.[48] The disciple did not come to him [any more to join him in his meal]. Therefore the Elder went to him and said to him: 'My Son, why don't you come so that we may eat our meal in love?'

He replied: 'By the Lord, the Living God, I will not let you go before you have told me what was the matter with that Elder!'

Abba Daniel said to him: 'My Son, do not think of things exalted, and do not worry about this matter. While we were on the way I had wanted to tell you that there is nobody who will know his story until that man dies. But now I will tell you that his name is Awlogiyos[49] and that he is a stonecutter. People give him gold every day, and with it he prepares dinners for strangers; he does not save anything for the next day. /10/ He is a hundred years old, but God gives him strength. Forty-eight years ago I went to that village and sold my handicrafts. When it became evening he took me[50] to his house, and I saw what he did. After I had returned home, I remembered the kindness of that man and fasted many days on his behalf, in order that God would bestow his blessing on that angel of the travellers. After I had fasted for three weeks I fell to the ground and slept, due to my great toil. And behold, a man clad in light appeared to me and said to me: "What is the matter with you, Daniel?" I said to him: "My lord, I made a pledge to God that I will not eat and drink on account of Awlogiyos the stonecutter, so that[51] He may bestow his blessing, as much as He can, on that angel of the travellers". The man clad in light then said to me: "Do not seek such a thing, his work is enough and well for him". I replied: "No, lord. Give him [an extra blessing] so he can do [more] good to the travellers. Everybody who sees him will praise God". He then said to me: "Look, he lives in good circumstances, but you want more for him. Shall I give him more, on the condition that you will be his guarantor?" I said to him: "I will serve as a guarantor for him, lord, because I desire the salvation of his soul".

'This I spoke in the dream, and I saw him as though we were in Jerusalem. Then suddenly there was an infant clad in light, and it said to me: "All this is not enough for Awlogiyos? Take heed for yourself, because I will demand his soul from you". While it said this to me, there suddenly were two men. They brought much money and poured it into Awlogiyos' lap.[52] I woke up right away and knew that God had answered my prayer, and I praised God.

/11/ 'That morning Awlogiyos got up and went to his work, and while he was hewing a stone he found a pot filled with gold. He was perplexed and terrified, and said to himself: "This must be money of the Ishmaelites,[53] and when I return to my house the prefect will arrest me. But I will go to a land where I am not known". So he took the gold, boarded a ship, travelled to Byzantium, and went to the city of Constantinople. He gave up almsgiving altogether, but instead went to the emperor Bastasiyos[54] and gave him that money. Thereupon the emperor appointed him as ruler over the entire city. He acquired great wealth and many chariots, and became haughty of heart and merciless.

'Many years later I had a dream in which I found myself in Jerusalem. I saw that infant clad in light, upon which I thought of Awlogiyos. Then I saw Awlogiyos as he was being dragged toward that infant clad in light and put in front of a court of justice. Immediately I awoke. When I got up in the morning I went to that village [where Awlogiyos used to live], saying "Woe is me! Wretched am I, because I have brought ruin on myself". Then I offered my handicrafts for sale and remained until evening fell, waiting for Awlogiyos; but I did not find him. Suddenly there was an old woman, to whom I said: "Give me some bread, for I have nothing to eat". She said to me: "You are a young man and should not stay in populated places! Is not hard toil incumbent upon a monk?" I said to her: "Forgive me, for I came to sell my goods". She said to me: "Tomorrow do what you need to do, and then return to your monastery".[55] I then said to her: "Is there not a man here who receives strangers and shows them hospitality?"[56] She said to me: "Indeed there used to live here such a man, and much good /12/ did he do to travellers and to the hungry. When God saw his good works he showed him his favor, and he was appointed to high office".

'When I heard this I said in my heart: "I, only I, am responsible for this sin". So I boarded a ship, went to Constantinople and inquired about him. People told me where he lived. Therefore I sat down at his gate so I would see him when he came out. When he came out, I saw him in great power, and I said to him: "May your mercy reach me! I want to speak a word to you". He, however, did not turn his face towards me, so I cried out to his retainers who were running around him, and my heart suffered on behalf of him. Therefore I went to a church, threw myself on the ground before an icon of Saint Mary, wept, and said: "My Lady, you who have given birth to the Lord, keep away from me the guilt of that man so that I will not perish on account of him!" Having said this, I fell asleep due to the suffering in my heart. And behold, [in my dream] there were many people, and they said: "Look, the Queen has come, and thousands upon thousands, indeed myriads of people, are marching around her". So I cried out and said: "My lady, my Queen, may your mercy reach me!" She said to me:

"What is your concern?" I said: "Order Awlogiyos the Captain, for whom I vouched, to come and absolve me from his guilt". She said: "I will not order it. Go and redeem your debt!"

'Immediately thereafter I awoke and said in my heart: "I will not leave his gate until I have spoken to him, or else I will die [there]". So I went to his gate, and when he came out I cried out for him, but the gatekeeper beat me and pounded my whole body until I almost died. So I said in my heart: "Okay now, after this I will go back to my country. God willing, he will save us, together with Awlogiyos". I boarded a ship /13/ and came to Alexandria in the country of Egypt. I returned to my dwelling place and fell asleep in sadness. In my dream it was as if I were in Jerusalem, and I saw that infant clad in light. He was[57] in a holy place and looked at me in anger. Before his majesty I trembled like leaves that are shaken by the wind[58] and could not open my mouth. He said to me: "Why did you not go to pay what is incumbent upon you?" He then ordered two of those standing around him to suspend me,[59] so they suspended me high up. Furthermore, he said to me: "Take care not to do anything that is not commensurate with your power, and do not be quarrelsome in your speech". While I was hanging there, there suddenly was a voice that said: "The Queen has come!" When I saw her I felt comforted[60] and said to her: "Have compassion on me, my Lady!" She said to me: "What do you want?" I said to her: "I am crucified on account of Awlogiyos' guilt". She said to me: "I will intercede for you". She then kissed that infant's feet. Thereupon he said to me: "Take care that from now on you do not do such a thing again, so nothing even worse than this happens to you". I said to him: "Lord, I have sinned, forgive me, your servant". Now they at once took me down, and he said to me: 'Go, Daniel, and bring him back to his former way of life'".

'After I had woken up I praised God because he had relieved me of the blame for Awlogiyos. After three months I heard that the emperor Bistiyanos[61] had died and that somebody else[62] had been appointed in his stead. Also, three of his high officials[63] had been accused, their names being Dikradis, Sisnos, and Awlogiyos.[64] The [new] emperor had ordered that all their possessions be confiscated and that their heads be cut off with the sword. When Awlogiyos heard this he left everything, at night fled from /14/ Constantinople, and came to the country of Egypt. The emperor then sent out people in order to kill him wherever they found him. The people of his village said to him: "We heard that you had been appointed to high office in the country of Byzantium". He said to them: "No, the fact is that I remained in my profession but went into the wilderness in order to pray. It must be another Awlogiyos, not me". After this he took off his clothes and put on sackcloth, as in the olden days, and said in his heart: "Oh, you miserable one, do not seek state office, so that they do not cut your head off". He then took his tools for stonecutting, went to where he had formerly lived and tried to earn money, but did not earn any. Thereupon he thought of his former money and prestige that had perished, and said in his heart: "I will work in my profession and sustain myself in this manner, and I will give to the poor". In his spirit he became firmly resolved to do so, through the [interceding] prayer of the Mistress over all of us, Holy Mary. Truly, there is no unfairness[65] in God; he had not forgotten Awlogiyos' earlier hard toil.

'A short time later, I went to that village in order to sell my handicrafts. Awlogiyos discovered me when dusk was setting in, and he joyfully took me to his house, together with many other people. I for my part, however, sighed and said: "You are so very righteous, Lord, and all your judgement is just. How great are your deeds, Lord, and everything you do is done with wisdom. O Christ, my Lord, you who lift up the poor one from the earth, who exalt the wretched one from the dust and make him sit together with the great among the people,[66] you who also for me, the sinner, have done many deeds, Lord: When my soul was about to descend to the lowest hell, you saved it". Awlogiyos then brought water, washed my feet, and set the table. After we had eaten I said to him: "How are you, my brother Awlogiyos?" He said to me: "Let me have your prayer, for I am poor and do not possess anything" /15/. I said to him: "It is better for you not to have anything than to have something". He said to me:[67] "Why is this, Father?" Thereupon I told him everything that had happened, and we wept together. He then said to me: "Father, pray for me to God that he may forgive my sin. I will not do [such] evil again".[68] I said to him: "God will certainly give you strength, and you will earn a living through your work".

[To his disciple Abba Daniel said:][69] 'Do not tell this story to anyone until I have died.[70] Let us now praise our Lord Jesus Christ who did not allow his labors to perish. As for us, may he help us to do good deeds. Let us praise him in eternity. Amen'.

[*Concerning a Holy Woman (Thomaïs) (I.6)*][71]

Once, while Abba Daniel was in Alexandria, there was an old man there whose wife had died, and he was left with a son.[72] He raised his son and took a christian girl for him in marriage. He worked in a vineyard,[73] and the couple lived with his father. But behold, the Devil turned the mind of the old man toward his son's wife. He constantly kissed her, while she, in all innocence, kissed him with a holy kiss, as her father.

Thereafter he called upon the young man to guard his vineyard at night. Then the old man rose up against his daughter-in-law. She said to him: 'Go away and make the sign of the cross over your face, because such a deed is from the Enemy!' When she further resisted him, he took his son's sword in order to frighten her. She said to him: 'Even if you cut off every one of my members I will not commit this sin!' He, while intimidating her, hit her flank [with the sword], whereupon she died. Immediately then the old man became blind. He searched for the door of the house, but could not find it. In the morning people came looking for his son, but did not find him. To them the old man said: 'I implore you, show me door!' When they entered they saw the dead woman. They said /16/ to him: 'What happened?' Weeping, he said to them: 'My sin is greater than anything on earth!' When they heard this, they knew that he had killed her. They took him to the magistrates, and they, hearing that he confessed his sin, condemned him to death.

When Abba Daniel heard this, he went with his disciple to the place where they were going to bury the girl, and as they brought her, he said to them: 'By the Living God, do not bury her anywhere else than in the cemetery of the Fathers!' Against this some people murmured in complaint. To them he said: 'This one is my mother and the mother of all of you, because she died for the sake of [her soul's] salvation'. When they heard this they did not argue with him any more, but buried her in the cemetery of the Fathers. He then returned home, constantly praising and glorifying God.

[*A Monk, Tempted by Sexual Sin, Receives a Blessing from Thomaïs (I.7)*][74]

Shortly thereafter lustful thoughts assaulted one monk [from Abba Daniel's community], and he told Abba Daniel. The Elder said to him: 'Go to the city of Alexandria, weep on the graves of the Fathers and say: "Oh Lord, help me through the prayer of Holy Dontiris!"[75] Then trust that God will deliver you from struggling with the Enemy'.

That brother then did as Abba Daniel had told him. After a little while he returned to the Elder and said to him: 'I give praise to God! Through your prayer I have been healed from evil thoughts'.

Abba Daniel said to him: 'What happened to you?'

He said: 'I prostrated myself twelve times, and then fell asleep at the grave. Then [in my dream] a girl[76] came and said to me: "Take this eucharistic bread and return to your monastic cell". When I took a piece of it, it immediately vanished from my hand'.

Abba Daniel said to him: 'From now on guard yourself against evil, and return [to your cell] in peace'.

[*Concerning the Woman Who Pretended to be Mad* (I.4)]

/17/ In another episode Abba Daniel, while he was wandering south, came to a monastery. There five hundred brothers with their abbot received him and prostrated themselves before him. They then kissed each other in salutation. Thereupon they said to him: 'Tell us a word!'

He said to them: 'He who wants to be saved shall preserve humility and silence. These two commandments are better than all'. He wrote this down and gave it to them. Then he went away from there, constantly praising God.

As he approached the city whose name is Armon,[77] he said to his disciple: 'Go to the nunnery and tell them: "A monk wants to pay you a visit"'.

The disciple went and knocked. The doorkeeper said to him in a humble voice: 'What do you want, Father?'

He said to her: 'I would like to speak to the abbess'.

The doorkeeper said to him: 'She never speaks to a man, but tell me, and I will bring you what you want'.

He said to her: 'We are travelling monks. Accept us until tomorrow, because night is falling'.

She went and told the abbess. The latter replied and had the doorkeeper say to him:[78] 'It is impossible for a man to spend the night in this place. It would be better for you if the animals of the wilderness devoured you than that the beast that is inside, Satan, devour you'.

The disciple said to her: 'But it is Abba Daniel!'

As soon as she heard that it was Abba Daniel she came out running, and with her all the virgins, approximately three hundred. They spread their garments [on the ground] until Abba Daniel had entered. The abbess then brought water in a basin and washed his feet.[79] When she had finished she said to the virgins: 'Take and drink [from this water] and sprinkle it on your heads!' And she also did so herself. Because they so honored him, and because of the silence, a great miracle occurred, as if the power of the exalted angels had been present, the virgins all the while rendering their service to them.

Abba Daniel said to the abbess: 'Do not make them toil on behalf of me'.

She said to him: 'Their work is like this every day. Father, pray for them, and for me together with them'.

The Elder said to her: 'May God preserve you all, and us as well, from all the evil of the Enemy'.

There was one virgin who was clad in sackcloth and lay stretched out at the gate. The Elder said to the abbess: 'What is the matter with this one?'

The abbess said to him: 'She is an insane one among her companions. I don't know what to do. I had wanted to chase her away so that the others wouldn't go astray on account of her, but I am afraid of God'.

The Elder said to her: 'Bring the water that remains in the basin and sprinkle it on her; then she will be healed'.

After this the abbess set the table, and they had supper. He then said to his disciple: 'Keep the vigil with me this night'. The virgins went to sleep, but Abba Daniel and his disciple retired on their own. They then saw that insane virgin as she raised her hands toward the sky, opened her mouth, praised God, and prayed much. All the while her tears flowed as if from a water fountain, because she was in great sadness for the sake of God. However, when she heard the sound of another virgin coming in her direction, she cast herself down, like one who is asleep. She acted like this every day. Thereupon the Elder said to his disciple: 'Call the abbess, quick!' She came and saw what was the matter with that righteous one, and she wept and said: 'Woe is me, sinner, on account of how I abused that virgin!' When they beat the church-gong, the abbess[80] told the virgins everything she had seen, and they all became agitated on account of that virgin.

Because she was aware of what had been said about her, the virgin for her part stealthily went to where the Elder was, /19/ grasped his gown and wrote the following words: 'Forgive me, you saints, for the trouble I brought upon you, and pray for me!'

When morning came, they looked for her,[81] but they did not find her. Then, when they saw what she had written, they all wept. But Abba Daniel told them: 'This is why I came here. As it is written: "God has indeed chosen those who are fools in this world"'.[82]

Thereupon all the virgins told him everything they had done against her. At last Abba Daniel rose, prayed for them and returned home, all the way praising God who had revealed to him many of his servants who live concealed in the world.

[*The Thief Who Repented* (Coptic)]

Abba Daniel's fame was heard in all the regions [of Egypt]; therefore many desired to receive his holy blessing, especially from among the priests. There was a monastery where there lived many virgins. They did good deeds, and of their food they gave to the hungry and to travelers. Hence Satan became aroused, on account of the mercy they showed towards all people. Therefore he entered into the heart of the head of the thieves of that region, in order that he should take with him all the thieves and go and plunder and tear down that monastery. The head thief told the other thieves [of his plan], and they rejoiced.

When they went, they could not enter [the monastery] because its wall was strong, so they became dejected. The head thief then said to them: 'Bring me a monk's garments and a black cloak that is fully covered with crosses, in the image of the one worn by Abba Daniel. When evening falls I will dress in those clothes, take a monk's staff in my hand and knock. Then they will open for me, and I will let you in right away, so that you will be able to pillage without any trouble'. When they heard this, they rejoiced and brought him what he had requested.

In the evening he dressed [in monastic clothing], took the staff in his hand, went to the gate and knocked. /20/ The gatekeeper said to him: 'Where do you come from, and what do you want?'

He said to her: 'Go and tell the abbess: "Abba Daniel, a priest from the land of Scetis,[83] is standing at the door"'.

As soon as the abbess heard this she swiftly rose up together with all the virgins. They ran towards him, kissed his feet and led him into the place. The abbess then brought water in a bowl, washed his feet, and wanted to raise him high up. He said: 'By the Living God, I will not go away from here until tomorrow'. When she had finished washing his feet, she took some of the water and, full of faith, sprinkled[84] it over her head and her face, and all did likewise, in sincere belief.

There was one among them who had been blind since childhood. When she heard their joy she said to them: 'I implore you to give me some of that water'. So they took her and brought her to that bowl. She rejoiced and said: 'Blessed are you, Abba Daniel, God's holy one. May your prayer be with me. Amen'. She then rubbed water onto herself and poured it over her face, and immediately her eyes were opened and she could see. There was great joy and much clamor as they all ran about and kissed the feet of that thief. Especially the blind one who now could see cried out: 'Blessed are you, saintly Father, because through the washing of your feet I again found light'.

As for the head of the thieves, a great fear and trembling took possession of him when he saw this. All the virgins then went to sleep. He, however, did not sleep but stayed awake, weeping, until he watered the ground with his tears. He then said to himself: 'Woe is me, miserable and a sinner am I, because I wasted all my days in great evil and in futility. If already the name of that man, when I am called by it, transformed the water /21/ of my feet so it gives light to the blind, how much more then will that man [himself be holy]!' He further said: 'Woe is me, wretched and a sinner am I, who repudiated my salvation!'

His companions, on the other hand, were waiting for him at the gate like dogs, that he would open it for them. With their swords in their hands, they waited until the next morning. When morning came they went away in great confusion and embarrassment.[85] He, however, left in peace, and his companions later met him on the road. They said to him: 'What happened to you while we were waiting for you all night long?'

He said to them: 'From now on I will have no more to do with you', and told them all that had happened. He then went to the monastery of [Saint] Macarios, to Abba Daniel, became a very fine monk, and renounced everything worldly till the day of his death.

[*The Female Hermit* (no known parallel)]

Furthermore, Abba Daniel related:

Once, while I was in the desert in order to find rest, I wandered at night by the light of the moon. Suddenly I saw a man[86] sitting on a hill; hair covered his whole body. I said in my heart: 'I will go [there] in order to see what this is.' So I went to him. When he saw me, he entered a crack in the rock. Immediately I understood that he was human,[87] and I said to him: 'I implore you, man of God, to come out to me so that I may have your blessing'.

He, however, patiently kept silent for a long time. He then said to me: 'Forgive me, Father, for not coming out'.

I said to him: 'Why?'

He said to me: 'Because I am a woman, and naked'.

When I heard this I took off the tunic in which I had wrapped myself and threw it towards her. After she had put it on she came out, and we prayed. I then said to her: 'Tell me, my mother, why you came here and how you found this crevice'.

She said to me: 'I was a virgin and lived in Jerusalem. There was a monk /22/ who always came to see me and spoke with me. After a short while I went to his place. There I heard him weep and confess his sin[88] before God. When I knocked he did not open [the door] for me, but instead continued to weep and to repent. Thereupon I said in my heart: "Why do I not also weep and repent on account of my shameful behavior and wretchedness?" So I quickly went to my dwelling place, clad myself in sackcloth, took a basket[89] of peas as well as a jug of water, and prayed at the grave of our Lord, saying: "O Lord, you who are powerful, wonder-working, eternal, you who save the lost ones, lift up the fallen, and listen[90] to those who cry out to you! Send your grace and your justice so that you save me,[91] your maid, who puts her trust in you. Look after me, the poor and sinful one, and accept my repentance. Bless these provisions and this jug of water so they may be with me for the length of my days, in order that I may not disregard for the sake of my belly what I ponder for the sake of my salvation".

'So I went to Golgotha and prayed this prayer, and went forth and gave up my soul to God. I came to Jericho and [from there] went as far as the Red Sea, and from there I came into this desert, found this crevice in the hill and stayed in it, saying "This shall be the dwelling place that God has prepared for me". Indeed, I have now been living in this place for thirty-eight years, and [during all this time] I haven't seen anybody except you. That basket and jug for my sustenance did not exhaust themselves or cease [to yield nourishment] during those thirty-eight years, but my clothes have been worn out. This location then served me as my hiding-place in substitution for my clothes. Therefore, during all my days, the heat /23/ of summer did not afflict me, nor the cold of winter'.[92]

She then implored me to eat and drink, and so I ate from that basket and drank from the jug. They did not cease,[93] and I praised God. I wanted to leave her my tunic, but she refused, saying: 'Bring me something that is better than this'. So I went to a [nearby] monastery and told the story to the abbot. He exclaimed: 'He who has two garments shall give one to him who has none!'[94] He brought him what he had wanted,[95] and immediately I went away to see that maiden of Christ. I spent much effort looking for her, but I did not find her, and so I returned.

After a few days some elders came and said: 'While we were traveling in the wilderness of Tanewos,[96] on the road leading to the Red Sea, around dusk we saw a woman sitting on rocky ground. We ran [towards her] in order to be blessed by her, but she fled and entered a cave. As we approached the entrance of the cave we could not see her, but we found a basket of peas and a jug of water. We ate from it, and it immediately was exhausted. We spent the night there until the next morning, and then searched for the saintly woman so that we could be blessed by her. We found her where she had died;[97] her hair covered her [whole] body. We prostrated ourselves before her. Then we buried her inside the cave and blocked its entrance with a stone. We then turned back [towards our original path], all the while praising God that he had considered us worthy to receive the blessing of that woman saint'.

When I heard this I became aware that she must have been the one whom I had met. I told them what she had spoken to me and praised God who helps the weak human vessel to vanquish[98] the Enemy and all his demons.

[*Abba Daniel Refuses to Accept the Tome of Leo* (Coptic)]

When Bastiyanos, the heretic, was emperor,[99] he molested all the churches on account of the perverted creed of the impure bishops of

/24/ the Council of Chalcedon[100] and dispersed the flock of Christ as well as the bishops and archbishops, whom he chased from their sees. He issued a decree to the land of Egypt that they should believe in the evil creed which is full of blasphemy, as a result of which there was great commotion in all the land. Abba Daniel in those days was bishop in the monastery of Abba Macarios,[101] and God revealed to him [the decree] before they brought it. Thereupon he assembled all the great men and the priests. He told them what had been revealed to him and instructed them to be steadfast until death in the true faith. Thereafter soldiers arrived and went to Abba Daniel and to all the great men who recognized him. When the soldiers found the fathers, they took out the decree and said to them: 'The emperor orders that you believe in the words of this decree, and that all of you sign that you agree with his creed'.

Thereupon Abba Daniel said to them: 'What is the faith professed in this creed?'

They said to him: '[It is] the creed of the great council of those who assembled in Chalcedon, six hundred thirty-four bishops'.

Upon [hearing] this Abba Daniel flared up through the grace of the Holy Spirit, grabbed that document, sprang away, tore it apart and said to the soldiers: 'Anathema on the impure council that took place in Chalcedon! Anathema on everybody who has fellowship with them, and everybody who remains[102] in their faith! Anathema on everybody who denies the sufferings of Christ! We for our part will never listen to that council of heretics and will [continue to] believe in[103] the Father and the Son and the Holy Spirit, a co-equal Trinity, one Godhead, until our end!'[104]

[*Abba Daniel Goes to Tambōk* (Coptic)]

When the soldiers saw the firmness of his heart, /25/ they became very angry. They seized him, beat him[105] and inflicted wounds upon him until he almost died. They then punished the [assembled] fathers, whereupon they dispersed into many different places. Abba Daniel went to a small village and built a church, and there he remained, serving Christ with great devotion and much mortification, until news about him spread and the people praised God who was with him.

[*Abba Daniel Returns to Scetis* (Coptic)]

Later on, God killed the heretical emperor Bastiyanos, whereupon Abba
Daniel set out and returned to his home in joy, adorned with the crown
of profession [of the true faith]. When his companions learned about this,
they welcomed him with great joy and praised our Lord Jesus Christ.

[*The Death of Abba Daniel* (Coptic)]

[Some time] after this an angel of God said to him: 'Your departure from
this world is drawing near. You will go to your Beloved One, Jesus
Christ'.

    After Abba Daniel had fallen ill, people would say to him: 'What is
the matter with you?'

    He then said: 'My fleshly body and my strength have grown weak.
Earth will return to earth, but [only] God knows where my soul will
be going'.

    His disciple then said to him: 'Are you, even though you are perfect,
also afraid?'

    He replied: 'If Abraham and Isaac and Jacob came and told me that
I was righteous, I would not believe it.[106] Woe is us on account of our
sinfulness! Let me tell you that Moses, who spoke with God five hundred
seventy times,[107] and also the prophets, and all the saints, were afraid of
this hour and tormented by it, even though they were saintly figures.
Look at the infants who still suck milk! When this hour comes to them,
they are tormented and suffer agonies, even though they do not know
sin. I do not know the path I am going to travel, and as to the attendants
who will receive me, I have not yet seen their faces, /26/ each of its
own kind.[108] Moreover, they will not take bribes and therefore spare
me, or behave reverently towards me, not even on account of my grey
hair; and they are perfectly entitled to conduct themselves in this
manner'.

    When he had said this he turned his face eastwards and said to his
disciple: 'Come near to me, because the time has come'.

    He then took his disciple's hands, placed them on his eyes and said:
'My Lord Jesus Christ, the Beloved of my soul, into your hands I

commit my soul'.[109] As soon as he had said this, his spirit left him, on the seventh of the month of Takhsas.[110] His disciple shrouded him, and they buried him with great honors.

Blessed are those who do acts of mercy in his name on the day of his commemoration;[111] they will be with him in the Kingdom of Heaven. May we all find mercy through the grace and compassion of our Lord Jesus Christ. To him be praise in eternity, together with his Father and the Holy Spirit. Amen.

APPENDIX I

ENTRIES FROM THE ETHIOPIC SYNAXARY (*Sinkissar*)

I. 16 Khidar[112] (November 25):
Abba Daniel of the Monastery of Saint Macarius[113]

On this day furthermore takes place the commemoration of Abba Daniel the monk and of Honorius the emperor.[114]

This Abba Daniel was a contender in spiritual struggles[115] in the desert of Scetis at the monastery of Abba Macarius.[116] He spent forty and a half years without tasting bread, fish, honey, or oil, but only herbs. After so many days, boastful thoughts came into his heart. He said: 'Who is like me among those living in the monasteries of Scetis?[117] Who has persevered [like me] in fasting and standing?'[118] When God saw the boasting of his heart, he sent to him his luminous angel. He said to him: 'Daniel, why do you boast in such an inappropriate manner? Jesus Christ, our Lord, does not desire boasting, but rather humility, fear [of God], and trembling'.

Daniel said to him: 'Tell me, my lord, whether there is someone more accomplished [in ascetic practices] than I am, so that I may go see him. Then I will humble myself before my Lord on account of my boasting'.

The angel said to him, 'Honorius, the emperor of Rome, that is, of Constantinople,[119] a pure, saintly, and god-fearing man, will be your companion in the Kingdom of Heaven'.

When Abba Daniel heard this, he prostrated himself, with his knees on the earth, put dust[120] on his head, and asked God that he, in his wisdom and power, bring him to that city[121] so that he should see him. While he was praying like this, a cloud came, by God's command carried him away, and brought him to the gates of Constantinople. There he

came upon a servant of the emperor Honorius. When the servant saw
Abba Daniel, he asked to be blessed by him.[122] Then he said to him, 'My
father, what is your desire that you have come here for'?

Abba Daniel said to him, 'My son, take me to one of the high officials
if you can, in order that he may gain me access to the Emperor'.

The servant said to him: 'If I gain you that access, will you not want
to enter?'

He replied, 'If that is within your powers, gain me access. May God
bless you'.[123]

The servant said to him, 'My father, what will be the use of your
seeing a mortal emperor? Would it not be better for you to see the
Kingdom of Heaven?'

Abba Daniel said to him, 'If my Lord had not ordered me, I would
not have come here'.

The servant said to him, 'Be patient, my father, until I have bought
what my master has need of'.

Right away then he bought bread, salt, herbs, and vinegar. He then
took him[124] to where Honorius was with his companion, a monk by
the name of Eulogius,[125] as was his custom. Honorius, after having returned from the court of justice, had put on clothes of sackcloth and a
clean monk's tunic. He was seated. The servant left Abba /88/320/
Daniel outside the gate and entered. When Honorius saw him, he said
to him, 'Are you foolish, that you keep Abba Daniel waiting?' Then
Honorius and Eulogius went out, welcomed him, and threw themselves
down at his feet. They exchanged greetings of peace among themselves,
then entered the house and sat down. At three p.m. the servant brought
them something to eat.[126] Together they got up and prayed. But Abba
Daniel was afraid to eat bread lest he harm his heart,[127] and said to them,
'My lords, do not grumble against me because I do not eat bread. It is
not on account of any haughtiness of mine, but because I fear sickness'.
Thereupon they gave him herbs, and he ate them, as he usually did.

After they had finished saying grace, Honorius inquired about Abba
Daniel's coming. Abba Daniel said to him, 'If it is within your powers,
I would like you to gain me access to the emperor. Truly, I have come
at God's command'.

Honorius said to him, 'Tomorrow I will gain you access'.

The next day Honorius dressed in his royal garments, which are
ravishing to the eye, sat down on his throne, and had Abba Daniel led

in. When Abba Daniel saw the emperor, he became afraid and trembled. When the servant saw his fear, he took him away and brought him back to his room.

After he finished passing judgement,[128] Honorius took off his [royal] clothes, put on the monastic garments, and returned to his dwelling. When Abba Daniel saw him, he said to him, 'Abba, why is it that you did not lead me to the emperor so I could tell him what is in my heart and then return to my country?'

Honorius said to him, 'Did you not enter [the emperor's hall]?'

He said to him, 'Your servant led me in'.

When he heard this, Honorius marveled [at him] and said to him, 'My father, I am that Honorius, whom they call emperor over this earth, and it was I whom you saw sitting on a transient throne'.

Upon hearing this, Abba Daniel threw himself at his feet and adjured him to tell him all about his life. Thereupon the emperor Honorius told him that for forty years he had not eaten or worn anything that he had not earned through the labor of his hands, which was the plaiting of branches.[129] In addition, whatever was left over from his daily bread he used to give to the poor. His food, for that matter, consisted of bread and salt. He did not abuse people, did not rob anybody of their possessions, and preserved his chastity.

Upon hearing this, Abba Daniel said to him, 'Forgive me for vaingloriously considering myself better than you'. Then Abba Daniel, contrite and weeping, returned home.

Two months later Honorius took leave from his master Eulogius and left his palace. God sent his angel, and he carried him away and brought him to Daniel. They completed their spiritual struggle together and passed away on one and the same day. Eulogius and the servant also passed away on that day.

May their intercessions be with our emperor Iyasu[130] and his Beloved One Zä-Mänfäs Qiddus[131] in eternity.

II. 7 Tahksas (December 16): *Abba Daniel of Däbrä-Sihat*[132]

In the name of the Father and of the Son and of the Holy Spirit, one God. On the seventh of Takhsas.[133] On this day passed away Abba Daniel of the Monastery of Sihat,[134] that is, the Monastery of Abba Macarius.[135] /92/634/ It was this Abba Daniel who buried the queen Patrika,[136] whom he called by the name Anastasius.[137] Nobody knew that she was a woman except her husband.[138]

One day, while Abba Daniel was travelling to Alexandria with his disciple and dusk fell, he came upon an insane man whose name was Mark; many other insane people followed him.[139] To the people of the city he appeared to be insane. But Abba Daniel took him by the hand and led him to the patriarch and told them about the fool's virtues.[140] When they put the fool under oath, he told them that he had fled from the onslaught of unchaste desire and had given himself the appearance of a madman. Upon hearing this they praised God.

One day Abba Daniel came into a town and met an old man whose name was Eulogius, who cut stone and sold it for bread, and from it fed the poor.[141] He led Abba Daniel into his house and entertained him gladly. When Abba Daniel saw the old man's goodness, he asked God to give Eulogius wealth, with which he could entertain /93/635/ the poor even more. Upon this request, our Lord appeared to Abba Daniel in a dream in the image of an infant and said to him, 'Will you vouch for him that he[142] will not change his character?' Abba Daniel said, 'Yes, I will vouch for him'. After this Eulogius found a pot full of gold, went to the king,[143] was appointed a high official, and abandoned his [previous good] character.

When Abba Daniel heard this he went to the king's town[144] in order to chastise Eulogius. But his soldiers[145] beat him up until he almost died. While he was very grieved on account of this, that infant appeared to him [again] in a dream, ordered that they suspend him,[146] and said to him, 'Why did you enter into someone else's business?' After this Our Lady Mary came, kissed the infant's feet, and also saved Eulogius.

When another king ruled he wanted to kill Eulogius.[147] He was frightened and fled to another region. When he came back to his country,[148] he returned to his previous manner of life.

One day, while Abba Daniel was traveling in moonlight, he came upon a woman on top of a hill whose hair covered her whole body.[149] /94/636/ She had lived a life of spiritual struggle[150] for thirty-eight years. She told him her whole secret, and then she passed away.

The Tome of Leo

One day, the Tome of Leo was brought and read before the people.[151] When this happened, Abba Daniel leapt forward, tore Leo's epistle apart, and said, 'Anathema on the Creed of Chalcedon!' When the emperor's soldiers heard this, they beat him severely and chased him from his monastery.

The Insane Female Monastic

One day he came to [a convent of] virgins and knocked on the door. When they learned that he was Abba Daniel, they opened it for him and received him with joy. But there was one of them who made herself appear insane and who used to sleep near the gate.[152] Abba Daniel inquired about her. The abbess said to him, 'She is insane'. Thereupon Abba Daniel told the abbess that [rather] she was a saint and was waging a spiritual struggle. The following night she wrote a letter in which she said, 'Forgive me, you saintly women, for the irritation I have caused you'. Having written this, she disappeared. When the virgins learned about this, they became exceedingly grieved and repented.

The Thief who Repented (Coptic)

There was a monastery in which many virgins lived and whose gate was strong. The Devil stirred up robbers against them to ravage their possessions.[153] /95/637/ The chief of the robbers said, 'I will pose as Abba Daniel, and they will immediately open [the gate] for me'. He did as he had planned and said to them, 'I am Abba Daniel'. When the nuns[154] heard this, they received him with joy, washed his feet and uncovered their faces. One of them was blind, and when she washed her face with that water,[155] her eyes were opened. When the other nuns saw this, they said to him, 'Blessed are you, Abba Daniel!' When, on the other hand, the chief of the robbers saw this, he repented and made himself a monk under Abba Daniel.

The Death of Abba Daniel (Coptic)

Abba Daniel continued to live a pious and ascetic life.[156] When the time of his passing away came near, an angel of God told him. He fell ill with a light illness, prayed to Christ, and passed away in peace.

May his prayer and his blessing be with our emperor Iyasu[157] in eternity.

Greetings of peace to you, head of the blessed priests
    Of the monastery of Scetis,[158]
Daniel. Clothed in palm-leaves, /96/638/
You await the adornment of the sky in flowers:
Something which on earth not even the most magnificent
kings obtain.
When he beseeched you [the Virgin Mary],[159] invoking
your name,
On behalf of troublesome Eulogius,
    You kissed Christ's feet for his benefit.[160]
Just as earlier you saved Daniel's soul,
Also work my salvation, Mary![161]

III. 8 Ginbot (May 16): *Abba Daniel of Scetis*[162]

On this day[163] furthermore passed away the saintly father Abba Daniel, abbot of a monastery in the desert of Scetis. This saint was pure and perfect. When his fame spread, saintly Anastasia,[164] the patrician lady, came to him, wearing the clothes of a [male] aristocrat.[165] She made herself a nun with his help and stayed in a cell[166] close to him for twenty-eight years, without anybody finding out that she was a woman.

This saint once saw a man whose name was Eulogius.[167] He hewed stones for one small gold coin every day, sustained himself from a little part of it, and fed the poor and the wretched from what remained; and what remained of that food he threw to the dogs. He never saved anything for the next day.[168] When this saint saw him, he found his struggle[169] a very fine thing and was pleased by his actions. Therefore he asked God to give Eulogius the riches of this world, so that through them the doing of good and merciful works would increase. Then he vouched for Eulogius. While the latter was hewing stones he came upon a treasure of gold, took it and went to the city of Constantinople. There he became an important military commander for the emperor and gave up the doing of good works that he had practiced before.

When saintly Abba Daniel heard [this] about him, he went to the city of Constantinople and saw how Eulogius had become an important military commander, riding on a horse and surrounded by many soldiers, in much haughtiness, and how he had given up the doing of good works. Afterwards this saint saw a vision: our Lord Jesus Christ sat judging all people, and he ordered saintly Abba Daniel to be suspended[170] and demanded from him Eulogius' soul, and Our Lady Mary implored our Lord Christ on his behalf.[171] When this saint then woke up, he returned to his monastery and beseeched God on behalf of Eulogius, that he return him to his former poverty. Then an angel /36/228/ of God appeared to him and exhorted him not to be defiant towards God with regard to his punishment for his creatures. Afterwards, the emperor of Constantinople died, and another emperor acceded to the throne in his stead. He turned against Eulogius, seized all his possessions, and wanted to kill him. Eulogius fled from him in order to save his life and returned to his [own] country.[172] He [now] hewed stones just as before. Saint Abba Daniel came to meet him and told him how, in a vision, he had been suspended[173] on account of him, and how Eulogius' soul had been demanded of him.

The spirit of prophecy resided in this saint, and through him God worked many wonders. When the heretics wanted to make him leave the orthodox faith,[174] he refused, grasped that written document which contained the creed of the heretics, and tore it apart.[175] Thereupon the emperor's soldiers punished him very severely.

After this, when God wanted to give him eternal rest, he sent him his angel and informed him about the time of his departure from this world. Thereupon Abba Daniel assembled the monks [of his community], gave them his last orders, encouraged them, consoled them, and passed away in peace.

May God have mercy on us through his prayer, and may his blessings be with us. Amen.

IV. 1 Ḥamlē (July 8): *Biyoka and Benjamin*[176]

On this day[177] furthermore passed away the saints and spiritual contenders,[178] the two priests and brothers /194/210/ Biyoka and Benjamin.[179] These saints were priests in the church of the village[180] of Tuna, of the region of Qīda in Upper Egypt, and they were brothers.[181] Their father was the steward of the church, a good and gentle man. These two children of his were perfect in holiness. Through their hands God worked many great wonders and miracles, and they healed the sick: they used to wash the sick with water from the cistern of the church, and they were immediately healed.

When their father was about to pass away, at that very time the priest Benjamin had put on his priestly garments and gone up to the temple[182] in order to celebrate the eucharistic offering. People informed him and told him, 'Your father is about to die, and he desires [to have] you [by his side]'. Saint Benjamin replied, 'But I cannot take off my priestly garments before I have completed the mass. Either God wishes me to see him before he passes away or not; God's will be done'. His father, wanting him, sent for him three times like this, but Benjamin [always] responded in the same manner.

When he had completed the mass, he found that his father had passed away. He was very grieved on account of the vessels for the divine service of the church, because they had been in his father's custody and the son did not know where he had put them. His brother Biyoka then counseled him to go to the desert of Scetis and ask the holy elders about the holy vessels of the church. /195/211/ When Saint Benjamin went to the desert of Scetis, he met holy Abba Daniel, abbot of the monastery of Scetis. Holy Abba Daniel told Saint Benjamin everything he had come to him for and ordered him to go to a certain righteous man; that one would let him know everything he had come for. So Benjamin went to that man, and that man revealed to him where the vessels for the divine service were [hidden], and so he took them. Afterwards, this saint, together with his brother, devoted himself to every kind of virtuous and perfect mortification.[183]

In those days the faithful used to keep whatever was left over from the Holy Flesh[184] for the sick; if the sick were about to die, the faithful would then give them some of it.[185] Then Satan entered into a serpent and stirred it up, and it slipped into the chest in which the Holy Flesh was kept. It entered into the chest and ate the Flesh that was in it. It became in fact a habit of that serpent to enter into that chest and to eat whatever Holy Flesh was in it. When the saints Biyoka and Benjamin found out what had been going on they were very grieved, and they killed that serpent. They then deliberated and agreed that they would eat that serpent, on account of the Holy Flesh.[186] They asked God to indicate to them whether this was his will. An angel of God then appeared to

them and ordered them to eat it. So they took that /196/212/ serpent
and ate it. After this they passed away,[187] and God revealed the story of
their pious lives[188] and everything they had done to a saintly virgin,[189]
and she related to the people everything[190] that had happened to the
saints. So they built them a beautiful church. From their dead bodies
sprang very many wonders and miracles, which are related in their written hagiography.[191]

   May God in all eternity show mercy towards us on account of their
prayer. Amen.

> Many greetings of peace to Binyamī and Biyok,
> Who were eager in prayer and in additional supplications
> Until there came to them from God,
> On account of the one who had eaten from the Blessed Flesh,
> An angel who ordered them to eat the serpent.[192]

V. 28 Hamlē (August 4): *Andronicus and Athanasia*[193]

On this day takes place the commemoration of Andronicus and his wife
Athanasia,[194] lovers of God; they were from the city of Antioch. They
were rich in gold and silver. Both of them gave [liberally] from their
many riches to the poor. After a short while[195] they had two children,
a boy and a girl; they called them John and Mary.[196] After this they deliberated and decided to give up marital intercourse and began to minister to the sick and the poor, with their possessions and their souls. He
ministered to the men, and she ministered to the women. In this manner
they labored for twelve years. Then their children fell sick with a fever[197]
and died on one single day.

   When Andronicus saw this, he fell on the ground and cast himself
down in tears before an image of our Lord Jesus Christ, saying, 'Naked
have I /419/435/ come from my mother's womb, and naked will I go.
God has given, and God has taken away; God's name be blessed from
now until eternity'.[198] Their mother, however, wanted to kill herself on
account of the enormity of her grief. In tears she entered the church[199]
where her children lay buried. During the night she saw there a figure
resembling a monk who said to her, 'Do not cry about the death of your

children, cry rather for yourself. As to your children, they are rejoicing in heaven'.

When she had heard this she went and told her husband. They deliberated and decided that they should renounce the world. Therefore they distributed their possessions among the poor and the wretched and left Antioch by night. They came to Alexandria, and there he left her, went to the desert of Scetis, and became a monk with Abba Daniel. He then returned, took his wife to Upper Egypt to a convent of virgins,[200] and left her there. After he had spent twelve years in Scetis, he asked Abba Daniel for permission to go to Jerusalem and receive the blessing of the Holy Places. While he was on his way, his wife unexpectedly appeared; she also wished to receive the blessing of the Holy Places. It was through God's will that she met him. As for her, however, her face had changed because of her many fasts and vigils, /421/437/ and so he did not recognize her as his wife. But she for her part recognized him because his face had not changed. After they had been to the Holy Places they returned to Alexandria.

Through the Holy Spirit, Abba Daniel was aware of what had happened. He said to Andronicus, 'Live in one place with that monk who accompanied you, because he is a saintly person'. They lived together twelve more years; nobody knew that she was a woman,[201] and they called her Athanasius. Abba Daniel used to visit them every once in a while and speak to them about their spiritual progress.[202] When Athanasia fell ill, Andronicus went to Abba Daniel and said to him, 'Since my companion will die, come take care of him'. When Abba Daniel came, he found her in great suffering. She said to him, 'Father, I want you to give me the Eucharist'. Abba Daniel attended to her in her sickness and gave her the Holy Sacrament,[203] and immediately thereafter she passed away.

At that time a smell of perfume came forth and filled the house. When they wanted to shroud her for burial, they found that she was of the female sex, and they found a letter in which she had written down her story and a mark of identification that she had left to her husband. When Andronicus read the letter and learned that she had been his wife, he lost his self-control[204] and began to beat his face and wail. When, after a few days, he fell ill, the elders[205] came to him /422/438/ and received his blessing. Then, after having received the Eucharist, he passed away and entered into the Kingdom of Heaven.

May God in all eternity show mercy towards us on account of their prayers.

Greetings of peace to Andronicus, who came to the Monastery of
  Scetis
After he had given away his possessions—which were not possessions
  unjustly acquired!
And also greetings of peace to Athanasia, with whom he dwelled as a
  companion
Without recognizing her face and thereby knowing that she was his
  wife,
Because her features[206] through fasting had dried up like grass.[207]

APPENDIX II

ETHIOPIC APOPHTHEGMS

PATERICON AETHIOPICE

The *Patericon Aethiopice* contains seven apophthegms attributed to an Abba Daniel, six of which belong to Daniel, the disciple of Arsenius. The seventh, translated below, is a story about Abba Daniel of Scetis found in the extended greek dossier.

Through a Miracle Abba Daniel Refutes Slanderous Charges (IV.1)[208]

/268 /196/[209] Abba Nēhē said: Abba Daniel [once] left the monastery in order to sell his handicrafts. On this occasion a young man asked him to come into his house and pray for him because his wife was barren. Thus Abba Daniel went and prayed over her, and she became pregnant that year.

There were people, however, who did not fear God, and they heaped slander on the Elder, saying, 'It is the young man who is sterile. The child is Abba Daniel's!'

Abba Daniel said [to the young man], 'Let me know when your wife has given birth'.[210]

When she had given birth,[211] the young man thus sent [word] to him. Abba Daniel came and said to him, 'Prepare food and invite your relatives and friends'.

While the guests were [sitting] at the table, the Elder took the infant and said to him, 'Tell me who your father is!'

With his hand the infant beckoned to his father and said, 'This is my father'. It had been twenty-five days since the child was born. All those present marveled [at this].

GERONTICON

The ethiopic *Geronticon* contains five stories about Abba Daniel.[212] It appears that the Gi'iz *Geronticon*, whose textual history has not yet been studied in detail, at least in its bulk goes back to an arabic original from medieval christian Egypt. For some of the following pieces an arabic origin can be conclusively demonstrated through linguistic peculiarities, which are pointed out and discussed in the endnotes.

No. 68. *The Holy Mendicant* (I.3)[213]

This is a story about Abba Daniel. One time he and his disciple came to Alexandria. There he saw sitting a blind and naked man, begging from the people. He said to his disciple, 'Do you see that blind man? He has attained many things,[214] I tell you the truth. If you want, stay[215] here and I will demonstrate it to you'.

He approached the blind man, saying, 'My brother, do me a work of charity, for I do not possess anything with which I can buy palm leaves in order to work and thereby feed myself'.

The blind man said to him, 'What do you see in me that you want me to give you something for your sustenance while I am blind and naked and beg for alms myself? Nonetheless, come'.

Thus Abba Daniel went with the blind man, saying to his disciple, 'Follow us'.

They came to the sanctuary[216] of Saint Mark, the blind man's abode. As he entered it,[217] the blind man said to the Elder, 'Do me the favor of waiting[218] here a little while'.

He then brought out a bag filled with raisins, pomegranates, and figs, as well as three small gold coins. From the bag's mouth he further brought out a *dinar* coin weighing three shekels.[219] He gave him all this, saying, 'Take this and pray for me'.

The Elder returned to his disciple in tears, saying, 'How many of God's servants live concealed! By the name of the Living God, I will not turn down any of his blessings!'

A few days after they had left him, it became known[220] that an illness of the liver had struck a high official.[221] He had been lying in the sanctuary[222] of Mark the Apostle. The saint[223] had then spoken to the high official, saying, 'Have the blind man so-and-so brought to you, and implore him to put his hand on the spot where you suffer; then you will recover'. And so it had happened.

The people heard about this, and the news also reached the Father Patriarch. When they went to him[224] in order to receive his blessing, they found that he had just passed away.

May his prayer and the gift of his help be with his beloved Matthew.[225] Amen.

No. 70. *The Patrician Lady Anastasia* (I.8)[226]

The story of the great female saint who was considered[227] a eunuch with the name of Anastasius.[228]

Abba Daniel told us that a man who appeared to be a eunuch once lived in the interior desert, eighteen *mïraf*[229] from Scetis. Abba Daniel used to care for him one night each week: the Elder used to have his disciple fill a pitcher of water each week and deliver it to the entrance of the eunuch's cave. The disciple then returned home to him, and he did not speak to Abba Daniel about anything at all except the hermit. If he found a potsherd at the entrance with something written on it, he brought it to his master.

One time he brought his master a potsherd on which the following was written: 'My father, bring a tool with you, also bring your disciple, and come to me!'

The Elder knew the meaning [of this message]. He said to his disciple, 'Bring a tool, and then let us hurry so that we find that man and obtain his blessing before he passes away'.

They set out, weeping as they hurried toward him. They found him afflicted with a strong fever. Abba Daniel said to him, 'Blessed are you who have [long] pondered this hour and have repudiated the worldly kingdom'.

That eunuch replied and said to him, 'It is rather you who are blessed, new Abraham, who have entertained God for dinner'.[230]

Abba Daniel then implored him, saying, 'Pray for us now, our father, before your departure'.

The eunuch said, 'Indeed, it is rather I who am in need of your prayer at this hour'.

To this the Elder responded, saying, 'If I had reached this hour first, I would have beseeched [God] on your behalf'.

At this the eunuch raised himself up,[231] took the Elder's head in his hands, kissed it[232] and said, 'May my Lord, who has led me to this place and watched over me up to this moment, bless you as he blessed Abraham'.

The Elder then took his disciple and presented him to the eunuch, saying, 'My father, also bless him, my son'.

Thereupon the eunuch kissed the disciple and said, 'O my Lord, who has ordained for me this hour to make me leave my flesh! O Omniscient One, how many paths did this brother walk in all circumstances[233] in order to bring me water, for the sake of your name! Let the spirit of his fathers[234] rest upon him, as you made the spirit of Elijah the prophet rest on his disciple Elisha.[235]

He then said to the Elder, 'I adjure you[236] not to undress me [after my death]; rather let me go to God like this. Nobody shall know about my condition[237] except you two'.

He further asked for the Communion of the Eucharist. Therefore Abba Daniel quickly administered it to him in that hour. When he took the Eucharist, they exchanged the peace among themselves.[238] He then turned toward the east, made the sign of the cross, blessed himself[239] and said, 'It is good that you have come to me'. His face then shone like fire, and he gave up his blessed soul into God's hands. At that moment a beautiful, sweet, and pleasant odor could be smelled; the whole place was filled with it. There is no way to explain this sweet odor.

He then dug a grave before his cave.[240] Thereafter the Elder took off the eunuch's [upper] clothes and said to his disciple, 'Shroud him on top of his [under]clothes'.[241] The eunuch's [under]clothes were made of palm-leaves[242] sewn together on top. When the disciple shrouded him, he saw that his breasts were like the breasts of a woman, except that both of them were fiery and parched, like dry leaves from a tree. He did not mention it, however. Then they buried him, said a prayer, and got ready to return home.

At this point, the Elder said to the disciple, 'Today we should suspend our fast and perform a work of love on the grave of that brother'. So they stepped up to it and ate dry bread and fresh[243] grapes. They then took away with them the plaited palm-leaves[244] that he had plaited. On their way home they praised God and marveled at him.

The disciple [at one point] said to his master, 'My father, I saw his breasts, like those of women'.

Abba Daniel said, 'My son, I knew that before today'.

The disciple said to him, 'For the sake of God, my father, let me know his story'.

Abba Daniel said, 'My son, that woman was a great patrician lady of royal descent; she had grown up[245] in a palace. When the emperor saw her beauty and her charm, he wanted to forcibly take her. Queen Theodora[246] informed her about this. The patrician lady thereupon became afraid of what actions the emperor might take in the future. Therefore at night she quickly went to the seashore, taking with her what she could of her valuables and jewels. She then hired a ship to Alexandria. There [she went] into a monastery. She later had a monastery built; it became known as the Monastery[247] of the Patrician Lady.

'Later Queen Theodora died, and news reached the patrician lady that the emperor [now] wanted to fetch her.[248] At this she left Alexandria and came here on her own. She implored me to assign her a remote dwelling place; she did not hide from me anything of her situation. Therefore I set aside for her this dwelling place and dressed her in men's clothes. Today the length of her stay is twenty-eight years. No one has found out about her secret except for unworthy me, another brother, and now you.

'How many, my son, have come from the emperor on account of her: military leaders, church leaders, and many nobles. But it was not only this, also an earlier[249] commander of Alexandria sent out spies, and still another [did the same]. Christ, however, did not let them find out anything at all about her circumstances. I tell you, my son, this woman has risen to the highest order and surpassed the saints, the spiritual contenders.

'Now you have heard her story: about her lineage,[250] her childhood, her beauty, her wealth; how she left everything and sought Christ, as you have seen with your own eyes over such a long time; and how she mortified her flesh on account of the longing for Christ, until she had come to such a state as you have seen when you shrouded her.

'We, on the other hand, used to live in a world in which it was not easy for us to find enough bread to satiate our hunger. When we then entered into monastic life, we had enough to eat and to drink, a good life and rest. In addition, we could not acquire one of her abundant luxuries [anyway]. Therefore we should now weep for ourselves[251] on account of our days that have passed, and through the prayer of this great

and chosen saint seek help from Christ, our Lord, with regard to those
things which are conducive to the salvation of our souls'.

No.71. *Andronicus and Athanasia* (Gk I.5)[252]

The story of Andronicus and his wife Athanasia, God-fearing people.[253]
In the large city of Antioch[254] there lived a young, God-fearing man by
the name of Andronicus. He was a money-changer,[255] and he had a
God-fearing wife who cared very much[256] for the poor. They possessed[257] many riches and much wealth. They used to divide the profits
which accrued to them into three parts: one third for themselves; the
second third for the monks[258] and their like, and the other third for alms.
They were blessed further with a son; they called him John. They also
begot a daughter; her they called Mary.[259]

After that they abstained from each other for the sake of the love of
God. He said to her, 'My blessed wife, the Fathers, [that is] the Apostles,
promised[260] beatitude to the married man who lives as if he did not
have a wife: they would inherit eternal life.[261] As for us, we have been
truly blessed with children, and even if we lived on for 1,000 years they
would be like one hour. If we are not satiated by the worldly pleasures
of the past, we will not be satiated by those that could still come,
either'.

Therefore they agreed on chastity. Every Wednesday, Friday and
Sunday they would now look after the sick and the ascetics,[262] and
equally after those suffering from leprosy or elephantiasis.[263] With their
goods and their souls, the wife ministered to the women and the husband
to the men. Like this they lived for twelve years.

Then suddenly a severe fever befell their children on one and the
same day. As a result, their mother was in grave sorrow. Their father for
his part went to the church of Saint Julian[264] in order to pray and implore
[God] on their behalf. He remained there until about the sixth hour.[265]
When he returned home, however, he found that, alas, both of them
had passed away in peace; they were lying stretched out on the bed.

Seeing this, he returned [to the church] and cast himself down before
an icon of our Lord and Saviour. In tears he said, 'Naked have I come
out of my mother's womb, and naked will I go again. God has given,
God has taken, God's will has been done. God's name be praised now
and in eternity!'[266]

As for the mother of the children, she wanted to kill herself on account of the enormity of her grief. She said, 'I want to die with my children because of my love for them'.

The patriarch,[267] the archbishops, bishops, and all the priests attended the burial of the two children. They were carried to the church of Saint Julian [and buried there]. Afterwards the patriarch took their father Andronicus by the hand and led him home in order to console him.

The children's mother, on the other hand, remained in the church at their burial place; she did not go back home. Her grief overwhelmed her, and she fell asleep there. At midnight a saint appeared to her in the guise of a monk. He said to her, 'Why are you in such deep grief?'

She said, 'My lord, how could I not grieve, having lost my children on one and the same day?'

[The monk asked], 'How old were they?'

She said, 'One was ten and the other twelve years old'.

He said, 'And yet do not weep on account of your children, rather weep on account of your sins! Truly, your children for their part duly and joyfully have gone to the Kingdom of Heaven. They are not besmirched by sin; they walk as clean and pure ones'.

She found relief in his words and consoled herself, saying, 'If indeed my children are alive now in the Kingdom of Heaven, I will not cry'.

Then she could no longer see the monk who had spoken to her. She walked around the whole church, but could not find anyone. Therefore she called out for the gatekeeper and said, 'Where is that monk who was here this [past] hour?'

He replied, 'The gate is locked and has not been opened. Nobody is here'.

She then understood that she had seen a vision, and she felt great fear. She asked the gatekeeper to escort her home. Thus he did.

When she came to her husband,[268] she informed him about what had happened to her. Then she said to him, 'I have it in my mind and I would now like to tell you that the two children have indeed gone to Christ and found rest. My lord, allow me,[269] if you please, to go to a monastery and live in it so I may weep for my sins among the nuns'.[270]

He said to her, 'What you say is blessed and good.[271] First, however, go and test yourself in a monastery. If you are strong enough for one week and thus find comfort, then we will both go, God willing'.

So she went out to one of the monasteries, stayed in it for a week, and then came back and informed her husband that her mind had felt most pleasantly comforted. At this he immediately sent [a message] to her father by which[272] he handed over to him all their possessions. They further informed him about what had come to pass between them, from the beginning to the end,[273] and wrote to him:[274] 'These possessions[275] we now entrust to you, so that with their proceeds you may do what is worthy of[276] us and of you. Leave this residence to the pilgrims[277] as well as to traveling monks and traveling worldly persons, and look after everything they need. Also the afflicted and ill shall be staying in it. May abundant blessings from God be with you! Be thus very watchful and circumspect. Christ is now witness between us, and the one who will requite us. Now it is time that you receive these possessions.[278] May peace be with you and on you'.

He then turned to his servants and attendants and gave each of them his share according to the duration [of his service]. Then all were dismissed.[279]

He and his wife then set out alone, leaving at night. Athanasia, the blessed woman, looked back at her home from a distance, lifted her eyes up to heaven, and said, 'My Lord, God of Abraham the righteous one, as you said to him and Sarah, his wife, "Leave your land and your family and come to the land that I will show you",[280] also now guide us, your servants, to the place that you wish! We indeed have gone forth and left our house and what is in it open. Do not therefore lock before us the gates of your mercy!'

They wept together, and then went on to the Holy Places.[281] At them they worshipped, and received blessings from them. Then they went to the church of Saint Menas in Alexandria.[282] When at the ninth hour[283] Andronicus emerged from the church gate, he saw a layman quarreling with a monk. He said to him, 'My brother, why do you quarrel with a monk?'

He replied, 'I will tell you. He hired my animal[284] so I would take him, riding on it, to Scetis. I said to him, "Let us set out now so we can travel that road in the cool of the night and are near the place when morning breaks". He said, "It doesn't suit me. I have experience with traveling in the desert at night"'.

Andronicus said to him, 'Do you have a second animal?'

He said, 'Yes'.

Andronicus said, 'Go and bring it to me so that I, too, can be your travel companion'.

He then said to his wife, 'As for you, remain here until I have returned from my trip to Scetis'.[285]

She said, 'My lord, take me with you'.

He said to her, 'It is not possible for a woman to go there'.

She said, 'How can you go and look for the salvation of your soul while you leave me here, all alone!'

He said, 'My sister, may God be with you and not depart from you, as his very true word [says]'.[286]

They then wept and said goodbye to each other, blessed each other once again, and off he went to Scetis. When he arrived there he visited the monastic fathers and received their blessings.

He then heard about the reputation of Abba Daniel and therefore wanted to go to him. With much effort he reached him, and he related to him all his circumstances. Abba Daniel thereupon said to him, 'Go and bring your wife, so I can prepare for you[287] letters [of recommendation] for Upper Egypt,[288] for the monastery of Il-Täbänsa'.[289]

He heeded Abba Daniel's word, returned [to Alexandria], took his wife, and [again] came to the Elder's abode.

Abba Daniel spoke to them about salvation and wrote them letters for that aforementioned monastery. Then Andronicus accompanied his wife there, left her at the monastery, and returned to Abba Daniel. The latter then conferred the monastic garment[290] on Andronicus and taught him the rules of the perfect monk.

When twelve years had passed, he asked permission from the Elder to go to the Holy Places.[291] Abba Daniel said[292] a prayer for him and let him go. He then tired while walking, so he sat down under the twigs of a thorn bush in order to seek shade against the heat and rest a little. Then suddenly his wife came by, through God's dispensation, but she was wearing men's clothes. She also wanted to visit the Holy Places. They greeted and embraced[293] each other, with their monk's hoods over their heads.[294] She for one recognized that it was him, because his appearance had not changed, and she had not forgotten it.[295] For him, on the other hand, it was not possible to recognize and identify her. Her condition had changed, her youth and beauty had perished, her flesh had suffered badly, and her color darkened on account of her mortifications during the aforementioned years. She indeed fully looked like a black slave.[296]

She said to him shyly and with reserve, 'Where are you headed, my brother?'

He said, 'It is my desire to visit the Holy Places'.

She said, 'It is the same with me. Would you like to travel together?'

He said: 'Yes'.

She said, 'However, it is a bit far. Let us therefore not behave like Bedouins'.[297]

He said, 'As you wish, my father'.

She then said to him, 'You look like Abba Daniel's disciple'.

He said, 'Yes'.

She said, 'Are you therefore indeed that Andronicus?'

He said, 'I am'.

She said, 'May the prayer of that father be with our father Matthew.[298] Amen'.

The saintly woman spoke to him all along the way, but she kept her face lowered.[299] [Like this] they went on until they arrived and worshipped at those Holy Places. They then returned to Alexandria as companions.

She had called herself Athanasius.[300] She said to him, 'My saintly father, would you like us to live together in one place?'

He said, 'By all means! But first I would like to go receive the Elder's blessing and prayer'.

She said, 'Go in peace, but remember me. I will expect you in the monastery on the 18th'.[301]

So he went to the Elder, greeted and embraced[302] him, and informed him about what had happened to him regarding the companion he had unexpectedly met on the way to visit the Holy Places.

The Elder said to him, 'My son, go and live with that brother. He is truly a good monk. But devote yourself to silence'.

The Father knew that she was his wife, but he did not disclose that to Andronicus.[303]

Thus the brother returned to the monastery where his companion awaited him. He found him there. They then lived united, in the fear of God, for another twelve years, and Andronicus never found out [the truth]. Abba Daniel, the Elder, visited them every once in a while in order to watch over their condition and speak to them about what was beneficial for their souls; but he never told Andronicus anything about his wife.

Once he had visited them, then taken his leave and returned home. Later, Andronicus made his way to the Elder and informed him that his companion was about[304] to pass away and go to his Lord. At this Abba Daniel rose and went with him. They found the companion weeping.

Abba Daniel said to him, 'Why are you weeping now? You ought to rejoice and be cheerful very much because you are about[305] to meet Christ'.

He said, 'But I weep because of my separation from the beloved brother, Abba Andronicus. In any case, do a work of mercy for me and give the Eucharist[306] to me'.

Abba Daniel thus cared for him and gave the Holy Sacraments to him. When he had received them, he lay down and gave up his pure spirit. A pleasant odor was then emitted by the dead body and filled the house.

When they came to shroud him, they found that he was of the female sex. On a papyrus leaf they further found written down the story of her life's struggle[307] which she had written down for her husband Andronicus as a piece of evidence[308] by which he could definitively identify her. When Andronicus read it and realized the situation, his heart became completely dark and he lost control of himself.[309] He began to slap his face, fell on his knees[310] and wailed for a long time. Abba Daniel then wanted to take him with him in order to console him, but he refused.

He said, 'My father, pray for me that I may remain here with my sister and brother and wife until I go to her'.

A little later Andronicus fell ill. They informed the Elder about his condition, so he came to him. With him were [many] elders, fathers; they received Andronicus' blessing. Andronicus then partook of the Holy Sacraments.[311] Then he lay down, gave up his blessed soul, and went to the heavenly dwelling.

May their prayer and the gift of their help be with their beloved Matthew.[312] Amen.

No.72. *Eulogius the Stonecutter* (Gk I.9)[313]

The story of Eulogius[314] the Stonecutter.

It says: Abba Daniel,[315] a priest of Scetis, and his disciple were once traveling to Upper Egypt[316] when they came to a village. At this the Elder said, 'Let us stay here for a day'.

His disciple grumbled about this, saying, 'How long will we remain unsheltered travelers?[317] Let us hurry on to Scetis!'

The Elder said, 'Let us stay here for a day, and may God's will be done'.[318]

So they stayed on in the village, like strangers.[319]

The disciple said, 'Does our staying in this place like beggars please God? Let us at least proceed to a church'.

Abba Daniel replied, 'For now, let us stay here', and so they stayed there.

As it became evening and darkness fell, that brother [again] argued with the Elder. Then suddenly an old man from among the villagers came up to them and began to kiss Abba Daniel's feet, with much weeping. He then also kissed the disciple, and asked them to go home with him. In his hand he held a lamp with which he went around in the village's public places, [seeing] whether he would find a traveler who had no shelter in order to then take him in; that was his constant practice. They then went home with him. Nobody was there who would keep him company.[320] He then served them a meal, and they ate. When it was time for them to retire for the night, he brought water and washed their feet. When they had had enough of their dish, he took what was left over, went out, and threw it before the village dogs; such was his commendable habit. After this, the Elder, Abba Daniel, took him aside and they sat alone, discussing God's wondrous deeds until near daybreak, when they rose for prayer. After they had completed it, they took leave from each other and [Abba Daniel and his disciple] went away.

After they had left the village, the disciple threw himself down before the Elder, his father, imploring him to inform him about the story of the old man who had given them shelter.[321]

Abba Daniel said: My son, the name of this man is Eulogius. His profession is to hew stones every day for one *dirhim*.[322] He does not taste any food until dusk. Then, when night falls, he goes out, circulates in the village's public places and does as you saw yesterday. Whoever he finds he takes to his home. Today he is nearly a hundred years old, but God has not diminished his strength to exercise his profession, the hewing of stones. When I was a young man, forty years old, I [once] came to this village in order to sell my handicrafts. In the evening he came to me and aided me as you saw him do to others.[323] It so happened that he that night also found other brothers. All of us came [to his home], and he took care of us. After I had set out the next morning, come home again, and thought about what that brother did, I judged myself harshly on account of the magnitude of that largesse. So I fasted for several weeks in a row, all the time imploring and beseeching God to grant Eulogius a thriving business so that through it he would be able to do good deeds to many. Three weeks I spent begging, then I sank to the ground on account of the fasting and the standing;[324] I was unconscious.[325] Then suddenly I saw a man standing next to me. He wore priests' clothes, and he said, 'Daniel, what is the matter with you?'

I replied, 'My lord, I have pledged to Christ that I will not taste any food unless he listens to my plea on behalf of Eulogius, that he bless him with riches so that with them he can do good deeds to many'.

He said: 'He lives in good conditions'.[326]

I said,[327] 'I implore you to be more generous toward him so he can manifest his deeds much more clearly'.

He said: 'Yet presently he finds himself well off. However, if you wish me to be more generous toward him, vouch for his soul to me: that you will be a guarantor for his soul when his circumstances improve and he becomes more affluent'.

I said: 'I for him, yes, my lord'.

Then, after this, I saw us as if we were standing in Holy Jerusalem, with a youth sitting on the saint's lap. I also saw Eulogius standing at his right. He[328] sent to me one of those standing before him.

He said, 'Is this the one who vouches for Eulogius?'

All said, 'Yes, our Lord'.

He said, 'Instruct him again that from now on I will claim him as security'.

I said, 'Yes, my Lord, he is my charge'.

Then I saw how they poured money into the lap of the aforesaid Eulogius, very much money indeed. After this I awoke and knew that God had granted[329] my request.

Eulogius [that day] went out to hew stones as usual. When he hit the rock, a [peculiar] sound could be heard. So he hit again, and inside it a gate appeared to him. He hit it, and had found a cave. In it was a great treasure. Eulogius was dumbfounded by it.

He deliberated:[330] 'This will date back to the days of the Children of Israel'.[331] But what shall I do with this? If I take it to the village, the prefect will take it away from me, and I will get into trouble. It will be best for me to take it and go far away, to a place where nobody knows me.

Consequently, he made arrangements and rented an animal in order to carry the precious stones and the money to the sea, onto a ship that he hired. He then headed for Byzantium, that is, Constantinople, and lived in its vicinity.

Justin[332] was emperor over it. Once Eulogius was well established, he began to build close relations with high officials and the nobility, to eat and drink with them, and to ride out with the emperor's court. He entertained them[333] assiduously and very liberally, and he also lent them money. When the emperor heard about this,[334] he invited and received him, and showed him favor. The emperor wanted [to give him] something big and expensive as a gift, as is fitting. He therefore approached him and gave him a big and beautiful palace,[335] and continually honored him [also in other ways]. That residence until today is known as 'the Egyptian's palace'.

Eulogius then forgot about his good deeds and did not think of them any more. When I thus later saw that youth in a dream [again], as he was sitting in Holy Jerusalem, I thought to myself, 'Where indeed may that Eulogius be?' Suddenly there were black men, and they dragged Eulogius away. On account of this I awoke, completely dismayed, and said, 'Woe is me, a sinner indeed! I have brought about my soul's perdition'.

I then quickly traveled to that village, in the guise of one who sells his handicrafts. I looked out for Eulogius until darkness fell, but he did not come. I was surprised and asked one of the old women of that village, saying, 'Mother, do you have some bread? Give me something to eat, for I have not eaten [yet]'.

She went and brought me some morsels [of bread], as well as a little [other] food. She sat down next to me and spoke to me, saying, 'Master, have you forgotten[336] that you are a young man? On account of your monastic habit it is not appropriate for you to come into a village. You should rather look for work'. She then reminded me of many worthy occupations.

I said to her, 'What, then, do you now command me to do? Actually, I have come here to sell my handicrafts'.

She said, 'Do not stroll around in the village and do not sit here with me, but quickly complete your work and then return to your place'.

I then inquired from her, saying, 'Do you happen to have news about Eulogius, the stonecutter?'

She said, 'He was a true benefactor. Therefore God showed him great favor. News about him has reached us, to the effect that he is a high official in Constantinople'.

Thereupon I accused myself for my shameful conduct, saying, 'I have sinned against my soul!'

Having heard this I could not stay on, but rather boarded a ship to Constantinople. After I had arrived and ascended [from the port] to the city, I inquired, 'Where is the palace of Eulogius the Egyptian?'

They indicated it to me, so I went and sat down at the gate. A great crowd was waiting for him there. After an hour he emerged with a large retinue: I could not get to him. Therefore I cried out to him: 'Have mercy on me, stop and listen to me!'

He, however, did not in the least turn around to me. People from his retinue[337] even beat me up and moved me away. I then approached him at another place and cried out for him, but I was beaten up again. In such a fashion I continued for four weeks. Yet I never got through to him, and my spirits sank.[338] Eventually I went and cast myself down before an icon of the Mother of God, in intense weeping and heavy suffering, saying: 'Savior, take away from me the responsibility for that man. Otherwise I, too, will enter into damnation'.

Suddenly I was overcome by sleep.[339] While asleep I heard a loud and forceful voice saying: 'Behold, the Good Queen!', and in front of her there went hundreds and multitudes. I cried out to her, saying, 'Lady, have mercy on me!'

She halted and said, 'What is your concern?'

I said: 'I have gone astray and vouched for Eulogius the Egyptian. Deliver me from responsibility for him'.

She said, 'I do not have the authority to decide this matter.[340] You desired it and requested it, now live up to your pledge'. Then she went away from me.

I awoke and said to myself, 'Even if I have to die, I will not leave his gate until I have spoken to Eulogius!'

Therefore I remained there until he emerged [again]. I cried out for him, and was beaten up very severely. Now I was badly depressed,[341] lacked [further] perseverance and wanted to return to Scetis. If God wanted, he would save Eulogius. I went to the seashore in order to look for a ship to Alexandria, found one, boarded it, threw myself on the ground, and immediately fell asleep due to many reasons, in particular due to the great woe I felt. In my sleep I again saw a vision: I was in holy Golgotha, in fright and panic. I trembled like palm leaves and could not open my mouth. Then I saw our Lord Jesus Christ. He was seated and said to me, 'Live up to your pledge!' I was devastated.[342] He then immediately ordered me to be bound, and I was suspended[343] by my arms.

He said, 'Why do you vouch for something that is beyond your capacities? Why do you oppose your Lord?'

I could not answer.

Suddenly somebody announced, 'Behold, the Queen is coming!'

I cried out to her, afflicted and with a crushed soul, 'Mistress over the world, have mercy on me! I am suspended because I have vouched for Eulogius'.

She said: 'I will plead for you in this matter'.

She approached the Saviour, kissed his feet, pleaded with him, and then said to me, 'Do not do anything like this again'.

I said: 'Certainly not, my Lady. I have indeed sinned; forgive[344] me'.

The Saviour then ordered that I be untied, and said: 'Go home, because you cannot comprehend how I will restore Eulogius to his previous state'.

I then woke up in great joy due to the salvation of my and his soul. During the sea journey I constantly praised God.[345] Three days later the news reached me that the emperor Justin[346] had died and somebody else been made emperor. This new emperor then killed high officials and followers of the former emperor, as well as confiscated their possessions. Among their number was Eulogius: all his possessions had been seized, and he had fled at night, saving only his life.[347] The emperor then ordered that they search for him and kill him wherever they find him. He evaded them by posing as a pauper,[348] as he [in fact] was, and returned to his village. All the villagers at this occasion assembled around him in order to have a look at him.

They said to him: 'It is good that you have come back. But news had reached us that you were a high commander'.

He said to them, 'It is strange that you would say that. If I had been a commander, I would not now be looking into your faces. However, I too have heard that a man whose name is the same as mine is a commander in Constantinople. I, on the other hand, was away at the Holy Places'.

Thus he came to his senses[349] and said, 'Poor and weary Eulogius, get up, take your tools, and go work as you used to! Here there is indeed no state palace for you—in which you later only barely escaped grave sin'.[350]

So he rose, took his tools, and went out as he used to do in order to hew stones. He also went to that quarry where he had found the treasure, hoping that he would find it.[351] He hit various rocks[352] for six hours, but did not find anything. Then he began to think of what had been in the cave[353] and consequently said, 'Eulogius, now finally rid yourself of that idiocy and return to your [previous] ways and habits. This is what is incumbent upon you, and what is best'.

Thus he returned to his lifestyle of old; and God did not want to regard as null and void his earlier good deeds.[354]

I for my part later once traveled up-country in order to sell what I had manufactured—and there indeed he came in the evening, like he used to! When I saw him with his changed appearance,[355] I was mortified. I wept and said, 'How great are your works, Lord, and everything you do with wisdom![356] You alone are the great God who lifts up the poor one from the dust, who does wonders and miracles, and nobody can dispute your verdicts.[357] I, sinner and wretched one, my soul just barely stepped back from [the path] which leads to hell'.

There were also other brothers who had come with us.[358] Eulogius, according to his habit, washed their feet and served a meal, which we ate.

I then separated myself from the others with Eulogius and said, 'What is your situation now, Eulogius?'

He said: 'Pray for me, for I am poor and a sinner'.

I said, 'It would have been better if the things that happened to you had not happened'.[359]

He said, 'What is this talk? Have I caused you sorrow with anything I have done?'

I said to him: 'Yes, my beloved son', and then told him everything that had happened to me and that I had had to go through for his sake. Then we wept together.

He said, 'Pray for me, that God may show me his grace and be merciful with me. From now on I will behave in a proper fashion'.

I said to him: 'Truly, my son, Christ will not entrust a thing to you as long as you live in this world. He will not give you anything except for a *dirhim*[360] [each day], as you are used to. But God has given you the strength to work, and by that to eat and to let others eat. You should abundantly praise our Lord Jesus Christ'.

See thus, brothers, how great the compassion of our Lord Jesus Christ is!

No. 472. *The Sister Who Pretended to be Insane* (Gk I.4)[361]

It says: While Abba Daniel[362] and his disciple once traveled to the city of Armimon,[363] he passed by a nunnery.[364] As he did so, he indicated to his disciple to go to the monastery and inform the mother[365] that he was outside. That monastery was known by the name of The Monastery of Jeremiah.[366] Three hundred virgins lived there.

When the disciple knocked on the monastery gate, the nun guarding the gate responded to him by softly saying, 'Who is it?'

He said, 'I would like to speak two words with the mother'.

She said, 'The mother never speaks with a man. Instead tell me [what you wish], and I will then inform her'.

He said, 'Tell her "There is a monk who wants to speak with you"'.

She went and reported it to the mother. The latter then came to the gate and spoke with him through the mouth of the gatekeeper.

The brother said to her, 'Do a work of charity and take me and my father in with you[367] for the night so the wild animals will not devour us'.

She responded by saying, 'It is not our custom to have a man sleep among us. It would be better for you if the wild animals devoured you rather than have the inner lions, known as devils, devour you'.

The brother replied, 'But Mother, it is the father Abba Daniel, from the monastery of Scetis.'[368]

As soon as she heard that it was Abba Daniel, she hurried out to the second gate, with all the virgins following her. They spread out their tunics where the Elder walked[369] and escorted him into the interior of the monastery. The mother then brought a water basin and washed his feet. Afterwards the virgins took some of that water and washed their faces with it, except for one whom they called 'the Ridiculous One'[370] and who was lying at the gate wrapped in her cloak. The father Abba Daniel went out to her and circled around her, but she did not turn toward him nor greet him. Therefore the sisters shouted at her that she should kiss his hand, saying to her, 'It is the father Abba Daniel! Rise!'[371] But she did not rise.

The mother then said to Abba Daniel, 'Our father, she is insane. I have many times desired to expel her, but I am afraid of sinning'.

They then brought him several foods to eat, which he did. After him they also ate.[372]

He then said to his disciple, 'My son, stay awake with me tonight so that you see the virtue of the one they call insane. She truly is a great saint!'

After one hour of the night had gone by, she rose until she stood upright, and stretched out her hands. Then she prostrated herself many times, while her tears flowed like a fountain, on account of her heart's fervor for God. She did this every night, but as soon as she heard any sound she quickly cast herself on the ground and appeared as if she were sleeping. Abba Daniel said to his disciple, 'Go into the mother's chamber and gently[373] summon her'.

She came, and she saw that that virgin was a true maiden of Christ: there was light between her hands, and angels prostrated themselves with her.[374] At this the mother wept and said, 'Woe is me, a sinner! How I have vilified, humiliated, and mocked her!'

When the morning bell was rung and the sisters assembled for prayer, she informed them about what she had seen.

When the allegedly insane one, on the other hand, noticed that they had found out about her, she wrote a note, fastened it to the beam on the interior of the monastery gate, and left the monastery.

What she wrote in the note is this: 'The Enemy and his attacks against me drove me, the wretched one, out of your midst and estranged me from you and your good will toward me. Your contempt for me is my reward, and your indignation at me has spiced my fruits. Your scorn and rejection of me were what kept me on my pilgrimage. Blessed is the hour in which you say to me, "You fool![375] You idiot!" You are absolved with regard to me, free of sin as far as I am concerned.[376] Before the throne of the Exalted One I will testify[377] in your favor. As for me, there is no scornful person among you, nor any one who [unduly] desires food, clothes or sexual pleasure. Rather, all of us are pure'. That was the end of her message.

After Abba Daniel had read it out, he said to them, 'I spent the last night here only in order to achieve this'.

Then all the sisters confessed to him how they used to humiliate and verbally abuse her. The father Abba Daniel relieved their hearts, but also instructed them that it was a grave sin to deride a creature of God, even if the creature was, to our minds, an insane woman. This was on account of the word of the Torah: 'Man was created in the image and likeness of God'.[378] 'It is incumbent on us, therefore', [he said,] 'that we treat the image and likeness of God with respect, honor, patience and forbearance'. He then prayed for them, blessed them and left, heading for his own monastery.

CHAPTER FOUR

Syriac Accounts

Translated by Sebastian P. Brock and Rowan A. Greer

Introduction by Tim Vivian

I N SYRIAC there is no 'Daniel dossier' extant as there is in Greek, nor is there a syriac 'Life' as in Coptic and Ethiopic.[1] The five stories gathered here come from disparate sources. The first four pieces— the insane female monastic (Syriac 1), Andronicus and Athanasia (Syr 2), Anastasia (Syr 3), and Eulogius (Syr 4)—bear close resemblance to their counterparts in the greek dossier. In the first story, however, the sister is supposedly simple-minded and insane, not drunk, as in the greek version. At the end of the story Abba Daniel makes her metaphorically drunk for God: 'Truly, God loves those who are insane like this; for they are mad and drunk with his love and his mercy.' The third syriac piece, the story of Anastasia, unlike the greek account, identifies Anastasia as a 'deaconess who lived in the days of the patriarch Severus' of Antioch (465-538).[2]

The fifth syriac piece, 'The Narrative of Abba Daniel Concerning a Monk and His Sister', occurs in much shorter form in Greek (Gr III.1); in three manuscripts Daniel is named as the brother of the prostitute while in one manuscript Daniel is neither the narrator nor the brother. The syriac version is roughly four times the length of the greek version, though Sebastian Brock believes the syriac manuscript is '(probably) the earliest witness to the story'.[3] If so, the syriac bears witness to a lost, longer, greek version.

SYNOPTIC TABLE

Syriac	*Greek*
1. The Woman who Feigned Insanity	[I.4] The Woman who Feigned Drunkenness
2. Andronicus and Athanasia	[I.5] Andronicus and Athanasia
3. The Patrician Lady Anastasia	[I.8] The Patrician Lady Anastasia
4. Eulogius the Stonecutter	[I.9] Eulogius the Stonecutter
5. A Monk and His Sister	[III.1] A Monk and His Sister

SYRIAC ACCOUNTS

1 (I.4) *The Woman Who Pretended to be Insane*[4]

[1.] Once blessed Abba Daniel left Scetis with his disciple to go to a monastery of sisters in the inner desert. They were called Tabennesians.[5] When the monks in the desert noticed him, they all went out to meet him at once, like sheep expecting their shepherd. Seeing him coming from afar, they threw themselves to the ground before him seven times. He then addressed them with profitable words. He sealed them with the sign of the cross and said to them, 'Seek after the renunciation of possessions and the renunciation of anxious thoughts, since by such renunciations a person sees the face of God'. He prayed for them and went away.

[2.] In the evening they arrived at the monastery of which we have spoken. The blessed one said to his disciple, 'Go, my son, and say to the superior of the monastery that there is an old man from Scetis with you, and that we are asking for lodging with them this night, even though it is not the custom for a man to be brought into this monastery.'

The disciple went and knocked on the door of the monastery. An old woman answered and said to him, 'At your service. What do you want?'

He said to her, 'Go and call the superior of the monastery to me'.

When the superior of the monastery came out to him, he said to her, 'There is an old man from Scetis with me, and we ask for lodging with you this night so we may not be eaten by wild beasts'.

She said to him, 'It is better for you, my son, to be eaten by wild beasts outside rather than by wild beasts inside'.

He said to her, 'Blessed Daniel of Scetis is with me'.

[3.] When the superior of the monastery heard this, she did not hesitate to open the doors of the monastery to the two of them. She brought all the sisters out to meet him and led him from the door of the monastery to the appointed place. They spread their veils on the ground. And so, walking on them, Abba Daniel and his disciple entered the monastery. After praying, he sat down. The superior of the monastery brought water in a basin and washed their feet, his and his disciple's. All the sisters passed by before him and were blessed by him. Then the superior of the monastery took some of the water with which she had washed the feet of the blessed one and poured it on the head of each of the sisters for a blessing. Finally, she poured some on her own head and her breast. This worked great profit for the whole monastery. A table was prepared before the blessed one with only dry bread mixed with water and before his disciple with cooked lentils and leavened bread. Then she brought cooked food and oil to all the sisters, together with wine mixed with water and other things.

When they had satisfied themselves, the blessed one said to her, 'Why have you given us meager fare and abundance to the sisters?'

The superior of the monastery said to him, 'You, my master, are a monk; and a monk's food is appropriate for you. And your disciple is the disciple of a monk, so also to him I brought food appropriate for a monk's disciple. But because we are weak we eat abundantly'.

The blessed one said to her, 'Love has been kindled'.

Then those sisters marveled and were so amazed that there was a great silence among them. Everything they did, their service and all their necessary work, they accomplished either by sign or by signal. There were more than three hundred of them.

The blessed one said to the superior of the monastery, 'Are the sisters always like this, or is it because of us that they work this way?'

The superior of the monastery said to him, 'Your servants are always like this. Pray for them, and give God glory.'

[4.] He got up right away from the cloister and returned to the hall. He saw a sister vomiting on the ground in the filth she had spewed forth. And he asked the superior of the monastery, 'Mother, what is wrong with this sister?'

The superior of the monastery said to him, 'She is a poor soul, my master, and it is through simple-mindedness and insanity that she throws herself down like this wherever she happens to be'.[6]

He ordered his disciple to bring the water that was in a basin. He poured it on her, and she stood up, as though delivered from her insanity and simple-mindedness. She then went away stealthily. Then the old man said to his disciple, 'My son, do a work of love and go see where this poor insane woman sleeps'.

The disciple left and went [to find her]. He discovered that she was sleeping near the monastery privy. He returned and reported this to his master. The blessed one said to his disciple, 'My son, do a work of love, and keep vigil with me tonight'. When everyone was fast asleep, the blessed one went with his disciple and they stood where they had seen the insane woman. But she did not see them. When she saw that all the sisters were asleep, she stood in prayer and spread forth her hands to heaven. There went out from them what seemed like flashes and fiery lamps. She prostrated herself and stood praying the whole night. Her tears flowed and fell on the ground like rivers of water. She spent all her days this way.

The blessed one said to his disciple, 'Go quietly, my son, summon for me the superior of the monastery, and bring her back'. When the blessed one showed her the miracles, he said to her, 'You have seen this insane woman. Truly God loves people who are insane like this. Strike the gong right away at midnight'. This news went out among the sisters, and there was a great disturbance among them, since they were wailing and weeping for the many ways they had afflicted the poor insane woman because they thought she was truly simple-minded and stupid. Then, because they had kept vigil, the blessed one and his disciple withdrew for a while and rested.

That blessed woman,[7] when she realized that news of what had happened had spread, got up in the night and went to the place where the blessed one was sleeping. She took off his cloak and left. She wrote a letter, opened the door of the monastery, and left the place. No one knew where she had gone or where she had slept. This was what she wrote in the letter: 'Let my sisters in Christ rest in peace and pray for me for our Lord's sake. Let them forgive me, for I have vexed them with great trouble'. The blessed one, then, right away called together all the sisters and spoke to them words of salvation. He consoled them and said to them, 'You have seen this insane woman. Truly, God loves those who are insane like this; for they are mad and drunk with his love and his mercy'. And he sealed them with the sign of the cross and withdrew from there with his disciple.

(I.5) *Andronicus and Athanasia*[8]

A story of holy Andronicus and Athanasia, his wife, and of the blessed ending of their life in this world.

There was a young man in the city of Antioch named Andronicus. By trade he was an *arguroprates*, that is, a money changer. He had a wife, the daughter of John who was also an *arguroprates* by trade. Her name was Athanasia, and her deeds agreed with her name, since 'athanasia' means 'immortal'. Andronicus was also perfect in all the deeds of virtue just as his wife was. They had great wealth. They administered their worldly goods the following way. Whatever they had from their property and whatever they earned in their business every year they divided into three parts: one for the poor, another for the monasteries, and the third for their own use.

The whole city loved Andronicus because of his virtue and his pious deeds. A short time after their marriage Athanasia gave birth to a son and named him John. She later gave birth to a daughter and named her Mary. Thereafter Andronicus no longer drew near to his wife for sexual intercourse, but all their care was for the love of the poor. On Sunday, Wednesday, and Thursday from evening till morning the illustrious Andronicus went to perform his service of washing the poor. In the same way his wife washed the women. By means of the Lord's love they kept at this work for a space of twelve years.

One day Athanasia came back from her service and went up to see her children. She found both of them crying. Since they aroused her pity, she got up into her bed and put both her children on her breast. When the illustrious and attractive Andronicus entered his house and saw her lying down with her children, he reproached her and said, 'How long are you going to take your ease in sleep? What you are doing is not seemly.'

She then said to him, 'Do not be angry with me, my husband, because these children have a high fever'.

When he drew near and touched them, he found that they had a raging fever. He groaned and said, 'May the Lord's will be done'. He went out to pray outside the city at the shrine of Saint Julian, since that was where his fathers were buried.[9] When he had kept up his prayers till the ninth hour,[10] he returned to the city and heard the sound of wailing and weeping and great affliction in his house. In his affliction he ran and found the whole city gathered inside his house and the children dead. When he saw the two of them placed in one bed, he went to the shrine that was in his house. He threw himself down before the icon of the Saviour[11] and said this: 'Naked I came from my mother's womb, and naked shall I go forth from this world. The Lord gave, and the Lord has taken away. Let it be as it has seemed best to the Lord. May the Lord's name be blessed now and forever.'[12]

His wife Athanasia, however, was trying to strangle herself, as she said, 'Let me die with my children!' Now the whole city was gathered together to accompany them for the burial. The patriarch with the entire holy order of priests accompanied them for the burial in the church of Julian, the martyr of God, in the graves of their fathers. The patriarch escorted Andronicus to his palace. Athanasia did not wish to return home but wanted to stay in the church to sleep there that night, weeping and mourning for her children.

In the middle of the night holy Mar Julian appeared to her in a monk's habit and said to her, 'Why do you not leave in peace those who are here?'

She said to him, 'My master, do not be angry with me, since mine is a woman's sadness of spirit. I had only two children, and I have buried them both today.'

The saint said to her, 'My child, how old were your children?'

She said to him, 'One was twelve years old, and the other was ten'.

The saint said to her, 'Why, then, are you weeping for them and not weeping for your sins? Truly I tell you, woman, that just as it is the nature of human beings to seek food and to be unable to exist without it, in the same way these children who have died will ask of Christ on that day the good things promised them. And they will say to him, "Righteous judge, since you have deprived us of earthly things that are visible, do not deprive us of heavenly things that are invisible."'

When she heard this, she took it to heart, changed her mourning to joy, and said, 'If my children are in every way alive and are in heaven, why am I weeping?' She turned around and tried to find the monk who had spoken with her, but did not see him. She went round the whole shrine, but did not find him. She called the church custodian and said to him, 'Where is the monk who just came in here?'

The custodian said to her, 'What is wrong with you? You saw no one, since the door of the shrine was shut. Why are you saying that a monk has just come in here?' The custodian realized that the saint had appeared to her. She was greatly afraid, and he persuaded her to go home. When she returned home, she told her husband what she had seen. Both of them were greatly afraid.

Then blessed Athanasia said to her husband, 'Believe me, my husband, while the children were still living, I wanted to speak to you, but I was ashamed to. But now that they are dead, I shall speak to you. If you will hear me, put me in a monastery of sisters, and I shall weep for my sins.'

Andronicus said to her, 'Go and think it over for a week, and if you wish to persist [with this plan], we shall talk it over with one another'.

A week later she came back and told him what she had considered.[13] Blessed Andronicus summoned his brother-in-law, handed over to him all their property, and said, 'We are eager to go to the holy places to pray, since this is God's command. But if anything happens to us because we are human beings, you know—you and God—what should be done with this property. I ask you, then, to do well for yourself and to make this house a hospital and guest house for monks.' He freed all his slaves, male and female, and gave them a legacy. Andronicus and Athanasia took with them a small sum of money and two mules. He and his wife left the city at night alone. Athanasia, seeing her house from afar, looked up on high and said, 'O God, you said to Abraham and Sarah his wife, "Leave your land and your kindred, and go to the land I shall show you".[14] May you, my Lord, guide our lives in fear of you. See, we have left our dwelling open for the sake of your holy name. Do not close the doors of your kingdom upon us.'

Both of them left there weeping. They made a tour of the holy places and prayed in them. They were in the company of many fathers and came to the church of Mar Menas in Alexandria.[15] They rejoiced in the prayers of the saint. About the ninth hour blessed Andronicus looked and saw a monk in a fight with a layman. The blessed one said to the layman, 'Why are you abusing this blessed one?'

The layman said to him, 'My master, he hired my mule as far as Scetis, and I said to him, "Get up, and let us travel all night and tomorrow till noon, so that we can get to Scetis before noon and the great heat". But he does not want to go.'

Andronicus said to him, 'Do you have another mule?'

He said to him, 'Yes'.

The blessed one said to him, 'Go and bring it to me here. I shall take one, and this blessed one the other, since I also wish to go to Scetis'.

Andronicus also said to Athanasia his wife, 'Wait for me here, my wife, near Saint Menas while I go down to Scetis, venerate the fathers and saints, and receive their blessings. And I shall come back to you.'

Athanasia said to him, 'I pray you, my husband, take me with you'.

He said to her, 'No, my wife, because a woman cannot enter the desert of Scetis'. She then said to him, weeping, 'You will have to deal with God and with my holy Mar Menas if you desert me. Put me in a monastery of sisters until you return.'

They gave one another the peace, and he went down to Scetis. He venerated the holy fathers and was blessed by them. While he stayed there, he heard about blessed Daniel. With great difficulty he was able to converse with him. He told him their whole story. Blessed Daniel said to him, 'Go and come back here with your wife. I shall prepare letters for you, and you will go to the Thebaid to a monastery of Tabennesians'.[16] Andronicus did as the old man had commanded him. Both of them came and heard words of salvation. He [Daniel] prepared letters for them and sent them to the monastery of which we have spoken. When Andronicus came back to Abba Daniel, the old man gave him the monastic habit and taught him the monastic rule and law. He remained with him for twelve years, devoting himself to the disciplines of the angels.

After the space of these years blessed Andronicus besought the old man, saying, 'Release me, father, if you think it fitting, so I may go pray at the holy places'. The old man let him go, prayed for him, and sent him away in peace. Then blessed Andronicus, while he was traveling through Egypt, sat down one day beneath a tree to rest for a while from the toil of his journey and from the severe heat. By a dispensation of God the thought had equally come to blessed Athanasia to leave the monastery and go to pray at the holy places. A few days into her journey, wearing men's clothing, she came to the place where Andronicus was. They blessed one another and gave each other the peace. The dove recognizes its mate, but he did not recognize her, though she was able to recognize him. This was because her appearance was withered, and the beauty of her face hardened by her great toil and abstinence. She seemed like an Ethiopian in appearance.[17] Looking like a man, she spoke with him and said, 'Where are you going, abba?'

Andronicus said to her, 'To pray at the holy places'.

She said to him, 'I too have left to go there'. And she then said to him, 'Do you want to travel together?'

He said to her, 'Yes, *abba*, as it seems fitting and pleasing to you'.

She said to him again, 'Very well, let us travel in silence as though we were not with one another'.

Andronicus said to her, 'As you command, *abba*'.

Afterwards she said to him, 'In faith, *abba*, are you not the disciple of Abba Daniel?'

He said to her, 'Yes'.

Then she said to him, 'Is not Andronicus your name?'

He said to her, 'Yes, that is what I am called'.

She said to him, 'The prayers of the blessed one will go with us'.

When Andronicus said 'Amen', they went their way. He also asked her, 'What is your name, *abba*?'

She said, 'Athanasius'.

When they had gone and made the tour of the holy places and prayed in the monasteries and martyrs' shrines, they returned to Alexandria. Abba Athanasius said to Abba Andronicus, 'Is it your pleasure, *abba*, that we should dwell together in a cell?' Andronicus said to her, 'Yes, as you command, *abba*. Only I shall go and be blessed by the old man Daniel. Then I shall return.'

Athanasius said to him, 'Go in peace. I shall wait for you in Oktokaidekaton alone in silence, as we were on the journey. If you learn that you are not meant [to live] in silence, you need not return, for I have a place to dwell in Oktokaidekaton'.[18]

When he went and made himself known to the old man, the old man Mar Daniel said to him, 'Go, love silence, and dwell with the brother who was with you, for he is a monk'.

When Andronicus returned and found Athanasius, he dwelt with him in the fear of the Lord for twelve more years. But she did not let Andronicus know that she was his wife Athanasia.

Many times the old man went up to visit them, and he let them hear the living words of salvation. One time the old man went up and visited them, as was his custom. He turned back home, but before he reached the shrine of Mar Menas, Abba Andronicus overtook him and said to him, 'Come back, *abba*, because Abba Athanasius is going to our Lord'. When the old man returned, he found him in anguish. Athanasius began to weep. The old man said to him, 'Why are you weeping instead of rejoicing, since you are going to take your share with Christ?'

Abba Athanasius said to him, 'I am not weeping for myself, my master, but am weeping for Abba Andronicus. But do me a favor, my father. When you bury me, you will find near my head a tablet with a note written on it. Read it to yourself and to my Abba Andronicus.'

After they had prayed and taken Communion, he fell asleep in peace. When they drew near to wash him, they discovered that she was a woman by nature; and the news was heard in all Alexandria. When Andronicus learned what had happened and knew that she was Athanasia his wife, he threw himself on her breast and with many tears embraced her, saying, 'Alas for me, I had my pearl near me and did not perceive it! My wife was within my cell, and I did not know her!' He said other things like this in his grief.

Then blessed Daniel summoned all of Scetis, all the fathers in the inner desert, and all the lavras of Alexandria. [They came] clothed in white and carrying palm branches, and with the entire city of Alexandria accompanied for burial that chosen and holy vessel, the body of Athanasia, glorifying God who gave such patient endurance to the race of women.

The old man remained there seven days after the saint's death. When he was leaving to go back, he asked Abba Andronicus to go with him. But he refused and said, 'I shall die with my wife'. So he gave him the peace and left him to go. But before he reached the shrine of Mar Menas, one of the brethren overtook him and said to him, 'Come back, my master, because Abba Andronicus is going to our Lord'. Again the old man summoned and assembled all of Scetis, saying, 'Come, come up, because Abba Andronicus is going to Abba Mar Athanasius'. When they heard this, they all came up and found him still alive. When he had blessed them, he fell asleep in Christ.

There was then contention between the fathers who dwelt at Oktokaidekaton and those in Scetis, who said, 'Because he is our brother, he will come with us to Scetis so that his prayers may help us'.

Those from Oktokaidekaton said, 'We shall place him beside his sister'.

Now those from Scetis were greater in number, and so the archimandrite and those from Oktokaidekaton said, 'We shall do whatever the old man Daniel says'.

The old man said, 'Let him be buried beside Athanasia'. But the monks from Scetis would not listen to him, saying, 'This old man has been delivered from bodily struggles and is not afraid. But we are children, and we demand our brother so his prayers may help us. It is enough for you that we leave you Abba Athanasius.'

When the old man saw this great tumult, he said to them, 'Truly, unless you quiet down, I shall also stay here, and I shall be buried with

my son'. Then they became quiet. After accompanying blessed Andronicus for burial, they said to the old man, 'Let us go to Scetis'.

The old man said to them, 'Let us observe a week of mourning for
our brother'. They did not leave him, but right away celebrated the ob-
servance. Then they went up to Scetis.

Therefore, my brothers, let us pray that our Lord may make us worthy
to equal the deeds of Abba Andronicus and blessed Athanasius. May we
take delight with them in the bridal chamber of light. As for those who
dwell in this monastery, may God make his tranquility and peace reign
over those who dwell here and over those who come to it, forever and
ever. Amen.

The end of the story of Andronicus and Athanasia his wife. May their
prayers be with us.

(I.8) *The Patrician Lady Anastasia*[19]

[5.] When they arrived at Scetis, the old man said to his disciple, 'Go, my
son, and visit the old man living near us'. For there was an old man, a
eunuch, in the inner part of Scetis eighteen miles away. The purpose of
the brother's visit was to take a vessel full of water and put it at the door
of his cell, to knock on the door and go away without saying anything,
but taking back with him the empty vessel. One day the blessed one said
to his disciple, 'Go look, my son, near the cave of the old man. When
you find a clay tablet with something written on it, bring it with you'.

The disciple went, and at the old man's cave he found a clay tablet
with writing and brought it back with him. This is what was written
on it: 'Bring your farming tools and come, you and your disciple'. When
the blessed one read what was written on the tablet, he wept greatly
and said to his disciple, 'There is mourning in the inner desert. What a
great pillar is falling today!' He said to his disciple, 'My son, take these
tools, that is, these irons and the axe and the shovel. Let us go quickly
to track down the old man before he dies lest we be deprived of his
prayers, since the old man is going to our Lord.'

[6.] The two of them, weeping, went and found the old man laid low
with an evil fever. The blessed one threw himself upon his breast and
wept bitterly. He said to him, 'Blessed are you, our father, for you have

kept this hour in mind. You have turned away from earthly things and have cared for heavenly ones.'

The eunuch said to him, 'Blessed are you, second Abraham. What great fruits of excellence has God received from your hands.'

The old man said to him, 'Pray for us, our father'.

The eunuch said to him, 'It is I who at this time am in need of much prayer'.

Abba Daniel said to him, 'Would that I had been with you at this time. I could have brought you comfort'.

Then the eunuch sat up on the mat on which he was lying, embraced the blessed one's head, and said to him, 'God, who led me to this place, will pour his full goodness and mercies on your old age, as he did to Abraham, the first of the patriarchs'.[20] Then the blessed one took his disciple, put him against the knees of the eunuch, and said to him, 'Pray also for your son, our father'.

And he kissed him and said to him, 'God has appointed for me this hour to deliver me from this body and its infirmity, and he knows how much it has run and grown weary to get to this cell for his name's sake. He will send forth the spirit of this master upon this disciple. And his name and the name of his fathers will be called upon him, just as the spirit of Elijah was sent forth upon Elisha.'[21]

After this the eunuch said to the blessed one, 'For the sake of our Lord and our Father, do me a kindness. Do not take off the clothes I am wearing, but send me to our Lord just as I am; and let no one else know about me except for you and your disciple'.

The old man said to the blessed one, 'Give me Communion, our father'.

And when he had received Communion, he said to them, 'Give me peace in the holy kiss of Christ, and pray for me'. And he turned his face to the east and to the right. He spread forth his hands and said, 'Blessed are you for coming'. His countenance shone brighter than the sun, and he said, 'O God, into your hands I commend my spirit'. And he made the sign of the cross on his mouth and gave up his spirit.

[7.] Weeping, the blessed one and his disciple dug a grave in front of the door of the cell. The blessed one took off the clothes the eunuch was wearing.[22] For he[23] was wearing only a thong made from a rope of palm fronds and over it a cloak. While the brother was clothing him, he saw that his breasts looked like two withered leaves. But he kept quiet and said nothing. When they had buried him and offered prayer, the blessed one said to his disciple, 'Let us break our fast today, my son, and break bread for the old man'. And when they had taken Communion, they found there a small flat cake of bread and dried bread mixed with water. When they had eaten and drunk, they took the old man's rope and returned to their cell, praising and confessing God.

[8.] While they were walking on their way, the disciple said to the old man, 'My father, did you know that that eunuch we buried was a woman? When I was clothing her, I touched her and saw that she had breasts that hung down like two withered leaves'.[24]

The old man said to him, 'My son, I did indeed know that she was a woman. If you wish me to tell you her story, hear then that she was once a patrician lady of the first rank. She was in the court of Emperor Justinian. This Emperor Justinian wanted to bring her into his palace because of her beauty and her great virtue. But when Empress Theodora became aware of this, she was enraged and demanded that she be banished to Alexandria. When the patrician lady learned this news, she fled by night. She bought a ship, took some of her riches, and came to the city of Alexandria. She lived in Enaton.[25] There she built a monastery which to this day is called the Monastery of the Patrician Lady.

'But when she found out that Theodora had died and that Emperor Justinian was sending after her to restore her to her imperial rank, she fled by night from Alexandria and came here. She asked me to acquire a cell for her on the outskirts of Scetis. When she explained to me everything that had happened, I gave her this cave. She changed her appearance to that of a man. And she has been here twenty-eight years today, and no one is aware of her except for me and you and one other old man. How many court officials were sent from the emperor to look for her! Not only the emperor, but even the patriarch and all of Alexandria, and no one has found her to this very day.

'See now, my son, how those in imperial courts have become great, have contested against the Enemy, have afflicted their bodies, and have conducted themselves by angelic deeds while on earth. We, on the other hand, though in the world, how many times do we not even have bread to receive? But though we have drawn near to the appearance of the monastic life, we are inflamed with drink and cannot acquire a single virtue. Pray then, my son, that the Lord will make us worthy of the same course and way [as she walked], that with our holy fathers we may find mercy this day, and that with our father and brother, the eunuch Anastasius (whose true name was Anastasia) God will deem us worthy of the kingdom without end'.[26]

[9.] When the blessed one arrived at his cell, he sat down and wrote what he had seen and heard. This Anastasia, the patrician lady, is the deaconess who lived in the days of the patriarch Severus, holy to God.[27] He wrote many letters to her in answer to the questions she asked him when she was in the monastery with the sisters before she went to the desert of Scetis.

Here ends the story of a sister who was thought to be insane[28] and [the story] of Anastasia, the patrician lady and deaconess.

3A. *Anastasia* (fragment of the opening only)[29]

Abba Daniel told about a certain eunuch who was in the inner desert of Scetis, whose cell was some eighteen miles distant from Scetis. Once a week he used to come to Abba Daniel during the night, and no one was aware of him except his disciple. The elder instructed his disciple to fill up a jug of water for him every week and put it out for him by the door. He would knock and go off without speaking with him, except that [if he found] an inscribed sherd at the entrance to the cave, he brought it back. Thus would our brother act, filling a jug of water each week, and the elder used to write down on a sherd what he needed. Then our brother would put the jug of water by the entrance of the cave and take away the inscribed sherd without speaking with him, in accordance with the Elder's instructions. Mar Daniel would read the Elder's message and provide for his needs.

One day the disciple found a sherd with the following message: 'Bring at once . . .'

(I.9) *Eulogius the Stonecutter*[30]

Abba Daniel, the priest of Scetis, said, 'I once went to Thebes with one of my disciples and we embarked on a boat and went down the river'.[31] On reaching a particular village the elder urged those in the boat, saying that we should by all means stay here today. So they stayed there, but his disciple began complaining, saying, 'How long are we going to go around? Let's go on to Scetis?'

But the elder said, 'No. Instead, let us remain here today'.

So they sat down in the middle of the village, after the custom of strangers. Our brother said to the Elder, 'Does it please God that we are sitting here like beggars? Let us go off to the martyrion.'

But the elder said, 'No; we are going to sit here'. Now the elder knew in the spirit that Eulogius would be coming from his high office back to his former state, and that was the reason why the elder was waiting for him.[32] Our brother, however, was not aware of the situation. They remained sitting there until evening, without eating or drinking. Our brother began arguing with the elder, saying, 'O what violence at the hands of our Lord's elder! All because of you, I am going to die.'

While they were talking, along came an old layman, tall in stature and of a great age; his head of hair was white and he was bent from old age. On catching sight of Abba Daniel, he rushed up and embraced him and was in tears as he began to kiss him. He then greeted his disciple and said to them, 'If you agree, my good sirs, come with me to my house'.

Now he was also carrying a lamp with a wick, and he was going around the village streets looking for strangers. So he led off the elder and his disciple, along with all the other strangers he had found, and took them to his house. There he washed the feet of the brethren and of the elder. He had no one else in his house—or anywhere else—apart from God alone. He set a table of food before them, and when they had had enough, he took up the crumbs and gave them to the village dogs. This was his normal practice, not leaving anything at all until the morning. He then took the Elder aside, by himself, and they sat down talking with each other until morning in spiritual delight and with many a tear. Then in the morning they bade one another farewell, and the Elder and his disciple set off on their journey.

While they were going along the road, our brother made a prostration to his *abba*, saying, 'Perform an act of love, *abba*, and tell me who that old man is, and how do you know him?' But the Elder did not want to tell him.

Our brother made a further prostration, urging him and saying, 'You reveal so many good things to me, *abba*. Aren't you going to reveal this matter to me, abba?' Now the elder used to tell our brother a great deal about the virtues of the saints—but the Elder was unwilling to tell our brother about that particular old man. Then our brother became upset, and did not speak to the elder until he had arrived at Scetis.

Now when our brother reached his cell, he did not bring the elder anything to eat in accordance with his usual custom (the elder used to eat at the eleventh hour[33] every day of his life). When it was evening the elder came to our brother and said, 'My son, why have you let your father die of hunger this way? '

He replied, 'I do not have a father. Had I a father, he would love his son.'

The Elder said to him, 'In that case, farewell!' And the Elder took hold of the door to open it and go off. But our brother rushed to grab him, and he began kissing him, saying, 'As God lives, I am not going to let you go until you tell me who that old man is'. Now our brother could not bear to see the elder upset, since he loved him a great deal.

Then the elder said to him, 'Make me some food, and afterwards I will tell you'.

Once he had eaten, the elder said to our brother, 'Don't be stubborn. Because you were arguing with me, I did not tell you when we were sitting in the village, and I did not reveal it to you. You too must not repeat to anyone what I am going to tell you.'

And he said to him, 'This old man is called Eulogius, and by profession he is a stone-cutter. He labors every day for one *keration*,[34] and fasts until evening, without tasting a thing. Then in the evening he goes to the village, and takes home and feeds every stranger he finds, and whatever they leave he gives to the dogs. He has been doing this up to this very day, and today he is one hundred twenty years old.[35] He works each day for one *keration*.

'When I was young, forty years ago, I went up to sell my handiwork in that village where we were, and in the evening he came and led me off along with the brethren who were with me, in accordance with his custom, and refreshed us strangers. Now when I came to my cell, recognizing this man's excellent way of life, I fasted for two weeks, and I begged God to give him a blessing so he might in this way refresh the brethren just as he pleased. Now when I had fasted for three weeks, I was lying prostrate, as if dead, for more than a day when I saw someone coming towards me in grand clothing. He said to me, "What is up with you, Daniel?" I said, "Sir, I have given my word to Christ that I will not eat any food until he listens to me concerning Eulogius the stonecutter, giving to him in such a way that he can also help others". He said to me, "It is all right". So I said to him, "I ask of you, sir, grant to him what he needs so everyone will praise your holy name because of him". He said to me, "I told you, it is all right. But if you are asking me to give him something, stand surety to me for his soul, that it will be saved amidst many possessions, and then I will give him what he needs". Then I said to him, "Require his soul at my hands".

'I then saw as if we were standing in the Church of the Holy Resurrection,[36] and there was a young man sitting on the Sacred Stone, with Eulogius standing on his right. The young man sent to me one of those standing in his presence, who brought me to him, whereupon he said to me, "Are you the one who has stood surety for Eulogius?" Everyone standing there answered, saying, "Yes, Lord". Again he said, "Tell him, 'Your surety will be required'". I said, "Yes, Lord, at my hands you may require it. But add a blessing for him". Then I saw two of them putting vast riches into Eulogius' lap, and his lap was able to hold whatever they put in it. Then I woke up, and praised God.

'Eulogius went out to his work as usual, and then, when he struck a rock, he heard a sound as if it were hollow. He then found a small hole, struck it again, and found a cave full of gold. In his astonishment he exclaimed, "This gold comes from the Children of Israel; what shall I do? If I take it to the village, the prefect will hear about it and take it away, and I too will fall into great danger. No, I will take it off to some other place where no one recognizes me". Accordingly, he hired camels to carry stones, but in the night he took the gold and conveyed it to the river bank. Thus he brought to an end the good work he was doing, and took a boat and went off to Constantinople.

'At this time the emperor Justin, <uncle>[37] of Justinian, was reigning. Eulogius presented a quantity of gold to the emperor and to all his nobles so he would be made eparch over the whole eparchy. And he bought this large estate which is still today called the estate of the Egyptian. Then it happened that two years later I again saw in my dream that young man in the Holy Church of the Resurrection, and I said to myself, "So where is Eulogius?" After a while I saw an Ethiopian[38] dragging Eulogius, placing him in front of the eyes of the consuls. When I woke up I exclaimed, "Alas for me, wretched sinner that I am! I have destroyed my own soul!" While I was there sunk in thought, I got up and took my basket, and I said to the young man, "I am looking for Eulogius". And I sat down here like someone selling his handiwork, waiting for Eulogius, as was my custom and that of all the brethren.

'When it was evening and had grown very dark, but no one had taken me in, I got up and found an old woman. I said to her, "In faith, mother, give me three rusks[39] so I may eat. I am hungry, for I have not eaten anything today." She said, "I'll give you something". And she went off and brought some cooked food and bread. She sat down beside me and began speaking profitable words, saying, "Don't you realize that you are young? It's not good for you to come to the village. Don't you know that a monk looks for stillness?" She spoke further good words to me, and I said, "What do you think we should do? I have come to sell my handiwork." She said to me, "Even if you are selling your work, don't linger in the village, but if you want to be a monk, go off to Scetis". I said to her, "In faith, keep silent about these stories. Is there no God-fearing person at all in this village who will gather in strangers?" She said to me, "O sir, what have you said! We had here someone who was a stonecutter, and he used to do many good things for strangers, and God saw his works and give him great riches: today he is a patrician."

'When I heard that he had become a patrician, I said to myself, "I am the one who has effected this murder!" I put myself on a ship and then went up to Constantinople. I asked where the house of the Egyptian was, and when they informed me, I sat down by the door of his house until he should emerge. I saw him come out with a large entourage. I called out and said, "Have pity on me and listen to what I wish to say to you!" He did not so much as look at me, but those who were going in front of him were striking me. I said the same thing on every other occasion I was there, but they used to strike me.

'I spent four weeks without being able to approach him. So when he came out to leave, I threw myself down in tears in front of an icon of my Lady Mary, saying "Lord Jesus Christ [. . .], have mercy on me; release me from being surety for this man, otherwise I will go off into the world". And when [. . .] that I saw and beheld with my eyes, I approached the people and heard the cry of a great crowd exclaiming, "Here is the Empress of the world!" Thousands and myriads of people were going in front of her, and I cried out, saying, "My lady, have pity on me!" She said to me, "What is the matter?" I said, "I acted as surety for Eulogius the eparch. Give the order for me to be released from being surety for him". She said, "I am unable to do what you want; fulfill your role as surety".

'I woke up, and then I said, "Even if I have to die, I will not go away from his door without speaking to him!" So I went and sat down by the door of his house. When he passed by, I approached, but the door-keeper made a rush for me and laid into me with blows until my skin was lacerated.[40] I grew faint from the blows, and from the abuse they were hurling at me. Then I said, "I will go to Scetis, and if God so wills, he will deliver both me and Eulogius".

'I then went off and looked for an alexandrian ship, to go to my home country. I found a ship and embarked, in order to return to my cell. Once I had embarked on the ship, I dozed off from my faintness of soul. While I was asleep I saw as though I was in the Church of the Holy Resurrection, and I saw that young man sitting on a stone in front of the Holy Tomb. He looked at me very fiercely, so that out of fear of him my whole body shook; I could not open my mouth, and my heart dried up inside me. He said to me, "Where is your surety?" He then told two of those standing before him to fetter me and suspend me with my hands tied behind my back. He told me, "Do not act as surety for someone who is too much for you. Would you strive with God?" I was unable to open my mouth.

'While I was suspended there, there came a shout, "The Empress has come out!" When I saw her I took heart, and said to her in a humble tone, "Have pity on me, Lady of the world!" She said to me, "What is it you want?" I told her, "It is because I made myself surety for Eulogius that I am hanging here." She said to me, "I will make supplication for you". I saw her go and kiss the feet of that young man [. . .]. Straightaway they took me down from where I was hanging. The young man said to me, "From now on don't do this sort of thing". I said, "No, my Lord. The reason I petitioned you was so that Eulogius might prove all the more diligent. I did wrong: forgive me." He gave orders for them to release me. He told me, "Go off to your cell, and I will bring Eulogius back to his former activity. Don't be distressed." When I awoke, I became full of great joy, seeing that I had been delivered from being surety for Eulogius. I set off by sea, thanking God.

'Three months later the emperor Justin died, and Justinian reigned. Hypatius, <D>exikrates, Pompeius, and Eulogius the eparch rebelled against him.[41] The former three were killed, and all their wealth was plundered, along with the estate of Eulogius and all his fortune. He fled alone by night in the clothes that were on his body, and left Constantinople. The emperor gave orders that wherever Eulogius the Egyptian might be found, he should be put to death. But he escaped and came to his village, where he changed his clothing into that of the villagers. The entire village gathered to see him, saying, "We have heard that you became a patrician", but he told them, "Indeed, if I had become a patrician, would I be seeing you here?" No, it was another Eulogius from the same region. I was praying in Jerusalem."

'So he came to his senses, and said to himself, "O destitute Eulogius, get up, take your iron tools and go off to work; this isn't the palace here! Furthermore, your head won't be removed here!" He took his iron tools and went off to the quarry where he had found the gold, imagining that he might find more gold there. He struck the rock for six hours without finding anything. He began to recall those dishes, that honour, and the deceptive delights that accompanied them, but he said, "Get up and work, Eulogius; here it is Egypt!" Thus little by little he returned to his former custom, through the grace of our Lord Jesus. For God is not unjust so as to forget those former good deeds that he performed.

'After a short time I went up to the village, and when he saw me in the evening, he led me off as was his custom, and when I saw him, I gave a sigh and wept, saying, "What mighty works have you done in the world, O Lord of all, bringing low and raising up.[42] Who can search out your judgements and mighty acts, O Lord God? I have sinned in what I have done wrong: my soul was almost abandoned in Sheol."

'Eulogius took water and washed my feet, in accordance with his former custom. Then he prepared the table. After we had eaten I said to him, "What have you become, Abba Eulogius?" He said to me, "Pray for me, my lord, for I am destitute and possess nothing". But I said to him, "Eulogius, what you had, you will not have again". He said to me, "What, my lord Abba, have I offended you in anything?" I told him, "In what have you not offended me!" Then I told him everything, including the part about the blows with which I was struck by the doorkeeper. And we wept together. He said to me, "Pray that God may send me a blessing; from now on I will make myself worthy". I told him, "Believe me, my lord Eulogius, from now on you should not expect to be entrusted with anything of this in the present world apart from a single *keration* each day".

'During all this time God provides for him and gives him strength as he toils each day for a single *keration*. See how I have told you where I recognized him from?'

The elder's disciple was astonished at all that the elder had endured as a result of being surety for Eulogius. Abba Daniel disclosed these things to his disciple after he had returned from the Thebaid. It falls to us to be amazed at God's mercies, how within a short time he has raised up and brought low in this way, in accordance with our dealings. Pray that we too may be humble in the fear of our Lord Jesus Christ, so that we may find mercy before the awesome tribunal of his majesty, through the prayers of all the saints. Amen.

(III.1) *The Narrative of Abba Daniel Concerning a Monk and His Sister*[43]

1. Abba Daniel used to relate how there was a certain brother who was living in the city of Alexandria, and he had a sister in the flesh. He left her behind in Alexandria and went out to the desert and, having made himself a cell in the mountain,[44] was dwelling there, living a life of praiseworthy conduct. He possessed humility beyond measure. This man's sister, on being abandoned in Alexandria, gave herself over to a loose life, standing publicly in the city playing the harlot, and being the cause of the perdition of many souls.

2. Now when the holy fathers in the desert heard that a great deal of sinful activity was taking place by means of the sister of that brother, they put pressure on him many times to go and rebuke his sister: maybe she would repent and the sin that was occurring because of her would be cut off. This blessed man, overcome by his profound humility, used to say to them, 'How can I rebuke those who are better than me? For I do not know of anyone at all whose sins are as many as mine'.

3. The fathers again replied and said to him, 'Brother, you know what is the sentence decreed against a brother who argues and is disobedient. We now tell you that if you do not go and rebuke your sister, you will be responsible for her sin and the sin of all those who are sinning because of her'.

4. When he heard these words, fear and trembling seized him. He immediately got up, asked for the prayers of the fathers, and travelled to

Alexandria. When he was close to entering the city, one of his acquaintances saw him and ran and told his sister. Now she was with her lovers, with her head uncovered, and no sandals on her feet. When she heard that her brother had come, she was paralyzed with a sense of shame and fear, and she left at once for the city gate to receive her brother.

5. When she saw him and rushed up to embrace him, her brother replied, saying, 'My sister and my lady, what is this that has happened to you? Why do you so despise God's judgements, showing hatred for your own soul, destroying many people as well, and cause grief to my old age too?'

Shaking and trembling, and with tears running from her eyes, she said. 'Alas for me a sinner who is lost, having spent the days of my life in vanity. Now what shall I do? For I am unable to offer up repentance to God, seeing that I have angered him so much'.

6. Her brother said to her, 'Sister, it was for this very reason that Christ our God came into the world—to save sinners.[45] For this was what he said in his life-giving Gospel: "I did not come to call the holy, but the sinners to repentance."'[46]

7. She replied and said to him, 'But who are there, brother, among sinners who resemble me? As for now, I supplicate you, holy man of God, if you know that God will accept the repentance of a woman who is unclean and a prostitute, do not leave me here, but take me with you and I will offer up to God repentance with all my heart.' She then fell at his feet, amid many tears. She refused to get up, but kept saying, 'I will die here in front of these holy feet of yours, unless you promise me that you will take me with you to the desert'.

8. In great joy the blessed man made this promise to her, and she got up from the ground to go with him. He said to her, 'Go back, sister, and cover your head; put sandals on your feet, for the road we are going to travel on is a rough one'. But she did not want to go back, and she said to him, 'As the Lord lives, rather, just as the Lord God brought me to you, so shall I go with you; I will not take with me anything from what belongs to Satan. It is preferable for me to go with you having my hair uncovered than that I should go back and see the riches gotten by wickedness'.

9. On hearing this, her brother rejoiced greatly and, taking her with him, set off for the desert. As they were travelling he encouraged her with many words about repentance, and about the many good things that God has prepared for those who approach him with their whole soul.

10. Her feet were lacerated by the roughness of the road, and much blood flowed from them as a result. She was running along all the time following her brother, soaking the ground with her tears and smiting her breast as she said with a great groan, 'Lord, receive the repentance of your sinful handmaid, just as you received the repentance of the prostitute'.[47]

11. After they had travelled for many days, one day her brother saw some people coming along the road. He said to her, 'My sister and lady, these people who are coming in our direction will not be aware that you are my sister, so turn aside from the road a little and withdraw somewhere until they have passed; otherwise they may be scandalized seeing you with me'.

12. She did as he had told her. Turning aside a little from the road, she found a rock and withdrew behind it. At that very moment she delivered up her spirit to God and slept in peace.

13. Once those people who were coming along the road had passed and gone some distance, her brother then called her, saying, 'Sister, get up, and let us travel on'. When he saw that she did not give any reply, he turned aside from the road and followed the blood that had been flowing from her feet; thus he found her having fallen asleep in peace. In grief he moaned greatly, saying, 'Alas for me, the wretch, who was unable to rescue her soul'.[48]

14. On that very spot he dug a hole and buried her, amidst great mourning. As a result of his great grief and sorrow he dozed off and fell asleep above her grave. In his dream he saw someone like an official sitting in great splendor with many troops standing around him, while peoples and races were being judged in his presence.[49] He then gave orders to those who were standing in his presence, saying, 'Bring before me that prostitute'. Now he was speaking about the sister of that solitary. At once they brought her before him. The solitary also saw an Ethiopian[50] with three other black men with him as he stood there accusing her. He had in his hand a document from which he was reading out her life of prostitution and uncleanness, and the place was filled with the smell of a great stench. Now she was standing with humbled countenance, her face bent down to the ground.

15. Straightaway the official who was sitting on the throne gave orders that the angel of repentance be summoned to his presence. The angel immediately entered with a joyful face, holding in his hand a document.

The resplendent official answered and said to him, 'You too read out what you have seen in this prostitute'. He then began to read out how she had obeyed her brother, and how she had followed him in repentance, bare-footed and with her head uncovered.

16. The Ethiopian, countering him, probed and said, 'Look how long she was with me, continuously doing my will, whereas now it has been only for a few days that she has gone along with you. Do you want to deprive me of her?' Then he stretched out his hand and, along with the men with him, seized her by the hair of her head, wanting to take her off with them in order to torment her.

17. The resplendent person sitting on the seat answered and said to them in anger, 'Do not touch her until her repentance comes too'. Then the angel of repentance came along, his face radiant with joy, holding in his hand a gold box in which were her tears and the blood that had flowed from her feet.

18. The official immediately gave orders saying, 'Bring before me the scales, and weigh her sins against her repentance'. When they had done as he had commanded them, her repentance was heavier and weighed down the balance, whereupon the Ethiopian and those with him fled in great shame.

19. The official straightaway gave orders that her dirty garments and ugly clothes be taken off her, and he bade them clothe her in a luminous robe, whereupon they handed her over to the angel of repentance and put her in a glorious and luminous region.

20. When her brother woke up he rejoiced exceedingly and gave thanks to God. He related all these things to the holy fathers in Scetis, and when they heard them they gave glory to God who does not spurn those who repent, but glorifies those who glorify him,[51] to whom glory, honour, worship, and exaltation is befitting for ever and ever. Amen.

Ended is the narrative of the brother and his sister.

CHAPTER FIVE

Armenian Accounts

Translation (from Latin)

Introduction by Tim Vivian

THE ARMENIAN COLLECTION of stories about Abba Daniel of Scetis preserves nine pieces, five of which exist in two versions. Most of the armenian stories are close to the greek versions: 1 (Mark the Madman) closely resembles the greek text. 2A and 2B (The Holy Mendicant) are both reasonably close to the greek; 2B is closer to Dahlman's greek text than 2A, though it has additions. 3A (The Drunken Nun), except for two additional lines at the end, is reasonably close to the greek version. 3A is closer to Clugnet's text than to Dahlman's, as is 3B, although 3B has more additions. 4 (Andronicus and Athanasia) follows Clugnet's text more closely than Dahlman's, but has numerous differences and additions.[1] It especially follows BN 232; for example (the sentence in italics represents additions in 232):

> The whole city gathered and the patriarch with his clergy and, bringing out the children, they carried them outside the city to the church of the martyr Julian and buried them in the tomb of their parents. *Who can describe such weeping and bitter lamentation, because the whole city was there as a body and everyone was equally afflicted?* The patriarch took Andronicus to the patriarchal residence.

The armenian version of the story of Andronicus and Athanasia also has pro-clerical and pro-monastic additions:

Greek: And they left, both of them weeping. When they reached
the Holy Land, they worshipped there and, joining the company of many fathers, went to the Shrine of Saint Menas near
Alexandria and had the benefit of the martyr.

Armenian: So both of them left together for Jerusalem and,
praying, they visited all the [monastic] communities, and they
saw many holy monks and were blessed by them, and they
gave alms to everyone. From there they went to Alexandria to
the shrine of Saint Menas and the clergy there received them
with honor.

5A (Thomaïs) is very different from the greek version, keeping only the
bare outline of the story. The armenian version adds a 'father', presumably the head of the monastery, who tries to talk the lustful old monk
out of seeing his daughter-in-law. The father and the old monk have
this memorable exchange:

> A father said, 'Do not go into town lest Satan find you'.
> The old man said, 'I am an expert in the Scriptures and an old
> man and I am going to see only my son'.
> The father said, 'You are not more senior than Satan, or more
> expert in the Scriptures than he'.

After the old man kills his daughter-in-law, instead of being sent to
prison and executed, he is brought back to the monastery by its head.
There he does penance, and in a vision the young woman tells him that
because of her intercessions he has been reconciled with God. Except
for the lust and the murder, none of this is in the greek versions. 5B,
except for a moral added at the end, follows Dahlman 4B.

6, the story of the monk bothered by sexual thoughts, follows Dahlman 4B.

7A (Anastasia) is shorter than the principle greek version and has
considerable differences. 7B follows the greek more closely and has
longer readings adopted by Clugnet in his edition rather than the text
preferred by Dahlman.

8A (Eulogius) is very truncated. The disciple is missing entirely, as
are virtually all narrative details. 8B follows the greek version fairly
closely, with some additions.

9A (A Monk in a Tomb) follows the greek, whereas 9B does not name Daniel and tacks on a moral at the end.

The Armenian collection completely lacks the extra coptic and ethiopic material.

SYNOPTIC TABLE

Greek	*Armenian*[2]
1. Mark the Madman (I.1)	Leloir, II (*Tractatus* V-IX); V (*De fornicatione*) 47 R.
2. The Holy Mendicant (I.3)	Leloir, IV (*Tractatus* XVI-XIX), XVIII (*De thaumaturgis patribus*), 43
3. The Drunken Nun (I.4)	Leloir, II (*Tractatus* V-IX), VIII (*Contra ostentationem*), 3.
4. Andronicus and Athanasia (I.5)	Leloir, II (*Tractatus* V-IX); VII (*De sustinentia*) 49 R.
5. Concerning Thomaïs (I.6)	Leloir, II (*Tractatus* V-IX); V (*De fornicatione*) 30.
6. A Monk Receives a Blessing (I.7)	Leloir, II (*Tractatus* V-IX); V (*De fornicatione*) 36 R.
7. The Patrician Lady Anastasia (I.8)	Leloir II (*Tractates* V-IX) VII (*De sustinentia*) 40A & B.
8. Eulogius (I.9)	Leloir III (*Tractatus* X-XV) XIII (*De hospitalite et misericordia*) 10.
9. A Monk in a Tomb (II.1)	Leloir III (*Tractatus* X-XV), XII (*De oratione*) 11A & B.[3]

Numbers in parentheses in the *Greek* column indicate the numbering of the stories in Chapter One: *The Greek Dossier.*

ARMENIAN ACCOUNTS

1. *Mark the Madman* (Gk I.1 Mark the Fool)[4]

There was a certain old man in Scetis whose name was Daniel, and he had a disciple, and there lived with that disciple a certain other brother whose name was Sergi.[5] After a while, Sergi departed to the Lord. After Sergi's death, the old man placed his trust in his disciple, to have him live with him, because he loved him.

One day, the old man, taking his disciple with him, left for Alexandria because it was customary for the superiors of Scetis to go see the patriarch for Easter. They arrived in the city about five in the afternoon and, as they walked about on the street, Daniel saw there a certain naked brother who wore only a small piece of cloth over his privates. That brother acted as though he were crazy. There were other madmen with him, and that brother would go along in front of them as if he were insane and would snatch things from the business stalls and give them to the other madmen. He was called 'Mark of the Horse' and was a 'horseman' at the public bath called 'The Horse'. There Mark the Madman would stand and there he would sit at night, and he earned each day one hundred drachmas and he slept sitting on a bench. From the one hundred drachmas he would buy necessities with ten drachmas and the rest he would give to his mad friends. The whole city of Alexandria knew about Mark on account of his demented madness.

The old man said to his disciple, 'Go see where Mark the madman is living'. He went and asked and found out and came back and told the old man that that madman had lived in the hippodrome a long time. The old man went to see the patriarch and stayed at the patriarchal residence. The next day, when the old man left the patriarch's, by divine dispensation Mark the Madman met him at the Great Gate. Hurrying, the old man took hold of him and began saying in a loud voice, 'Men of Alexandria, help me!' The madman, however, made fun of him and the whole city congregated there. The old man's disciple stood at a distance and watched in fear. Others were saying, 'Don't be insulted, father: he's mad and insane'. The old man said, 'It is we who are mad and insane, children. I have not found anyone in this city better than this fellow'.

Then some clergy from the church who knew the old man came and said, 'What has this madman ever done to harm you, father?' The old man said to them, 'Take this fellow behind me to the patriarch, because there is not in this city today such a holy vessel as he'. The patriarch recognized that this had been revealed to the old man by God and he fell at the madman's feet and adjured and implored him and said, 'Tell us about yourself and the work you are doing'.

Giving in to their request, and coming to himself, he said to them, 'I was a monk and was ruled by the demon of sexual sin for sixteen years. Coming to my senses, I said, "Mark, you wretch, for sixteen years you've been a slave to the Enemy.[6] So go now and likewise serve Christ your King". So I went to the Pempton Monastery and remained there eight years in a deep ditch, and after eight years I said to myself, "Mark, you poor fellow, go to the City and there be a madman another eight years". See, today my eight years of madness are completed'. When they heard this from him, all of them wept over what he had said.

After Mark had told his story, he fell asleep in death that day near the old man in the home of the patriarch. Early in the morning, when they saw that Mark had gone to sleep and was lying dead, the old man told the patriarch and the patriarch explained matters to the ruler and the ruler ordered business to stop and the whole city gathered there. The old man sent his disciple to Scetis and said, 'Gather all the brothers and tell them what has happened so they may come here and be blessed by him'.

All of Scetis came, dressed in white, bearing palm branches in their hands. The Enaton[7] and Kellia did likewise, and those in the monastic settlements of Nitria and all the lavras around Alexandria. Such a large multitude of monks gathered that they were not able to bury Mark's body for five days. The city of Alexandria, likewise gathering with palm branches, watered the face of the earth with its tears. And so they bore out of the city for burial the remains of blessed Mark the Madman, and they glorified God, who gives grace and abstinence to all who run to him.

2. A. *A Holy Mendicant* (Gk I.3)[8]

Abba Daniel, along with his disciples,[9] went to Alexandria and saw a blind man who, sitting naked in the street, was saying, 'Give me something; have pity', and the old man said to his disciples, 'Do you see this blind man? He is a great man. I want to show you his way of life'. Going over to him, the old man said, 'Do me a favor. I don't have the means to buy myself palm branches so I may [work and] feed myself', and the blind man said to him, 'What are you saying, abba? You see me naked and begging, and you say to me, "Give me something with which I may buy palm branches so I may eat"? Nevertheless, wait here a minute'.

The old man motioned to his disciple and they went to Saint Mark's Outside-the-City (that blind man had a dwelling there) and the blind man said to the old man, 'Wait for me here, abba', and going to his cell he brought out to the old man a small basket: in it were raisins and figs and pomegranates; also in that basket were three gold coins. Taking a silver coin out of his mouth, he gave it to the father and said to him, 'Pray for me'. The old man went to his disciple, wept, and said, 'How many hidden servants God has! As the Lord lives, I will never turn my back on any blessing that this man offers!' And they left.

At that time the steward of the cathedral fell ill and was suffering terribly in his side and was lying down in the Church of Saint Mark. Saint Mark the apostle appeared to him and said, 'Bring[10] the blind man and let him place his hand on you and make you well'. He sent for his sons and they forcibly brought the blind man. When he placed his hands on the steward, the steward was immediately made well.

News of what had happened spread throughout the city and when the patriarch heard about it he got up in order to go see the blind man and found him going to the Lord. They heard about this in Scetis and the old man went up to Alexandria, along with his disciple, and many other fathers followed in order to receive the old man's blessing. And the whole city gathered there, with much praise, and they buried the blind man next to Abba Mark, who had been a fool for Christ.[11] And this was the blind man's way of life: Whenever people asked him for alms, he would buy something from passersby and give it to the sick. After thirty-eight years, he completed his life.

2B. One time Father Daniel and his disciple went up to Alexandria, and the old man saw a blind and naked man lying in the street, and he was crying out and saying, 'Give alms to me!' The old man said to his disciple, 'Do you see this blind man? I tell you, my son, that he is a great man. If you want to see, I will show you. Stay here and wait for me'. The old man went and said to the blind man, 'Do me a favor, father. I don't have the means to buy palm branches so I may work and feed myself'. The blind man said to him, 'Why are you looking at *me*, father? You see me blind and naked and you still make requests of me? But wait here a minute'.

Then the old man and his disciple went with him outside the city to the Church of Mark the Evangelist, following the blind man, for his cell was there. The blind man said to the old man, 'Stay here and wait for me', and he went inside his cell, brought his bag to the old man and gave it to him; in it were raisins and a kind of pomegranate and figs and three gold coins. And he took out of his mouth three other gold coins and gave them to the old man and said, 'Pray for me, father'. The old man went to his disciple and wailed and said, 'Do you see, my son, how many servants of God are hidden from sight? As the Lord lives, I will never turn my back on this man's gold, because that is what love is'.

A few days later, the patriarch's steward grew ill with fierce pains in his liver and Mark the evangelist appeared to him and said to him, 'Send for such-and-such blind man, and let him place his hand where your liver hurts and you will be healed there'. So the steward sent his servants and they brought the blind man by entreaty and force and when he prayed and placed his hand over the afflicted spot, the steward was immediately made well. The blind man quickly left: he was a man of God and returned to his cell.

What had happened spread throughout the city and when the patriarch heard about it, he left and went to see the blind man and when he came he found that the blind man had died. The whole city heard about his death, and Scetis too, and the old man went up to Alexandria, and many of the fathers with him, and they went to the blind man's tomb and were blessed by that blessed man. Bearing his corpse, praying and glorifying God over and over, they placed him in the tomb of Mark the Madman.[12] This was his life: He would take whatsoever came his way in the form of almsgiving on any given day and use what he needed that day and with the remainder he would buy apples, pomegranates, and raisins and distribute them to the sick in the hospitals. He kept up this work for forty-eight years. Indeed, he would beg on behalf of the indigent while he himself remained abstinent and was crowned with virtue in the contest.

3A. *The Drunken Nun* (Gk I.4)[13]

Abba Daniel of Scetis arose one time with his disciple and went to the Upper Thebaid for the feast day of Abba Apollo. The fathers came out to meet him for seven miles around and there were upwards of five thousand of them. Their appearance was that of choirs of angels expecting Christ, gathered together on the sand. Certain fathers were spreading out their clothing before him while others were spreading out their cowls, pouring forth tears like rivulets from a fountain. The head of the lauras came and venerated Abba Daniel seven times as he approached him. After they had greeted one another, the brothers begged to hear some word from him, since the father would not readily speak with anyone.

So they stayed there outside on the sand, since the church would not hold them. And Abba Daniel said to his disciple, 'Write this: "If you want to live, pay serious attention to yourselves and pursue poverty and silence, for the monastic way of life depends on these two, the complete source of strength for the solitary"'. So his disciple gave what he had written to a certain brother and the brother translated it into Coptic. All of them were made captive by what the old man had said and said goodbye to him, escorting him off. No one dared to say 'Please, do us the favor of staying'.

The old man went to Hermopolis and said to his disciple, 'Go, knock at the monastery for virgins and tell the mother superior I am here'. There was a monastery called the Monastery of Abba Jeremiah; there were about three hundred souls living there. The disciple left, knocked, and the doorkeeper said to him, 'How are you? We are pleased that you have come. What is your command?'

He said to her, 'I wish to speak with the mother superior'.

She said, 'She never speaks with anyone; but tell me what you command and I will tell her'.

He said, 'Tell her, "A certain solitary wishes to speak with you"'.

She left and told the mother superior everything he had said and returned and said to him in a faint voice, 'The mother superior ordered me to ask "What is your request?"'

The brother said, 'I wish you to do us a favor and give us lodging, for me and for the other old man, since it is night: we are afraid that if we spend the night in the fields the wild beasts will eat us'.

The mother superior said to him, 'No man has ever entered here. It would be better if the wild beasts outside devoured you rather than the ones inside'.

Then the brother said, 'It is Abba Daniel'.

When she heard this, they immediately opened the two doors of the gate and she came hurrying out, with the whole community, and they spread their outer garments from the door out to where the old man was, rolling themselves at his feet and kissing the soles of his feet.

After they had taken Abba Daniel and his disciple inside the monastery, they brought a basin and poured warm water into it, with fragrant herbs, and stood the sisters in two rows and they washed the feet of the old man and those of his disciple. They took earthenware jugs and gave them to the sisters and, holding their heads above the basin, poured water from the pitchers over their heads. Afterwards, the mother superior herself took a pitcher and poured water over her head. They looked like stones, not moving or speaking, and when they gathered together all their movements were those of angels. The old man said to the mother superior, 'The sisters do us wrong if they are always like this', and she said, 'Your servants are always like this. But pray for them'. The abba said, 'May the Lord bring these sisters life'.

One of the sisters, clothed in sackcloth, lay in the middle of the courtyard sleeping. The old man said, 'Who is this sleeping?' One of the sisters said, 'She is a drunk, and we don't know what to do with her. If we throw her out of the monastery, we are afraid of sinning, and if we take pity on her and let her stay, she makes the sisters sad'. The old man said to his disciple, 'Take the basin of water and pour it over her', and he did so. She staggered as if she were drunk and got up. The mother superior said, 'Lord, this is how she always is'.

After this, the mother of the monastery took the old man and led him to the refectory for dinner. After gathering the sisters, she said to the old man, 'Bless your servants so they may eat in your presence' and he blessed them. When they sat down together at the table, only she and her second-in-command sat with the old man. They set before the old man a bowl with moistened raw vegetables and dates and water and to his disciple they served warm lentils and a small loaf of bread and wine. To the sisters they served fish and wine in abundance. They ate very well and no one spoke at all. After they left for the church, giving thanks, the old man said to the mother superior, 'What is this you have done?

I would have preferred for us to eat fish and the foods that you ate'. The mother superior said to the old man, 'You are a solitary, and I served you a solitary's food; your disciple is a solitary's disciple and I set before him a disciple's food. We are ordinary monastics and we ate ordinary food'. The old man said, 'May your charity be remembered. You have helped us'.

When the sisters left to go to bed, Abba Daniel said to his disciple, 'Go see where the drunk sleeps'. He went and [returned and] said to the old man, 'She's by the exit to the toilets'. The old man said to his disciple, 'Keep watch with me this night'. When all the sisters had gone to sleep, the old man took his disciple and stood behind a lattice. The reputed drunk stood up and stretched her hands to heaven and tears gathered and flowed like a river; she fell to the ground and knelt down. Whenever she perceived one of the sisters coming to use the toilet, she threw herself down on the ground and snored. This was her pattern living in their midst. Then the old man said to his disciple, 'Call the mother superior for me quietly, with her second-in-command too'. They came and spent the whole night watching to see what she would do. The old man said, 'God loves drunks like this, and it's on her account that I have come here'.[14] The mother superior began to weep and said, 'Oh! How much abuse we've heaped on her!' When the signal sounded to mark the hour, a rumor concerning her spread among the sisters. She, however, secretly went to where the old man was sleeping, took his staff, and left the monastery. She wrote on the gate: 'Pray for me, and forgive me for whatever I have done to sadden you', and she disappeared.

They looked for her but did not find her and, finding the gate open and her note, the monastery erupted into weeping and the whole community confessed to the old man what they had done to her. The old man offered prayer for the sisters and returned with his disciple to his place in the desert, glorifying God for the way in which he alone knows how many servants he has. So too with this woman, who never tasted wine and yet appeared to be a drunkard. May we, since we have nothing good, beseech God for the goodness possessed by those servants of his.[15]

3B. One time mighty Daniel left Scetis with his disciple for the Upper Thebaid on the feast day of Father Apollo. All the fathers gathered and came out from seven *stades* around to meet him and there were about five thousand of them. They seemed to him to be like angels and all of them fell on their faces with fear and reverence and welcomed him as though he were Christ the Lord. Some of them were spreading out their clothing before him as he walked while others were adding their cowls to the clothing and still others were bearing palm branches. There seemed to be a fountain of tears there, like flowing, inundating streams of water. Their archimandrite came and venerated the old man seven times before he reached him. After they greeted one another, they sat down.

Then the archimandrite implored the old man, that he might hear words of life from his mouth, for the old man did not readily speak to anyone. So all of them sat outside the monastery on the ground, since the monastery would not hold them. Then Father Daniel said to his disciple, 'Write and say this to the fathers: "If you want to live, acquire poverty and silence, for a monk's whole life depends on these two virtues"'. So the disciple wrote this down and gave what he had written to one of the brothers to translate into Coptic since it had been written in Greek. This was done and when all the fathers read and heard what had been written, they wept exceedingly and they accompanied the old man off, displaying great sorrow in leaving him, and no one dared say to him, 'Do us the favor of staying'.

Afterwards, the old man Daniel went to the city of Hermopolis, and he said to his disciple, 'Go to the monastery for women and tell the deaconess that I am here', for there was a monastery for women there called the Monastery of Jeremiah, in which three hundred sisters lived. So the old man's disciple went and knocked on the door of the monastery. The doorkeeper within said in a quiet voice, 'It is good that you have come. What is your request?'

The brother said to her, 'Call for me your mother superior. I have something to say to her'.

The doorkeeper said, 'She never speaks to anyone, but tell me what you want to say to her and I will tell her'.

The brother said, 'Tell her, "A monk wants to speak with you"'.

The doorkeeper left and told her, and she sent him her second-in-command and she came and said, 'The deaconess sent me and said to say to you, "Who are you, and what do you want?"'

The brother said, 'Please do me a favor and give us lodging here; it's getting late'.

The deaconess said, 'No man has ever entered here; it would be better for you if the wild beasts outside ate you rather than those inside'.

Then the brother said, 'Father Daniel of Scetis is here'.

When she heard this, one sister opened the two doors of the monastery and she quickly came out to meet him, along with a multitude of sisters, and they spread the cords from their cassocks on the road from the monastery door to the church and they kissed the old man's feet and wiped the dust from his sandals.

When they entered the monastery, the mother superior personally took a serving bowl and a jug and filled the bowl with warm water and fragrant flowers and stood the sisters in two choirs and she washed the feet of the old man and his disciple. Then the mother superior took the water for washing and poured it over each of the sisters and after all of them she poured it over her own head. The sisters had the appearance of unmoving stone and incorporeal angels standing silent without uttering a word. Truly, they signaled to each other with only a few signs when it was necessary to work. The old man said to the deaconess, 'Are these sisters honoring us, or do they always stand mute and silent like this?' The mother superior said, 'They are always like this, father, but pray for them'. The old man said, 'May the Lord with his compassion bring these sisters life'.

One of the sisters lay asleep in the middle of the monastery, covered with torn sackcloth. The old man said concerning her, 'Who is this, so wild and forlorn, who lies sleeping here?' One of the sisters said to him, 'She is a fool, father, and is always listless, and we don't know what to do with her: if we throw her out of there, it will count as a sin against us, so we let her stay; and if we allow her to stay here, she makes the sisters feel ashamed in the eyes of guests. The old man said to his disciple, 'Take a cup and throw water on her'. When they threw water on her, she got up as though she were a drunk. The mother superior said to the old man, 'She is always acting foolish like this, father'.

The mother superior of the monastery then led the old man to dinner and all the sisters came at the same time and the old man celebrated an *agapē* for everyone and the mother superior said to the old man, 'Bless these your servants, lord, so they may eat the *agapē* in your presence'. The old man blessed them and only the mother and her second-in-command sat with the old man while the other sisters sat separately at dinner. And she set before the old man soaked lentils and raw, uncooked vegetables and dates and a flask of water. She served the old man's disciple cooked lentils and bread and wine mixed with warm water. She served the sisters various dishes and fish and wine; they dined well and everyone ate and no one spoke.

After they got up from the table, the old man said to the deaconess, 'What is this you've done? The good food should have gone to us as guests and the food of lesser quality to you, but you and the sisters ate the good food'.

The mother of the monastery said to him, 'You are monks and we served you food befitting a fighter; your disciple is an old man's disciple and we served him food appropriate to his station. We, however, are novices and ate food appropriate for those who are weak, just as it was appropriate for us to dine and be strengthened in celebration of your arrival'.

The old man said, 'We will certainly remember your charity, for we have profited greatly from it'.

When the sisters left to rest and go to sleep, Father Daniel said to his disciple, 'Go see where the listless and foolish sister who was lying in the courtyard sleeps'.

The brother went, looked, and returned and told the old man, 'She's lying sluggishly by the door to the latrines'.

The old man said to his disciple, 'Keep watch with me and keep vigil this night', and when everyone had gone to sleep, the old man and his disciple got up and left and stood secretly behind a lattice and watched that listless sister: she would stand up and stretch her hands to heaven and tears flowed from her eyes like flooding waters and her lips moved in prayer but not a whisper was heard from her mouth; she sighed and groaned and fell on her face. When she perceived that one of the sisters was coming from anywhere to take care of the body's business, she immediately fell to the ground and started snoring. She did this all night and stood this way every day of her life, and no one knew about it.

The old man said to his disciple, 'Go secretly and call here the deaconess and her second-in-command', so he went and called them. And they came and watched all night and saw what she was doing. The mother superior began to weep and say, 'Woe is me! How often I've treated this woman badly!'

When the hour for prayer arrived, the whole community of sisters heard about her and fear spread through the monastery. That holy woman, however, perceived it before daybreak and secretly went where the old man was sleeping and stole the old man's cloak and staff. She silently opened the monastery door and, writing a letter, placed it at the door to the monastery and here is what it said: 'Pray for me, and forgive me whatever sins I have committed against you'. And going out, she left and disappeared.

When dawn came, they looked for her but nobody could find her. Then they brought the letter they had found at the monastery door and read it and great weeping and wailing erupted in that monastery among the sisters. The old man said to them, 'This was the reason I came here, because God has chosen fools such as this woman and loves them'.[16] Then they began to tell the old man how many bad things each of them had done to her. The old man offered prayer for them, left, and withdrew to his cell.

4. *Andronicus and Athanasia* (Gk I.5)[17]

There was a certain moneychanger in the city of Antioch, a young man, whose name was Andronicus. He had a noble wife, whose name was Athanasia. Both had been brought up in the fear of God from the time they were children and had accomplished numerous good works, and the two of them were very wealthy. This was their way of life: they divided all their wealth into three parts—one part for the poor, another part for the monks and clergy, and one for their own needs and the needs of their servants. The whole city and its rulers loved them and the patriarch loved Andronicus on account of his clemency and beneficence and sanctity and multitudinous virtues.

Andronicus' wife bore him a son, and they named him John; she had already borne a daughter, and they named her Mary. Both of them then vowed themselves to God and no longer knew one another sexually; they both vowed to God to live in chastity in accordance with the monastic way of life until their children grew up and inherited their parents' estate and then to withdraw [to the desert]; and this was the will of God. All of their care and concern was in doing acts of mercy for the poor and serving the clergy and monks. On the holy day of the Lord,[18] from evening on they passed the night in vigil in prayer in the church and in giving gifts to the poor and the priests and the monks. They fasted on Tuesdays and Thursdays and Saturdays, and from morning until evening they walked through the streets of the city, the hospitals and prisons, and fed and filled the hands of the poor and the sick and the captive.[19] Such was their way of life for many years.

One day after twelve years Athanasia returned home worn out from ministering to the sick; entering the house, she found her children burning up with fever and near death, for they were groaning in bed with labored breathing. She got into bed with them and sat grieving until she fell asleep. When Andronicus came home from the church, he saw his wife grieving and his children burning up with fever. When he touched the children and saw that they were boiling with fever and burning hot, he was stunned and sighed and said, 'May God's will be done in everything'. He immediately left the city for the church of the martyr Julian, where the tomb of his parents was, and stood vigil for six hours, weeping and praying. When he returned home, he heard great wailing and lamentation: in the middle of the night both children had died at the same time and the whole city was gathered there mourning them. When he saw his children lying lifeless together, placed atop boards, he went into his bedroom, knelt down before an image of the Saviour and, weeping, said, 'Naked I came from my mother's womb and naked shall I return there. The Lord gave; the Lord has taken away. Let it be as has seemed best to the Lord'.[20] The children's mother, however, was trying to strangle herself and said, 'Bury me as a mother with my children!'

The whole city gathered, the patriarch with his clergy too, and, bringing out the children, they carried them outside the city to the church of the martyr Julian and buried them in the tomb of their parents. Who can describe such weeping and bitter lamentation? The whole city was there as a body and everyone was equally afflicted. The patriarch took Andronicus to the patriarchal residence. The children's mother, however, refused to go home but instead remained in the church of the martyr Julian at her children's sepulcher and wept. In the middle of the night the holy martyr Julian appeared to her, dressed as a monk, and said to her, 'Why, mother, do you not let sleep those who are here?'

She replied, saying, 'Do not be angry with me, my lord, since my heart is grieving. I had only two children and today I buried both of them together'.

The holy martyr said, 'How old were they?'

She said, 'One was twelve and the other ten'.

The holy martyr said, 'Why do you weep this way, since they are innocent and holy, instead of weeping for your own sins? I tell you, mother, just as a person requires food in order to live and it is impossible for that person not to give himself something to eat, so too will your children come before Christ [to ask for] the good things to come and they will say to him, "Holy and righteous Judge and Lord, you deprived us of the good things of this life, but do not deprive us of your kingdom", and he will give then what they ask for'.

Saying this, the monk withdrew in a vision. When Athanasia heard this, she was comforted and said, 'Since my children are in the kingdom of heaven, why am I mourning like this? And what will I gain by weeping for their deaths?' So she got up and looked for the monk but did not find him; the doors of the church were closed and, while looking for the monk, she heard a voice from the altar say, 'He is Julian the martyr, not just some old man'.

Joyfully giving thanks for the vision, she went home and told Andronicus about the vision, saying, 'In truth, believe me: while the children were alive I wanted to speak to you every day about this matter and was embarassed to do so for I had to wait for my children to grow up. It has now been ten years—I swear to God—and now I will say to you, "Listen to your servant and put me in a monastery for women that I may be a monk and there weep for my sins"'.

Andronicus said to her, 'Think for a week about what you have said. If you are still resolved to do this, we will do whatever is appropriate'.

And this they did. A week later she returned and said the same thing. Then Andronicus called his father, John,[21] and said, 'We are leaving for Jerusalem in order to pray at the holy places there so I am placing all our possessions in your hands. If we happen to die, if you take care of us and our possessions you will have your reward from God here and in the future. Now I want you to build hospitals and lodgings and a monastery here where our house is'. And Andronicus entrusted all his possessions to him and, taking part of their possessions with them, along with two horses, they left the city at night.

As they left, Athanasia looked back at her home, raised her eyes to heaven, and said, 'God, who told Abraham and Sarah to leave their land and people and home,[22] you have done the same with us. Now, Lord, lead us in your fear, because on account of your name we have left open the doors to our home. Do not close to us the doors to your kingdom'.

So both of them left together for Jerusalem and, praying, they visited all the [monastic] communities, and they saw many holy monks and were blessed by them, and they gave alms to everyone. From there they went to Alexandria to the shrine of Saint Menas and the clergy there received them with honor.

At three o'clock in the afternoon Andronicus left the refectory and was looking about in the city when he saw a monk arguing with someone. Andronicus said to the man, 'Why are you upset with the monk and harassing him?'

That man said, 'He hired my animal to take him to Scetis, and I said to him, "Come on, let's leave at night lest we roast in the heat, but he doesn't want to go'.

Andronicus said to him, 'Do you have another animal?'

He said, 'Yes, I do, father'.

Andronicus said to him, 'Go, bring it here and I will hire it and we will go together, because I too am on my way to Scetis'. Andronicus returned [to the shrine] and said to Athanasia, 'Stay here at Saint Menas until I go up to Scetis and pray there and see the fathers and return'.

The woman said to him, 'Take me with you'.

Andronicus responded, saying, 'A woman cannot enter Scetis'.

Weeping, she said to him, 'You will have to answer to God and Saint Menas if you do not return and place me in a monastery for women'. Then they kissed one another goodbye.

So Andronicus left and went up to Scetis and saw all the holy fathers living in the lauras of the monastic community, and he went to Father Daniel in the desert; with great weariness and much effort he was able to see him and he told the old man everything. The old man said to him, 'Go and bring your wife here and I will write a letter for you so you can take her to the Thebaid to the monastery for women in Tabennisi'.

Then Andronicus did as the father had told him and he left and brought Athanasia to the old man. The old man spoke life-giving words to her and sent her to the monastery for virgins. And Andronicus returned to Father Daniel and the father clothed Andronicus in the monastic habit and taught him about the monastic life and Andronicus remained with the old man twelve years. After twelve years, Andronicus asked the old man if he could go and pray in the holy places of Jerusalem. The old man warmly kissed him, offered a prayer for him, and sent him off.

It happened that while Andronicus was traveling within the borders of Egypt he sat in the heat of summer in a place filled with bramble bushes in order to get a little relief from the harsh heat. Suddenly, through the will of God, Athanasia came, dressed in men's clothing; she too was leaving for Jerusalem. They questioned one another and the dove recognized her mate. Andronicus, however, did not recognize her, whose appearance and beauty had wasted away from so many austerities and whose skin had turned black like an Ethiopian's. Athanasia said to him, 'Where are you going, father?' and he said, 'To Jerusalem; I am leaving to see the holy places of the Lord'.

She said to him, 'I too am traveling there and, if you want, let the two of us go together, but let us go in silence so that we say nothing at all'.

Andronicus said, 'Let us do as you say'.

Athanasia (for this was her name) said, 'Aren't you the disciple of Father Daniel?' and he said, 'Yes, indeed'.

Athanasia said, 'And isn't your name Andronicus?'

He said, 'Yes, it is'.

She said, 'The old man's prayer will be our helper'.

Andronicus said, 'Amen'.

So they traveled together. Arriving in Jerusalem, they prayed at all the holy places and returned to Alexandria without saying a word to one another. Athanasia said to Father Andronicus, 'If you want, we will live together', and Andronicus said, 'Let us do as you say', since he thought she was a eunuch. He added, 'First I want to go up to Scetis and ask my father about it'.

Athanasia said, 'Go, and I will wait for you at the Duodecim monastery.[23] But if you return, let us keep the same silence that we maintained on the road: let us stay together and never say a word. If you cannot be silent, however, do not return here, for I want to live at the Oktokaidekaton'.

So Andronicus left and saw his father and told him everything the eunuch had said. Father Daniel said to him, 'Go and stay with him and keep silence, for he is a great fighter'. When Andronicus returned and found Athanasia, they lived together, relying on the fear of God, for twelve years. Neither one spoke to the other, nor did Andronicus discover who she was.

Father Daniel would go to see them occasionally and would speak with them to their profit and then return. One time when he went to visit them, after he had said goodbye to them and left, he went to Saint Menas. Andronicus caught up with him and said, 'Father, Brother Athanasius is ill; he is going to the Lord and asks for you'. When the old man heard this, he turned around and came and found her with a violent fever and weeping bitterly. The old man said to her, 'You should be rejoicing that you are going to the Lord, and you are wailing like this?'

Athanasius said, 'I am not wailing for myself, father, but for Andronicus. When you bury me, you will find a note at my head; take it and read it and give it to Brother Andronicus'.

So Athanasia partook of the Sacred Mystery[24] and after these words slept the sleep of the righteous. When the brothers came to wrap her for burial, they discovered that she was a woman. The old man, reading the note, gave it to Andronicus. When Andronicus realized from the note that Athanasia was his wife and was not a eunuch, he blessed the Lord and they gave thanks to him for giving endurance to his servants in everything. News of what had happened spread through all the lavras and the old man summoned [all the monks of] Scetis and all the monks of Scetis came, dressed in white. Whole bands of monks came there with palm branches and, carrying [the body of Athanasia] with honor, they placed her in the tomb of the fathers and gave thanks to God who gave such virtue and fortitude to the female body. And everyone returned home. Father [Daniel], however, remained seven days at the tomb of Athanasia.[25]

Afterwards, Father Daniel wanted to take Andronicus with him, but he refused to go with him and said, 'I will die on top of Athanasia's sepulcher'. Then Father Daniel said goodbye and went to Saint Menas. When he arrived there, another brother caught up with him and said to him, 'Father Daniel, Brother Andronicus is going to God'. When the old man heard this, he informed [the monks of] Scetis and said, 'Let us travel there, for Elder Andronicus is following Elder Athanasia'. When the brothers heard this, they immediately went up and found him still alive and received his blessing and he went to sleep in peace in the Lord.

Then war broke out between the fathers of Scetis and of that lavra called Oktokaidekaton where the saints had been perfected. The monks of Scetis were saying, 'The brother is ours; we are going to take his body to Scetis'.

The brothers of Oktokaidekaton, however, were saying, 'He ordered us to bury him with his sister'.

The monks of Scetis were numerous and they were battling for Andronicus' body. Then all the monastic leaders said, 'Let them do whatever Father Daniel says'.

Father [Daniel] said, 'The brother entrusted me with burying him here'.

The old men of Scetis rejected this and were saying, 'Father Daniel is in heaven and does not fear warfare with the demons, but we fear it. We have among us inexperienced monks and it is necessary for Andronicus to be near us, that he may help us. His sister Athanasia should be enough for you, for she is here with you'.

When Father Daniel saw the quarrel, he said to the brothers, 'If you do not leave him here, I will not return with you but will stay with my children and will be buried with them'.

When the brothers heard this, they were silent and they brought out Blessed Andronicus and buried him with Saint Athanasia. Then the brothers said to Father Daniel, 'Come, let us leave for Scetis', and he said, 'Allow me to complete here his seven days of mourning'. They did not allow him to do this but took him and left.

Father Daniel told this story to his disciples.

Let us entreat the Lord to have mercy on us too, through the prayer and intercession of Andronicus and Athanasia and of all the saints. Wondrous are their acts of courage and endurance and their love of God.

5A. *Concerning Thomaïs* (Gk I.6)[26]

A monk at the Oktokaidekaton Monastery had a son who had a wife and the monk frequently went to visit his son.

A father said, 'Do not go into town lest Satan find you'.

The old man said, 'I am an expert in the Scriptures and an old man and I am going to see only my son'.

The father said, 'You are not more senior than Satan, or more expert in the Scriptures than he'.

When the old man would not agree to stay, the father took him to the brothers and said, 'With you as witnesses, I am innocent of this old man's blood.[27] If he wants to eat a little food, I will not prevent him. I have no answer to give God for him; I will not be a witness to what he is doing'.

One day, the old man went to his son's home, found his son's wife alone, lusted after her, and said, 'Come, be with me'.

The young woman said, 'Fear God and consider your position. What you are saying is no small evil. Crucify what is causing these feelings in you and put away Satan'.

When the young woman would not give in to the old man, he struck her with a sword and killed her and was himself struck blind. Neighbors came and saw what had happened. The old man said, 'Woe is me! Because of fornication I killed my sweet daughter, and I have been struck blind'.

They took him to the ruler and, after severely torturing him, put him in prison. Word of what had happened reached the monastery. The father came and took the old man back to the monastery and they buried the holy young woman with great honor. In a vision they said to the father, 'If any of the brothers here is disturbed by an evil thought, send him to the tomb of Christ's young woman and there let him pray and be healed'. This they did, and great happiness came about because of it.[28]

After having done two years of penance, the old man washed away his sins through hard work and tears and the young woman appeared in a vision to the father and said, 'Tell the old man for me not to be sad. He has reconciled with God because I interceded for him'. From that time on the father did not allow a single monk to go anywhere, not even for a short while.

5B. One of the fathers went with his disciple to Alexandria and while he was there the following occurred: a monk lived there in Alexandria in the Duokaidekaton Monastery.[29] He had a son who lived in the world who had a very beautiful wife, twelve years old,[30] and she lived with her husband, who was a fisherman. But the Demon who from the beginning has been the enemy of our souls was waging war against the old father by stirring up in him the desire for fornication with his son's young wife and he was looking for an opportunity to have sexual intercourse with her and did not succeed. He would frequently kiss her and embrace and hug her. She, however, with a pure heart accepted his attentions as from a father in the flesh.

One day some other fishermen came by and called the young man so they could go out at night and catch fish. When the young man left, the young man's father got up and stood over his son's wife and tried to force her to sin. The young woman said to him, 'What is this, father? Go to your room and make the sign of the cross on your face and over your heart, for what you are doing is some work of the Devil'.

But he refused to leave and struggled violently with her and beat her but the young woman did not allow him access to herself. Hanging at the head of his bed was a double-edged sword belonging to his son; taking it, he unsheathed it as though he were going to frighten her. He brandished the sword above her and said, 'If you do not obey me and do what I want, I will kill you with this sword'.

The young woman said to him, 'Even if you tear me apart by mangling all my joints, I will not commit this iniquitous sin!'

He immediately became agitated and, drunk with rage through the deception of the Evil One,[31] violently struck the young woman in the stomach and cut her in two. The Lord immediately struck him blind. He attempted to leave and go away but was not able to find the door to the house in order to exit.

After this had happened, some other fishermen came and called his son to come fishing with them. The young man's father said to them, 'He left in the evening to go fishing but show me the door because I can not see it'.

They said, 'Look, here's the door', and when they opened the door and went inside and saw the horrible thing that had happened and the body lying in a pool of blood, they said to him, 'What is this?'

He said, 'Seize me and take me to the magistrate, for I am a murderer'. They seized him and took him to the city magistrate and the magistrate interrogated him and heard the truth from him and, torturing him, subjected him to a severe whipping.

After all these things, the old man about whom I spoke earlier said to his disciple, 'Come, my son, let us go and see the remains of the holy young female athlete'. So they came to the Duokaidekaton Monastery, because that was where her corpse was, and the elders of the monastery came out to greet him and they received her [*sic*] with great honor. The old man said, 'Offer a prayer, for this young woman's body is not to be buried elsewhere but is to be placed in the sepulcher of the holy fathers'.

Some of the brothers began to grumble, [saying] that it was not right to place there the body of a woman murdered like this.

The old man, however, said, 'This young woman is a martyr; she died protecting her purity'. When the fathers heard this, they bore witness to what he had said and, treating the young woman's body with great honor, they placed her in the cemetery of the fathers. The old man returned to his desert [home] in Scetis with his disciple.

Thus, those who give in to the drunken folly of concupiscence and commit murders like this and do such unrestrained and fearful acts are neither terrified nor disturbed by their drunken madness. Because of this, it is appropriate that before they become drunk with madness they cast away little by little and remove from themselves this concupiscence and passion.

6. *A Monk Receives a Blessing from a Young Woman* (Gk I.7)[32]

A certain brother in Scetis was embattled by the ferocious demon of sexual sin and he went and told the old man about it. The old man said to him, 'Go to the Duodecim Monastery in Alexandria[33] and, entering it, prostrate yourself on top of the tomb of the fathers and say, "God of our fathers, help me and deliver me from these temptations to sexual sin!" and I have faith that the Lord will deliver you from this temptation'.

The brother accepted what the old man had said and went to the Duodecim Monastery and did everything the old man had instructed and after three days returned to Scetis. Falling at the old man's feet, he said, 'Thanks to God and your instructions, father, I have been delivered from the demon of sexual sin'.

The old man said, 'How? By what means?'

The brother answered, 'Just as you said, father, I knelt down twelve times and prostrated myself on top of the tomb of the fathers and slept a little and a young woman came and said to me, "Monk, take this blessing and go in peace to your cell". When I received that blessing, the warfare immediately lessened, but what the blessing was, I don't know'.

The old man said, 'That young woman had such confidence in God that she died on behalf of chastity'.

7A. *The Patrician Lady Anastasia* (Gk I.8)[34]

A certain eunuch was in the inner desert eighteen miles from the monastic community of Scetis. Daniel, the great old man, gave orders to one of his disciples and in the evening the disciple filled a small vessel with water and placed it outside the cave and re-entered the cave. At night the eunuch would come the eighteen miles secretly each week, take the water, drink it, and return to his dwelling made of stone, neither seeing nor speaking with anyone. After eighteen years, Daniel's disciple found an inscribed potsherd in the courtyard to the cave: 'Father Daniel, come with one of your disciples and bring me a hatchet and a branch'.[35] When the old man read what was written, he said, 'What woe there is in the inner desert! What great pillar the desert is losing!' And he said to his disciple, who had put the water outside the cave for eighteen years, 'Take the hatchet and the branch and let us immediately go; perhaps we can reach the old man while he is still alive and receive his prayer, for he is going to Christ'.

They took to the road, weeping. When they arrived, they found the eunuch burning up with fever. The old man fell on the eunuch's breast and wept many tears and said, 'Blessed are you who are giving your attention to this day and have looked with contempt on the world's glory!'

The eunuch said, 'Blessed are *you*, Daniel: your spirit has been placed with the patriarch Abraham because you have offered to Christ many fruits by your labors'.

Daniel said, 'Offer a prayer for us and bless us'.

The eunuch said, 'It would be better for you to offer prayer for me and bless me'. The old man said, 'If I had gone to Christ beforehand, I would have offered prayer for you. Now that it is you who are going on ahead, bless us'.

Stretching forth his hands, the eunuch blessed them intensely and, embracing the old man, kissed him on the forehead. Receiving Communion, he ordered the old man not to carry the reed mat by himself and he immediately commended his spirit to God and his face shone like fire.

They wept and wept and dug a grave in front of the cave and placed him in it. The old man, taking his tunic, gave it to his disciple to drape over the corpse. When the disciple stripped the clothing from the eunuch's breast in order to kiss it, he saw a woman's breasts like dried leaves and he buried him, placing a very strong rock on top, and they heaped up earth and with psalms and [songs of] praise[36] they committed him to Christ and returned to Scetis.

The disciple said to the old man, 'Did you know, father, that the eunuch was a woman?'

The old man said, 'Now I will tell you about him' and he began explaining that the eunuch was the wife of a great and very wealthy nobleman from the royal city of Constantinople. When her husband died, because of her outstanding beauty, Emperor Justinian coveted her and secretly sent messengers to her with riches. Abandoning all her wealth, her name, and her male and female servants, she secretly fled alone at night, came to the city of Alexandria, and built on a mountain a great monastery and gathered multitudes of women. It is called the Monastery of the Patrician Lady to this day. With great virtue she contended and reports of her divine way of life spread to every corner of the empire, even, because of her sanctity, to the emperor's ears. Many people went to her to ask for her prayers and to be blessed by her. Putting on a monk's clothing, she fled at night from her monastery and came to me and told me all her thoughts and asked me for that cave and I gave it to her. Her name was Anastasia, and absolutely no one for twenty-eight years knew what you alone know. The emperor and the patriarch of Alexandria sent numerous investigators to find her and receive her blessing but they were not able to find her. In like manner, the female religious of her monastery sought her with great longing but were not able to find her since God had hidden her and preserved her until her death'.

7B. A certain eunuch was living in the interior desert of Scetis and his remote cell was twelve miles from Scetis. Once a week he would go to Father Daniel at night and no one knew about it except Abba Daniel

and his disciple. The old man ordered his disciple to take water in a pot
to the eunuch once a week; taking it, he would place it outside his door
and knock just to indicate to him that he was there and then secretly
return, for the old man had ordered his disciple to speak to no one but
to return immediately. He had also said, 'If you find an ostracon with
writing on it outside his door, bring it with you'. So the old man's disciple did this for many days and years, just as his father had ordered.

One day, while he was bringing the water, the old man's disciple
found a potsherd with writing on it outside, in the forecourt to the cave,
and this was written on it: 'Father, hurry and come see me, you and your
disciple, and bring your hatchet with you'. When the old man read the
potsherd, he wept bitterly and said, 'Woe, my son, what great and resplendent pillar is leaving us today!' He added, 'Take the hatchet and
these tools, and follow me, and let us go to him; perhaps we can reach
the old man and not be deprived of his prayer, for he is going to the
Lord'.

So they went and found the eunuch burning up with fever. The old
man, placing his head on the old man's breast, greatly wailed and said,
'Blessed are you because you have focused all your attention on this
hour and have dismissed with contempt your royal way of life and
worldly glory'.

The eunuch said to him, 'And blessed are *you*, the new Abraham,
because you have received Christ and welcomed him as a guest.[37] Christ
has received many hidden servants from your hands'.

The old man said, 'Pray for me before God'.

The eunuch said, 'It is I who need many prayers at this hour'.

The old man said, 'If I had gone on before you, I would have prayed
for you'.

The eunuch sat on a rush mat and kissed the old man and said, 'God,
who brought me to this place, will bring to fulfillment your old age,
just as he did with Abraham'.

The old man pushed his disciple forward at the eunuch's feet and
said, 'Bless him too'. The eunuch raised him up and kissed him and said,
'May God, who stands beside me as I commend my spirit,[38] who knows
how many steps you have taken in coming to the cell from which I will
depart this life, in his mercy cause the spirit of your father to rest upon
you, as the spirit of Elijah rested upon Elisha'.[39] Then the eunuch said
to the old man, 'For the sake of the hope and love that we have in the

Lord, do not take off the clothes I am wearing but place me in the tomb as I am, give dust to dust,[40] and let no one else know about me except the two of you alone'. And he said to the old man, 'Bring me a portion of the Body of Christ, that I may have communion with him'. After he received the Holy Mystery, he said, 'Give me the kiss of Christ's love and pray for me' and, looking to his right, he said, 'It is good that you have come'. His face shone like a lighted lamp and he made the sign of the cross on his face and said, 'Into your hands I commend my spirit', God my Father'.[41] And so he gave his spirit into the hands of God the Father.

The old man, Abba Daniel, wept deeply. And they dug a grave in front of the forecourt to the cave and, stripping off his clothing, the old man said to his disciple, 'Clothe him with more than what he is wearing'. (The eunuch was wearing clothing made from palm fibers and a hairshirt.) When the brother dressed him, he saw that his breasts were those of a woman, and that they were like a tree's withered leaves, but he kept silent and did not say anything. After they had prayed and buried the eunuch, the old man said to his disciple, 'Let us break our fast today and celebrate an *agapē* in the old man's sepulcher'. After participating in Communion, they found soaked lentils and a little bread and they ate next to the sepulcher, and taking up the rope that the eunuch had made, they returned to their cells and gave thanks to God.

As they traveled, the disciple said to that old man, 'I know, father, that that eunuch was a woman. As I dressed him, I saw that his breasts were like dried leaves like those of a woman'.

The old man said to him, 'I know, my son, that he was a woman. Come now and I will tell you about her life. She was a virgin of the highest rank at the royal court, the daughter of a leader among the nobility, and Emperor Justinian wanted to marry her because of her beauty and wisdom and nobility. Queen Theodora, however, hearing about it, became very angry and wanted to persecute her. When the virgin found out, she boarded ship at night and, taking her wealth with her, came to Alexandria and lived in the Pempton, a monastery for woman.[42] She built another monastery for women, which to this day is called the Monastery of the Patrician Lady. When Empress Theodora died, she knew that the emperor would look for her and would want to seize her. Then she fled from Alexandria at night and came to me by herself and told me everything and begged me to give her a remote cell in Scetis.

So I gave her this cave and gave her a man's clothing. She lived twenty-eight years in Scetis and no one knew about her except me and, today, you, except for one other person and his disciple. They knew because when I had to go somewhere I would order them to take water to her, and no one knew about her, who she was or what sort of person she was except you and me alone. The emperor sent numerous magistrates looking for her, but they could not find her; similarly, the patriarch of Alexandria and all the rulers also looked for her but were not able to find her.

'Do you see, my son, what sort of things she devoted herself to for God's sake, although she was raised among kings, and how she fought against demons and defeated them by means of her contrite and humble body? We, however, born and raised in mean circumstances, being the sons of paupers, never having enough bread to eat, have come here for solitude and live in peace and luxury and fight for nothing. But now let us too pray that we may be deemed worthy to run the race of the righteous, with Saint Anastasia the eunuch (for that was her name), and may we too find mercy on the day of judgement, through her prayers, before the throne of Christ'.

8A. *Eulogius* (Gk I.9)[43]

Father Daniel related this story: 'A certain stonecutter used to labor for one gold coin a day and did not eat until evening. At that time he put food on the table with the money he had earned and ate with strangers and the poor and threw the leftovers to the dogs. He kept nothing for the next day except his chisel. It so happened that he took me in with the strangers and when I understood his way of life I asked God for three weeks to give him money so he might bear much good fruit and the Lord spoke to me in a vision, for he was standing on top of a rock in the appearance of a king, and he said, "What he has is sufficient". I persisted in asking him to give him possessions and the Lord said to me, "Will you act as guarantor that he will follow my commandments?" I said, "Yes, I will", and he said to the throng standing next to him, "Listen to what he is saying".

'When Eulogius was hauling rock, he found a wine jar filled with gold. Not able to show the money in town, he got draft animals and left for Constantinople to where Justin was emperor and acquired a house and became prefect of the city. When I once again saw my Lord [in a vision], he looked at me sharply and when I understood why, I left for the village; when I found out where Eulogius was, I went to Constantinople but for four years I was unable to see him. I stood at the door to his house until his servants beat me and wounded me and left me half dead. I threw myself down in supplication and entreated the holy Mother of God to release me from this pledge and I saw her take hold of the Lord's feet and entreat him on my behalf. And the Lord said to me, "I absolve you. Get up and go home and I will return him to his former way of life".

'It happened that Justin died and they seized Eulogius the stonecutter and three of his friends and confiscated all their wealth and they wanted to kill Eulogius.[44] He dressed in beggar's clothing and returned to his village and begged for a mallet and began again his stonecutting and works of hospitality. When I heard about this I went to see him and we wept together a long time and I told him everything that had happened. He said to me, "Pray now, father, for a few possessions and I will be satisfied", and I said to him, "Get away from me, you who trouble me and dare to speak to my Lord! 'Great are his works, and there is no end to his wisdom!'"[45]

8B. Father Daniel, the priest of Scetis, went one day to the Thebaid, and he had with him one of his disciples. When they returned by ship on the river, they came to a village somewhere; getting out there, the old man said to his disciple, 'This is a good place to stay today'.

The disciple said, 'No, let's return to Scetis today'.

The old man said, 'No, let's stay here today', and they stayed in the middle of the street as foreigners. The disciple said to the old man, 'It's not right for us to stay here like beggars; let's go to the village church and stay there'.

The old man said, 'No, we're not leaving; let's stay here until evening'. His disciple, however, got upset and contentious and said to the old man, 'How long are we going to waste our time here because of you? I'm going to die a miserable death here in the street'.

While they were talking there, an elderly layman came, a large man, with hair as white as snow. When he saw Father Daniel, he began to weep and kiss his feet and they lovingly kissed one another. He led them to his home; holding a torch in his hand, he went ahead of them through the streets and behind him came Father Daniel and his disciple, and many other paupers who met him on the way. He led them home and washed the old man's feet. He had no other family or relatives or relations in his house, no one but God. He set the table for them and everyone ate. After dinner, he collected their leftovers, went outside, and threw them to the dogs. He would not put this off till the next day, nor would he leave a crumb inside; it was his custom not to leave anything in the house till the next day. He and the old man went outside, sat together, and did not sleep the whole night; rather, the old man spoke spiritually beneficial things, and that fellow listened to his commandments with fervent tears. Early in the morning they said goodbye to one another and, taking their leave, Father Daniel and his disciple left.

While Father Daniel and his disciple were on the road to Scetis, his disciple entreated the old man, saying, 'Please, father, tell me who that man is and where he is from. Where do you know him from?'

The old man refused to tell him. Again the disciple fell before him and said, 'You've told me many other things, father. Why won't you tell me about this person?' (The old man had told him about the virtues of many men.) The old man, however, refused to speak or tell him anything, until the brother became very sad and did not speak another word to the old man until they reached Scetis.

Standing [in prayer?] until evening, the old man got hungry but the brother would not bring him anything to eat for his evening meal (the old man took dinner at 6 pm every day of his life).[46] When the old man saw that the brother was not coming in the evening to bring him his dinner as was the custom, he got up and went to the brother's cell and said to him, 'Why have you allowed your father to die of hunger, my son?'

The disciple said, 'You aren't my father, and you don't love me. If you did, you would tell me about that man'.

The old man said to him, 'Why are you so hardhearted and proud?' and he got up to leave the cell. The brother, however, filled with compunction, grabbed his feet and begged him not to go away upset. Because of this, the old man did not want to make him sad, since he loved him dearly, so he said to him, 'Cook me a little something to eat, and I will tell you about that old man'. The disciple, overjoyed, did what the old man had said, and after dinner the old man began to tell the disciple

about him: 'That man', he said, 'is called "Eulogius", and he is a craftsman, a stonecutter and worker in stone. He works at his trade and earns
one *sisterce* a day, because he is very skilled in that trade. He does nothing
but work until darkness and when evening comes he goes into the village and summons home with him whatever paupers and foreigners
and needy he finds on the streets and feeds them and he himself eats
with them. Whatever leftovers remain on the table he takes outside and
throws to the dogs and he leaves nothing till the morning, He's been
doing this work and performing these services for a hundred years now
and Christ gives one gold coin each day for his work, as I said earlier.

'When I was a young man, forty years ago, I went to set out my handiwork for sale and when I arrived in the village in the evening, he took
me and other foreigners home with him, as was his custom and, treating
us hospitably, made himself my disciple. I went up there often and came
to know his virtue and with fasting began to entreat God on his behalf,
saying, "Lord, give this man more possessions so he may give more in the
way of necessities to those without". I fasted three weeks with this purpose
in mind until I was suffering from starvation and fell on my bed. And I
saw a certain dignified-looking priest dressed in white; he came and stood
next to me and said, "Daniel, what are you doing starving yourself?" I said,
"I made a vow to Christ not to eat anything until he heard me and gave
possessions to Eulogius the stonecutter so he might benefit many with
them". He said to me, "What you're doing isn't good; leave things be and
matters will go better for him". I said, "Lord, give him more, so he may
give more to others and your name may be glorified more through him".
He said to me, "I'm telling you, it's for the best that he live as he is now.
If you want me to give him more, act as guarantor for his soul so he may
live under the rule of his soul, and I will give him more". And I said to
him, "Seek his spirit from my hands".

'I saw that we were in the Church of the Resurrection of the Lord
and that young man was sitting upon the stone of the sepulcher and
Eulogius was standing at his right and thousands of angels were standing
beside him. The Lord spoke to them about me, "Is this the one who has
pledged himself for Eulogius?" and they responded, "Yes, Lord, this is
the one who pledged himself for him". The Lord said, "Truly, I will demand from you your pledge for him", and I in turn said, "Yes, Lord, let
the guarantee for him be upon me and give him the money". And I
saw that they were placing a large amount of money in Eulogius' lap,

and his lap was able to hold however much they were putting into it, and more. This was the vision, my son, and when I woke up I knew that the Lord had heard my entreaties and I gave glory to God.

'Eulogius came out to do his work and when he struck rock he found beneath the rocks a large wine jar filled with gold and excavated it; when he saw it, Eulogius said, "This money belonged to the Israelites! What should I do with it? If I take it home with me, the ruler will hear about it and will torture me. No, I will take it and go to a foreign land where no one knows me, and there I will do with it as seems appropriate". Hiring mules as though he were hauling stones, hauling the gold out he went down to the seashore and, hiring a boat, left for Constantinople, giving up the good husbandry he had been doing. Justin, an old man, reigned at that time in Constantinople and Eulogius gave a large part of the money to the emperor and to his nobles so they would make him procurator of the great praetorian guard. Then he bought a very large house, which to this day is called "the house of the Egyptians", and this is the way things happened.

'Two years later I saw the vision again of that young lord sitting in the same place in the Church of the Resurrection. There was a throng with him, and Eulogius was not there at his right, and I saw black demons dragging Eulogius by his hair and pulling him out of there. When I awoke from sleep, I said, "Woe is me, wretch that I am! I have lost my soul!" Taking my staff in my hand, I went to that village to look for Eulogius and I stayed there until evening, expecting to see him, but he did not appear. When evening came, I said to a woman, "Isn't there an inn in this village?" She said, "No, there isn't". That woman asked me to follow her for the sake of hospitality and I obeyed her. She led me to her home and prepared a meal and bread for me; sitting down, she welcomed me hospitably, then took hold of me and said to me, "It is not appropriate for you to come to town. A monk should have peace and quiet". She said this and many similar things to me, and I said, "I've come to sell my handwork". She said to me, "Even if you offer many such excuses, I will not be persuaded. You should never come to the village after dark". I asked her, "Tell me, for the Lord's sake, my good mother, what happened to Eulogius the stonecutter, the fellow who shows hospitality to strangers?" She said to me, "That man was generous and just and very hospitable. God accepted his good works and, so I hear, he is now a great prefect at the imperial court".

'When I heard this, I said, "Wretch that I am, I killed him!" Then I thought about it, collected myself, and went to find him. Boarding a ship, I went to Byzantium to look for him and made inquiries at the home of the prefect Eulogius the Egyptian and they showed me where he lived, so I sat at his gate and waited for him to come out so I could see him. Suddenly he came out, with many knights and soldiers, and I said in a loud voice, "Have mercy on me, prefect! I have something to say to you in private!" He never paid any attention to me but those who went before him whipped me. I continued to call out this way for four weeks whenever he went in or came out and his soldiers would whip me and I was never able to speak with him. Feeling very dejected, I threw myself down before an image of the Mother of God and with tears I said, "My Lord Jesus Christ, either release me from the pledge I made for Eulogius or I will return to my own country and region".

'While I was pondering things, I fell asleep for a little while and saw in my sleep that a great crowd was coming and that as they were approaching they were saying, "Her Ladyship the Augusta is coming!" and there came before her thousands upon thousands and tens of thousands upon tens of thousands. I roared out to her, "Your Ladyship, help me!" She said to me, "What is the matter with you? What is bothering you?" I said, "I pledged myself for Eulogius the procurator. Now order him to release me from this pledge".

'I woke up and said, "Even if I have to die, I am not leaving Eulogius' gate until I speak with him!" So I went to his gate once again and cried out again, and his doorkeeper grabbed me and badly beat me with a whip until he had broken every bone in my body and I was seriously wounded. Then I decided to leave for Scetis. Going down to the seashore, I found a ship leaving for Alexandria and boarded it and sat on board. Feeling discouraged, I fell asleep. Once again I saw that I was standing in the Church of the Resurrection of the Lord and that same young lord was sitting upon a rock and he looked at me in a threatening manner and I was terrified with fear and shook like a dried out leaf in the wind and was unable to look him in the face, for my heart quaked with fear.

'He said to me, "In pledging yourself for Eulogius, have you not gone astray?" Then he ordered two of them to hang me on a cross and tie my hands behind me and they did as the young king had ordered and they flogged and pounded me and said, "Why did you pledge yourself for someone, beyond your ability? Why did you oppose God's gracious intentions?" I was unable to answer them because I considered myself worthy of punishment and believed the king's orders just.

'Suddenly there was a voice, saying, "Her Ladyship the Augusta is coming!" and when I saw her, I recovered my spirits and said to her in a subdued voice, "Lady, help me". Then she spoke to me with her sweet tongue: "I am making entreaties on your behalf". And I saw her ladyship go and kiss the young lord's feet and make entreaties for me. Then that young man and king said to me, "Never dare to do this again!" and I said, "No, lord, I will never do this again!" I added, "I had hoped to make things better for him. Now forgive me and release me, my Lord and my God".[47] He ordered them to release me and as they released me he said to me, "Return to your cell and you will see and marvel at how I return Eulogius to his former way of life". When I woke up, I was deliriously happy at being set free from my pledge and, crossing the sea in peace, I returned to my cell.

'Three years later, I heard that Emperor Justin had died and a few days later four of his nobles had evil designs: the count Hypatius, and Hypokratius, and Pompeius, and Eulogius. The first three were immediately beheaded and all their property seized. Eulogius, however, fled alone and naked from the city. When they could not find how Eulogius had fled, then the new emperor, Justinian, who was ruling in place of the old man Justin, gave the order that they were to kill Eulogius wherever they found him. Eulogius escaped from their hands and, fleeing, returned home and put on the tattered clothing of a pauper. That whole village gathered at the sight of Eulogius and said to him, "We heard that you had been made prefect", and he said, "It wasn't me you heard about: if I had been made a noble, I would not be here looking at you. Those who hold high office live in royal palaces. The person you heard about was another Eulogius from here; I too heard about him. I, however, was in the Holy Land, going from place to place offering prayers and petitions".

'A few days later Eulogius came to himself and said, "Eulogius, you wretch, take up your mallet and go do your work and wear yourself out doing it—there is no palace here—lest you lose your head along with your wealth". Taking his mallet, he went out to the rock, thinking that he would find more treasure there. He exhausted himself digging until evening and when he did not find it he sat down disconsolately and thought about his wealth and all the pleasures he had enjoyed while he lived in the palace. Again he said, "This is Egypt, and not Constantinople". So he worked and took in foreigners as he was previously accustomed to do and, through the grace of Christ, he returned to his former way of life.

'A few days later, I went up to that village in order to sell my handwork and when evening fell Eulogius came and took me home with him as he had been accustomed to do previously. When I saw him covered with dust and dirt and worn out from stonecutting, looking at him I sighed and wept and said, "How great are your works, Lord! You have done everything with wisdom.[48] What god is as great as our God? You are God, who alone does wonders.[49] You raise up the poor from the earth and the wretched from the dungheap.[50] When I, a pauper, presumed to do something great, it turned out to be very little, and my soul perished in Hades".[51]

'[And taking me, along with the others he had found,] Eulogius washed our feet and fed us. After dinner I said to him, "How are you, old man Eulogius" and he said, "Pray for me, father, because I am very poor". I said, "It would have been better for you if you had not even had what you had", and he said to me, "Why, my lord father? Have I offended you?" I then began to tell him everything that had happened to me and the two of us wailed and wept profusely, without anyone knowing about it. Then Eulogius said to me, "My lord father, beseech Christ to give me what I need and I will not do what I did before". I, however, said to him, "Do not expect Christ to ever entrust you with wealth as long as you live, except for one gold coin, your day's pay". We wept saying goodbye to one another and I took to the road and returned to my little cell here, giving thanks to God who restored Eulogius to his former way of life; the Lord gave him the virtue to work hard each day and he did not lack anything he needed.

'Look, my son, I have told you how I came to know him and what sort of works he undertook. You, however, are not to tell this to anyone else'.

So Father Daniel told this story to his disciple as they returned to the Thebaid, and I,[52] having heard the story, have written it down to the glory of God. It is fitting to stand in awe before God's profound wisdom, for everything difficult is easy for him, and wonder at how through his goodness he first raised up Eulogius and through his loving mercy humbled him again. Let us pray therefore that we too may be humbled like this so we may find mercy on the fearful day of Christ our God.[53]

9A. *A Monk in a Tomb is Ignored by Two Demons* (Gk II.1)[54]

Abba Daniel of Scetis told this story: 'A brother was in Egypt[55] and one day while he was walking on the road evening approached and, because it was getting dark, he went inside a tomb on account of the cold and remained there. When two demons passed by, one said to the other, "Do you see this solitary's audacity? He's sleeping in a tomb! Come on, let's harass him". The other said, "Why should we harass him? He belongs completely to us and even serves us, doing what we want: he eats and drinks and disparages others and is lazy in prayer. Rather than hinder him, come on, let's bother those who bother us and who vie with us night and day with their prayers"'.

9B. A certain old man told us about a certain brother who lived in Egypt.[56] That brother was on the road one day and when evening fell he went into a tomb in order to sleep there because it was cold. Demons were walking nearby at night and one demon said to the other, 'Do you see how bold this monk is, how he's sleeping in a tomb? Come on, let's terrify him'. The other demon responded and said to him, 'No, let's not terrify him. He belongs to us and does what we want: he eats and drinks and disparages everyone and is lazy about his prayers. Why should we deceitfully hinder this fellow who belongs to us? Come on, let's go and harass those who harass us and who continually fight against us with prayers and fasting and vigils and all kinds of austerities'. When the brother heard what they were saying, he became terrified and came to his senses and, repenting from that day on, became a chosen fighter.

CHAPTER SIX

Latin Accounts

Translated by Jeffrey Burton Russell

Introduction by Tim Vivian

F IVE OF THE SIX stories preserved in Latin are reasonably close to the greek accounts. (The first account does not occur in Greek; it may, in fact, not refer to the Daniel of Scetis who is the subject of the greek dossier.) In the two stories about Thomaïs (told as one in Latin 4), Daniel is not named as he is in Greek; in Lat 5, the monk falsely accused of theft is given the name of Dulas, whereas in Greek Doulas tells the story of the falsely accused monk. But these are relatively minor differences.

One amusing difference occurs: in the story of Eulogius the stone-cutter, Eulogius comes on stage as 'an old hunchbacked layman, many days into his long old age', whereas the best greek text describes him as 'a large man, completely gray-headed'. How did Eulogius acquire a hump? One greek text describes him this way: 'an elderly lay person came, with long gray hair, very advanced in age, humpbacked'. 'Hump-backed' (*hupokurtos*) is a corruption of a variant reading in yet another greek manuscript: 'very old, advanced in years, holding a fishing-basket (*kurtēn*)'. The latin translator, using a corrupt, secondary, greek text, and misreading the Greek, has turned Eulogius 'holding a fishing-basket' (*kurtēn*) into a humpback or hunchback (*hupokurtos*) for his latin-speaking audience.

SYNOPTIC TABLE

Latin	*Greek*
1. (8) About a Young Man	-----
2. (27) The Marvelous Holiness of Abbot Daniel	[I.9] Eulogius the Stonecutter
3. (28) About a Eunuch	[I.8] Anastasia
4. (36) About a Monk	[I.6] Thomaïs & [I.7] A Monk, Tempted by Sexual Sin, Receives a Blessing from Thomaïs
5. (38) About a Monk	[II.2] A Monk Accused of Theft
6. (40) Abba Daniel and a Nun	[I.4] The Drunken Nun

LATIN ACCOUNTS

1. (8) *About a Young Man* [-----][1]

Abba John, who was staying at a place called Petra, tells this story about Abba Daniel the Egyptian:

'When the Old Man went up to the place called Terenuthis in order to sell some things that he had made, a young man came to him and besought him: "For the sake of God, Father, I beg you to come to my house and pray over my wife, because she is barren". The Old Man, seeing that the younger man had asked him to help in the name of God, was persuaded by his request and went with him. When he had prayed over the young man's wife, he left and went back to his cell.

'Not long afterward, the woman conceived. When vicious people who did not fear God saw this, they disparaged the Old Man, saying, "We know for sure that this young man is sterile and cannot beget children, so the woman must have conceived the child by Abba Daniel". This rumor reached the Old Man. When he heard it, he sent a message to the woman's husband telling him to let him know when the woman gave birth.

'When the woman had borne the child, the young man sent a message to Abba Daniel in Sitheus [Scetis] reporting that with the help of God and Daniel's prayers his wife had given birth. Then Abba Daniel went and told the young man to have a feast and invite all his relatives and friends. When they were all eating, the Old Man took the child in his hands and, in front of everyone, asked the baby a question: "Who is your father, Child?" The boy replied, "There he is", pointing his finger at his father. The boy was twenty-five days old. When they saw this, all who were present glorified God.

'From that moment, those who spoke evil, disparaging the man of God, were forced to keep their mouths shut'.

2. (27) *On the Marvelous Holiness of Abba Daniel* [Gk I.9 (Eulogius the Stonecutter)]

There was in the Thebaid an Abba Daniel, who was a priest in Sitheus [Scetis].[2] One day he sailed down the river, taking one of his disciples with him. And when they had sailed, they came to a town, where the Old Man commanded the sailors, saying, 'We have to stay here today'. But his disciple began to grumble and said, 'How long do we have to hang around? Let us go to Sitheus now'. The Old Man said, 'Absolutely not: we have to stay here today'. And they went and sat down in the middle of the town like strangers. The disciple said to the Old Man, 'How does it please God for us to sit here like begging brothers?[3] Let us at least go into the church'. But the Old Man said, 'Absolutely not: we have to be here'. They continued to sit there until the dark of evening. The disciple grew depressed and began to complain to the Old Man, saying, 'Ah, I am going to die for you and because of you. What are we going to accomplish just sitting here?'

While they were talking together, an old hunchbacked[4] layman, many days into his long old age, appeared. Seeing Abba Daniel, he embraced him and, weeping, kissed his feet. He also greeted the disciple, saying, 'Whatever pleases you!' He was carrying a lantern and roaming all the streets of the town looking for strangers. He took the Old Man, his disciple, and others whom he found there to his home. There he poured water into a bowl and washed the feet of the brothers and the Old Man, for he had no other person in his house or anywhere else other than God himself. He brought them dinner, and when they had eaten, he took the bits that were left over and gave them to the village dogs, for that was his custom. Not even a morsel did he set aside for the next day. After that, he took the Old Man aside into a private place, where, sitting up until dawn, they spoke saving words, weeping abundantly. Next morning, they bade farewell to each other and went their separate ways.

When the Old Man and his disciple were on their way again, the disciple threw himself at the Old Man's feet, saying: 'For the love of God, Father, tell me who that old man is and where you know him from'. But he did not want to tell him. Again the disciple asked him, saying, 'You have entrusted many matters to me, yet you will not trust me about that old man? For he had numerous virtues of many saints ascribed to him'. But the Old Man would not speak to the brother about the other old man. The brother was so depressed by this that he would not speak to the Old Man any more.

The brother, going to his own little cell, did not offer the Old Man even a small meal, as he had been accustomed to do—throughout his whole life the Old Man observed the eleventh hour[5] as his mealtime.

When evening came, the Old Man came to the brother's cell and said to him, 'What is the matter, son? Would you send your father away to die of hunger?' The brother replied, 'I have no father. If I had a father, he would love his son as he ought to. Now wait on me'. The Old Man took hold of the cell door to open it and go out. But the brother, running after him, seized the Old Man and began to kiss his feet, saying, 'As the Lord lives, I will not let you go unless you tell me who that old man is'. (The brother could not bear to see the Old Man upset, for he loved him greatly.) Then the Old Man said to him, 'Make me something to eat, and I will tell you'.

When he had eaten, the Old Man told the brother, 'Do not be stiff-necked. It is because you were recalcitrant while we were in the town that I did not explain it to you. See: you do what you are told. That old man is called Eulogius, and he is a stonecarver. Every day he takes up stoneware that he made that day to sell. He eats nothing at all before evening. When evening comes, he goes into town. He takes as many strangers as he can find into his house and feeds them, and then, as you saw, he gives whatever is left over to the dogs. He has been a stonecarver from his youth to the present. He is a hundred years old and more. And God grants him the strength that he had as a youth, and he always makes his stoneware every day.

'When I was a young man forty years ago, I went up into that town to sell the work of my hands. It became late, and Eulogius gathered me and my companions up according to his custom and ministered to us assiduously. For my part, when I saw the kindness of the old man, I began to fast for weeks at a time, begging God to give the old man abundant goods so he might have the wherewithal to do good by giving fully to others.

'When I had fasted three weeks or more, I was lying on the ground almost dead from fasting. And I saw someone hoary and venerable standing next to me and saying to me, "What is the matter, Daniel?" I replied: "I gave my word to Christ not to taste bread until He heard me about Eulogius the stonecarver and bestowed blessings upon him that he might share with many others". And he said to me, "By no means! It is enough already". And I replied, "All right, Lord, but give to him so that all may glorify your holy Name". He again said to me, "I tell you, it is enough as it is. Still, if you want me to grant him more, stand as the guarantor of his soul, so he may be saved by the abundance of his good deeds, and I will give to him". I responded: "All right, make me responsible for his soul".

'Then it seemed to me that we were standing at the day of divine judgement.[6] And a Child was sitting atop the holy rock, and I saw Eulogius standing at his right hand. The Child sent one of those who were present all around him to ask me: "Is it you who are taking responsibility for Eulogius?" And all said, "Yes, Lord".[7] And he said again, "Tell him that I have to demand this guarantee". I replied, "Yes, Lord, from me, only just please multiply his blessings". And I saw two of those who were present pouring a lot of money into Eulogius' pocket, and however much they poured in, his pocket held it. When I awoke, I knew that my prayers had been answered, and I glorified God.

'Now when Eulogius was at his work, he struck a stone and heard a kind of ringing, and he found a small fissure. He struck again and found a cave full of money and treasure. Gripped by profound fear, he said, "What shall I do? Shall I take this treasure into town? But the ruler of the place will hear about it and will seize it, and I will be in danger. Rather, I will covertly take it someplace outside of town, as if I were transporting stones by night". So he carried the money to the riverbank. He ceased his daily labors and stopped giving out what he had earned for the support of the poor.

'He hired a ship, into which he put the treasure, and sailed to Byzantium. At that time, Justin, Justinian's uncle, was reigning. Eulogius gave a great deal of money to the emperor and his nobles, so much in fact that they made him prefect of the sacred palace and bought him a magnificent house, which is still called even today "The Egyptian House".

'Two years later, I saw another vision of the Child at the day of divine judgement, and I said to myself, "Where is Eulogius now?" And after a while, I saw Eulogius being taken away from before the face of the Child by an Ethiopian.[8] When I awoke, I cried, "Woe is me, a sinner! What have I done? I have lost my soul". Taking up my staff, I went into town as if to sell my wares. Sitting down, I waited for Eulogius to come according to his custom. And it became quite late in the evening, and no one had yet received me. Finally I got up and approached an old woman, asking her, "Mother, please bring me three loaves so that I may eat, for I have had nothing to eat today". She said, "I will go". She went and brought me a little hot food and, sitting down by me, began to offer me useful spiritual advice: "Do you not know that an ordered monastic life requires peace and quiet?"—and other helpful words. I said to her, "What are you telling me to do? I have come to sell what I have made." She said, "Even if you sell your work, you should not remain in the city. If you really want to become a monk, go to Sitheus [Scetis]". I said to her, "Please stop telling me these things and instead tell me whether there is not in this town a God-fearing man who receives strangers". And she said to me, "Oh, what have you said, Lord Abba! We once had a stone-carver, who did many good deeds for strangers, and God, seeing that, rewarded him, and now he is a nobleman". Hearing this, I said to myself, "I am the one who committed this murder".

'Taking ship myself, I went to Byzantium and asked some people where I could find the house of the Egyptian, and they pointed it out to me, and I sat at the door waiting for him to come out. Then I saw him in rich and elegant garb. Crying out, I said, "Pity me, for I want to tell you something important". But he would neither hear me nor look at me; instead, his servants beat me with sticks. Again setting proper behavior aside, I ran after him, shouting, and again his servants beat me. I went on risking this behavior for four weeks, but there was no way I could ever speak to him.

'When I was worn out, I went and threw myself down, grieving and weeping before an icon of our Lord Jesus Christ, and I said, "Lord, absolve me from this guarantee; if not, I too will become worldly". While I was saying this in my heart, I fell asleep. At that point a great excitement began to break out, with people saying, "Here comes the empress". Those in her service who preceded her were thousands and millions of thousands in their ranks. And I called out, "Have mercy on me, my lady". She stopped and said to me, "What is your problem?" I replied, "I made surety for Eulogius the eparch. Please free me from this guarantee". Then she said, "This is no concern of mine; fulfill your promise if you like".

'Upset, I said to myself, "Even if I have to die, I will not go away from his door unless I speak to him". And I went in front of his door and stood there waiting for him to come out. When he appeared, I shouted to him again. His porter laid so many blows on me that my whole body collapsed from the multitude of my wounds. When I had become so weak that I could not take any more, I said to myself, "Let us go to Sitheus, and if God wants to save Eulogius, he will".

'Going to look for a ship, I found one from Alexandria and, embarking in order to sail, I found myself a place somewhere on board, almost dead from weakness. And in a vision of the holy resurrection,[9] I saw myself, and the Child sitting on the holy rock and looking indignantly at me, so that I trembled like a leaf and was unable to open my mouth to say anything. My heart became like a stone. And he spoke to me threateningly, saying, "Why do you not go and fulfill the duty that you have taken upon yourself?" And he ordered two of those present there to stretch me with weights, and he said to me, "Do not presume to undertake things that are beyond your strength, do not pledge yourself as a mediator for others, and do not resist God's will". And I could not open my mouth or even mumble.

'After I had been racked, a voice was heard: "The Empress is coming". Seeing her, I recovered my confidence and said to her in a plain voice, "Have mercy on me, Queen of the World!" And she said to me, "What do you want?" I replied, "I am suffering punishment on account of my guarantee for Eulogius". She replied, "I will intercede for you". And I saw that she went and kissed the feet of the Child. And the Child spoke to me, now not indignantly but gently, "You do not want to continue to be his guarantor anymore?" I said, "No, Lord. I made that petition so Eulogius might be improved, but I sinned. Be gentle with me". And he ordered them to let me go and said to me, "Go to your cell and do not concern yourself with how I return Eulogius to his ordered life". I was raised up immediately, and I rejoiced with great joy that I was relieved of such an obligation, and I threw myself down and gave thanks to God.

'Three months later, I heard that the emperor Justin had died, that Justinian was now the ruler, and that Justinian had deposed Ypacium and Deiocratum along with my Eulogius, who had been a prefect. The former two were executed, and all their property was sequestered along with that of Eulogius. But Eulogius fled Constantinople by night, and the emperor ordered that he be detained wherever he was found. Fleeing, Eulogius came to the town in which he had lived. Changing his clothes, he put on peasant's garb, for he had previously been a peasant. All the inhabitants of the town came together and saw him and said to him, "We heard that you had become a noble". He replied, "A noble? If I had been a noble, would I have seen *your* faces anywhere? No, it is another Eulogius from this region, for I myself have been in the Holy Land".

'Having reflected, Eulogius said to himself, "Eulogius, take up your stonecarver's tools and go to work. There is no imperial palace here, so you are not likely to lose your head". Taking his tools, he went out and rushed to the rock where he had found the money, hoping to find another treasure, but although he worked cutting away till the sixth hour,[10] he found nothing. Then he began to lament those delicacies and indulgences and seductions and ostentatious pomps of his, and was tormented by the memory of them. And, talking to himself again, he said, "Eulogius, get up and work: this is Egypt, not Constantinople". Then gradually the Lord and the Mother of God restored him to his former modest state. For God is not unjust and did not forget Eulogius' earlier good works.

'After a little while, I went up to that town. When evening came, Eulogius received me according to his earlier custom. When I saw him, I cried aloud, sighing and weeping, and said: "How glorious are your works, O Lord, for you take care of everything wisely. What God is great like our God, who raises the needy from the dust and the poor from the dung heap,[11] who brings low and raises up?[12] Wonderful are your judgements, Lord; who can fathom them?[13] I would have become a sinner in what I was about to do, and if you had not heard me, my soul would very soon have been in hell". Taking a bowl of water, Eulogius washed my feet and brought me dinner, as was his custom. After we had eaten, I said to him, "How are you, Brother?" He replied, "Pray for me, Lord Abba. I am a humble man and have no possessions". I said to him, "It would have been better if you had not had what you did have". He replied, "Why, Lord Abba? Have I scandalized you in any way?" And I responded, "How have you *not* scandalized me?"

'Then I told him all that had been said and done, and we both wept and sobbed. Eulogius said to me, "Pray that God may command me something, so I may amend my life". I replied, "Surely, my son, you will in no way again expect the Lord to entrust you with anything other than this stonework as long as you are in this life". And behold, God granted him his stonework every day for many years. I am telling you how I know him, but please do not disclose it to anyone else, for Abba Daniel of the Thebaid has entrusted you with it'.

And the disciple saw to it that he did not entrust anyone with it before the death of the blessed Old Man. It is right for us to marvel how the mercy of God in such a short time raised up and again cast down as is needed. Let us pray, therefore, that we may be humbled in the fear of our Lord Jesus Christ, so that we may find mercy before that Dread Tribunal through the prayers of our Lady the holy Mother of God—the Virgin Mary—and of all the saints. Amen.

3. (28) *About a Eunuch* [Gk I.8 (Anastasia)]

There was a eunuch who lived deep in the desert of Sitheus [Scetis]. He lived by himself in a cell about eighteen miles away from the brothers. Once a week he would come at night to Abba Daniel, unbeknownst to anyone but Daniel and his disciple alone. The Old Man ordered his disciple to fill a bottle with water and carry it once a week out to the eunuch and place it outside in front of the door, knock on the gate, and go away without saying anything to him, except that the disciple, if he should find a note next to the opening of the cave, was to pick it up and bring it back with him.

One day he found a tablet with this written on it: 'Bring your tools and come'. Reading this, the Old Man wept grievously and said to his disciple, 'Take this equipment here and come follow me. Oh no! Let us go so that perhaps we may reach the eunuch in time, lest we be deprived of his prayers, for he is going to the Lord'.

Making their way, the two of them arrived and found the eunuch suffering with fever. The Old Man threw himself down on the eunuch's breast and wept copiously, and the Old Man said: 'You are blessed because you have meditated on this moment. You have despised the kingdom of this world and of man, and so you have obtained the kingdom of heaven'.

The eunuch replied, 'You are blessed too as the new Abraham and the bearer of Christ, for Christ has received much good work from these hands of yours'.

The Old Man said to him, 'Pray for us, Father'.

The eunuch replied, 'It is I who am more in need of the prayers of many people at this time'.

The Old Man responded, 'If I should precede you in this hour, I would intercede for you'.

The eunuch, lying on his pallet, took the Old Man's hand and kissed it, saying, 'May God, who led me to this place, grant you a long life, just as he did Abraham'. Leading his disciple forward, the Old Man made him kneel at the knees of the eunuch, saying to the eunuch, 'Bless him, Father'. And the eunuch kissed the disciple, saying, 'God, you are standing by me at this hour in order to separate me from my body, and you know how long a journey this brother made coming to this cell in your holy Name: please make the spirit of his fathers rest on him, just as you made the spirit of Elijah rest upon Elisha,[14] and may the names of the fathers be called down upon him'. The eunuch said to the Old Man, 'For the sake of God, do not take what I am wearing off me, but send me to the Lord as I am, so no one but you two knows about me'. And he asked the Old Man to give him Communion, and when he had taken Communion, he said, 'Give me a blessing in Christ and pray for me'.

Looking toward the east and to the right, the eunuch said, 'You have been welcome; let us go'. And his countenance became like fire, and, making the sign of the cross on his face, he said, 'Into your hands, God, I commend my spirit'.[15] Thus he gave his soul over to the Lord. And Daniel and his disciple wept.[16] They dug a grave in front of the cave and, when the Old Man had taken off the eunuch's clothes, he said to his disciple, 'Put something on her to clothe her'. The eunuch was wearing a waist-cloth without linen underneath, and on top a patched garment. When the brother was dressing him, he noticed that his breasts were female and hung down like two dry leaves, but at that point he said nothing.

While they were burying him and praying, the Old Man said to his disciple, 'Let us break our fast today and say grace over the body of this old person'. Preparing food to share, they found that he had some small loaves and boiled vegetables. Saying grace over him, they took the weaving that he had been working on and went off to their own cells, giving thanks to God.

As they were walking along the way, the disciple said to the Old Man, 'Father, do you know that that eunuch was a woman? When I was dressing him, I saw his breasts, and they were female and like withered leaves'. The Old Man replied, 'I know, my son, I know that he was a woman. Shall I tell you what happened to him?' The disciple replied, 'I would like to know'.

'This is what I heard about her: she was the foremost noblewoman of the emperor Justinian, and the emperor wanted to introduce her into the palace household on account of her great prudence. When the empress Theodora learned about it, she wanted her to be exiled, but when the woman found out about that, she took ship at night, bringing with her whatever of hers that she could, and fled. She came to Alexandria and lived in the fifth district of Alexandria,[17] where there was a monastery, and right up till today that place is called "the place of the noblewoman".

'After the death of the empress Theodora, the woman learned that the emperor wanted to bring her back, so she fled again during the night, this time from Alexandria, and eventually she came here alone and asked me to give her a cell near Sitheus [Scetis]. She recounted the story to me, informing me of the reason. So I gave her this cave and dressed her in a man's clothing. She was in Sitheus twenty-eight years, and no one knows except you, one other brother there, and me. How many officials did the emperor send looking for her! And not only the emperor Justinian, but also the patriarch of Alexandria, yet no one has been able to find out where she was up till the present day.

'See how those who are nobly brought up struggle against the Devil by mortifying their bodies. Let us pray, then, that perhaps the Lord will grant that we too can run that course and share it with Father Anastasius—for Anastasia was her name while she was in the outside world. May we be aided by the prayers and merits of the blessed Mother of God—the Virgin Mary—and of all the saints when we stand before the Dread Tribunal of our Lord Jesus Christ, to whom all glory is due forever and ever'.

4. (36) *About a Monk* [Gk I.6 (Thomaïs)]

One of the fathers, along with his disciple, went up to the city of Alexandria. While they were staying there, an event of this sort occurred:

A certain monk of the eighteenth district of Alexandria[18] had a son who had a very young wife, eighteen years old. The monk lived with his son, who was a fisherman. The enemy of our souls—the Devil— aroused a lustful struggle within the monk against his daughter-in-law. He sought the opportunity to come together with her but found none. He began to kiss her frequently, which the girl permitted as if he were her father.

One day at evening, fishermen who were comrades of the young man came and called on him to go out fishing together with them, and when the young man had departed, his father rose up against her. The girl said to him, 'Father, what are you trying to do? Go and examine your heart, for what you are doing is the Devil's work'. He would not let her go, but the girl, resisting him, refused to yield. Now, there was a sword above the son's bed; unsheathing it, the monk tried to terrify the girl, saying, 'If you do not listen to me, I will strike you with this sword'.

But she replied, 'Even if I risk being cut to pieces, I will not commit this disgusting crime'. Enraged with terrible fury and overwhelmed by the Devil, he struck the girl near her shoulders and cleaved her in two. Immediately God blinded him, so that he went around the house groping for the door but could not find it.

Other fishermen came looking for the young man, for it was dawn already. The father spoke to them from inside, saying, 'He went fishing. Where is the door? I cannot see'. They replied, 'It is here'. Opening the door, they saw the crime that he had committed. Then he said to them, 'Take hold of me and hand me over to the authorities, for I have committed murder'. Seizing him, they handed him over to the ruler of the city. The ruler, examining the matter, learning the whole truth, and weighing the case according to the law, sentenced him to many tortures.

After these events, the Old Man said to his disciple: 'Let us go and look at the girl's corpse'. When they came to the eighteenth district of Alexandria, the fathers heard about the Old Man's arrival and went out to meet him, for he was very famous. The Old Man said to them, 'Say a prayer, fathers and brothers'. After the prayer, he said to them, 'The body of this girl shall not be buried anywhere but with the remains of the fathers'. Some of them grumbled that he was arranging to bury the remains of a woman—and a murdered one at that—with the bodies of the fathers. The Old Man said to them, 'This girl is my mother and yours, for it is because of her chastity that she was killed'. After that, no one opposed the Old Man, and they buried her with the bodies of the fathers. Taking leave of the fathers and brothers, the Old Man went back with his disciple to Sitheus.

[Gk I.7 (*A Monk, Tempted by Sexual Sin, Receives a Blessing from Thomaïs*)]

One day a certain brother in the same Sitheus [Scetis] was gravely assaulted by the spirit and demon of fornication and went to report this to the Old Man. The Old Man said, 'Go to the eighteenth district of Alexandria, stay in the cemetery of the fathers, and say, 'God of Thomaïs, help me; free me from this temptation to fornication, and I hope in God that you will free me from this temptation'. The brother, accepting the prayers and orders of the Old Man, went to the eighteenth district and did what the Old Man had commanded.

After three days, he returned to Sitheus, threw himself at the feet of the blessed Old Man, and said to him, 'With the help of God and your prayers, holy father, I have been freed from the temptation of fornication'.

The Old Man said, 'How were you freed?'

The brother replied, 'I knelt ten times and stretched out on the ground in the cemetery and fell asleep, and a girl came to me and said, "Abba, abba! Receive this blessing and return to your cell". As soon as I accepted her blessing, the struggle was over, and I realized that I had been freed. Yet what that blessing was I do not know'.

The Old Man said to him, 'Those who have struggled on account of purity have such great credit with God'.

From that time on, whoever among the brothers was tempted by a spirit of this kind went to the cemetery and was cured.[19]

5. (38) *About a Monk* [Gk II.2 (The Monk Falsely Accused of Theft)]

Abba Daniel told this story:

'Once there was a monk named Dulas, who was considered to be among the great fathers. This Dulas lived in a monastic community forty years, for he reflected and found that monks advance more fully and quickly in the works of virtue when they are in a community, so long as they stay there with an honest heart.

'Now, there was a certain brother in the community who was really repulsive and contemptible in his appearance, although he was beautiful enough in mind and spirit, for although he was despised and insulted by all, he rejoiced and exulted.[20] From the very time of his entry into the community, all the brothers were his enemies and went around talking against him, spitting on him, hurling epithets at him, and steeping him in a variety of curses. But he patiently endured this treatment for twenty years and more.

'The Great Enemy,[21] unable to bear his patience and longsuffering in these trials, put it into the heart of one of the brothers to go into the church while the others were resting and to steal all the sacred vessels and then to leave the monastery—and this he did. When the time for psalms came, the sexton came to get incense and found that everything had been stolen. He went out and reported this to the abbot. The bells were rung, and all the brothers were called together, became agitated, and said, "No one but such and such brother did this, for he did not come when the bells rang. If he had not committed the crime, he would have been the first to come, as he always used to be". Ordering a search party, they found Dulas standing and praying somewhere.[22] They went in, striking him and grabbing him, and dragged him off by force. He asked them, "What is this, my lord brothers?" But they, cursing and insulting him, said, "You sacrilegious and worthless man, is it not enough that you have bothered us for so many years? And now you have broken into our very souls!" He replied, "Spare me, for I have sinned".

'They led him to the abbot and said, "Abbot, here is the one who has been upsetting the community from the outset". And they began to speak against him one after the other. One said, "I saw him secretly eating the vegetables"; another said that he had stolen bread and given it to people outside the monastery; yet another said, "I saw him covertly drinking better wine than the other brothers had". They told many other lies against him, and the lies were believed; but he told the truth, and it was not believed. Taking him away, the abbot stripped him of his monastic habit, saying, "These crimes are not the acts of a Christian".

'Taking him off, they gave him to the provost of the lavra. The provost, stripping him and flogging him with leather straps, interrogated him as to whether what was said about him was true. But the monk only laughed and said, "Spare me, for I have sinned". Enraged by these words of his, the provost ordered him to be whipped again even harder and to be shackled and thrown into prison. The provost wrote to the commandant about the matter. And next they came and put the brother bareback on an animal, for he was unable to walk because of the tortures they had inflicted on him and the irons that they had placed on his neck and feet, and thus they led him through the middle of the city.

'When he had been taken before the commandant, he was asked who he was, where he was from, and how he had made his profession as a monk; but he replied nothing more than "Spare me, for I have sinned". Enraged, the commandant ordered him to be drawn and quartered and to have his back completely flayed with rawhide thongs. While he was being drawn and quartered and mercilessly beaten with thongs, he smiled and said to the commandant, "Go ahead and beat my aging silver head so that you may be all the more happily occupied". The commandant said, "All right, stupid, I will plaster you whiter than snow". And he ordered coals to be placed under his belly and vinegar mixed with salt to be poured into his wounds. But those standing and observing admired the monk's patience and strength and said to him, "Tell <us>[23] where you put the sacred vessels and what you did with them, and you will be set free". The monk simply replied, "I have no reason to". Then the commandant ordered him to be released from his torments and to be thrown into prison and to be kept there fasting without any treatment for his wounds.

'The next day, the commandant sent orders to the monastery that all the monks should assemble, including the abbot. When they had come, the commandant said to them, "I have done many things to him and tortured him with a variety of torments, and I have been unable to find out anything more". The brothers replied, "But, my lord, he did many other bad things, and we put up with him for the sake of God, hoping that he would be converted from his criminality—and look, he just sank to even worse deeds instead". The commandant asked, "What shall I do with him?" They replied, "Whatever the laws demand". The commandant said, "The law prescribes death for sacrilege". They said to him, "Let him be executed".

'The commandant sent them away and ordered the accused brother to be brought out. Seated on his official chair, he said: "Confess, you wretch, and you will be spared death", but the brother replied, "If you order me to say what is not true, I will say it". The commandant responded, "I do not want you to tell lies against yourself". The brother said, "I do not recall having ever done any of those things that you were interrogating me about". Seeing that the brother would say nothing else about the matter, the commandant ordered him to be beheaded, and the executioners took him and led him out to behead him.

'When he was being led to execution, the conscience of the monk who had stolen the sacred vessels was stung, and he said to himself, "Sooner or later this matter is going to come to light, and if you hide here, what will you do on Judgement Day? What reason do you have for such cruel viciousness?" And he went to the abbot and said to him, "Send word quickly so that the brother may not die, for the sacred vessels have been found". The abbot swiftly reported the message to the commandant, the brother was released, and they took him to the monastery. And they all began to throw themselves at his feet, saying, "Spare us, for we have sinned against you". Then he began to weep and say, "Spare *me*, please; I thank you greatly because through this small pain you have offered me great comfort. I was always enormously happy when I heard the evil that you spoke against me, for by these tiny insults and this contempt of yours, you have prepared great honors and advancement for me. I rejoiced beyond measure that you did such things to me, but still I was troubled on your account: you who were unjustly persecuting me, because I foresaw the good things and rewards that were being prepared for me in the kingdom of heaven, and I joyfully endured everything".

'He survived three days and then went to the Lord. One of the brothers, coming to see how he was, found him lying forward over his knees, for he had been there kneeling in prayer and while praying had given up his spirit. His body remained as if it were still kneeling in prayer, thus testifying, though lifeless, the posture that it was accustomed to be in while it was still alive. The brother who found him reported these things to the abbot. The abbot ordered that his body be brought into the church so that it could be buried there. When they had placed him before the altar, the abbot ordered the bells rung so that all who were in the monastery might come together in order to lay his body to rest with glory and honor. When they had congregated, one of them wanted to take a relic from his remains. Seeing this, the abbot put his body into a place apart,[24] locked it up carefully, and put the key into his pocket until the other abbots should come, so that they might bury him together.

'When the father of a great monastery came with his clerics, they prayed in the customary way and then said to the abbot, "Open the door and bring out the body so that it can be buried, for it is already the ninth hour.[25] Opening the door, the abbot found nothing but the brother's clothing and sandals.[26] Then everyone, seized by terrible fear, began to marvel and to glorify God, weeping and saying: "You see, brothers, what longsuffering, humility, and patience confer on us? According to what you have seen, so you yourselves strive to endure sneers and adversities, because the kingdom of heaven is prepared for us by the grace of our Lord Jesus Christ—to whom is honor and glory, with the Father and the Holy Spirit forever and ever. Amen"'.

6. (40) *Abba Daniel and a Nun* [Gk I.4 (The Woman Who Pretended to be Drunk)]

Abba Daniel went up from Sitheus [Scetis] to the upper Thebaid with one of his disciples to attend the memorial service for Abba Apollonius.[27] All the fathers went out about seven stades—about five miles—to meet him. And he saw them stretched out on the sand, lying on their faces like angels of God awaiting him fearfully as if he were Christ. Some strewed their clothes before him, others their hoods. It was a marvel to see that tears were pouring down like rivers from their eyes.

The archimandrite went out and, before he met the Old Man, he knelt before him. Greeting one another, they sat down. The archimandrite begged that a word from the Old Man's lips might be heard, for the Old Man seldom spoke much. When they came to sit on the sand in front of the monastery—for the church could not hold them all, they were so many— Abba Daniel said to his disciple, 'Write this down: "If you want to be saved, follow poverty and silence, for upon these two virtues the entire monastic life depends"'. His disciple gave the writing to a monk to translate into Coptic for the brothers. When it had been read to the brothers and fathers, all wept and said goodbye to the Old Man, for no one presumed to speak to him in an effort to show him christian charity.

When the Old Man came to Hermopolis, he said to his disciple, 'Go knock at the gate of that women's monastery over there, which is called the Monastery of Saint Jeremiah. About three hundred sisters lived there. The disciple went and knocked. The portress said to him in a quiet voice, 'Greetings and welcome. What may I do for you?' He said to her, 'Go call the mother archimandrite for me: I wish to speak with her'. But she replied, 'She never speaks to any man; just tell me what you want, and I will give her the message'. He said, 'Say to her, "A monk wishes to speak with you"'.

The portress went away and reported to her. The abbess came and said to the brother in a quiet voice, 'The mother superior sent me to ask you what you want'. The brother said, 'I want you out of charity to let me sleep here, along with an Old Man, since it is late, lest the wild beasts devour us'. The abbess replied, 'No man ever enters here. It would be much more fitting for you to be devoured by the beasts outside than by the beasts within you'.[28] The brother said, 'It is Abba Daniel of Sitheus'.

When she heard this, she opened both gates and ran out to meet Abba Daniel, and so did the entire congregation of sisters. They laid down their headdresses all the way from the gate of the monastery to the place where the Old Man was, and they rolled at his feet and licked his footprints.[29] When they went into the monastery, the mother superior brought a bowl, filled it with warm water mixed with fragrant herbs, arranged the sisters in two groups on one side and the other, and washed the feet of the Old Man and his disciple. Then, taking a small cup, she brought the sisters before the Old Man and, using the cup, dipped water from the bowl over their breasts and heads. Behold, they were like stones, motionless and unspeaking, for this was their angelic manner of life.

The Old Man, however, said to the abbess, 'Are the sisters afraid of us, or are they always like this?' She replied, 'Your handmaidens are always like this, lord, but pray for them'. The Old Man said, 'Tell that to my disciple, who is raising himself up cunningly against me'.[30]

One of the sisters was lying in the middle of the hall of the monastery, ragged, half-naked, with her clothes torn. The Old Man asked, 'Who is that sleeping there?' One of the sisters said, 'She is drunk, lord. We do not know what to do with her. We do not want to expel her from the monastery, for we fear God's judgement if we do so. If we let her be, she disturbs the sisters'. Then the Old Man said to his disciple, 'Take the bowl and pour it out over her'. When he had done this, she got up drunkenly. The abbess said, 'Lord, she is always as you see'.

Then, helping the Old Man up, the abbess took him into the refectory and had a dinner for the sisters, saying, 'Bless your handmaidens, Father, so that they may dine in your presence', and the Old Man blessed them. The abbess sat apart with him with only her provost. And the sisters who were serving the men brought the Old Man a little dish with boiled vegetables, raw herbs, dates, and water; they brought his disciple boiled lentils, a morsel of bread, and wine mixed with water. But they served the sisters a variety of dishes, fish, and all the wine they wanted. They ate well, and no one said anything, but when they had risen, the Old Man asked the abbess, 'What were you doing? We are the ones who ought to have been served good food, but you were the ones who were eating well'. The abbess replied, 'You are a monk, and I served you the food of a monk, but we are only novices and ate the food of novices'. The Old Man said, 'Your charity is memorable, and you have truly helped us'.

When they had begun to take their rest, Abba Daniel said to his disciple, 'Go see where that drunken nun who was lying in the middle of the hall is sleeping'. The disciple went out and saw and reported to him: 'Next to the lavatory door'. The Old Man said to his disciple, 'Keep watch together with me'. When all the sisters had got up,[31] he roused his disciple and they went silently back down to the lavatory door and saw that the drunk had got up and stretched her hands toward heaven, and her tears flowed like rivers, and her lips were moving slightly: what she was saying was inaudible. She frequently knelt, praying to God; falling to the ground, she praised God's majesty. Whenever she noticed one of the sisters coming down to the lavatory, she would throw herself on the ground and snore loudly. Thus she behaved every day of her life.

The Old Man said to his disciple, 'Go quietly and call the abbess for me'. Going out, the disciple called her with her second-in-command,[32] and all night they watched what the nun was doing. The abbess began to weep, saying, 'Oh, how much wrong I have done to her'. And when she had rung the bell, she inquired among the sisters about her. When the nun discovered this, she rushed into the room where the Old Man had been staying and stole his staff and his cowl. Opening the gate of the monastery quietly, she wrote a note and stuck it on the outside locks of the gate. The note said: 'Pray for me and spare me, for I have sinned against you'. She went out and was never seen again. When day came, they looked for her, but she was not to be found. Going to the gate, they found it open and the note that she had written. Therefore great lamentation arose throughout the monastery. The Old Man said, 'It is for her that I came here, for God loves such drunks'.

The community of sisters began to confess to the Old Man each of the evils that they had done to her, begging absolution from him. He prayed over the sisters and then went back to his cell [in Scetis] with his disciple, glorifying God and giving thanks to him, who alone knows how many unrecognized servants and handmaidens he has.

CHAPTER SEVEN

Old Church Slavonic Accounts

Translated by Vitaly Dudkin and Jehanne Gheith

Introduction by Tim Vivian

OLD CHURCH SLAVONIC sources refer to a number of stories from the greek Daniel dossier: Mark (Gk I.1), Daniel's 'crime' (I.2), a drunken monastic (I.4), Andronicus (I.5), 'a certain virgin and holy girl' (Thomaïs? I.6), Anastasia (I.8), Eulogius (I.9), and Abba Doulas (II.2).[1] Only the story about the 'eunuch' Anastasia, however is reasonably complete. It is translated below in two versions, **W** (Wiener Codex slavicus 42) and **B** (Berliner Alphabetikon (Wuk 40).[2] Version **W** contains about ninety percent of the story in the greek dossier and **B** contains about eighty percent. Neither has significant variants from the greek version.

Anastasia (I.8)[3]

W /340/ *Of the same Father Daniel, about a Eunuch who was in Scetis.*

A certain eunuch was in the inner desert of Scetis. He was in a cell far from Scetis and used to come on Sundays to Father Daniel at night and nobody saw him except Daniel's disciple. The elder commanded his disciple to take water to the eunuch who was alone in his cell and leave it in front of the door of his cell and then, giving a knock [at the door], to leave [immediately] and say nothing /341/ to him, and to follow this rule carefully. If there was a clay potsherd with a note written on it at

263

the door of the cave cell, he should bring it back with him. He obtained the clay with writing on it: 'Come and bring tools with you'. The elder read the writing on the clay and wept with great sorrow and said to his disciple, 'Woe to the inner desert! What [great] pillar will be destroyed today!' And he said to his disciple, 'Take the tools and follow me. Soon we will see the elder. Let us not be deprived of his prayers, since he is going to the Lord', and they left together.

So they left, and found the elder burning with fever. Abba Daniel threw himself on the elder's breast and, weeping profusely, said, 'Blessed are you, father, at this hour, /342/ since you prepared for it by rejecting the worldly kingdom and human glory'.

The eunuch said to him, 'Blessed are you, the new Abraham, who welcomes Christ and strangers.[4] You have labored so hard with your hands'.

Abba Daniel said to him, 'Pray for us, father', and the eunuch said to him: 'I have need of many prayers at this hour'.

Abba Daniel said to him, 'If you have expected this hour, then you should want to pray'.

Then the eunuch leaned down from his bed and took the elder's head and kissed him, saying, 'God instructed me and led me to this place. He will finish your old age as he did Abraham's'.[5]

Then the elder took his disciple and knelt him down before the eunuch's feet and said, 'Bless your child, father'. The eunuch accepted the kiss and said, 'I stand before God at this hour when I am taking leave of my body and he knows how many prostrations I have made in this cell. May the Lord give you rest with his saints, just as he caused Elijah's spirit to rest on Elisha'.[6] And the eunuch said to the elder, 'For the sake of the Lord, do not take my clothing off me, but bury me as I am dressed now. And may no one know about me except you'. Then he said to the elder, 'Give me Communion'. After Communion he said, 'Give me love in Christ and pray for me', and having looked to the east and to his right, he said, 'To the Good I am going'. /344/ His face was like fire and he made the sign of the cross on his lips and said, 'God, into your hands I commit my spirit'.[7] And at this moment he gave up his spirit into God's hands.

After weeping profusely, the elder and his disciple dug a grave in front of his cell. And the elder took off his cassock and said to his disciple, 'Dress him in this cassock'. So his disciple dressed him. The eunuch's breasts were as thin as two leaves. They said nothing. They buried him and prayed. The elder said to his disciple, 'Let us break our fast and let us celebrate an *agapē* on the elder's casket'. In the eunuch's cell there was a little /345/ dried bread and some soaked grain. They celebrated an *agapē* on top of his casket. Taking a rope that he had in his cell, they left his cell, giving thanks to God for everything.

As they were going, the disciple said to the elder, 'Did you know, father, that the eunuch was a woman? When we dressed him, I saw his breasts; they were like a woman's. I saw that his breasts were like two leaves'.

The elder said to the disciple, 'I know that she was a woman, and if you wish, listen, and I will tell you about her. She was a patrician lady at the court of Emperor Justinian. The emperor wanted to make her an empress because she was so wise. When his empress, Theodora, saw what was happening, she became angry with her /346/ and decided to put her in jail. When the patrician lady realized it, she boarded a ship at night, having paid part of her riches, and fled. She reached Alexandria, and stayed there. Then she went to the monastery that to this day is called [the Monastery of the] Patrician Lady. After the death of Theodora, knowing that the empress wanted to take her as his wife, she fled Alexandria at night and came here. She begged me to give her a cell outside Scetis and she told me everything. I gave her this cave and made her look like a man. She lived in Scetis twenty-eight years and nobody knew about her, only you and the other brother here. The emperor sent court officials and envoys /347/ to get her, not only the emperor but even the patriarch of Alexandria did so, and nobody knew where she was, even up to today.

'You can see, child, that even those brought up in the emperor's palace are tempted by the Devil and afflict their bodies. Let us pray and ask the Lord to allow us to become like them and with Father Anastasius to become a eunuch. For her name was Anastasia'.

By the prayers of the Holy Mother of God and all the saints. Amen.

B /341/ . . . [disc]iple of Abba Daniel found an ostracon that had written on it 'Bring tools and come, along with your brother'. The elder read what was written and wept greatly and said, 'Woe to the inner desert! What [great] pillar will fall today!' He said to his disciple, 'Take what you need, and let us go as soon as possible in order to see if the elder is still alive. He is going to the Lord'.

They both wept, and they went and found the elder burning with fever. Abba Daniel threw himself on the elder's breast and, weeping, said, 'Blessed are you at this hour of remembrance and prayer for the dead and dying. You despised the worldly kingdom and all human [glory]'.

The eunuch said to Abba Daniel, /342/ 'Blessed are you, the new Abraham, for many will be born from your hands'.[8]

Abba Daniel said to him, 'Pray for us', and the eunuch answered him, 'It is I who have need of many prayers at this hour'.

Abba Daniel said to him, 'I myself wanted to have a prayer and offer a prayer'.

So the eunuch sat on the carpet, took the elder's head and kissed it and said, 'God instructed me in this place and he will do the same with your old age as with Abraham'.[9] And the elder took his disciple, raised him to his feet, and said, 'Bless my child, father'. Kissing him, [the eunuch] said, 'We stand before God in his hour and he knows how many prostrations I have made in this cell for your [*sic*] name's sake. Give him rest in the spirit of the fathers, as he caused Elijah's spirit to rest on Elisha.[10] And may the name of the Father be on him'.

And [the eunuch] said to the elder, 'For the sake of the Lord, do not take off my clothing, for I was vested by God. Let me go to the Lord as I am. And may nobody know about me except you'. Then he said to the elder, 'Give me Communion', and after Communion he said, 'Give me love in Christ and pray for me'. Then he looked to the east, saying, 'Goodness has come'. /344/ And his face was lighted like flame and, having made the sign of the cross on his lips, he said, 'Into your hands I commit my spirit and also my soul'.[11]

Then both [Abba Daniel and his disciple] wept and dug a grave in front of the cave and then the elder took off his clothes and said to his disciple, 'Dress him in this'. So his disciple dressed him and saw he was a woman, but said nothing. After they buried him and offered a prayer, the elder said to his disciple, 'Let us break the fast and let us celebrate an *agapē* on top of the elder's casket'. And having had Communion, they found in his cell a little dried bread and some soaked grain. They celebrated an *agapē* on top of the casket and took the rope he had made and they left giving thanks to God.

As they were going on their way, the brother said to the elder, 'Do you know, father, whether he was a eunuch or was a woman?'

The elder said, 'I know, child, that he was a woman. If you want, I will tell you about her'. And the elder said, 'This is what I heard about her: She was a patrician lady who lived at the palace. Emperor Justinian wanted to take her into the palace due to her great wisdom. When Empress Theodora saw, she became angry and decided to get rid of her. When she [Anastasia] learned about this, she hired a ship and took her riches and went to Alexandria and reached the monastery which became "[The monastery of] the Patrician Lady". After the death of Theodora, when the emperor wanted to take her back, she left Alexandria at night and came here to me, and told me everything and asked me to give her a cell. I gave her this cave and dressed her in men's clothing and she lived in Scetis for twenty-eight years and nobody knew about her except you and the other brother. The emperor sent envoys, and even the Pope of Alexandria, but nobody knew where she was up to today.

'See for yourself, child, that even the emperor's retinue are tempted by the Devil and afflict their bodies. As for us, when we lived in the world we could not even get our fill of bread. Now that we have entered monastic life, we eat and are not able to acquire virtue! We pray for the Lord to make us worthy of the way of his saints and we pray to acquire mercy with our fathers and with Abba Anastasius the eunuch, for she was named Anastasia.'

CHAPTER EIGHT

Arabic Accounts

Translation and Introduction by Mark N. Swanson

IN THE CENTURIES following the islamic conquest of the eastern
byzantine provinces and the sasanid domains, the arabic language
came to serve as a 'catchment field' for the older literatures of the
Christian East.[1] As early as the eighth century AD, arabic-speaking chalcedonian ('melkite') monks in the monasteries of Palestine and Sinai
were producing arabic translations of scripture and saints' lives from
greek and syriac originals.[2] Three centuries later in Egypt, a wave of
translation of christian texts into Arabic from Coptic began.[3] In its turn,
the developing 'reservoir' of arabic christian texts was drawn on by
monks making translations into Georgian (in melkite circles)[4] and Ethiopic (in coptic orthodox ones).[5]

The arabic 'Daniel dossier' provides an example of this complexity.
Arabic translations of the Daniel stories were made from greek, syriac
and coptic originals,[6] and in turn were translated into Ethiopic. While
a full description of this arabic dossier is a project beyond the scope of
this introduction, I will attempt to give a sense of its shape before pro-
viding english translations of two stories, 'The Woman Who Pretended
to be Mad' and 'The Thief Who Repented'. These two stories appear
in the most common collection of arabic *apophthegmata*, known as *Bustān
al-ruhbān* ('The Garden of the Monks'), which is widely available in
Egypt in an inexpensive published edition.[7]

Arabic Daniel among the Melkites

Antonius, *hegumenos* of the Monastery of Saint Simeon near Antioch (*fl.*
before the end of the tenth century AD), is one of the few early translators

of greek patristic texts into Arabic whose name has come down to us.[8]
His translations include such substantial works as a series of sermons on
Saint John's Gospel by Saint John Chrysostom,[9] most of *The Fount of
Knowledge* by Saint John of Damascus,[10] and a *paterikon* preserved in a
parchment manuscript at the Bibliothèque Nationale: Paris, B.N. ar. 276.[11]
Among the eighty-one separate pieces preserved in the first part of the
manuscript are five of the Daniel stories:

	Story	Folios
#43	(the very end of) Anastasia	(lacuna) f. 169r
#44	Andronicus and Athanasia	ff. 169r–173r
#45	The Woman Who Pretended to be Drunk	ff. 173r–175r
#46	Eulogius the Stonecutter	ff. 175r–179v
#77	The Monk Accused of Theft	ff. 153v–155v[12]

These arabic stories correspond very closely to the greek texts published
by Clugnet;[13] more specifically, the first four provide a useful witness to
a greek original similar to those preserved in the eleventh-century
manuscripts Paris BN Coislin 232 or Coislin 283.

As Sauget has pointed out, three of Antonius' translations of Daniel
stories, 'Andronicus and Athanasia', 'The Woman Who Pretended to be
Drunk', and 'Eulogius the Stonecutter', made their way into an ampli-
fied collation (in 31 stories) of the 'Edifying Tales' (*Akhbār Nāfi'ah*) of
Paul, bishop of Monembasia. Sauget found this collection represented
in a number of arabic manuscripts in the Vatican Library.[14]

Antonius' translations do not exhaust the melkite Daniel dossier. A
perusal of Aziz Suryal Atiya's checklist of arabic manuscripts at the Monastery of Saint Catherine at Mount Sinai[15] reveals copies of 'Eulogius
the Stonecutter' in Sinai ar. 445 (ad 1175)[16] and 448 (thirteenth century),[17] and of 'Andrianus [*sic*] and Athanasia' in Sinai ar. 542 (parchment,
ninth-tenth century).[18] A glance at these copies is sufficient to ascertain

that they differ from the translations of Antonius and are not literal translations of the known greek texts. They deserve to be edited and studied.

Arabic Daniel among the Coptic Orthodox

The fullest study of the Daniel materials based on copto-arabic sources is a 1964 arabic-language publication by Yūsuf Ḥabīb, *Saint Abba Daniel, Hegumenos of the Wilderness of Scetis: From the Oldest Coptic Manuscripts*.[19] The author's goal was to provide, for the first time, an arabic translation of the coptic *Life of Daniel*. However, he discovered that his coptic sources were incomplete, and aimed to 'make up for what is lacking from some manuscripts of the Syrian Monastery' in the Wadi al-Natrun in Egypt—arabic manuscripts, that is.[20] Although Yūsuf Ḥabīb did not usually specify his source when relating one of the Daniel stories, and did not distinguish clearly between transcription and his own introductions, paraphrases, or glosses, he offers texts that, for the most part, appear to be carefully transcribed from manuscripts at the Syrian Monastery.[21] The following table lists the Daniel stories related by Yūsuf Ḥabīb and whether he himself translated them into Arabic from Coptic, or whether he found them already in Arabic. For the sake of comparison, I have added columns indicating the presence of these stories in Greek, Coptic and Ethiopic.

Greek	Title	Coptic *Life*	Yūsuf Ḥabīb, *Abba Daniel*	Language of YH's source manuscript	Ethiopic *Life*
I.1 [3]	Mark the Fool	x	pp. 58–60	Arabic	X
I.3 [4]	A Holy Mendicant		pp. 61–62	Arabic	
I.4 [7]	The Woman Who Pretended to be Drunk/Mad		pp. 78–80	Arabic	X
I.5 [10]	Andronicus and Athanasia		pp. 65–68	Arabic	
I.6 [5]	Thomaïs		pp. 63–64	Arabic	X
I.7 [6]	The Tempted Monk		p. 65	Arabic	X
I.8 [2]	Anastasia		pp. 84–86	Arabic	X
I.9 [9]	Eulogius the Stonecutter	x	pp. 24–31	Arabic	X
II.1 [1]	A Monk and Demons		p. 70	Arabic	
Not in Greek					
1	The Thief Who Repented	x	pp. 70–73	Coptic	X
2	Abba Daniel Refuses to Accept the Tome of Leo	x	pp. 93–97	Coptic	X
3	Abba Daniel Goes to Tambōk	x	p. 98	Coptic	X
4	Abba Daniel Returns to Scetis; Its Destruction	x	pp. 98–100	Coptic	X
5	Abba Daniel Returns to Tambōk; the Death of Abba Daniel; Doxology	x	pp. 104–105	Coptic	X

The table indicates that, on the basis of manuscripts at the Syrian Monastery, there is a fairly extensive copto-*arabic* Daniel dossier, to which we can add 'The Thief Who Repented', found in the most common collection of arabic *apophthegmata*, *Bustān al-ruhbān* ('The Garden of the Monks').[22] As for the anti-chalcedonian and biographical material found at the end of the coptic *Life*, its presence in the ethiopic *Life* indicates that it probably existed in Arabic.[23]

The two pieces translated below are the final two stories found in the widely-available edition of *Bustān al-ruhbān*. They are of interest for a variety of reasons, not the least being that they provide points of comparison with the corresponding stories in Coptic and Ethiopic.

EXCURSUS: ABBA DANIEL ON FILM

While visiting coptic orthodox bookstores in Cairo in the summer of 2003, I regularly asked the clerks if they knew anything about Abba Daniel of Scetis. To my surprise, while they knew of no books dedicated to Abba Daniel, several did know some of the Daniel stories, having seen them enacted on video! Abba Daniel has become known as a character in the life of another saint, Anāsīmūn, 'the queen of seven provinces', who renounced her throne in order to become a wanderer in the desert, 'the queen of the beasts'. Her story is told in an arabic-language videotape that has been distributed widely since its release in 2000.[24] Vignettes within the film relate the stories of 'The Woman Who Pretended to Be Mad' (who is Saint Anāsīmūn herself), 'The Thief Who Repented', and 'Eulogius the Stonecutter'.

A *vita* of Anāsīmūn does exist, and was published (for example) in 1986 on the basis of manuscripts in the Syrian Monastery.[25] One episode of the *vita* is an echo of 'The Woman Who Pretended to be Mad': Anāsīmūn pretends to be demented and is taken in by an (unnamed) convent of three hundred sisters. She is sought out by 'one of the fathers' who has learned in a vision that none of the fathers has achieved the degree of holiness achieved by this queen who renounced her throne. This unnamed father visits the convent and promptly reveals Anāsīmūn's identity (without a night vigil held near the privy!). In recent years, however, the Anāsīmūn story has been enriched through incorporation of all the dramatic detail of 'The Woman Who Pretended to Be Mad' as known from *Bustān al-ruhbān*, including the identity of the monk who discerned her holiness.[26] And thus renewed attention has been attracted not only to this story, but also to other stories involving Abba Daniel of Scetis. It remains to be seen whether this renewed attention will lead to a deeper knowledge of and reflection upon the Daniel dossier among Coptic Orthodox Christians, or whether—through Daniel's subordination to the fictional Anāsīmūn—the figure of Abba Daniel will be trivialized for the present generation.

ARABIC ACCOUNTS

THE WOMAN WHO PRETENDED TO BE MAD²⁷

Abba Daniel was once going along the road with his disciple. When they approached the place called *Ārmūn al-Madīnah*,²⁸ he said to his disciple, 'Go to this convent belonging to these virgins, and inform the mother superior²⁹ that I am here'. The convent was known as the Convent of Abba Armiyūs,³⁰ and three hundred virgins were in it.

When the disciple knocked on the gate, the gatekeeper said to him in a low voice, 'Who is that? What do you want, my father?'

The father said to her, 'I want to speak with the mother superior'.

She said to him, 'The mother superior does not speak with anyone, so inform me of what you want, and I will inform her'.

He said to her, 'Say to her, "There is a monk who wishes to speak with you"'.

So she went and called the mother superior, and she came to the gate and spoke with him through³¹ the gatekeeper. The brother said to her, 'Perform an act of love and receive us to yourself this night, I and my father, lest the wild beasts devour us'.

She responded, saying, 'We have no custom that a man spend the night with us. It is better for you that the wild beasts of the wilderness devour you than that the interior beasts of prey, who are the enemy demons, devour you!'

Then the brother said to her, 'Our father Abba Daniel sent me to you'.

When she heard that it was Abba Daniel, she went out in haste to the second gate. The virgins ran behind her, spreading out their head-coverings³² upon the path to where the old man was. He had hardly entered the monastery before they brought him a pan containing water and washed his feet. When they had finished washing them, the virgins began to take the water and wash their faces, except for one sister whom they called 'The Imbecile',³³ who lay at the gate in very miserable rags. When they had finished washing, the father, Abba Daniel, went out to the gate. He looked at that sister, but she did not greet him, nor did she pay any attention to his speech. The sisters cried out for her to 'kiss the hands of /357/ our father Abba Daniel', but she did not stand up. The mother superior said to Abba Daniel, 'Our father, she is insane. I have been asked many times to throw her outside the gate of the convent, but I have feared sin'.

Then they offered Abba Daniel food that he might eat, and after that they ate.[34] Then he said to his disciple, 'Keep vigil with me tonight, to see the greatness of the virtues of this saintly woman whom they call insane!'

A watch of the night had not passed before the 'insane' woman arose and drew herself up. She lifted her hands towards heaven, opened her mouth, and blessed God. She performed many prostrations,[35] and her tears flowed like a flowing spring, on account of the burning of her heart[36] for God. This was her labor every night, and if she heard any sound coming towards her she would throw herself on the ground and pretend to be asleep. This was how she conducted herself all the days of her life. And he said to his disciple, 'Call the mother superior, quickly!' When she came and saw the sister, the servant of Christ, with light between her hands and angels prostrating themselves with her, she wept and said, 'Woe is me, a sinner! How often have I offered her insult, contumely, and reproach!'

When the clapper[37] was sounded and the sisters gathered for prayer, the mother superior informed them of what she had observed. But when [the 'insane' sister] learned that they had come to know her story, she wrote a note, hung it from a reed at the gate of the convent, and left the convent. In the note was written: 'Wretched woman that I am, because of my wretchedness and the stubborn opposition of the Enemy! He has expelled me[38] from you and banished me from your faces, so full of life. Your insulting me was the fruit[39] of my soul; your vexation with me was fruit to be gathered daily; your contempt of me was my gain, capital which increased every day and hour. Blessed is that hour in which it was said to me: "Imbecile! Madwoman!" For my part you are absolved, innocent of sin. Before you and before the judgement seat[40] I will answer on your behalf, for my sake, that no one among you offers mockery, or loves the sound of her voice,[41] or clothing, or desire; but that all of you are pure'.

That is the end of her letter. When Abba Daniel had read it, he said, 'My stay here last night was for this purpose alone'.

/358/ All the sisters confessed to him the ways in which they had scorned and slandered her. Then the father Abba Daniel absolved them, and taught them not to mock any creature of God—even if an imbecile!—for that is the greatest of sins. The Torah[42] of the prophet Moses says, 'He created the human in the image and likeness of God', with dignity, honor, patience and longsuffering'. Then the father prayed over them and headed away, seeking his own monastery.

THE THIEF WHO REPENTED[43]

Near the Mountain of Scetis—the translation of which is 'the balance of hearts'—there was a convent in which there were many virgins. They had few provisions, and they used to distribute part of them to the poor and strangers. The Hater of the Good[44] could not bear the righteous deeds they were performing, so he entered into the heart of the chief of a tribe near them and incited him to rob the convent. How great was the joy of his men when he informed them of his intention!

When they came to the convent, they schemed as to how they could take it, but [realized that they] could not because the fortifications of the convent were impregnable. Their chief said to them, 'Do what I tell you. Go and bring me a monk's robe, a black headcovering[45] and a hood[46] embroidered entirely with crosses, like the appearance of Abba Daniel who is from Scetis. When evening falls I will dress myself in all that, and taking a palm staff in my hand will knock on the gate. When they look at me they will open [the gate] to me for his sake, and in that way I will prepare the place for you so that you may pillage it at leisure'. When they heard this they rejoiced and brought him the robe he had requested.

When evening fell, the chief arose, dressed himself in the robe, took a palm staff in his hand, and knocked on the gate. The gatekeeper responded to him, 'Who are you, my master and father?'

He said to her, 'Go and inform the mother superior[47] that the poor priest Daniel, who is from Scetis, is standing at the door and says, "Receive me among you until the morrow, that I may rest"'.

The gatekeeper reported this speech to the mother superior. No sooner had the mother superior heard that Abba Daniel was standing at the gate than she arose in haste, the sisters following her, and they kissed that man's foot. Because it was evening they did not make sure of his person, but rather made haste, brought water in a pan and washed his feet. And when they wanted to spread a bed for him in the upper part of the convent,[48] he prevented them saying, 'I will not leave this place'.

/359/ The mother superior and the sisters took the water in which his feet had been washed, and placed it before him. Each one of them began to wash her face in it while he made the sign of the cross upon her. Among the sisters there was a virgin girl who had been blind from her mother's womb. And it happened, as they grasped her by her hands and brought her to that man, that it was the father Abba Daniel who had come among them in the Spirit at that very hour, and who grasped the virgin by the hand and brought her to that man! And they said to him, 'Our father, we request from your holiness that you make the sign of the cross upon her eyes'.

He said to them, 'Give her what's left of the water in the pan'. (He said this in mockery of the water and with contempt for their intellects.)[49]

When the sister took the water, she made the sign of the cross upon it in the name of Christ, saying, 'By the prayer of the saint, Abba Daniel'. Immediately her eyes were opened while that man looked on.

What fear and trembling then possessed him! How great the cry with which they cried out at that hour! They began to kiss the feet of that robber, saying to him, 'Our father, blessed is the hour that you came in to us!'

As for the robber, he said, 'O woe is me! How far I am from God! If the eyes of the blind are opened by the [mere] name of Abba Daniel, how great must be that one who does the work of the Lord! Indeed, how I have squandered my time doing unclean works! By the truth of Abba Daniel's prayer, from now on I shall not return to walk the path that I used to walk!' He was saying this while weeping and plucking out the hair of his beard.

As for the virgins, they were repeatedly saying to him, 'Blessed is the hour in which you came here!' And as for him, he was saying, 'Truly it is a blessed hour!'

As for the men who were waiting for him to open the gate for them, they had been standing with their swords in their hands, restless for the gate to open.[50] From inside he heard them saying: 'Night has drawn near. Perhaps he wants to become a monk and live with them!' Another one of them was saying, 'Perhaps a nun from among them has made him a Christian!' They were saying these things in mockery, but he heard them and said, 'Truly, a prophet of God has spoken through their mouths, because I will become a monk, and a nun from among them has made me a Christian!'

When he kindled the light and their hope in him had failed, they were afraid and sadly departed to their own place, /360/ gnashing their teeth against their chief. As dawn broke, that robber stretched out his hands towards the East, saying, 'O Lord, you did not come to call the righteous, but sinners. Accept me to yourself, through the prayer of those who have exerted themselves for the sake of your name'. Then he bade farewell to the women and went out, they [still] being sure that he was Abba Daniel.

When he was mid-way through his journey, his companions came out against him and said to him, 'What's got into you? Did you wait around because you found beautiful jewels? Do you intend to reveal yourself to us? Show us what you have!' But when they searched him, they found him to be in the worst condition: his face had changed and his eyes had swollen from great weeping. He had changed altogether; the predatory spirit had gone out of him. Then they were afraid and trembled, and began to ask with fear and shame that he let them know the reason for the change of his entire life.

Then he began to let them know what had happened, from the time that he entered among the women and the matter of the blind virgin up to that very hour. When they heard [this], fear came over them, and they were silent.

Thereupon he turned his face to the wilderness, to the place of the father, Abba Daniel, and some[51] of his companions followed him. He related to him what had taken place in the convent of the virgins. Abba Daniel said to him, 'It was I who brought the blind virgin to you. From the time that you entered among the women, I was present in your midst, in the spirit'. After that Abba Daniel made him a monk, and he resided near him, [living] in beautiful worship and surpassing asceticism until the day of his death. That robber performed great miracles, and through his prayer came to dwell in the Paradise of bliss. May the blessing of his prayers be with us. Amen!

Primary Sources
& Translations

Alcock, Anthony, ed. and trans. *The Life of Samuel of Kalamun*. Warminster: Aris & Phillips, 1983.

Amélineau, Emile. 'L'histoire des deux filles de l'empereur Zénon', *Proceedings of the Society for Biblical Archaeology* 10 (1888) 181–206.

————. *Monuments pour servir à l'histoire de l'Egypte chrétienne aux IV, V, VI et VII siècles*. Mémoire de la Mission archéologique Française au Caire, vol. IV, fasc. 1–2; Paris: 1888–1895.

Arras, Victor, ed., *Geronticon*, CSCO 476–477, Scriptores Aethiopici 79–80. Louvain: E. Peeters, 1986.

————. *Patericon Aethiopice*, CSCO 277–278, Scriptores Aethiopici 53–54. Louvain: Secrétariat du CorpusSCO: 1967.

Azéma, Yvan, ed. *Théodoret de Cyr: Correspondance*. Sources chrétiennes; Paris: Cerf, 1965.

Bedjan, Paul. *Acta Martyrum et Sanctorum Syriace*. Hildesheim: G. Olms, 1968 [1890–1897].

Bell, David N., trans. *The Life of Shenoute by Besa*, CS 73. Kalamazoo: Cistercian Publications, 1983.

Brock, Sebastian P. 'A Syriac Narratio Attributed to Abba Daniel of Sketis', *Analecta Bollandiana* 113 (1995) 269–280.

Brock, Sebastian P., and Susan Ashbrook Harvey, *Holy Women of the Syrian Orient*, 40–62. Berkeley: University of California Press, 1987.

Brooks, E. W. *A Collection of Letters of Severus of Antioch from Numerous Syriac Manuscripts*, Patrologia Orientalis 14.1: 75–103, 107–117, 117–127; Paris: Firmin-Didot, 1920.

Bustan al-ruhban: 'an aba' al-kanisah al-qibtiyyah al-urthudhuksiyyah tibqan nuskhah al-khattiyyah al-asliyyah [*The Garden of the Monks: From the fathers of the Coptic Orthodox Church, according to the original manuscript*], 2nd edition. Cairo, 1956.

Chaîne, Marius. 'Une lettre de Sévère d'Antioche à la diaconesse Anastasie', *Oriens Christianus*, 3rd ser., 11 (1913) 32–58.

Charles, R.H., trans., *John of Nikiu, Chronicle*. London & Oxford: Williams & Norgate, 1916.

Clugnet, Léon. 'Vie et Récits de L'Abbé Daniel, de Scété', *Revue de l'Orient Chrétien* 5 (1900) 49–73, 254–271, 370–391; *Revue de l'Orient Chrétien* 6 (1901) 56–87.

Colin, Gérard, ed. *Patrologia Orientalis* 44.3 (no. 199) (Turnhout: Brepols, 1988) 318–321 [86–88].

———. *Patrologia Orientalis* 47.3 (no. 211) (Turnhout: Brepols, 1997) 226–229 [34–37].

Cyril of Scythopolis. *Lives of the Monks of Palestine*, trans. R. M. Price. Kalamazoo: Cistercian Publications: 1989.

Dahlman, Britt. *St Daniel of Sketis: A Group of Hagiographic Texts*. Acta Universitatis Upsaliensis. Studia Byzantina Upsaliensia 10. Lund: Wallin & Dalholm, 2007.

Drescher, James, ed. and trans. *Vita Sanctae Hilariae*, in Drescher, *Three Coptic Legends: Hilaria, Archellites, The Seven Sleepers*. Supplément aux annales du service des antiquités de l'Égypte 4; Cairo: IFAO, 1947.

Evagrius Ponticus: Praktikos and Chapters on Prayer, trans. John Eudes Bamberger, Cistercian Studies 4. Spencer—Kalamazoo: Cistercian Publications, 1972.

Evergetinos, Paul. *Synagoge Rhematon*. Constantinople: 1861.

Forget, I., ed., *Synaxarium Alexandrinum*. Corpus Scriptorum Christianorum Orientalium 47–49, 67, 78, 90, Scriptores Arabici, ser. 3, 18–19; Romae: K. De Luigi, 1905–1926.

Gingra, George E., trans., *Egeria: Diary of a Pilgrimage*, ACW 38. New York: Newman, 1970.

Goldschmidt, Lazarus and F.M. Esteves Pereira. *Vida do Abba Daniel do Mosteiro de Sceté: Versão Ethiopica*. Lisbon: Imprensa Nacional, 1897.

Grébaut, Sylvain, ed. *Patrologia Orientalis* 15.5 (Paris, 1927) 633–638 [91–96].

Guidi, Ignazio. 'Texte Copte', *Revue de l'Orient Chrétien* 5 (1900) 535–552.

Guy, J-C. *Les apophtegmes des Pères: Collection Systématique. Chapitres I-IX*. Paris: Cerf, 1993.

Huber, Michael. *Johannes monachus. Liber de miraculis. Ein neuer Beitrag zur mittelalterlichen Mönchsliteratur*. Sammlung mittellateinischer Texte 7; Heidelberg: C. Winter, 1913.

John of Ephesus. *Lives of the Eastern Saints*, ed. E. W. Brooks. Patrologia orientalis 17; Turnhout: Brepols, 1923.

Johnson, D. W., ed. and trans., *A Panegyric on Macarius, Bishop of Tkôw, Attributed to Dioscorus of Alexandria*. CSCO 415–416 [Scriptores Coptici 41–42]; Louvain: Secrétariat du CorpusSCO, 1980.

Kuhn, K. H., ed. and trans. *A Panegyric on Apollo, Arcimandrite of the Monastery of Isaac, by Stephen, Bishop of Heracleopolis Magna* 10. CSCO 394, Scriptores

Coptici 39 [Coptic], CSCO 395 and 40 [English]; Louvain: Secrétariat du CorpusSCO, 1978.

Kuhn, K. H., and W. J. Tait. *Thirteen Coptic Acrostic Hymns*. Oxford: Oxford University Press, 1996.

Leloir, Louis. *Paterica armeniaca a P.P. Mechitaristis edita (1855) nunc latine reddita*. CSCO 316, subsidia tomus 43; Louvain: Secrétariat du CorpusSCO, 1975).

Lewis, Agnes Smith. *The Forty Martyrs of the Sinai Desert and the Story of Eulogios from a Palestinian Syriac and Arabic Palimpsest*. Horae Semiticae No. IX; Cambridge: Cambridge University Press, 1912.

Lippomano, Luigi. *De vitis sanctorum ab Aloysio Lipomano* [Venice: Aldo Manuzio, 1581], volume 5.

Meyer, Robert T., trans. *Palladius: The Lausiac History*. New York: Newman Press, 1964.

Mikhail, Maged S. and Tim Vivian. 'Life of Saint John the Little', *Coptic Church Review* 18: 1 & 2 (Spring/Summer, 1997).

Mioni, Elpidio. 'Il Pratum Spirituale di Giovanni Mosco', *Orientalia Christiana Periodica* 17 (1951) 61–94; 92–93 (XI [151]).

Moschus, John. *The Spiritual Meadow (Pratum Spirituale)*, trans. John Wortley. Kalamazoo: Cistercian Publications, 1992.

Müller, C. Detlef G. *Die Homilie über die Hochzeit zu Kana und weitere Schriften des Patriarchen Benjamin I. von Alexandrien*. Heidelberg: C. Winter, 1968.

Müller-Kessler, Christa and Michael Sokoloff. *The Forty Martyrs of the Sinai Desert, Eulogios the Stone-Cutter, and Anastasia*. A Corpus of Christian Palestinian Aramaic III; Groningen: Styx, 1996.

Nau, F. 'Histoires des solitaires égyptiens', *Revue de l'Orient Chrétien* 12 (1907) 174–175.

Petitmengin, Pierre, ed., *Pélagie la pénitente: Métamorphoses d'une légende*, Tome I, *Les textes et leur histoire*. Paris: Études augustiniennes, 1981.

Price, R. M., trans. *A History of the Monks of Syria*. Kalamazoo: Cistercian Publications, 1985.

Ramsey, Boniface, trans. *John Cassian: The Conferences*. Mahwah, NJ: Paulist, 1997.

Regnault, Lucien. *Les sentences des Pères du désert: Nouveau recueil*, 2nd ed. Solesmes: Abbaye Saint-Pierre du Solesmes, 1977.

———. *Les sentences des Pères du désert: Série des anonymes*. Solesmes: Bellefonatine, 1985.

Russell, Norman, trans. *The Lives of the Desert Fathers: The Historia Monachorum in Aegypto*. Kalamazoo: Cistercian Publications, 1980.

Stewart, Columba. *The World of the Desert Fathers*. Fairacres, Oxford: SLG Press, 1986.

van Wijk, N. 'Die Erzählungen des Sketioten Daniel im Kirchenslavischen', *Slavia* 12 (1933–1934) 335–352.

Veilleux, Armand, ed. *Pachomian Koinonia*, volume one, *The Life of Saint Pachomius*. Kalamazoo: Cistercian Publications, 1980.

Vivian, Tim. 'The *Ascetic Teaching* of Stephen of Thebes', *Cistercian Studies Quarterly* 34.4 (1999) 425–454. Repr. in Vivian, *Words to Live By*.

———. 'Humility and Resistance in Late Antique Egypt: *The Life of Longinus*', *Coptic Church Review* 20.1 (Spring 1999) 2–30. Repr. in Vivian, *Words to Live By*.

———. *Journeying into God: Seven Early Monastic Lives*. Minneapolis: Fortress, 1996.

———. '"A Man Holy and Perfect": The *Life of Paisios/Bishoy* Attributed to John Kolobos', *Studia Monastica* (forthcoming).

———. 'The Monasteries of the Wadi Natrun, Egypt: A Personal and Monastic Journey', *American Benedictine Review* 49:1 (March 1998) 3–32. Repr. in Vivian, *Words to Live By*.

———. 'Monks, Middle, Egypt, and *Metanoia*: The *Life of Phib* by Papohe the Steward', *Journal of Early Christian Studies* 7.4 (Winter 1999) 547–572. Repr. in Vivian, *Words to Live By*.

———. *Paphnutius: Histories of the Monks of Upper Egypt and the Life of Onnophrius*. Rev. ed., Kalamazoo: Cistercian Publications, 2000.

———. *Saint Macarius the Spiritbearer*. Crestwood, NY: St. Vladimir's, 2004.

———. 'Saint Paul of Tamma: Four Works Concerning Monastic Spirituality', *Coptic Church Review* 18:4 (Winter 1997) 105–116. Repr. in Vivian, *Words to Live By*.

———. *Words to Live By: Journeys in Ancient and Modern Egyptian Monasticism*. Kalamazoo, MI: Cistercian: Publications, 2005.

———, and Apostolos N. Athanassakis, trans., *The Life of Antony*. Kalamazoo: Cistercian Publications, 2003.

Ward, Benedicta. *Harlots of the Desert*. Kalamazoo: Cistercian Publications, 1987.

———, trans., *The Sayings of the Desert Fathers*. Kalamazoo: Cistercian Publications, 1975; rev. ed., 1984.

Bibliography

Alcock, Anthony, ed. and trans. *The Life of Samuel of Kalamun*. Warminster: Aris & Phillips, 1983.

Amélineau, Emile. 'L'histoire des deux filles de l'empereur Zénon', *Proceedings of the Society for Biblical Archaeology* 10 (1888) 181–206.

———. *Monuments pour servir à l'histoire de l'Égypte chrétienne aux IV, V, VI et VII siècles*. Mémoire de la Mission archéologique française au Caire, vol. IV, fasc. 1–2; Paris: 1888–1895.

Anastasi al-Samu'ili. *Firdaws al-Athar* [*The Paradise of the Pure Ones*], 2nd printing. The Monastery of Saint Samuel the Confessor, n.d.

Anson, J. 'The Female Transvestite in Early Monasticism: Origin and Development of a Motif', *Viator: Medieval and Religious Studies* 5 (1974) 1–32.

Arras, Victor, ed. *Geronticon*, CSCO 476–477, Scriptores Aethiopici 79–80. Louvain: E. Peeters, 1986.

———. *Patericon Aethiopice*, CSCO 277–278, Scriptores Aethiopici 53–54. Louvain: Secrétariat du CorpusSCO: 1967.

Aziz Suryal Atiya. *The Arabic Manuscripts of Mount Sinai: A Hand-List of the Arabic Manuscripts and Scrolls Microfilmed at the Library of the Monastery of St. Catherine, Mount Sinai*. Baltimore: The Johns Hopkins Press, 1955.

Atiya, Aziz S., ed. *The Coptic Encyclopedia*. 8 volumes. New York: Macmillan, 1991.

Azéma, Yvan, ed. *Théodoret de Cyr: Correspondance*. Sources chrétiennes; Paris: Cerf, 1965.

Bedjan, Paul. *Acta Martyrum et Sanctorum Syriace*. Hildesheim: G. Olms, 1968 [1890–1897].

Bell, David N., trans. *The Life of Shenoute by Besa*, CS 73. Kalamazoo: Cistercian Publications, 1983.

Berry, Wendell. *Another Turn of the Crank*. Washington, D.C.: Counterpoint, 1995.

———. *Life is a Miracle: An Essay against Modern Superstition*. Washington, DC: Counterpoint, 2000.

Bolman, Elizabeth S., ed. *Monastic Visions: The Wall Paintings at the Monastery of St. Antony at the Red Sea*. New Haven: Yale University Press, 2002.

Bonnet, Max. Review, *Byzantinische Zeitschrift* 13 (1904) 166–171.

Bradley, K. R. *Slaves and Masters in the Roman Empire: A Study in Social Control*. Oxford: Oxford UP, 1987.

Brakke, David. *Athanasius and the Politics of Asceticism*. Oxford Early Christian Studies Series. Oxford: Clarendon Press, 1995.

Brock, Sebastian P. 'A Syriac Narratio Attributed to Abba Daniel of Sketis', *Analecta Bollandiana* 113 (1995) 269–280.

Brock, Sebastian P. and Susan A. Harvey. *Holy Women of the Syrian Orient*. Berkeley: University of California Press, 1987.

Brooks, E. W. *A Collection of Letters of Severus of Antioch from Numerous Syriac Manuscripts*, *Patrologia Orientalis* 14.1: 75–103, 107–117, 117–127; Paris: Firmin-Didot, 1920.

Brown, Peter. 'The Rise and Function of the Holy Man in Late Antiquity', *Journal of Roman Studies* 61 (1971) 80–101.

———. 'The Rise and Function of the Holy Man in Late Antiquity: 1971–1997', *Journal of Early Christian Studies* 6:3 (1998) 353–376.

———. 'The Saint as Exemplar in Late Antiquity', *Representations* 2 (1983) 1–25.

———. *Society and the Holy in Late Antiquity*. Berkeley: University of California Press, 1982.

Budge, Ernest A. Wallis. *The Paradise or Garden of the Holy Fathers*. London: Chatto & Windus, 1907.

Burton-Christie, Douglas. *The Word in the Desert*. New York-Oxford: Oxford University Press, 1993.

Butler, A. J. *The Arab Conquest of England*, ed. P. M. Fraser. Oxford: Oxford University Press, 1978.

Bustan al-ruhban: 'an aba' al-kanisah al-qibtiyyah al-urthudhuksiyyah tibqan nuskhah al-khattiyyah al-asliyyah [*The Garden of the Monks: From the Fathers of the Coptic Orthodox Church, according to the original manuscript*], 2nd edition. Cairo, 1956.

Calderini, Aristide. *Dizionario dei nomi geografici e topografici dell' Egitto greco-romano*. 5 vols.; Cairo, Società reale di geografia D'Egitto, 1935–1987.

Chaîne, Marius. 'Une lettre de Sévère d'Antioche à la diaconesse Anastasie', *Oriens Christianus*, 3rd ser., 11 (1913) 32–58.

Charles, R. H., trans., *John of Nikiu, Chronicle*. London-Oxford: Williams & Norgate, 1916.

Clédat, Jean. *Le Monastère et la Nécropole de Baouît*. Mémoires publiés par les membres de L'Institut Français d'Archéologie Orientale du Caire 12 [one volume in two parts]; Cairo: IFAO, 1904.

Clugnet, Léon. 'Vie et Récits de l'Abbé Daniel de Scété', *Revue de l'Orient Chrétien* 5 (1900) 49–73, 254–271, 370–391; *Revue de l'Orient Chrétien* 6 (1901) 56–87.

Colin, Gérard, ed. *Patrologia Orientalis* 44.3 (no. 199) (Turnhout: Brepols, 1988) 318–321 [86–88].

—————. *Patrologia Orientalis* 47.3 (no. 211) (Turnhout: Brepols, 1997) 226–229 [34–37].

Constable, Olivia Remie. *Housing the Stranger in the Mediterranean World: Lodging, Trade, and Travel in Late Antiquity and the Middle Ages.* Cambridge: Cambridge University Press, 2003.

Coquin, René-Georges. 'Apollon de Titkooh ou/et Apollon de Bawit?', *Orientalia* 46 (1977) 435–446.

Crum, W. E. *A Coptic Dictionary.* Oxford: Clarendon, 1979.

—————. 'Der hl. Apollo und das Klöster von Bawit', *Zeitschrift für ägyptische Sprache und Altertumskunde* 40 (1902) 60–62.

Cyril of Scythopolis. *Lives of the Monks of Palestine*, trans. R. M. Price. CS 114. Kalamazoo: Cistercian Publications: 1989.

Cyrillus, Salvator. *Codices graeci manuscripti regiae bibliothecae Borbonicae.* Naples: De regia typographia, 1826–1832.

Dahlman, Britt. *St Daniel of Sketis: A Group of Hagiographic Texts.* Acta Universitatis Upsaliensis. Studia Byzantina Upsaliensia 10. Lund: Wallin & Dalholm, 2007.

Davis, Stephen J. 'Crossed Texts, Crossed Sex: Intertextuality and Gender in Early Christian Legends of Holy Women Disguised as Men', *Journal of Early Christian Studies* 10:1 (Spring 2002) 1–36.

Delcourt, Marie. 'Appendix: Female Saints in Masculine Clothing', in Delcourt, ed., *Hermaphrodite: Myths and Rites of the Bisexual Figure in Classical Antiquity*, trans. Jennifer Nicholson, 84–102. London: Studio Books, 1961.

Delehaye, Hippolyte. 'Bulletine des publications hagiographiques', *Analecta Bollandiana* 22 (1903) 96.

—————. 'Catalogus Codicum Hagiographicorum Graecorum Bibliothecae Nationalis Neapolitanae', *Analecta Bollandiana* 21 (1902) 381–400.

—————. *Les origines du culte des martyrs.* 2nd rev. ed.; Brussels: Société des Bollandistes, 1933.

—————. 'Quelques saints du propre de Naples', *Analecta Bollandiana* 59 (1941) 1–33.

—————. 'Saints de Chypre', *Analecta Bollandiana* 26 (1907) 161–301.

Dembinska, Maria. 'Diet: A Comparison of Food Consumption between some Eastern and Western Monasteries in the 4th–12th Centuries', *Byzantion* 55 (1985) 431–462.

de Ricci, Seymour and Eric O. Winstedt. 'Les quarante-neuf vieillards de Scété', *Notices et extraits des manuscrits de la Bibliothèque nationale*, vol. 39:2. Paris, 1910–1911.

Desprez, Vincent. *Le monachisme primitif: Des origines jusqu'au concile d'Éphèse.* Spiritualité orientale 72; Begrolles-en-Mauges: Abbaye de Bellefontaine, 1998.

Downey, Glanville. *A History of Antioch in Syria: from Seleucus to the Arab Conquest.* Princeton: Princeton University Press, 1961.

Drescher, James, ed. and trans. *Vita Sanctae Hilariae,* in Drescher, *Three Coptic Legends: Hilaria, Archellites, The Seven Sleepers.* Supplément aux annales du service des antiquités de l'Égypte 4; Cairo: IFAO, 1947.

Drew-Bear, Marie. *Le nome Hermopolite: Toponymes et sites.* American Studies in Papyrology 21; Missoula, Montana: Scholars Press, 1979.

Emmel, Stephen, et al., eds. *Ägypten und Nubien in spätantiker und christlicher Zeit: Akten des 6. Internationalen Koptologenkongresses, Münster, 20.–26. Juli 1996.* Sprachen und Kulturen des christlichen Orients, Bd. 6; Wiesbaden: Reichert, 1999.

Evagrius Ponticus: Praktikos and Chapters on Prayer, trans. John Eudes Bamberger. CS 4. Spencer-Kalamazoo: Cistercian Publications, 1972.

Evelyn White, Hugh G. *The Monasteries of the Wadi 'N Natrun,* vol. 2, *The History of the Monasteries of Nitria and Scetis.* Rpt New York: Arno Press, 1973.

Evergetinos, Paul. *Synagoge Rhematon.* Constantinople: 1861.

Festugière, A.-J. 'Lieux communs littéraires et thèmes de folk-lore dans l'Hagiographie primitive', *Wiener Studien* 73 (1960) 123–152.

Forget, I., ed., *Synaxarium Alexandrinum.* Corpus Scriptorum Christianorum Orientalium 47–49, 67, 78, 90, Scriptores Arabici, ser. 3, 18–19; Romae, K. De Luigi, 1905–1926.

Frank, Georgia. *The Memory of the Eyes: Pilgrims to Living Saints in Christian Late Antquity.* Berkeley: University of California Press, 2000.

Frazee, Charles A. 'Late Roman and Byzantine Legislation on the Monastic Life from the Fourth to the Eighth Centuries', *Church History* 51/3 (September 1982) 263–279.

Freeman, Laurence. *Jesus: The Teacher Within.* New York–London: Continuum, 2000.

Frend, W. H. C. *The Rise of the Monophysite Movement.* Cambridge: Cambridge University Press, 1972.

Frost, Peter. 'Attitudes toward Blacks in the Early Christian Era'. *The Second Century* 8 (1991): 1–11.

Garitte, Gérard. *Catalogue des manuscrits géorgiens littéraires du Mont Sinaï,* CSCO 165/subs. 9. Louvain: L. Durbecq, 1956.

———. 'Daniel de Scété', *Dictionnaire d'Histoire et de Géographie* 14.70–72.

Gascou, Jean. 'Enaton, The', *The Coptic Encyclopedia,* ed. Aziz S. Atiya, 3.954–58. New York: Macmillan, 1991.

Gingras, George E., trans. *Egeria: Diary of a Pilgrimage.* ACW 38; New York: Newman, 1970.

Goehring, James E. *Ascetics, Society, and the Desert: Studies in Early Egyptian Monasticism.* Harrisburg, Pennsylvania: Trinity, 1999.

Goldschmidt, Lazarus and F.M. Esteves Pereira. *Vida do Abba Daniel do Mosteiro de Sceté: Versão Ethiopica*. Lisbon: Imprensa Nacional, 1897.

Gould, Graham. 'Lay Christians, Bishops, and Clergy in the Apophthegmata Patrum', *Studia Patristica* 25, ed. Elizabeth A. Livingstone. Leuven: Peeters, 1993.

Graf, Georg. *Geschichte der christlichen arabischen Literatur*, I, *Die Übersetzungen*, Studi e Testi 118. Vatican City: Biblioteca Apostolica Vaticana, 1944; II, *Die Schriftsteller bis zur Mitte des 15. Jahrhunderts*, Studi e Testi 133. Vatican City: Biblioteca Apostolica Vaticana, 1947.

Grébaut, Sylvain, ed. *Patrologia Orientalis* 15.5 (Paris, 1927) 633–638 [91–96].

Griffith, Sidney H. *Arabic Christianity in the Monasteries of Ninth-Century Palestine.* Brookfield, Vermont and Aldershot, Hants: Variorum, 1992.

Grossmann, Peter. *Abu Mina: A Guide to the Ancient Pilgrimage Center.* Cairo: Fotiadis, 1986.

———. 'The Pilgrimage Center of Abû Mînâ', in David Frankfurter, ed., *Pilgrimage and Holy Space in Late Antique Egypt*, 281–302. Leiden: Brill, 1998.

Guidi, Ignazio. 'Corrections de quelques passages du texte éthiopien', *Revue de l'Orient Chrétien* 6: 54–56.

———. *Patrologia Orientalis* 7.3 (Paris: 1911) 209–212 [193–196].

———. *Patrologia Orientalis* 7.3 (Paris 1911) 435–438 [419–422].

———. 'Texte Copte', *Revue de l'Orient Chrétien* 5 (1900) 535–552.

Guillaumont, Antoine. 'Le depaysement comme form d'ascèse dans le monachisme ancien', in Guillaumont, *Aux origines du monachisme chrétien: Pour une phénoménologie du monachisme*, 89–116. Spiritualité Orientale 30. Bégrolles-en-Mauges: Bellefontaine, 1979.

———. 'La folie simulée, une forme d'anachorèse', in *Études sur la spiritualité de l'orient chrétien*, 125–130. Spiritualité Orientale 66. Bégrolles-en-Mauges: Abbaye de Bellefontaine, 1996.

———. 'La séparation du monde dans l'orient chrétien: ses formes et ses motifs', in Guillaumont, *Études sur la spiritualité de l'orient chrétien*, 105–112. Spiritualité Orientale 66; Bégrolles-en-Mauges: Abbaye de Bellefontaine, 1996.

Guy, J-C. *Les apophtegmes des Pères: Collection Systématique. Chapitres I-IX.* Paris: Cerf, 1993.

———. *Recherches sur la tradition grecque des Apophtegmata Patrum*, Subsidia hagiographica 36. Brussels, Société des Bollandistes, 1962.

Haas, Christopher. *Alexandria in Late Antiquity: Topography and Social Conflict.* Baltimore: Johns Hopkins University Press, 1997.

Habib, Yusuf. *al-Qiddis al-Anba Daniyal, qummus barriyyat Shihit: 'an aqdam al-makhtutat bi-l-lughah al-qibtiyyah.* Cairo: Maktabat Markaz al-dirasat al-qibtiyyah, 1964.

Hardy, Edward R. 'The Egyptian Policy of Justinian', *Dumbarton Oaks Papers* 22 (1968) 21–41.

————. 'Gaianus', *The Coptic Encyclopedia*, ed. Aziz S. Atiya, 4.1138. New York: Macmillan, 1991.

Harmless, William, SJ, 'Remembering Poemen Remembering: The Desert Fathers and the Spirituality of Memory', *Church History* 69:3 (September 2000) 483–518.

Harvey, Susan Ashbrook. *Asceticism and Society in Crisis*. Transformation of the Classical Heritage 18; Berkeley: University of California Press, 1990.

Holman, Susan R. *The Hungry are Dying: Beggars and Bishops in Roman Cappadocia*. Oxford Studies in Historical Theology; Oxford-New York: Oxford University Press, 2001.

Huber, Michael. *Johannes monachus. Liber de miraculis. Ein neuer Beitrag zur mittelalterlichen Mönchsliteratur*. Sammlung mittellateinischer Texte 7; Heidelberg: C. Winter, 1913.

Innemée, Karel C. *Ecclesiastical Dress in the Medieval Near East*. Leiden: Brill, 1992.

John of Ephesus. *Lives of the Eastern Saints*, ed. E. W. Brooks. Patrologia orientalis 17; Turnhout: Brepols, 1923.

Johnson, D. W., ed. and trans., *A Panegyric on Macarius, Bishop of Tkôw, Attributed to Dioscorus of Alexandria*. CSCO 415–416 [Scriptores Coptici 41–42]; Louvain: Secrétariat du CorpusSCO, 1980.

Kosack, Wolfgang. *Historisches Kartenwerk Ägyptens*. Bonn: Rudolf Habelt, 1971.

Krueger, Derek. *Symeon the Holy Fool: Leontius' Life and the Late Antique City*. Berkeley: University of California Press, 1996.

Kuhn, K. H., ed. and trans. *A Panegyric on Apollo, Arcimandrite of the Monastery of Isaac, by Stephen, Bishop of Heracleopolis Magna* 10. CSCO 394, Scriptores Coptici 39 [Coptic], CSCO 395 and 40 [English]; Louvain: Secrétariat du CorpusSCO, 1978.

Kuhn, K. H., and W. J. Tait. *Thirteen Coptic Acrostic Hymns*. Oxford: Oxford University Press, 1996.

Lampe, W. G. H. *A Patristic Greek Lexicon*. Oxford: Clarendon, 1961.

Lane, Belden C. *The Solace of Fierce Landscapes: A Journey into the Spirituality of Desert and Mountain*. Oxford, Oxford University Press, 1998

————. 'The Spirituality and Politics of Holy Folly', *The Christian Century* (15 December 1982) 1281–1286.

Lane Fox, Robin. 'The *Life of Daniel*', in M.J. Edwards and Simon Swain, eds., *Portraits: Biographical Representation in the Greek and Roman Literature of the Roman Empire*. Oxford: Clarendon, 1997.

Leloir, Louis. *Paterica armeniaca a P.P. Mechitaristis edita (1855) nunc latine reddita*. CSCO 316, subsidia tomus 43; Louvain: Secrétariat du CorpusSCO, 1975).

Leslau, Wolf. *Comparative Dictionary of Geʿez (Classical Ethiopic)*. Wiesbaden: Harrassowitz, 1987.

Lewis, Agnes Smith. *The Forty Martyrs of the Sinai Desert and the Story of Eulogios from a Palestinian Syriac and Arabic Palimpsest*. Horae Semiticae No. IX; Cambridge: Cambridge University Press, 1912.

Liber de vita moribusque sanctorum Patrum ex gemina interpretatione veterum scriptorum. Venice, 1855.

MacCoull, Leslie S.B. "'When Justinian Was Upsetting the World': A Note on Soldiers and Religious Coercion in Sixth-Century Egypt', in *Peace and War in Byzantium: Essays in Honor of George T. Dennis, S.J.*, ed. Timothy S. Miller and John Nesbitt. Washington, DC: The Catholic University of America Press, 1995.

Marincola, John. *Authority and Tradition in Ancient Historiography*. Cambridge: Cambridge University Press, 1997.

Martindale, J. R., ed. *The Prosopography of the Later Roman Empire*. Cambridge: Cambridge University Press, 1971–1992.

Mathews, Thomas F. *The Clash of the Gods: A Reinterpretation of Early Christian Art*. Princeton: Princeton University Press, 1993.

McGuckin, John. *Saint Gregory of Nazianzus*. Crestwood, New York: St. Vladimir's Seminary Press, 2001.

Meier, John P. *A Marginal Jew: Rethinking the Historical Jesus*, Volume One, *The Roots of the Problem and the Person*. New York: Doubleday, 1991.

Meinardus, Otto F.A. *Two Thousand Years of Coptic Christianity*. Cairo: American University of Cairo Press, 1999.

Meyer, Robert T., trans. *Palladius: The Lausiac History*. New York: Newman Press, 1964.

Mikhail, Maged S. and Tim Vivian. 'Life of Saint John the Little', *Coptic Church Review* 18: 1 & 2 (Spring/Summer, 1997).

Mioni, Elpidio. 'Il Pratum Spirituale di Giovanni Mosco', *Orientalia Christiana Periodica* 17 (1951) 61–94.

Moorhead, John. *Justinian*. London-New York: Longman, 1994.

Moschus, John. *The Spiritual Meadow (Pratum Spirituale)*, translated by John Wortley. CS 139. Kalamazoo: Cistercian Publications, 1992.

Moussa, Mark R. 'Abba Moses of Abydos', Unpublished M.A. Thesis. Washington, DC: The Catholic University of America, 1998.

Muilenberg, J. 'Holiness', in *The Interpreter's Dictionary of the Bible*, 616–625. Nashville: Abingdon, 1962.

Müller, C. Detlef G. *Die Homilie über die Hochzeit zu Kana und weitere Schriften des Patriarchen Benjamin I. von Alexandrien*. Heidelberg: C. Winter, 1968.

———. 'John of Parallos, Saint', in *The Coptic Encyclopedia*, ed. Aziz. S. Atiya, 5.1367–68. New York: Macmillan, 1991.

Müller-Kessler, Christa and Michael Sokoloff. *The Forty Martyrs of the Sinai Desert, Eulogios the Stone-Cutter, and Anastasia*. A Corpus of Christian Palestinian Aramaic III; Groningen: Styx, 1996.

Nau, F. 'Histoires des solitaires égyptiens', *Revue de l'Orient Chrétien* 12 (1907) 174–175.

Nugent, Andrew. 'Black Demons in the Desert', *American Benedictine Review* 49.2 (June 1998) 209–221.

O'Connor, Flannery. *Collected Works*. New York: Library of America, 1988.

Petitmengin, Pierre, ed., *Pélagie la pénitente: Métamorphoses d'une légende*, Tome I, *Les textes et leur histoire*. Paris: Études augustiniennes, 1981.

Price, R. M., trans. *A History of the Monks of Syria*. CS 88. Kalamazoo: Cistercian Publications, 1985.

Quibell, J. E. *Excavations at Saqqara (1908–1909, 1909–1910)*, vol. 4, *The Monastery of Apa Jeremias*. Cairo: IFAO, 1912.

Ramsey, Boniface, trans. *John Cassian: The Conferences*. Ancient Christian Writers 57. Mahwah, New Jersey: Paulist Press, 1997.

Rapp, Claudia. '"For next to God, you are my salvation": reflections on the rise of the holy man in late antiquity', in James Howard-Johnston and Paul Antony Hayward, eds., *The Cult of Saints in Late Antiquity and the Middle Ages: Essays on the Contribution of Peter Brown*. Oxford: Oxford University Press, 1999.

———. 'Storytelling as Spiritual Communication in Early Greek Hagiography: The Use of *Diegesis*', *Journal of Early Christian Studies* 6.3 (1998) 431–448.

Rassart-Debergh, Marguerite. 'Trois Peintures', in *Acta ad Archaeologiam et Artium Historiam Pertinentia*, ed. Hjalmar Torp, *et al.*, 193–201. Rome: Bretschneider, 1981.

Regnault, Lucien. *The Day-to-Day Life of the Desert Fathers in Fourth-Century Egypt*. Petersham, Massachusetts: Saint Bede's Press, 1999.

———. *Les sentences des Pères du désert: Nouveau recueil,* 2nd ed. Solesmes: Abbaye Saint-Pierre du Solesmes, 1977.

———. *Les sentences des Pères du désert: Série des anonymes*. Solesmes: Bellefontaine, 1985.

———. *La vie quotidienne des pères du désert en Égypte au IVe siécle*. Paris: Hachette, 1990.

Rousseau, Philip. 'Ascetics as mediators and as teachers', in James Howard-Johnston and Paul Antony Hayward, eds., *The Cult of Saints in Late Antiquity and the Middle Ages: Essays on the Contribution of Peter Brown*. Oxford: Oxford University Press, 1999.

———. *Ascetics, Authority, and the Church in the Age of Jerome and Cassian*. Oxford Historical Monographs; Oxford: Oxford University Press, 1978.

Rubenson, Samuel. 'Translating the Tradition: Some Remarks on the Arabization of the Patristic Heritage in Egypt', *Medieval Encounters* 2 (1996) 4–14.

Russell, Norman, trans. *The Lives of the Desert Fathers: The Historia Monachorum in Aegypto*. CS 34. Kalamazoo: Cistercian Publications, 1980.

Sauget, Joseph-Marie. 'Le paterikon du manuscript arabe 276 de la Bibliothèque Nationale de Paris', *Muséon* 82 (1969) 363–404.

Saward, John. *Perfect Fools: Folly for Christ's Sake in Catholic and Orthodox Spirituality*. Oxford: Oxford University Press, 1980.

Shaw, Teresea M. *The Burden of the Flesh: Fasting and Sexuality in Early Christianity*. Minneapolis: Fortress, 1998.

Sim'an al-Suryani. *al-Aba' al-Sawah* [*The Wandering Fathers*]. Metropolitanate of Bani Suwayf and al-Bahnasah, 1986.

Snowden, F. M. *Blacks in Antiquity: Ethiopians in the Greco-Roman Experience*. Cambridge: Harvard University Press, 1970.

Stewart, Columba. *The World of the Desert Fathers*. Fairacres, Oxford: SLG Press, 1986.

Stewart, Randall. 'Theodosians', *The Coptic Encyclopedia*, ed. Aziz Atiya, 7.2240–2241. New York: Macmillan, 1991.

Tarchnisvili, Mik'el. *Geschichte der kirchlichen georgischen Literatur: auf Grund des ersten Bandes der georgischen Literaturgeschichte von K. Kekelidze*, Studi e Testi 185. Vatican City: Biblioteca Apostolica Vaticana, 1955.

ten Hacken, Clara. 'Coptic and Arabic Texts on Macrobius, an Egyptian Monk of the Sixth Century', in Stephen Emmel, et al., eds., *Ägypten und Nubien in spätantiker und christlicher Zeit*. Wiesbaden: Reichert, 1999.

Timm, Stefan. *Das christlich-koptische Ägypten in arabischer Zeit: eine Sammlung christlicher Stätten in Ägypten in arabischer Zeit, unter Ausschluss von Alexandria, Kairo, des Apa-Mena-Klosters (Der Abu Mina), der Sketis (Wadi n-Natrun) und der Sinai-Region*. Wiesbaden: L. Reichert, 1984–1992.

Tougher, Shaun F. 'Byzantine Eunuchs: An Overview, with Special Reference to their Creation and Origin', in Liz James, ed., *Women, Men and Eunuchs: Gender in Byzantium*, 168–184. London and New York: Routledge, 1997.

Urbainczyk, Theresa. *Theodoret of Cyrrhus: The Bishop and the Holy Man*. Ann Arbor: The University of Michigan Press, 2002.

Van Cauwenbergh, Paul. *Étude sur les moines d'Égypte depuis le concile de Chalcédoine (451) jusqu'à l'invasion arabe (640)*. Paris: Imprimerie Nationale, 1914.

van Wijk, N. 'Die Erzählungen des Sketioten Daniel im Kirchenslavischen', *Slavia* 12 (1933–1934) 335–352.

Veilleux, Armand, ed. *Pachomian Koinonia*, volume one, *The Life of Saint Pachomius*. CS 45. Kalamazoo: Cistercian Publications, 1980.

Vivian, Tim. 'A Journey to the Interior: The Monasteries of Saint Antony and Saint Paul by the Red Sea', *American Benedictine Review* 50.3 (September 1999) 277–310.

————. 'Ama Sibylla of Saqqara: Prioress or Prophet, Monastic or Mythological Being?' *Bulletin of the Saint Shenouda the Archimandrite Coptic Society* 5 (1998–1999)1–17.

————. 'The *Ascetic Teaching* of Stephen of Thebes', *Cistercian Studies Quarterly* 34.4 (1999) 425–454.

————. 'Humility and Resistance in Late Antique Egypt: *The Life of Longinus*', *Coptic Church Review* 20.1 (Spring 1999) 2–30.

————. *Journeying into God: Seven Early Monastic Lives*. Minneapolis: Fortress, 1996.

————. 'The Monasteries of the Wadi Natrun, Egypt: A Personal and Monastic Journey', *American Benedictine Review* 49:1 (March 1998) 3–32.

————. 'Monks, Middle, Egypt, and *Metanoia*: The *Life of Phib* by Papohe the Steward', *Journal of Early Christian Studies* 7.4 (Winter 1999) 547–572.

————. *Paphnutius: Histories of the Monks of Upper Egypt and the Life of Onnophrius*. Revised edition. CS 140. Kalamazoo: Cistercian Publications, 2000.

————. *Saint Macarius the Spiritbearer*. Crestwood, New York: St Vladimir's Seminary Press, 2004.

————. 'Saint Paul of Tamma: Four Works Concerning Monastic Spirituality', *Coptic Church Review* 18:4 (Winter 1997) 105–116.

————. *Words to Live By: Journeys in Ancient and Modern Egyptian Monasticism*. Kalamazoo: Cistercian Publications, 2005.

———— and Apostolos N. Athanassakis, trans., *The Life of Antony*. CS 202. Kalamazoo: Cistercian Publications, 2003.

Ward, Benedicta. *Harlots of the Desert*. CS 106. Kalamazoo: Cistercian Publications, 1987.

————. trans., *The Sayings of the Desert Fathers*. CS 59. Kalamazoo: Cistercian Publications, 1975; revised edition, 1984.

Wijk, van N. 'Die Erzählungen des Sketioten Daniel im Kirchenslavischen', *Slavia* 12 (1933–34), 335–352.

Wipszycka, Ewa. 'Les clercs dans les communautés monastiques d'Égypte', *The Journal of Juristic Papyrology* 26 (1996) 135–166.

————. 'Le monachisme égyptien et les villes' in Ewa Wipszycka, *Études sur le christiansime dans l'Égypte de l'antiquité tardive*. Studia Ephemeridis Augustinianum 52, 257–278. Rome, 1996.

Wortley, John, trans. *John Moschus: The Spiritual Meadow*. CS 139. Kalamazoo: Cistercian Publications, 1992.

Yusuf, Sa'id, and Majid Tawfiq. *Qissat hayat al-Qiddisah Anasimun al-Sa'ihah* [*The Story of the Life of Saint Anasimun the Wanderer*]. Cairo: The Church of Saint George and Saint Abraham in Heliopolis, 2000.

Zanetti, Ugo. 'Les chrétientés du Nil: Basse et Haute Égypte, Nubie, Éthiopie', in Robert F. Taft, ed., *The Christian East, Its Institutions and Its Thought: A Critical Reflection*, OCA 251, 181–216. Rome: Pontificio Istituto Orientale, 1996.

Notes

Introduction

1. Wendell Berry, *Life is a Miracle: An Essay against Modern Superstition* (Washington DC: Counterpoint, 2000) 8.

2. Lev 11:44. For an overview of holiness in the Bible, see J. Muilenberg, 'Holiness', in *The Interpreter's Dictionary of the Bible* (Nashville: Abingdon, 1962) 616-625. See now John Webster, *Holiness* (Grand Rapids: Eerdmans, 2004).

3. Douglas Burton-Christie has recognized and acknowledged this by subtitling his excellent study of the apophthegmata, *The Word in the Desert* (New York & Oxford: Oxford University Press, 1993), 'Scripture and the Quest for Holiness in Early Christian Monasticism'. For a general overview, see Burton-Christie, 'Quest for Holiness in [the] Fourth Century: Pagan and Christian Approaches', in *The Word in the Desert,* 48–62.

4. In the AP, see Arsenius 5, Agathon 3, Agathon 9, Amoun of Nitria 2, Elias 8, Theodore of Pherme 13, John the Dwarf 22, 26, 34, James 3, Poemen 119, 130, 134, 208, Pambo 3, Rufus 2. English translation in Ward, *Sayings.*

5. Wendell Berry, *Another Turn of the Crank* (Washington, D.C.: Counterpoint, 1995) 76.

6. See Evagrius, *Praktikos* 6-14 for the evil thoughts and 15–39, apparently, for the antidotes; english trans. by Bamberger, *Evagrius Ponticus: Praktikos and Chapters on Prayer.*

7. See Jean Clédat, *Le Monastère et la Nécropole de Baouît,* Mémoires publiés par les membres de L'Institut Français d'Archéologie Orientale du Caire 12 [one volume in two parts] (Cairo: IFAO, 1904) 23. On Ama Sibylla, see Tim Vivian, 'Ama Sibylla of Saqqara: Prioress or Prophet, Monastic or Mythological Being?', *Bulletin of the Saint Shenouda the Archimandrite Coptic Society* 5 (1998–1999) 1–17, reprinted as an Appendix in Vivian, *Words to Live By.* These Virtues in medallions become even more striking when one sees the prophets of the Hebrew Bible similarly placed in medallions in the dome above the altar in the old church at the Monastery of Antony; see Elizabeth S. Bolman, ed., *Monastic Visions: The Wall Paintings at the Monastery of St. Antony at the Red Sea* (New Haven: Yale University Press, 2002) 69, 141.

8. See Marguerite Rassart-Debergh, 'Trois Peintures', in *Acta ad Archaeologiam et Artium Historiam Pertinentia*, ed. Hjalmar Torp, *et al.* (Rome: Bretschneider, 1981) 193–201.

9. Paul of Tamma, 'On Humility' 9. See Vivian, *Words to Live By,* 141–164.

10. Stephen of Thebes, *Ascetic Discourse* 37; Vivian, *Words to Live By,* 283–322.

11. The *Virtues of Saint Macarius* 12; Vivian, trans., *Saint Macarius the Spiritbearer.* See also AP John Kolobos 34. The Greek Systematic Apophthegmata I.13 also attributes the saying to John; see also I.16, which is given to Macarius.

12. AP Arsenius 5.

13. See Peter Brown, 'The Rise and Function of the Holy Man in Late Antiquity', *Journal of Roman Studies* 61 (1971) 80–101 (rpt in Brown, *Society and the Holy in Late Antiquity* (Berkeley: University of California Press, 1982) 103–152; see also his later reflections in 'The Rise and Function of the Holy Man in Late Antiquity: 1971–1997', *Journal of Early Christian Studies* 6:3 (1998) 353–376.

14. In II.2 of the Daniel dossier (see Chapter One), 'each monk wished to receive a blessing' from a deceased holy fool. *Eulogia*, 'blessing', may suggest here that the monks wanted to take a 'relic'—hair or clothing—from the deceased brother. This is how Lat 5 (Chapter Six) understands matters: 'one of them wanted to take a relic from his remains'. See Hugh G. Evelyn White, *The Monasteries of the Wadi 'N Natrun* (3 vols.; rpt. New York: Arno Press, 1973), vol. 2, *The History of the Monasteries of Nitria and Scetis*, 292: 'In the earlier period of the history of Nitria and Scetis, pilgrims made their way into the desert to be edified by the discourse of the fathers, to beg for their prayers, and to receive their blessing. . . . In the seventh century a change seems to have come over both pilgrims and monks. The former seek out holy places believing that prayer there will, through the mediation of some departed saint, lead to a cure or to some other benefit; the latter are drawn more and more to realize the advantages presented to them by such an attitude, and come to look upon relics as an attraction bringing renown and wealth to their monastery. In proportion, then, as the sanctity of the living grew less remarkable, the veneration of the dead increased.'

15. See Georgia Frank, *The Memory of the Eyes: Pilgrims to Living Saints in Christian Late Antiquity* (Berkeley: University of California Press, 2000).

16. On the monasteries of the Wadi al-Natrun (Scetis), see Vivian, *Words to Live By*, 25–57.

17. See Britt Dahlman's discussion of holiness, 'Chapter II: The Theme of Secret Holiness', in Dahlman, *St Daniel of Sketis*.

18. For a fuller discussion, see Dahlman, Chapter I.2, 'The Daniel Texts', and Chapter III, 'The Textual Tradition'.

19. The georgian material is not translated in this volume. There are no georgian stories about Abba Daniel among the georgian manuscripts of Mount Sinai (at least, according to Gerard Garitte, *Catalogue des manuscrits géorgiens littéraires du*

Mont Sinai, CSCO subsidia hagiographica 9 [Louvain: 1956]. Michael Tarchnisvili, ed., *Geschichte der kirchlichen georgischen Literatur*, Studi e Testi 185 (Vatican City: 1955) makes one rather vague reference to Daniel on page 422 (the index incorrectly says 420) with a claim that among the texts of the early period of georgian christian literature (up to AD 980) there is an ascetic collection of sixty-six reports which displays some similarities to the Daniel accounts: 'Die Sammlung weist verwandtschaftliche Züge mit den bekannten Narrationes de Daniele Scetiota aus den Vitae Patrum auf'. He refers to an article by K. Kekelidze in *Hristianskii Vostok* 4 (1916) 252. (These may just be formal similarities; Tarchnisvili does *not* say that Daniel is mentioned by name in the collection.) Much more concretely, in an appendix, Tarchnisvili gives a list of 204 *vitae* from the early period of georgian literature, among which is #15, p. 469, 'Andronicus and Athanasia', found in the greek dossier (Chapter One). Two manuscripts are mentioned (Peeters does not give the manuscript numbers) of the Bodleian Library, ff. 491–495, described by P. Peeters, 'De codice hibernico Bibliothecae Bodleianae Oxoniensis', *Analecta Bollandiana* 31 (1912) 301–318. 'Andronicus and Athanasia' is the 46th piece in a collection of 50. The manuscript dates to around AD 1039. Tarchnisvili lists another manuscript only as A. Nr. 95 (pages 1314–1316); this must mean Mount Athos, Iviron 95. See Blake's catalogue of the georgian manuscripts at the Iviron in *Revue de l'Orient Chrétien* 28 (1931–32) and 29 (1933–34). Tarchnisvili makes some interesting comments, 32–34, about the sources of the translated georgian works. The monks, he says, were catholic in their sources, translating from Armenian, Syriac, and Arabic as well as Greek, although Greek takes pride of place. The georgian version of 'Andronicus and Athanasia' is presumably translated from Greek. It is not impossible, though, that it was translated from Arabic. I wish to thank Mark Swanson for the above material on the georgian versions. The Bodleian collection includes some pieces that are clearly translated from arabic originals. See Dahlman, 2.11–2.13, 56–59, for a brief discussion of the non-greek stories.

20. Paul Van Cauwenbergh, *Étude sur les moines d'Égypte depuis le concile de Chalcédoine (451) jusqu'à l'invasion arabe (640)* (Paris: Imprimerie Nationale, 1914) 10: 'un ramassis d'anecdotes sans cohésion'.

21. Van Cauwenbergh, 10.

22. As Dahlman has independently observed in Chapter II, 'The Theme of Secret Holiness'.

23. G. Garitte, 'Daniel de Scété', *Dictionnaire d'Histoire et de Géographie* 14.70–72; 72.

24. Max Bonnet, review, *Byzantinische Zeitschrift* 13 (1904) 166–171; 166.

25. Brock and Harvey, *Holy Women of the Syrian Orient* 142.

26. Clugnet, ROC 5 : 49–73, 254–271, 370–391. Clugnet's introduction appears in ROC 6 (1901) 56–87.

27. Dahlman, *St Daniel of Sketis*, 'Text and Translation', 114–190.

28. Clugnet, ROC 6 (1901) 535–553. See Dahlman, 56–58.

29. Nau, ROC 5 (1900) 391–406; ROC 12 (1907) 174–175. See Dahlman, 59.

30. Lewis, *The Forty Martyrs of the Sinai.*

31. Goldschmidt-Esteves Pereira. Guidi provides corrections for the ethiopic text, ROC 6 (1901) 54–56. See Dahlman, 56–58.

32. *Liber de vita moribusque sanctorum Patrum ex gemina interpretatione veterum scriptorum,* 2 vols. (Venice: 1855).

33. Brock, 'A Syriac Narratio' 269–280; Müller-Kessler and Sokoloff, *Forty Martyrs.*

34. Latin: M. Huber, ed., *Johannes monachus* 335–352.

35. L. Clugnet, *Bibliotheca Hagiographica Orientalis* 1 (1901) xxvii.

36. See Dahlman's discussion, 43–46, and her textual discussion of individual stories, 46–55.

37. Bonnet, 167: 'une mauvaise édition'. He goes on to say that it is not a critical edition, has no commentary, and no index of proper names or subject index. In Bonnet's opinion Cluget's edition falls considerably short because the latter did not consult all the available manuscripts and because, instead of collating textual variants in a single apparatus criticus, he listed them separately at the bottom of each MS. Bonnet lists some of Clugnet's errors on pages 169–170. Professional jealousy or rivalry may have had a part in Bonnet's attack: he had long been working on publishing the Daniel Dossier (Bonnet, 166). Bonnet's research was also noted by Van Cauwenbergh in 1914 (11 n. 2). Bonnet, however, died in 1917 and apparently his work was never published. See also the criticisms of Hippolyte Delehaye, 'Bulletin des publications hagiographiques', *Analecta Bollandiana* 22 [1903] 95–98.

38. Dahlman generously supplied me with copies of her then unpublished, now published, work and I have used her text to supplement Clugnet's as the basis for my translation from Greek. New manuscripts have added to the textual information available for the ethiopic and syriac versions; see the introductions to Chapters Three and Four, respectively.

39. Claudia Rapp, 'Storytelling as Spiritual Communication in Early Greek Hagiography: The Use of *Diegesis*', *Journal of Early Christian Studies* 6.3 (1998) 431–448; 433. The examples Rapp adduces, the *Historia monachorum*, the *Lausiac History* of Palladius, and the *Religious History* of Theodoret of Cyrrhus, as she notes, relate stories about 'a number of holy men and women', not just one, as in the Daniel dossier.

40. Van Cauwenbergh, 12.

41. See Brock, 'A Syriac *Narratio*', and the Introduction to Chapter Four.

42. See Clugnet, ROC 6 (1901): 86, and Brock, 'A Syriac *Narratio*'.

43. See the tables in Clugnet, ROC 6 (1901): 83–87.

44. See Dahlman's brief discussion, 57–58. She hypothesizes that the episodes unique to Coptic 'were originally written in Greek versions which have not

survived, as in the case' with 'a great deal of other literature defending anti-Chalcedonian views'.

45. Bonnet, 167.

46. Coislin 282; see Clugnet, ROC 6 (1901) 84. Dahlman puts Mark's story second and begins with the story of Daniel's atonement for a 'murder' he committed (I.2 in this volume).

47. Dahlman, 120, does not include this sentence in her text.

48. As Bonnet notes, 170; he observes that another MS, Naples Codex II. C.27, also begins with the tale about Mark; see AB 21 (1902) 390 (#5). One MS designates the collection as 'eight chapters' (κεφάλαια); Bonnet, 170.

49. Numbers (e.g., I.1) indicate the numbering used in Chapter One; numbers in brackets refer to those used by Clugnet in ROC 5 (1900): 50–73, 254–271. An "X" in a column indicates that a story is preserved in that language. See Clugnet's tables in ROC 6 (1901): 83–87. As a supplement to Clugnet's tables, I note the following. In an article in AB 21 (1902): 381–400, 'Catalogus Codicum Hagiographicorum Graecorum Bibliothecae Nationalis Neapolitanae', on greek hagiographical MSS in the National Library of Naples, H. Delehaye (390–391) describes Codex II.C.27, fol. 235v–291. Salvator Cyrillus, *Codices graeci manuscripti regiae bibliothecae Borbonicae* (Naples: De regia typographia, 1826–1832) I:290-291, lists the incipits of five pieces from the Daniel dossier (XXVII–XXXI): Anastasia (I.8 in the present volume), Andronicus and Athanasia (I.5), The Woman Who Pretended to be Drunk (I.4), Eulogius (I.9), and The Monk Falsely Accused of Theft [Abba Doulas] (II.2). XXXII then appears to be about Abba Doulas, not Daniel. I wish to thank A. Garofalo of the Biblioteca Nazionale in Naples for supplying me with a photocopy of the relevant pages of Cyrillus' volume.

50. See also Dahlman's discussion, 60–69.

51. Hugh G. Evelyn White, *The Monasteries of the Wâdi 'N Natrûn*, Part II, *The History of the Monasteries of Nitria and of Scetis* (New York: Arno, 1973 [1932] 241).

52. A Daniel was the disciple of Paphnutius Bubalis, who died at the end of the fourth century; see Guy, *Les apophtegmes des Pères: Collection Systématique* 56. The Daniel of Alphabetical AP Daniel 1–8, Arsenius 14, 23, 39, 42, 43, and Agathon 28 is a disciple of Arsenius, who died in 449 (see Guy, 74–79), and a contemporary of Cyril of Alexandria, who died in 444. The Daniel of Alphabetical AP Poemen 138 is a contemporary of Poemen, who died after Arsenius (see Guy, 77–79).

53. On the *Pratrum spirituale* texts by John Moschus, see Dahlman, 55–56.

54. For analogous examples, see Mikhail and Vivian, 'Life of Saint John the Little', and 'Life of Longinus' in Vivian, *Words to Live By* 247–275. For a homily on a monastic saint where any historical sense of the saint almost completely disappears, see 'A Discourse on Saint Onnophrius by Saint Pisentius', in Vivian, *Paphnutius* 167–188.

55. See the lists in Clugnet, ROC 6 (1901) 83–87 and Synoptic Table I above. See also Dahlman's discussion, 56–59.

56. Van Cauwenbergh, 26, believes that only the stories of Anastasia (I.8) and Eulogius (I.9) belong with certainty to Daniel of Scetis.

57. Clugnet, ROC 6: 56; and Van Cauwenbergh, 24.

58. Goldschmidt-Esteves Pereira, viii; see also Garitte, 71, who says that it is 'probable' that not all the stories refer to the same Daniel. The ethiopic sources, upon which Goldschmidt and Pereira base their conclusions, show confusion regarding Abba Daniel; see below and, for a fuller discussion, the Introduction to Chapter Three.

59. Van Cauwenbergh, 25.

60. Evelyn White intriguingly raises the possibility, 244, that Daniel was a partisan of one splinter group within the anti-Chalcedonians in Egypt, the 'Theodosians', and that 'his absences from Scetis were due to the hostility' of an opposing group, the Gaianite majority. But White also acknowledges that we do not know enough about his attitude toward 'current controversies' to support such suppositions. On these groups see John of Nikiu, *Chronicle* 94.1–9; E. R. Hardy, 'Gaianus', *The Coptic Encyclopedia*, ed. Aziz Atiya (New York: Macmillan, 1991) 4:1138; and Randall Stewart, 'Theodosians', *Coptic Encyclopedia* 7:2240–2241. In the sixth century, Apa Daniel of Scetis visited the memorial (*mnēmē*) of Apa Apollo; P. Bal. 611, W. E. Crum, 'Der hl. Apollo und das Klöster von Bawit', *Zeitschrift für ägyptische Sprache und Altertumskunde* 40 (1902) 60–62, at 60.

61. For example, in the bohairic *Life of Shenoute,* 68, some monks from Scetis come to visit Shenoute; in the syriac version, they become 'Some monks from the monastery of the holy and illustrious apa Macarius'. See Bell, trans., *Besa: The Life of Shenoute* 61–62 and 103 n. 55.

62. See the *Synaxary* entries in the Appendix to Chapter Two.

63. See C. Detlef G, Müller, 'John of Parallos, Saint', in *The Coptic Encyclopedia*, ed. Aziz. S. Atiya (New York: Macmillan, 1991) 5.1367–1368; for the synaxary entry on John, see the Appendix to Chapter Three.

64. For these synaxary entries and an expanded discussion of this material, see the Introduction to Chapter Three.

65. Garitte, 71, comments that many of the stories 'seem to appear to belong more to the folklore of Alexandria than to that of Scetis'.

66. A latin version places this story in the time of Theodosius the Great; see Chapter One, n. 60.

67. The syriac version (Chapter Four) identifies these locations while the greek does not.

68. Ἐκ παιδόθεν ἀπετάξετο ἐν τῇ Σκήτῃ. While not unknown, children at Scetis were rare, it seems, so this could well be a hagiographical topos.

69. When Daniel and his disciple travel to the Thebaid (I.4), 'his disciple gave what he [Daniel] had written to one of the brothers and he translated it into

Coptic [literally: into Egyptian]', Clugnet, BHO iv, believes from this that Daniel was Greek and did not know Coptic, but Evelyn White, 241, says this is unlikely: Daniel was a monk from childhood in Scetis and hēgoumen there so he 'must certainly have known Coptic'. Evelyn White believes, 242, that the translation was from bohairic into sahidic Coptic.

70. Dahlman, 63, comes independently to similar conclusions.

71. See also Dahlman's discussion, 63–69.

72. Evelyn White, 242 n. 4, places the visit in 520 and also believes, 243 n. 2, that the pope mentioned in I.3 is also Timothy. He suggests that Daniel was thus superior of Scetis before 535, but the chronology of I.3 is so vague and elliptical that one can not deduce that Daniel was the superior of Scetis when he went to visit Timothy; in fact, the story seems to suggest that the events described took place in Daniel's youth.

73. I.1, in fact, states that Daniel went to Alexandria 'because it is customary for the superior of Scetis to go up to see the pope for the Great Feast [of Easter]'. Unfortunately, this story does not supply the name of the pope.

74. Codex Paris. Coislin 283, ff. 130v-132.

75. Regnault, *Les Sentences des Pères: série des anonymes*, item 1409/2, K296.

76. Dahlman, 63, agrees.

77. On these events see below, pages 17, 98–103, 115–118.

78. Hippolyte Delehaye, 'Quelques saints du propre de Naples', *Analecta Bollandiana* 59 (1941) 1–33; 32.

79. Letters LXIX, LXXI, LXXII; Brooks, *A Collection of Letters of Severus of Antioch* 75–103, 107–117, 117–127. See also Chaîne, 'Une lettre de Sévère d'Antioche' 32–58. Unfortunately, these letters are commentaries on Gospel passages and tell us nothing about the addressee (other than that she was intelligent and biblically literate).

80. A ὑπατίσσα; see Evelyn White, 247, who suggests that she is 'perhaps identical with the mother of Georgia to whom Severus writes'. Syriac MSS in London and Paris (BM Add. 14601; Paris, Coislin 23, 25, 195) contain fragments of letters from Severus to Anastasia, wife of a counsel (ὑπατίσσα) or deacon (διάκονος).

81. Van Cauwenbergh, 15.

82. Severus of el-Ashmunein, *History of the Patriarchs*, PO 1:453.

83. Seymour de Ricci and Eric O. Winstedt, 'Les quarante-neuf vieillards de Scété', *Notices et extraits des manuscrits de la Bibliothèque nationale* (Paris, 1910–1911), 39:2, 27. I was unable to obtain the manuscsript and have translated from the french translation of Van Cauwenbergh, 14–15, who says (citing de Ricci and Winstedt) that chronologically nothing opposes this identification. On Hilaria, see Evelyn White, 224–227, and see Emile Amélineau, 'L'histoire des deux filles de l'empereur Zénon', *Proceedings of the Society for Biblical Archaeology* 10 (1888) 181–206.

84. Some MSS identify the house as an 'estate'.

85. On folklore and hagiography, see A.-J. Festugière, 'Lieux communs littéraires et thèmes de folk-lore dans l'Hagiographie primitive', *Wiener Studien* 73 (1960) 123–152.

86. See John Moorhead, *Justinian* (London—New York: Longman, 1994) 14, 21–22, 46–47. On the conspirators, see J. R. Martindale, ed., *The Prosopography of the Later Roman Empire* (Cambridge: Cambridge University Press, 1971–1992) vol. 2, under Eulogius 9, Dexicrates, Hypatius 6, and Pompeius 2.

87. Some versions of Eulogius' story have Daniel say when he was 'younger, forty years old' (four manuscripts say 'about forty years old or less') rather than 'forty years ago'.

88. See Evelyn White, 241–242.

89. On the dates, see Evelyn White, 249–251.

90. Dahlman, 64, concurs: 'Thus we may merely state that he was born at the end of the fifth or at the beginning of the sixth century, and died after 576'.

91. Antony and Shenoute, to name just two, lived very long lives, 105 and 115 years respectively. The major figures in the *Lives of the Monks of Palestine* by Cyril of Scythopolis—Euthymius, Sabas, John the Hesychast, Cyriacus, Theodosius, Theognius, and Abraamius—lived from 82 to 106 years, with an average of 97!

92. Otto F. A. Meinardus, *Two Thousand Years of Coptic Christianity* (Cairo: American University of Cairo Press, 1999) 302.

93. See also Dahlman, 66–69.

94. For the biblical resonance of *parrēsia*, an important monastic concept, see Jn 16:25 and 1 Jn 3:21, among many.

95. See III.1 in Chapter One.

96. It is perhaps not coincidental that one MS, Mount Athos 2541.208 (seventeenth century), gives this story to Ephrem Syrus; see Clugnet, ROC 6 (1901) 85. I do not know whether it is Ephrem or Daniel in this version whom Andronicus visits. Legend did associate Ephrem with Scetis; see Evelyn White, 114–115.

97. Bonnet, 167. He did not develop this insight, which was surprisingly unnoticed by other early scholars. John Wortley has recently concurred with Bonnet. One argument for a disciple's authorship is that in the Daniel dossier there is no monastic deference to clergy, as there is in the *Life of Antony* and other early monastic texts. Thus it seems unlikely that a priest—or bishop—wrote the dossier. On monastic-clerical relations, see David Brakke, *Athanasius and the Politics of Asceticism*, Oxford Early Christian Studies Series (Oxford: Clarendon Press, 1995); Philip Rousseau, *Ascetics, Authority, and the Church in the Age of Jerome and Cassian*, Oxford Historical Monographs (Oxford: Oxford University Press, 1978); and Theresa Urbainczyk, *Theodoret of Cyrrhus: The Bishop and the Holy Man* (Ann Arbor: The University of Michigan Press, 2002) 115–129.

98. See Derek Krueger, *Symeon the Holy Fool: Leontius'* Life *and the Late Antique City* (Berkeley: Univ. of California Press, 1996); he mentions Mark on pp. 59–60, 64. See also Belden C. Lane, 'The Spirituality and Politics of Holy Folly', *The Christian Century* (15 December 1982) 1281–1286. See also Dahlman, 78–80.

99. Brock, *Holy Women*, 142. Brock believes that the story about 'the mad nun' (I.4) 'is clearly modeled' on a figure in Palladius' *Lausiac History* (¶ 34 in the greek version), but I do not believe that this is the case. Brock also observes that the theme of the transvestite 'was always a popular one among hagiographers'. For a circumspect and unadorned account of the post-mortem discovery of one transvestite, see Alphabetical Apophthegmata Bessarion 4, and for the story of Saint Apollonaria Syncletica, who reportedly lived in Scetis in the fourth-fifth century, see Evelyn White, 117–118. On monastic transvestites, see Lucien Regnault, *The Day-to-Day Life of the Desert Fathers in Fourth-Century Egypt* (Petersham, Massachusetts: Saint Bede's, 1999), who notes, 25, that 'hagiography records many such cases whose historicity is hard to evaluate'; Ward, *Harlots of the Desert*; Marie Delcourt, 'Appendix: Female Saints in Masculine Clothing', in Delcourt, *Hermaphrodite: Myths and Rites of the Bisexual Figure in Classical Antiquity*, trans. Jennifer Nicholson (London: Studio Books, 1961) 84–102; J. Anson, 'The Female Transvestite in Early Monasticism: Origin and Development of a Motif', *Viator: Medieval and Religious Studies* 5 (1974) 1–32; and Teresa M. Shaw, *The Burden of the Flesh: Fasting and Sexuality in Early Christianity* (Minneapolis: Fortress, 1998), esp. 235–247, and the bibliography cited on 240, n. 79. On female monastic 'transvestites', most recently, see Stephen J. Davis, 'Crossed Texts, Crossed Sex: Intertextuality and Gender in Early Christian Legends of Holy Women Disguised as Men', *Journal of Early Christian Studies* 10:1 (Spring 2002) 1–36. Davis, 4 and 4 n. 5, notes that there are at least eleven *Vitae* of transvestite female saints from the fifth through the seventh centuries. For a brief history of the scholarship on this subject, see Davis, 5–11.

100. For an account of a modern 'fool' and holy man, see Vivian, 'A Journey to the Interior' in Vivian, *Words to Live By,* 59–98.

101. Dahlman's felicitous phrase, p. 73.

102. AP Or 14; PG 65.440C. 'Mock' translates *empaixon* from *empaizein,* which also means 'make sport of' or 'delude'; therefore, one could translate it as 'fool'. 'Making yourself for the most part foolish': *mōron seauton eis ta polla poiōn.*

103. See John Saward, *Perfect Fools: Folly for Christ's Sake in Catholic and Orthodox Spirituality* (Oxford: Oxford University Press, 1980). As Saward observes, 12: 'Holy folly is nearly always in close historical relation to monasticism; indeed, it might almost be said that the history of folly for Christ's sake is but the history of monasticism under a certain description . . . . the two forms of following Christ have a common inspiration'. On the early monastic relationship with

the city, see James E. Goehring, 'The World Engaged: The Social and Economic World of Early Egyptian Monasticism', Chapter 2 of Goehring, *Ascetics, Society, and the Desert: Studies in Early Egyptian Monasticism* (Harrisburg, Pennsylvania: Trinity, 1999).

104. Ewa Wipszycka, 'Les clercs dans les communautés monastiques d'Égypte', *The Journal of Juristic Papyrology* 26 (1996) 135–166, at 153, even suggests that the famous fourth-century figure Abba Moses 'seems to have been composed of *topoi* and literary inventions' and that 'we cannot even be completely sure that the literary construction had a real ascetic for its model'.

105. Such is the dilemma faced by Krueger (see n. 83) who does not deny that Symeon existed but virtually despairs of knowing anything about the historical person. See Dahlman, 66–67 and 198–200.

106. *Dēmosion* was used of any public building, such as an amphitheater or public bath. Christopher Haas, *Alexandria in Late Antiquity: Topography and Social Conflict* (Baltimore: Johns Hopkins University Press, 1997), cites a fourth-century source to the effect that there were no less than 1,561 baths and 845 taverns in the city. Aristide Calderini, *Dizionario dei nomi geografici e topografici dell' Egitto greco-romano,* 5 vols. (Cairo: Società reale di geografia D'Egitto, 1935–1987), vol. 1: *Alexandreia*, 96, has an entry, 'Balaneia, thermai, loutra', where mention is made of the *demosion loutron to kaloumenon Ippon en Alexandreia* in an epigram attributed to John the Scribe.

107. A visit confirmed elsewhere. In the sixth century, an Apa Daniel of Scetis visited the memorial (*mnēmē*) of Apa Apollo; see P. Bal. 611, in W. E. Crum, 'Der hl. Apollo und das Klöster von Bawit', *Zeitschrift für ägyptische Sprache und Altertumskunde* 40 (1902) 60-62, at 60. On Apollo, see René-Georges Coquin, 'Apollon de Titkooh ou/et Apollon de Bawit?', *Orientalia* 46 (1977) 435–446, and Vivian, 'The *Life of Phib* by Papohe the Steward' in Vivian, *Words to Live By,* 218–236.

108. This monastery, also called the Monastery of Abba Jeremias, is well known because of excavations undertaken there early in the last century; see J. E. Quibell, *Excavations at Saqqara (1908–1909, 1909–1910)*, vol. 4: *The Monastery of Apa Jeremias* (Cairo: Institut français d'archéologie orientale du Caire, 1912). To my knowledge, Quibell's findings do not point to a double monastery or separate monasteries for men and women, but there are some inscriptions by women and the fascinating personage of Ama Sibylla figures prominently; see Vivian, *Words to Live By,* 379–393.

109. John P. Meier, *A Marginal Jew: Rethinking the Historical Jesus*, vol. one, *The Roots of the Problem and the Person* (New York: Doubleday, 1991).

110. Meier, 180.

111. Meier, 183.

112. Meier, 184.

113. On the theme of remembering in early monasticism, see William Harmless, SJ, 'Remembering Poemen Remembering: The Desert Fathers and the Spirituality of Memory', *Church History* 69:3 (September 2000) 483–518.

114. Philip Rousseau, 'Ascetics as mediators and as teachers', in James Howard-Johnston and Paul Antony Hayward, edd., *The Cult of Saints in Late Antiquity and the Middle Ages: Essays on the Contribution of Peter Brown* (Oxford: Oxford University Press, 1999) 51. Rousseau continues, 'without necessarily a reliable balance being achieved between the two'. In this essay, Rousseau criticizes Peter Brown on a number of matters, but one wonders what criteria Rousseau uses to find his hypothesized 'reliable balance'. How do we determine, at this distance and late date, what is 'promotion' and what is 'recording'?

115. See Joyce Tanner's icon based on this scene on the cover to this volume.

116. Some MSS add 'in accordance with God's divine dispensation'.

117. Susan R. Holman, *The Hungry are Dying* (Oxford—New York: Oxford University Press, 2001) 161.

118. Harmless (above, n. 113), 517.

119. See Catherine Bell, *Ritual Theory, Ritual Practice* (Oxford: Oxford University Press, 1992).

120. Vivian, 'Monasteries of the Wadi Natrun', in Vivian, *Words to Live By*, 25–57.

121. Tradition and history blend together in the story of the keep at the Syrian Monastery in the Wadi al-Natrun. According to tradition, the keep was built in the fifth century by Emperor Zeno (450–491), whose daughter, Saint Hilaria, lived as a monk at Scetis under the name Hilarion. Scholars regard the story of Hilaria as apocryphal, but the story fits the current understanding of when keeps came into existence. As Evelyn White, 224–227, observed, 'It is clear that the story of Hilaria *as a whole* is a pious legend and no more. . . . But the benefactions bestowed upon Scetis by Zeno cannot be similarly dismissed'.

122. See John Marincola, *Authority and Tradition in Ancient Historiography* (Cambridge: Cambridge University Press, 1997) 63–86.

123. *Palladius: The Lausiac History*, trans. Meyer 23. On the historical/hagiographical nature of such narratives as the *Lausiac History*, see Frank, *The Memory of the Eyes* (note 15, above).

124. Claudia Rapp, 'Storytelling as Spiritual Communication in Early Greek Hagiography: The Use of *Diegesis*', *Journal of Early Christian Studies* 6.3 (1998) 431–448, at 432.

125. Rapp, 432.

126. See Rapp, 432.

127. Robin Lane Fox, 'The *Life of Daniel*', in M. J. Edwards and Simon Swain, edd., *Portraits: Biographical Representation in the Greek and Roman Literature of the Roman Empire* (Oxford: Clarendon, 1997) 206.

128. Urbainczyk, 118.

129. Marincola, 74.

130. Marincola, 74.

131. Rapp, 443-444.

132. Some MSS add: 'He had his cell about eighteen miles from Scetis itself'.

133. Some MSS have 'and saw that his breasts were those of a woman and were like two withered leaves'.

134. Monks usually ate at the ninth hour or about 3 PM, especially if they ate once a day.

135. Just as Antony's two anonymous disciples in the *Life of Antony* later receive names and just as two unnamed monks in Macarius' community later become 'Maximus' and 'Domitius'.

136. Cod. Paris graec. 1596, p. 652; see Chapter One, V.1.

137. The fact that Abba Isaac is called 'the superior of Scetis' complicates matters since in the Daniel dossier Abba Daniel holds this position.

138. Rapp, 441.

139. Dahlman, Chapter II, 'The Theme of Secret Holiness', also discusses the theme of holiness in the Daniel dossier, especially on how 'all the (eight) stories deal with secret holiness' (p. 71).

140. Berry, *Life is a Miracle* (above, n. 1), 8, crediting Kathleen Raine, *The Inner Journey of the Poet* (Braziller: 1982), 180–181, with reminding us of this.

141. Burton Christie, *The Word in the Desert*, 54.

142. Antoine Guillaumont, 'La séparation du monde dans l'orient chrétien: ses formes et ses motifs', in Guillaumont, *Études sur la spiritualité de l'orient chrétien*. Spiritualité Orientale 66 (Bégrolles-en-Mauges: Abbaye de Bellefontaine, 1996) 105–112; 105.

143. See James E. Goehring, *Ascetics, Society, and the Desert: Studies in Early Egyptian Monasticism* (Harrisburg, Pennsylvania: Trinity, 1999) 13–25.

144. On this theme, see the powerful meditation of Belden C. Lane, *The Solace of Fierce Landscapes: A Journey into the Spirituality of Desert and Mountain* (Oxford, Oxford University Press, 1998).

145. Vincent Desprez, *Le monachisme primitif: Des origines jusqu'au concile d'Éphèse*. Spiritualité orientale 72 (Begrolles-en-Mauges: Abbaye de Bellefontaine, 1998) 184. The bracketed words are Desprez'.

146. For a deep recent meditation on this theme, see Laurence Freeman, *Jesus: The Teacher Within* (New York—London: Continuum, 2000).

147. See the *Life of Saint George of Choziba* 33: 'Child, do not think that it is the place [*topos*] that makes you a monk; it's the way you live [*tropos*]'; Vivian, *Journeying into God* 94.

148. AP Antony the Great 24; Ward, 6.

149. Regnault, *Les sentences des pères du désert: série des anonymes* N 490. In a sense, he reverses the curse against the city first seen, as least in biblical tradition, in the fall of Sodom and Gomorrah (Gen 19:24).

150. Vivian, 'The Coptic Sayings of Saint Macarius of Egypt' in Vivian, *Saint Macarius the Spiritbearer*, 75–76.

151. The conclusion of the story of Thomaïs (I.6) shows this: when Abba Daniel orders her to be buried at the monastery, 'Many began to grumble' (some MSS have 'Some of them began to grumble because he was ordering a woman's corpse to be buried with the fathers, and she a victim of murder'). But the old man says to them, 'This young woman is my *amma*, and yours. Indeed, she died to protect her chastity'. Afterwards, the story reports, 'no one opposed the old man'.

152. Rapp, 432.

153. Graham Gould, 'Lay Christians, Bishops, and Clergy in the Apophthegmata Patrum', *Studia Patristica* 25, ed. Elizabeth A. Livingstone (Leuven: Peeters, 1993) 399.

154. *Systematic Apophthegmata* III.33 (= Alph. AP Silvanus 2); Guy, ed., *Les Apophtegmes des pères*, 166–169.

155. Flannery O'Connor, *Collected Works* (New York: Library of America, 1988) 654.

156. Stewart, *The World of the Desert Fathers* 12–13.

157. AP Syncletica 19; *Life of Syncletica* 97 (PG 28.1438A).

158. See, for example, the *Historia Monachorum*; see Benedicta Ward's excursus in Russell, trans., *Lives of the Desert Fathers* 39–45.

159. Marincola, 82. For a christian example, see the Preface to the *Life of Antony,* in Vivian & Athanassakis, translation (CS 202), 51–55.

160. By contrast, see the stories about Abba Aaron in Vivian, trans., *Paphnutius,* 114–141.

161. Patron: Peter Brown, 'The Rise and Function of the Holy Man in Late Antiquity', *Journal of Roman Studies* 61 (1971) 80–101; exemplar: Brown, 'The Saint as Exemplar in Late Antiquity', *Representations* 2 (1983) 1–25; intercessor: Claudia Rapp, '"For next to God, you are my salvation": reflections on the rise of the holy man in late antiquity', in James Howard-Johnston and Paul Antony Hayward, eds., *The Cult of Saints in Late Antiquity and the Middle Ages: Essays on the Contribution of Peter Brown* (Oxford: Oxford University Press, 1999).

162. Charles A. Frazee, 'Late Roman and Byzantine Legislation on the Monastic Life from the Fourth to the Eighth Centuries', *Church History* 51/3 (September 1982) 263–279, at 265.

163. As Antony the Great reportedly said, 'A time is coming when people will go mad, and when they see someone who is not mad they will attack him, saying, "You are mad, you are not like us"'. AP Antony 25; Ward, 7, slightly modified.

164. In his zeal to intercede for Eulogius, he oversteps his bounds, gets himself into trouble, and is reproved for his *hubris* by an angelic being in a vision.

165. Gould, 399.

166. Jerome came to define the 'true' monk not as the ascetic living in town or city but as the anchorite; see Goehring, 53–72.

167. Guillaumont, 'La séparation' 105. Guillaumont's essays, cited here and below, have greatly influenced the discussion in this paragraph and the next.

168. See Antoine Guillumont, 'La folie simulée, une forme d'anachorèse', in *Études sur la spiritualité de l'orient chrétien*. Spiritualité Orientale 66 (Bégrolles-en-Mauges: Abbaye de Bellefontaine, 1996) 125–130.

169. See Antoine Guillaumont, 'Le depaysement comme form d'ascèse, dans le monachisme ancien', in Guillaumont, *Aux origines du monachisme chrétien: Pour une phénoménologie du monachisme*. Spiritualité Orientale 30 (Bégrolles-en-Mauges: Bellefontaine, 1979) 89–116. See also Dahlman, 73–74.

170. See 'A Woman in the Desert: Syncletica of Palestine', in Vivian, *Journeying into God* 37–52. See Dahlman, 72–73.

171. Guillaumont, 'Le dépaysement', 100, speaking of Isaiah.

172. Guillaumont, 'La séparation', 107.

173. AP Macarius the Great 2 (Ward, 126); PG 65:261A.

Chapter 1: The Greek Accounts

1. I wish to thank Britt Dahlman for much of the information here, given to me via e-mail. See now Dahlman, *Saint Daniel of Sketis* (Uppsala: Uppsala UP, 2007), especially Chapter III.

2. Dahlman notes, 90, that there are more than one hundred manuscripts.

3. Numbers in this chapter, and throughout, such as I.2, with a roman numeral followed by an arabic numeral, refer to the numbering of the greek stories that I have used throughout this volume.

4. See Clugnet, 83-86, for his list of texts consulted. Eight tales from the Daniel dossier (I.1, I.3, I.4, I.5, I.6 & I.7 (conjoined), I.8, I.9, and II.1, as numbered in this volume) can also be found in Coislin 126, which was not consulted by Clugnet. See Lucien Regnault, *Les sentences: Nouveau Recueil,* 131; and J.-C. Guy, *Recherches sur la tradition grecque des Apophtegmata Patrum*, Subsidia hagiographica 36 (Brussels, Société des Bollandistes, 1962).

5. See Dahlman 95.

6. See Dahlman 94.

7. Abbreviated references to primary material (e.g. Dahlman) may be found alphabetically in 'Primary Sources' in the Bibliography.

8. Numbers in parentheses following the roman numeral + arabic numeral—e.g. I.1—before the title of each story indicate Dahlman's enumeration of the stories;

numbers in square brackets indicate Clugnet's. Similarly, numbers in parentheses within the translations indicate page numbers in Dahlman's text, whereas numbers in square brackets within the translations indicate page numbers in Clugnet's.

9. For the opening words, Paris BN 283 has 'This blessed Daniel of Scetis had a disciple'. BN 282, f. 232 (if one removes #1, which is really an apophthegm), and Naples IIC27 place the story of Mark the Fool first (see Guy, *Recherches sur la tradition grecque des Apophtegmata Patrum* [Brussels, Société des Bollandistes, 1962]) and, as Max Bonnet, in his review in *Byzantinische Zeitschrift* 13 (1904) 166–171, notes, 170, the greek text does suggest that this story was intended to be first: ἦν τις γέρων ἐν τῇ Σκήτει, ὀνόματι Δανιήλ, καὶ εἶχε μαθητήν. Dahlman begins this story (#2 in her ordering) 'A certain brother named Sergius lived for a short time with his disciple', but 'his' is ambiguous, referring either to Sergius or, as in the text translated above, to Abba Daniel. The next sentence, however, makes it clear that 'his' refers to Abba Daniel. See n. 41 at I.2.

10. Dahlman, 121, lacks 'There was an old man in Scetis by the name of Daniel'.

11. That is, he died. 'To go to sleep' is a common greek euphemism in late antiquity, like our 'pass away'.

12. Text: τελευτὴν (*teleutēn*). Dahlman has 'death', which is customary and accurate but misses the important nuances of τελέω (*teleō*). The verb τελέω (*teleō*) in monastic usage can mean 'accomplish, execute, perform', but takes on the added meanings 'fulfill, bring to fulfillment', 'finish', then 'perfect, make perfect' (see Lampe, 1386ab–1387a). Thus, Jesus' final word in John 19:30, τετέλεσται (*tetelestai*), means far more, especially in the perfect aspect (tense), than the usual 'It is finished' (RSV and NRSV).

13. *Abbas* (ἀββᾶς) was a title of respect given to well-respected and usually venerable monks, but the term could also mean the abbot of a monastery. It is commonly used in the AP as an honorific and not as an abbatial title.

14. *Parrēsia*. For the biblical resonance of *parrēsia*, see Jn 16:25 and 1 Jn 3:21, among many.

15. Text: γέρων. In monastic parlance, 'old man' was an honorific indicating a wise, esteemed monk, often, though not always, older.

16. Text: τῷ ἡγουμένῳ. *Hēgoumenos* indicates a ruler or, more specifically, a bishop or monastic superior, the head of a monastery. See Lampe, 601a–b.

17. The word 'pope' was used early in Alexandria for the head of the Church in Egypt. See Petro Belaniuk, 'Pope in the Coptic Church', *The Coptic Encyclopedia*, ed. Aziz S. Atiya (New York: Macmillan, 1991) 6:1998b–2000b.

18. Easter.

19. 'Brother' (ἀδελφός) originally indicated a natural brother, a blood brother, but in monastic usage came to mean a monastic brother, so much so that many

texts offer further clarification when they mean a natural, non-monastic brother. That Mark is a monastic brother soon becomes clear.

20. The *kampsarikon* was a loincloth worn by a *kapsarios* (Latin *capsarius*) or bathroom attendant. LSJ Supplement, p. 82, says that a capsarius was a 'slave in charge of clothes, esp. at baths'.

21. Dahlman points out, 198 (l. 11), that the ὤμων of the MSS, 'shoulders', must be a mistake for ψυῶν (LSJ 2025a s.v. ψόα, ψύα). Two manuscripts with ψοιῶν (= ψυῶν, due to itacizing) confirm her emendation.

22. Gk. *Salos.* Saward, *Perfect Fools: Folly for Christ's Sake in Catholic and Orthodox Spirituality* (Oxford: Oxford University Press, 1980) 15, suggests 'crackpot' as an english translation. Dahlman, 121, correctly translates *salos* as fool. I have chosen, however, to try to indicate the word's double meaning: to an outsider, a secular, a non-Christian, Mark would appear to be a 'fool'; that is, half-witted or imbecilic. To Daniel and his disciple, however, as to Christians and to readers of this story, Daniel would indeed *appear* to be acting idiotically but would in reality be a 'holy fool'. For this biblical theme, see 1 Cor 1–3 and 2 Cor 11:16–21.

23. Ἐξηχευόμενος < ἐξηχευόμαι. See Dahlman's extensive discussion, 198 (l. 13). Dahlman translates the participle as 'madman'; I prefer to render it as a participle corresponding to the two that follow it.

24. On 'holy fools' see Derek Krueger, *Symeon the Holy Fool: Leontius'* Life *and the Late Antique City* (Berkeley: University of California Press, 1996), and Saward, *Perfect Fools*; the former mentions Mark on 59–60, 64, and the latter on 17–18. Dahlman, 198 (ll. 12–13), makes the point that the other *saloi*, 'imbeciles', 'half-wits', are really that, as opposed to Mark, who is a 'holy fool'.

25. Interestingly, Paul Euergetinos (+ 1054), in *Synagōgē* 3.16.7), translates *balaneion* into Modern Greek as *dēmosion loutron*. Van Cauwenbergh, *Étude sur les moines d'Égypte depuis le concile de Chalcédoine (451) jusqu'à l'invasion arabe (640)* (Paris, Imprimerie Nationale, 1914) 15, believes that Mark lived at the Hippodrome, hence his name, 'Mark of the Horse [*hippos*]'.

26. The greek word *noumion* (plural: *noumia*) is an adaptation of the latin word *nummus* (plural: *nummi*), generally 'a piece of money, coin, money' or, more specifically, a roman silver coin, the *sesterius*. Clugnet has here *folleis*. The *phollis* (Latin *follis*) was a small coin, 1/288th of a *solidus*. In the next sentence the *noumion* appears to be considered its equivalent. The *keration* (1/24th of a gold piece) was worth twelve copper coins (variously known as *folleis, noumia, lepta, pholera,* or *obols),* of which there were thus 288 to the gold piece. One hundred *folleis* was more than eight times the earnings of Eulogius the stonecutter (I.9). See Dahlman, 199–200 (ll. 15–16) for further discussion. She observes that one hundred may be a symbolic number.

27. Some (many? most?) Christians came to regard public baths—like the theater an integral part of greco-roman society—as places of licentiousness and

sin; this apparently was especially true for monks. In V.1 [5] below, an Abba Palladius disparages a monk: 'Moreover, if this fellow were not self-centered, self-indulgent, and lecherous, he would not shamelessly strip naked in the baths, or look at others as naked as himself. Our holy fathers Antony and Pachomius, Amoun, Serapion, and the rest of the God-bearing fathers inspired by God decree that no monk should ever strip naked other than for reasons of severe illness and necessity'.

28. Dahlman notes, 200 (l. 17) that some manuscripts have 'twelve' while others have 'ten'. She argues that it was more likely that a scribe dropped δω from δώδεκα, 'twelve', making δέκα, 'ten', than that a scribe added it. See her further discussion.

29. Literally, a building with four doors. Dahlman suggests, 200 (l. 24) 'a four-sided arch in the Agora [central square or marketplace]'. John Moschus says that 'the Tetrapylon is held in very high esteem by the citizens of Alexandria for they say that Alexander (who founded their city) took the relics of the Prophet Jeremiah from Egypt and buried them there'; see Moschus, *The Spiritual Meadow* 77 (Wortley, trans., p. 59). Haas, 368 n. 27, says that the Tetrapylon 'probably resembled the roughly contemporary tetrapylon in Thessaloniki (the so-called arch of Galerius), which was also centrally located in the city's design'. See also Calderini, I:1, 154.

30. The Greek is ambiguous and may also be translated (Wortley) 'The elder ran up and laid hands on him, and [the fool] began to call out: "O men of Alexandria, help me!"' In the coptic account, 'the old man ran and grabbed him [Mark] and cried out with a loud voice, "Come and see, people of Alexandria!"'

31. The Coptic is clearer: 'You are the imbeciles, for there is no one in this city, including me, like this fellow!' For a similar response, see *Lausiac History* 34.6; see further Dahlman's discussion, 200 (ll. 27–30).

32. On 'vessel' see BDAG 927b–928a (3); see Acts 9:15.

33. In *Life of Antony* 6.2 the Devil yells, 'I am the friend of fornication. I am the one who has undertaken to trap young people into fornication and entice them with its blandishments. I am called "the spirit of fornication"!' See Vivian and Athanassakis, 71. Chapter five of the *Systematic Apophthegmata* is concerned with sexual sin, 'fornication' (*porneia*). In I.7 below the demon of sexual sin wages war against a monk.

34. That is, Satan, the Devil.

35. The monastic settlements at the fifth milestone west of Alexandria; see note 42 below and I.2.

36. The coptic account has Mark spend ten years as a fool, all in Alexandria.

37. See LSJ 1652b; *stratēlatēs = magister militum*, though Dahlman notes, 202 (l. 54), that 'In the East the power of the stratēlatēs weakened, and in the 6th-7th centuries this term had become very vague and could designate the head of a military office (the *magisterium militum*), but also (as is shown from papyri [in] Egypt) an honorary title for any kind of military officers or for functions in the

civil administration such as the praetorian prefect, the duke of a province, the tribune of a city, or for any distinct member of a great family'.

38. The coptic account has the Enaton (see n. 42 below).

39. On receiving a blessing from a deceased holy person, see I.3 below.

40. For another example of this custom, see I.5 below. The narrator seems to be suggesting that white dress was unusual here, although that is not certain. HM 2.12 and 8.19 suggest that monastic dress was white, although the angelic context in both places indicates that the author intends the color to be understood symbolically.

41. See Jn 12:13.

42. For similar details, see I.10 below. The Enaton, or Ennaton, nine miles west of Alexandria, was one of the most famous monastic settlements of the sixth and seventh centuries; it was a collection of monasteries, hermitages, and churches, rather than a single monastery. It is mentioned twice by Moschus, *Pratum spirituale* 177, 184. See van Cauwenbergh, 64–72; A. J. Butler, *The Arab Conquest of England*, ed. P. M. Fraser (Oxford: Oxford University Press, 1978) 500–504; and Jean Gascou, 'Enaton, The', CE 3:954–958. Nitria, forty miles south of Alexandria and west of the delta, was, according to monastic tradition, founded by Amoun about 330; within ten years, Nitria had become too crowded for Amoun, so he and Antony the Great together founded Kellia, the Cells, about ten to twelve miles south of Nitria.

43. Or: the corpse of Mark of blessed memory.

44. Dahlman, 204–205 (ll. 63-64), suggests that 'this would be [the] Via Canopica, the great colonnaded boulevard which ran from the Gate of the Sun in the east to the Gate of the Moon and the Necropolis in the west. Processions and ceremonies along the main east-west street were frequent'. See *loc. cit.* for references.

45. Or: the precious body of Mark the imbecile, he of blessed memory.

46. Dahlman, 114–155, entitles this piece 'Abba Daniel from Sketis'.

47. Dahlman, who places this story first, notes, 191 (l.2) that 'the word οὗτος may suggest that this story was not the first in order in the original Daniel dossier. Possibly it was the second after the story of Mark the Fool', which is where I have put it. See also Dahlman, 196 (l.2).

48. Ἀπετάξετο < ἀποτάσσω. Ἀποτάσσω (*apotassō*), 'to renounce (the world)', is a key word in early monastic thought; see Lampe, 216a(D).

49. On children and child monks in the desert, see Lucien Regnault, *The Day-to-Day Life of the Desert Fathers in Fourth-Century Egypt* (Petersham, Massachusetts: Saint Bede's, 1999) 34–38. Apollo 'withdrew from the world' when he was fifteen (HM 10.3); Abba Helle 'had persevered since childhood in the ascetic life' (HM 12.1); see also AP Zacharias 2. The Apophthegmata contain numerous warnings against having young boys in the desert: see Isaac of the Cells 5, Poemen 176, and Macarius the Great 5. On bandits such as the ones who snatch and abuse Daniel, see Regnault, 147–148.

50. Clugnet's text identifies this man as a *nauklēros*, a shipowner. As John Wortley has noted, the God-fearing shipmaster is not an unknown figure in monastic tales, e.g., in *The Spiritual Meadow* (where there is far more about shipping than in any other collection of tales) one shipowner buries dead monks (91), one prays for rain (174), and one discerns that he has a sinful woman aboard and casts her adrift (76).

51. Barbarian sacks of Scetis took place from 570–580. See Evelyn White, 2.250.

52. Dahlman, 192 (l. 10), notes that one manuscript 'has a more explicit description': 'and one of the men who had taken him prisoner was sitting down to pass water'. See her discussion of the possible meanings of the Greek.

53. This would seem to be Patriarch Timothy III, 517/519–535/536. Codex Paris Coislin 283, ff. 130v–132, gives an episode (it is scarcely a story) that links Daniel with this pontiff. It begins: 'Abba Silvanus said: "When I was with Abba Longinus the wonder-worker I went with that elder to Alexandria where we were met by Abba Daniel of Scetis. We took him into our company and were then received by Abba Isidore, noted for his hospitality. When Pope Timothy heard about Abba Longinus and Abba Daniel he sent his *syncellus* and had the elders brought to him."' For this account, see V.3 below. See also Regnault, *Les Sentences des Pères: anonymes*, item 1409/2, K296. The other near-contemporary patriarchs of Alexandria who bore the name of Timothy (Timothy II Ailouros ['the Weasel' or 'the Cat'] and the Chalcedonian Timothy II Salofaciole) date from the third quarter of the previous century.

54. Timothy opposed the Tome of Leo accepted by the Council of Chalcedon in 451. The pope of Rome, by contrast, as the successor of Leo, was pro-Chalcedonian. See Dahlman, 193 (l. 19), for a list of possible popes for this 'pope of Rome'—if, indeed, this is a historical fact, which seems exceedingly unlikely.

55. Text: ὁ φονεύων φονεύεται. The traditional translation of φονεύω (*phoneuō*) and related words is 'to kill', which Dahlman, 115, uses. But the NRSV translates μὴ φονεύεις (*mē phoneueis*) as 'You shall not murder' (Ex 20:13), and related words in LSJ (1949a-b) and Lampe (1488a) suggest that 'murder' is better. Dahlman later translates φόνος as 'murder' (116 l. 39; 117).

56. Text: διακρίσει. Dahlman, 117, given the context, nicely translates διακρίσις as 'scrupulousness', whereas I, immersed in monastic studies, originally had 'discernment'. The word actually has both meanings here. Discernment, rather than scrupulousness, is an extremely important monastic virtue and tool; see *Life of Antony* 22.3 and 36.1-3. See also 1 Cor 12:7, 10. But the *Life of Antony* and other early monastic sources see discernment primarily as 'discerning between good and bad spirits', which does not fit the context here as well as 'scrupulousness'.

57. See *Lausiac History* 21 for a striking parallel. There, 'a certain Eulogius, an Alexandrian solitary', '[b]ored with himself, and not wishing to enter a

community . . . found someone lying at the marketplace, a cripple who had
neither feet nor hands'. Eulogius 'prayed to God and made a compact with Him:
"Lord, in your name I will take this crippled man and look after him until death,
so that I may be saved through him. Graciously grant me to endure this under-
taking"' (trans. Meyer, 72). Any similarity with the story about Daniel and the
leper ends there. John McGuckin, *Saint Gregory of Nazianzus* (Crestwood, New
York: St. Vladimir's Seminary Press, 2001) 153, notes that '[t]he image of the
leper stands, of course, as the supreme example of the loss of [classical] "balance"
in the human condition: a loss of wealth, status, and even the very image of the
human form'. 'Who is there even among the most gracious and humane of
men', Gregory asks (in *Oration* 14.10 [PG 35:869], cited by McGuckin, 153),
'who does not habitually show himself hostile and inhuman to the leper?' On
lepers and the Church, see Susan R. Holman, *The Hungry are Dying* (Oxford—
New York: Oxford University Press, 2001) 135–167. The greek word for leper,
lelōbēmenos, literally means 'a damaged, maimed, mutilated person'.

58. In monastic literature 'Egypt' commonly designates (non-monastic) areas
away from Scetis, that is, Alexandria, the Delta, or Babylon (Cairo).

59. In I.9, Abba Daniel eats at 5 PM, an unusual time. The monks usually
ate around 3 PM, the ninth hour.

60. Text: πρὸς τὸ διακονῆσαι αυτῷ τιποτε. Dahlman, 117, reasonably translates διακονέω (*diakoneō*) as 'perform some service', whereas I have emphasized
the original sense of the word, 'to serve tables'. In Lk 12:37 and 17:8 this is
precisely what the verb means. Acts 6:2, as BDAG 230a says, 'poses a special
problem' (see the entry). The NRSV translates Acts 6:2 as 'to wait on tables' but
a note there says it may also mean 'keep accounts'. With my translation I am
visualizing that Abba Daniel calls to his disciple for something to eat, which the
disciple brings, then goes away to resume his duties. As Abba Daniel feeds the
leper the food brought by the disciple, the disciple returns and unexpectedly
sees what his abba is doing. Because monks in Egypt generally ate in mid-af-
ternoon, this suggests that the disciple brought food not for Abba Daniel but
for the leper.

61. The scene may be confusing unless one knows something about early
monastic architecture. Abba Daniel is not literally in his cell but rather outside
the cell in a courtyard in the sun. Many anchoritic and semi-anchoritic buildings
had a cell, usually with two rooms, and outside the cell a small courtyard surrounded by a fence or wall. One may see modern monastic dwellings like this
near Deir Anba Bishoy in the Wadi al-Natrun (Scetis). The disciple finds open
the door to the courtyard, not to the two-roomed cell itself.

62. For an icon by Joyce Tanner depicting this story, see the cover of this volume.
Dahlman notes, 194–195 (ll. 53–55), that one manuscript gives more detail: 'The
old man entered his cell and brought the finest wheat flour and fed the leper himself
because the latter did not have hands and because he could not swallow his food

because he had completely rotted away. The old man wiped the leper's mouth with his own hands and put [the food] into the leper's mouth' (my translation).

63. Dahlman entitles this story 'The Blind Man' (Περὶ τοῦ ἀπὸ ὀμμάτων).

64. Γυμνός, 'naked', but this is not meant literally, since below the story mentions 'the fold of his garment'. See LSJ 362b (5), 'lightly clad, i.e. in the undergarment only'.

65. Dahlman, 126 (l. 4) translates τὴν πλατεῖαν as 'street' but suggests, 206 (l. 4) that this may be the Via Canopica mentioned in I.1 above. Since πλατύς means 'broad' or 'wide', the word probably indicates more of a thoroughfare rather than an alley.

66. See n. 15 above.

67. That is, by using the palm leaves to make baskets, mats, ropes, etc., a common monastic practice. Numerous apophthegmata mention monks exchanging their 'handiwork' for money or supplies.

68. Saint Mark's Outside-the-City was the church associated with the martyrium of Saint Mark the Evangelist in Boukolou (Baucalis). By the third century the city had shrunk, and the church was a suburban one. See Haas, 213 and 271.

69. Dahlman notes, 206 (l. 16), that MS. Paris Coislin 238 has 'and three *keratia* in change, and he took out of his mouth', and notes that 'The fold of the garment [*kolpos*], used as a pocket, as well as the mouth, was a common place to keep small coins'.

70. A small gold coin worth 1/3 of the *aureus*. Earlier in the sentence 'coins' (Clugnet) translates *keratia*; the *keration* was another small coin. According to Moschus, *Spiritual Meadow* 184, twenty-four *keratia* equaled one *tremissis*.

71. This same exclamation is uttered about Pelagia; see the *Life of Pelagia* 49 (Petitmengin, 93; Brock and Harvey, 61). Dahlman translates *kruptous,* hidden, as 'secret'; see her discussion of the 'secret servant', 70–74 and 74–78. See I.4.

72. The *oikonomos* ('steward') was a high official chosen among the clergy at a church or monastery to take care of the financial administration. He was ranked second to the bishop (or patriarch) and was the head of an office of subordinate clerical officials working on e.g. the distribution of alms to the poor and the sick. Later on the epithet μέγας ['great'] was attached to the title'; Dahlman, 207 (l. 22).

73. It was common practice among both non-Christians and Christians in Antiquity and Late Antiquity to lie or sleep in sacred places—shrines, churches—associated with healing.

74. For a similar story about the healing of a person's liver, see Vivian, *Paphnutius*, 150.

75. See n. 11 above.

76. The text may also mean 'the fellow-brother of blessed memory'. On receiving a blessing from a deceased holy person, see I.1 above.

77. On Mark, see I.1 above.

78. 'Among the foreigners to the sick': 'the institution called ξενῶν (*xenōn*), as well as the ξενοδοχεῖον (*xenodocheion*), was a hostel which provided food and lodging for free to travelling strangers, preferably pilgrims and monks. Gradually they become combinations of hostels and sick bays, and in the sixth century they are often referred to as "hospitals"': Dahlman, 207 (l. 39). She refers the reader to Olivia Remie Constable, *Housing the Stranger in the Mediterranean World: Lodging, Trade, and Travel in Late Antiquity and the Middle Ages* (Cambridge: Cambridge University Press, 2003) 35-37 and 36 n. 88. Dahlman accidentally omits 'foreigners' in her translation, p. 129.

79. For a strikingly similar story of a female monastic who feigns madness at 'the women's monastery at Tabennisi', see *Lausiac History* 34; there the monk who encounters her is Saint Piteroum.

80. The Upper Thebaid formed the southern province of the roman administrative province of the Thebaid; its capital was Thebes (modern Luxor).

81. Text: εἰς τὴν μνήμην. Clugnet, 6:72, who also reads εἰς τὴν μνήμην, translates as I have (see Lampe 874A[2a]), but Van Cauwenbergh takes μνήμη as 'tomb' or 'sanctuary' and thus believes that Daniel and his disciple are going 'to the tomb of Abba Apollo' at the monastery at Bawit. BN Ar. [PA] 276 has 'to the remembrance', which is ambiguous but probably indicates an *act* of remembrance rather than a *place* of remembrance. The story later mentions Hermopolis, and Hermopolis Magna was near Bawit. Apollo was born around 305, and lived most of the fourth century. His monastic activity centered around Hermopolis Magna in the Lower Thebaid (Shmoun; al-Ashmunein in the Middle Sa'id) between modern-day al-Minya and Asyut (Lycopolis). According to HM 8.2, 'when he was eighty years old he established on his own a great monastery of five hundred perfect men' at Bawit, about fifteen miles south of Hermopolis (which is mentioned in this story). His feast day is the twenty-fifth of Paope [October 22 on the Julian calendar]. On Apollo, see René-Georges Coquin, 'Apollon de Titkooh ou/et Apollon de Bawit?', *Orientalia* 46 (1977) 435-446, and Tim Vivian, 'Monks, Middle, Egypt, and *Metanoia*: The *Life of Phib* by Papohe the Steward', JECS 7.4 (Winter 1999) 547–572, repr. in Vivian, *Words to Live By,* 218–236.

82. Thomas F. Mathews, *The Clash of the Gods: A Reinterpretation of Early Christian Art* (Princeton: Princeton University Press, 1993) 30, has distinguished such actions as these, modeled on Jesus' triumphant entry (Mt 21:8; 2 Kgs 9:13), from those that take place during the imperial *adventus*.

83. See Mk 11:8.

84. The archimandrite (a term still in use) was the head of a monastery.

85. Care with speech is a characteristic of Pambo of Scetis (*Lausiac History* 9 and 10.6).

86. See Mt 22:40 which has the same sentence structure and some of the same vocabulary.

87. Hermopolis Magna, modern el-Ashmunein, on the west bank of the Nile in the Thebaid, between al-Minya and Asyut (Lycopolis).

88. Marie Drew-Bear, *Le nome Hermopolite: Toponymes et sites.* American Studies in Papyrology 21 (Missoula, Montana: Scholars Press, 1979) 132, identifies two monasteries dedicated to Apa Jeremiah, one south of Antinoë, and the other, this monastery for women, which she believes had no connection with the other. Syr 1 identifies these female monastics as 'Tabennesians'. On this term, see n. 125 below.

89. Dahlman notes, 214 (l. 25), that 'in hagiographical literature three hundred is a standard number of members of a cenobitic community in Egypt' and refers to *Lausiac History* 29 and Wipszycka, 'Monachisme égyptiene', 321.

90. The terms are interesting here: the head of the monastery, the superior, is referred to as τὴν ἀμμὰν τὴν ἀρχιμανδρίτην (*tēn amman tēn archimandritēn*) and then simply as ἀμμάς (*ammas*) here and below. Her assistant, the abbess, is called ἡ ἡγουμένη (*hē hēgoumenē*) here. Later, Daniel and his disciple sit at dinner with the *hēgoumenē* and her second-in-command, ἡ δευτεραρία (*hē deuteraria*), but this seems to be the superior and the abbess, so the terms are apparently not being used consistently. BN Ar. [PA] 276 indicates that the mother superior and the abbess are one and the same person. She conceals her identity when she first speaks with Abba Daniel's disciple. Later on, her 'second [in command]' is mentioned, but she remains silent.

91. It appears that the superior of the monastery (*ammas*) is now present, or came with the abbess. She is referred to below (in some MSS) as ἡ κυρία ἡ μεγάλη (*hē kuria hē megalē*), 'the great lady'.

92. BN Ar. [PA] 276, which is clearly secondary, spiritualizes the wild beasts: 'No man has ever entered here. It is better for you that the wild beasts devour your outer selves, so that your inner selves not be destroyed'. In *Novel* 133, promulgated in 539, contemporary with Daniel's visit, Emperor Justinian ordered that men should never be permitted inside a women's monastery; the only exception allowed a priest to enter in order to celebrate the funeral liturgy of a female monastic. Syr 1 makes this prohibition explicit. See Charles A. Frazee, 'Late Roman and Byzantine Legislation on the Monastic Life from the Fourth to the Eighth Centuries', *Church History* 51:3 (September 1982) 263–279, at 274.

93. For similar rites, see 'The Thief who Repented' in the coptic *Life*, Chapter Two.

94. At a monastery a signal (the *krouma*, or *krousma*) was given by striking metal or wood in order to call the monks together for the divine office or some other occasion. In BN Ar. [PA] 276, the word for 'signal' is clearly a hand gesture,

not a clapper or gong. The point in the arabic text is that the sisters do not speak but communicate by gesture.

95. Clugnet: ὅτι ὡς λοτθός μοι ἐπέρχεται, which must be corrupt; 232, 282, and Dahlman: ὅτι ὡς Γοτθός μοι ἐπέρχεται, 'he assaults me like a Goth'; BN Ar. [PA] 276: 'Speak to my disciple, for he comes to me crying out like a Persian'. The point is that Abba Daniel is commending the sisters' silence. His disciple, by contrast (he seems to be saying), is constantly screeching like a barbarian (like a 'Goth' to Greek-speakers and like a 'Persian' to Arabic-speakers). Other translators had difficulty with the sentence. Lat: The Old Man said, 'Tell that to my disciple, who is raising himself up cunningly against me'. Arm: The abba said, 'May the Lord [*var.* with his compassion] bring these sisters life'. Syr: The blessed one said to her, 'Love has been kindled'. Eth lacks.

96. Syr 1 calls her simple-minded and insane. The Greek (λέγει αὐτῷ μία τῶν ἀδελφῶν) is ambiguous, depending on punctuation. An alternative translation could be 'One of the sisters said to him, "She's a drunk"', but the one above is preferable, and Dahlman, 143, agrees.

97. Text: κρίμα. The sense may be stronger, 'judgement', as Dahlman, 143, has, or 'condemnation'; see Lampe, 777b(1 & 3), but also 778a(4), 'responsibility'.

98. For an analogous figure, less fully developed, see Palladius, *Lausiac History* 34; the female monastic there simulates madness, not drunkenness, as does the female monk in the ethiopic Daniel account.

99. Lentils were a staple in the monastic diet. Wine mixed with water was the norm in the ancient world but many monastic communities forbade wine; the AP, however, has examples of apparently normal wine consumption. See Regnault, *Day-to-Day Life*, 61–81, and Maria Dembinska, 'Diet : A Comparison of Food Consumption between some Eastern and Western Monasteries in the 4th-12th Centuries', *Byzantion* 55 (1985) 431–462, at 440–442.

100. Καὶ τὰς μετανοίας ἐποίει. Probably prostrations, elsewhere in early monastic literature called *metanoias*, literally 'repentances'. This egyptian practice appears to have traveled to Syria: John of Ephesus, in 'Lives of Thomas and Stephen' [*Lives of the Eastern Saints* 13, PO 18:204], describes one act of penance this way: 'During every [interval], he would make thirty Egyptian metunâyê [= *metanoiai*] which are called prayers, until he accomplished five hundred during the night with the service of matins, and these I myself on many nights secretly counted'. See further Vivian, 'Monks, Middle Egypt, and Metanoia', 547-572, rpt. Vivian, *Words to Live By*, 325-331.

101. Here *hēgoumenos* clearly indicates the superior because she brings her second-in-command with her.

102. For Matins?

103. This part of the story has strong parallels with *Lausiac History* 34.7. There Abba Piteroum asks to see one who was more holy than himself at the convent.

They assembled all the sisters, but produced only a mad woman (*salē*; see I.1 above) when all else had failed. He fell down before her, proclaiming her 'my *amma* and yours'. She then went away, and no more was ever heard of her.

104. In Syr 1, Daniel earlier says, 'Truly God loves people who are insane like this' and here adds, 'Truly, God loves those who are insane like this; for they are mad and drunk with his love and his mercy'. The armenian version ('because God has chosen fools such as this woman and loves them') ties what Daniel says explicitly to 1 Cor 1:27. BN Ar. [PA] 276: God loves the one drunk with such sweetness.

105. An almost identical phrase occurs at the end of the first paragraph of the story of the blind beggar (I.3 above). The same thought is frequently expressed (e.g., *The Spiritual Meadow* 37), especially in connection with holy fools (Symeon *salos*, Andrew *salos*), but it is not found in connection with the tale of Mark the Fool (I.1). Dahlman translates *kruptous* as 'secret'; see her discussion of the 'secret servant', 70–74 and 74–78.

106. Van Cauwenbergh, 20, points out that a latin version of this story (Lippomano 5:605-607) begins 'In the days of Emperor Theodosius the Great' (*In diebus Theodosii Magni imperatoris*), which would place the events at the end of the fourth century during the reign of Theodosius I (379–395). Clugnet, 6: 76 n. 2, dismisses the latin time frame because it is lacking in Greek, Syriac, and Arabic. Hippolyte Delehaye points out, however ('Bulletine des publications hagiographiques', AB 22 [1903] 96), that Clugnet failed to consult two MSS that also place the story in the days of Theodosius (Ἐν ταῖς ἡμέραις Θεοδοσίου τοῦ μεγάλου βασιλέως. Van Cauwenbergh concludes, 27, that it is thus very doubtful that the Daniel of this account belongs to the sixth century and terms it a 'charming legend that offers no verisimilitude'. Evelyn White, however, 245, equates this Daniel with the sixth-century monk. He states, 245 n. 3, that a fourth-century date 'is impossible (at any rate for Clugnet's recensions)'. No Daniel, he says, was eminent in Scetis in the fourth century, and details point to the sixth-century commonplace visits of Syrians to Egypt, references to the laurae (plural) of Scetis, the importance of the Oktokaidekaton, and the general topography. One might also add that the shrine of Saint Menas, mentioned in the story, though existing in the fourth century, was much more impressive, and popular, in the sixth, during the reign of Justinian; see Peter Grossmann, 'The Pilgrimage Center of Abū Mīnā', in David Frankfurter, ed., *Pilgrimage and Holy Space in Late Antique Egypt* (Leiden: Brill, 1998) 281-302. Andronicus and Athanasia are also remembered, rather surprisingly, in a brief *Laudatio* or *Encomium* by the monk and priest Neophytus of Cyprus. Apparently, their remains (*leipsomena*) were interred on the island. See Hippolyte Delehaye, 'Saints de Chypre', AB 26 (1907) 161–301, at 178–180.

107. In Greek *athanasia* means 'immortal'.

108. This motif of dividing possessions into thirds occurs elsewhere in monastic literature. In AP Eucharistus the Secular 1, Eucharistus and his wife divide

their profits into three parts: one for the poor, one for hospitality, and one for their own needs.

109. The biblical 'knew': ἔγνω. Gen 21:2, Is 8:3, Lk 1:24.

110. Literally 'approached', 'came near', a circumlocution (as is the biblical 'knew' earlier), for saying that they no longer had sexual relations. For a striking parallel to the way of life of Andronicus and Athanasia, see AP Eucharistus the Secular 1 (Ward, 60): After they married, Eucharistus says, they did not have 'sexual intercourse with one another'.

111. Dahlman, 230–231 (ll. 17–19), says that such ministry took place at night, and she refers to Paul of Ephesus for the practice in Syria: For Paul, 'the object of his zeal was to carry poor and old and sick persons by night, and he would take them and bathe them and anoint them', doing this 'also for women'.

112. *Philoponias.* A *philoponos* was a lay person with specific duties in the Church; see Lampe 1480A; see further Dahlman, 231–232 (l. 12).

113. Mt 6:10, Lk 22:42, Acts 21:14.

114. It is not certain who this Julian is, but it is probably Julian of Cilicia. In Letter 131, to Bishop Timothy, written in 450, Theodoret of Cyrrhus speaks of 'the shrines dedicated to the glorious martyrs' and names 'the martyr Julian or Romanus or Timothy' as examples of those buried in such shrines; see Azéma, ed., 3.121. According to John Chrysostom, who wrote a *Laudatio Sancti Juliani* (*In Praise of Saint Julian*), Julian was a martyr from Cilicia whose body the Antiochenes claimed to possess. See also H. Delehaye, *Les origines du culte des martyrs*, 2nd rev. ed. (Brussels: Société des Bollandistes, 1933) 121, 166, and 189. Delehaye notes, 200, that Julian's 'presence in Antioch remains unexplained', and that Chrysostom gives no indication of the saint's feast day, 'perhaps December 26'. Theodoret, *Religious History* 10.8, says that the monk Theodosius, also from Cilicia, was 'buried in the shrine of the holy martyrs, obtaining the same abode and roof as Julian the victorious contestant in piety . . . [and] also the inspired and blessed Aphrahat' (*A History of the Monks of Syria*, trans. Price, 92). Aphrahat died between 407 and 413; about ten years later the hermit Macedonius was buried in the same shrine (Theodoret, *Religious History* 13.19; Price, 93 n. 6. and 107). Numerous shrines were dedicated to a Julian in the East, but it is not certain that these all refer to Julian of Cilicia; see the index in Delehaye, 426. During Justinian's reign the remains of the martyr Saint Marinus were brought to Antioch and were buried outside the city in the church of Saint Julian, which is probably to be associated with a 'Gate of Saint Julian' mentioned by one account written following the earthquake of 526; see Glanville Downey, *A History of Antioch in Syria: from Seleucus to the Arab Conquest* (Princeton: Princeton University Press, 1961) 531 and n. 127. The Persians invaded Antioch in 540 and burned the city and 'the suburbs, except for the sanctuary of St. Julian and the dwellings attached to it, about three miles outside the city' (Downey, 544–545). Downey notes, 545 n. 180, that the direction of Saint Julian's outside the city

is unknown but that 'there were accommodations for visitors connected with the church and on at least one occasion a small local synod met there'. About 570 the pilgrim Antoninus visited Antioch and among other churches saw one dedicated to Saint Julian (Downey, 561). Dahlman, 232 (ll. 28–29), says that the Church of Saint Julian was three miles from Antioch, 'probably on the road to Daphne', and believes that the Julian referred to above was Julian of Anazarbos, martyred in Cilicia during Diocletian's persecution (the 'Great Persecution') in the early fourth century.

115. Syr 2 and Arm 4 say that he threw himself down 'before the icon of the Saviour'. Recension B says that he threw himself before the Saviour.

116. Job 1:21 LXX, Ps 112:2 LXX.

117. Text: ἐζήτει πνῖξαι. Dahlman, 169, prefers 'tried to strangle herself' (LSJ 1425a), but I prefer 'drown' (LSJ 1425b (III)).

118. The day of judgement.

119. On the manumission of slaves, see K. R. Bradley, *Slaves and Masters in the Roman Empire: A Study in Social Control* (Oxford: Oxford University Press, 1987), esp. 'Manumission', 81–112.

120. Text: Ἐυλόγιαν. Eulogia has a wide variety of meanings (see Lampe, 569a–570b) but seems to mean 'blessed bread' here. It is a word that recurs in the dossier; see the Index.

121. Gen 12:1.

122. The shrine of Saint Menas (Abū Mīnā in Arabic) was the most popular pilgrimage site in Egypt in Late Antiquity; see Peter Grossmann, *Abu Mina: A Guide to the Ancient Pilgrimage Center* (Cairo: Fotiadis, 1986), and Grossmann, 'The Pilgrimage Center of Abū Mīnā', in David Frankfurter, ed., *Pilgrimage and Holy Space in Late Antique Egypt* (Leiden: Brill, 1998) 281–302. Evelyn White, 245 n. 4, believes that the genitive 'of Alexandria' means that the couple visited a site in or very near Alexandria and not the famous shrine of Saint Menas further away from the city, but this seems unlikely: the greek genitive can indicate a wide locale (in I.6 and I.7 the Monastery of the Oktokaidekaton, although eighteen miles outside Alexandria, is in Greek literally 'the Monastery of the Oktokaidekaton *of* Alexandria') and if the couple had been seeing 'the holy places', they would have made sure to visit the most important pilgrimage site in Egypt.

123. Dahlman, 234 (l. 94), suggests there may be a lacuna here. None of the other versions of this story in any language supply a lacuna, so if there is one here it occurred very early in the text's transmission.

124. See n. 15 above.

125. Although the term 'the monastery of the Tabennisiotes' could be referring to one of Pachomius' monasteries, it seems probable that 'Tabennisiote' came to be used in an almost general way for cenobitic communities that followed the pachomian form or rule and does not necessarily mean that they belonged to a formal *koinonia* as in the time of Pachomius and Theodore. The use here may

mean nothing more than 'cenobitic'. Jim Goehring has observed that the term 'Tabennisiote' 'had come to be used by this period of any monastery that used the Pachomian *Rule*. The use of the *Rule*, however, did not necessarily mean that the monastery belonged to the Pachomian koinonia or system centered at the Middle Egyptian monastery of Pbow, and notes as examples the White Monastery at Atripe, Ammon's monastery (HM 3) and, probably, the monastery of Metanoia at Canopus. See James E. Goehring, *Ascetics, Society, and the Desert* (Harrisburg: Trinity, 1999) 258. As a sixth-century example, the monastic communities founded by Macrobius in Sarga, twenty-five km south of Asyut, included separate monasteries for men and women; see Clara ten Hacken, 'Coptic and Arabic Texts on Macrobius, an Egyptian Monk of the Sixth Century', in Stephen Emmel, *et al.*, edd., *Ägypten und Nubien in spätantiker und christlicher Zeit* (Wiesbaden: Reichert, 1999) 2:122. Since the stories about Daniel often refer to 'lavras' or semi-anchoritic communities, a contrast is probably being made here between these and cenobia. In the *Lausiac History*, 'Tabennisiote' is used vaguely (Prologue 2, 18.1) and then explicitly of Pachomius and his monastery at Tabennisi (18.12, 32). The pachomian sources mention two female communities, and *Lausiac History* 33 specifically refers to a tabbenisiote monastery 'of some four hundred women'. This monastery for women may in fact be the same as the monastery in I.4 above. Lampe, 1370a, is not much help.

126. 'Egypt': see n. 58 above.

127. See Jonah 4:6.

128. This motif occurs elsewhere: in one saying from the AP, a man whose wife has left him to become an ascetic does not recognize her because, as an ascetic, she has become as dark as an Ethiopian; see Regnault, ed., *Les sentences: Série des anonymes* 241 (no. 1596, 10). Early monastic literature often regards Ethiopians and Nubians, because of their darker skin, with suspicion and fear. See n. 236 at I.9 below for further discussion and references. Dahlman observes, 236 (ll. 131–132), that female ascetics are often described as dark to emphasize their loss of beauty and cites the *Life of Saint Mary of Egypt* 10 and the *Life of Saint Theokiste of Lesbos* 17 in Alice-Mary Talbot, ed., *Holy Women of Byzantium: Ten Saints' Lives in English Translation* (Washington DC: Dumbarton Oaks, 1996).

129. The monastery or collection of monastic communities at the eighteenth milestone west of Alexandria. See notes 35 and 42 above.

130. Literally, 'love silence' (ἀγάπα τὴν σιωπήν), but Dahlman's 'devote yourself to silence' is good.

131. *Episkepsis* suggests an official visit or inspection made by a monastic superior.

132. For a similar discovery, see I.2 above. Syriac adds here: 'When Andronicus learned what had happened and knew that she was Athanasia his wife, he threw

himself on her breast and with many tears embraced her, saying, "Alas for me, I had my pearl near me and did not perceive it! My wife was within my cell, and I did not know her!" He said other things like this in his grief.'

133. See I.1 above. Again, it is not clear whether the narrator intends to mean it was the monks' custom to wear white for a special (funerary?) occasion or whether white was the normal color of monastic dress.

134. According to Clugnet's text, with improvements from Dahlman's text.

135. That is, he died. 'Go to sleep' is a common designation for 'to die'. The story of Lazarus in the New Testament shows that there could be ambiguity about the word 'sleep' (Jn 11:11–16).

136. Eph 5:19.

137. According to Dahlman, with variants from Coislin 232, 282.

138. Daniel, the monks are saying, has no fear of combat with the Enemy—Satan—while they do, so they need the body of the dead saint as a holy relic to protect them from evil.

139. MSS 232 and 282.

140. The feminine form of 'deathless' in Greek is *athanasia*. MSS 232 and 282 have this play on words on her name.

141. Mt 6:10, Lk 22:42, Acts 21:14.

142. Job 1:21.

143. On this saint, see n. 114 above.

144. Literally, 'the holy places', throughout this story.

145. Gen 12:1.

146. See n. 122 above.

147. See n. 125 above.

148. See above, n. 58.

149. Jonah 4:6.

150. See n. 128 above.

151. See n. 129, above.

152. From the Greek Synaxary, 9 October.

153. A circumlocution for saying that they no longer had sexual relations.

154. Job 1:21.

155. See n. 114 above.

156. The day of judgement.

157. Gen 12:1.

158. This would technically place them in Antioch, but it is clear that they are now in Egypt. See I.5A above, p. 34.

159. See n. 125 above.

160. Jonah 4:6.

161. See n. 129 above.

162. See n. 129, above.

163. According to monastic sources it was not uncommon for men, at least, to leave families and become monks, sometimes when they were widowers and the children were grown. But it is not clear why an *abba* would be living with his son and daughter-in-law. The armenian version (Chapter Five) has a strikingly different beginning, below, page 226.

164. Literally 'loins', *psoiōn*, probably with a sexual connotation.

165. See n. 15 above.

166. Apparently this refers to Thomaïs' father-in-law.

167. Van Cauwenbergh notes, 16 n. 2, that the 'Acts of Saint Thomaïs were published by the Bollandists according to the greek synaxary (*Acta SS.*, April 2:214), and that that account is in perfect agreement with the one in the Daniel collection'.

168. 'Soberly', *sōphronōs*, is closely related etymologically to *sōphrosunē*, 'chastity', for which Thomaïs dies.

169. Here Daniel is *prōtos*; see Lampe, 1201a(B). Earlier he is called *hēgoumenos*, 'superior', of Scetis.

170. In Modern Greek φωταγωγός means 'skylight'; Lampe, 1508a(B) suggests 'window', taking φωταγωγός as an adjective, 'giving light', and supplying θυρίς. The oil seems to have been kept near a source of sunlight in order to soften it and keep it liquid.

171. Or: Thomaïs of blessed memory.

172. Translated from Latin, *Acta sanctorum*, April 2:213–214.

173. Paris BN Coislin 283, f. 169; variants from BN Gk. ff 190-191, with improvements by Dahlman (4A). This story, as Bonnet observed, 170, was probably detached from the one above (as the latin version demonstrates) and numbered separately. Dahlman, 4A, ll. 43-57, has this story as the conclusion to I.6 (in the numbering used in this volume). All the MSS that contain I.6 also have this story following it. Note that here Daniel is identified only as 'the old man', suggesting that this story served as a sort of instructive appendix to I.6. As Dahlman rightly sees, 210 (4A: 43-57), 'The first part [I.6 in this volume] shows the virtue of the woman during her life and the second how her virtue works after her death'. Dahlman notes further that in all the MSS she has studied, 'this part of the text [I.7 in this volume] is directly connected with the previous part, and it is never given a title of its own, although some of the MSS' begin the second part with a capital letter.

174. See n. 15 above.

175. See above, note 129.

176. *Koimētērion*, which usually means 'cemetery', but here and below seems to mean 'tomb'; see I.5 [**A**] above and Lampe 760b (2).

177. Text (Dahlman 4A, p. 132, ll 49-50): διὰ τοῦ Θεοῦ <καὶ> τῶν εὐχῶν, 'through God <and> [your] prayers', which is also the text of I.4**B** (136, ll. 58-59), so I have adopted it. However, the other reading, διὰ τοῦ Θεοῦ τῶν εὐχῶν, 'through

the God of your prayers', is in fact the *lectio difficilior* and fits in well with the monastic understanding of the power of the abba's prayers. On this theme, see Tim Vivian, 'Holy Men and Businessmen', repr. in Vivian, *Words to Live By,* 325–331.

178. *Metanoias,* literally '(acts of) repentance', which probably meant saying a prayer and then prostrating oneself. See Vivian, 'Monks, Middle, Egypt, and *Metanoia*', JECS 7.4 (Winter 1999) 547–72; rpt. in Vivian, *Words to Live By,* 205–236. See n. 100 above.

179. *Eulogia* could also mean consecrated eucharistic bread or a gift of blessed bread, so it is possible that the young woman is giving the monk such blessed bread; see Lampe 570D-E. The fact that the monk later says that he does not know what the blessing was would seem to indicate that the *eulogia* was not a gift of bread. See n. 120 above and the Index for further references to *eulogia.*

180. *The Life of Pelagia* has interesting parallels with the story of Anastasia. Pelagia, a prostitute, after her conversion flees to the desert disguised as a male monk with the name of Pelagius. See Petitmengin, ed., and, for an english translation of the syriac version, Brock and Harvey, 40-62. On Appolinaris/ Doritheus, see Evelyn White, 117–118, and for Hilaria/Hilarion, 224–227.

181. On eunuchs in byzantine society, see Shaun F. Tougher, 'Byzantine Eunuchs: An Overview, with Special Reference to their Creation and Origin', in Liz James, ed., *Women, Men and Eunuchs: Gender in Byzantium* (London and New York: Routledge, 1997) 168–184.

182. In early monastic literature, 'inner' designates not movement towards the Nile but movement away from it and thus may be translated as 'further' or 'remoter' desert; see *Life of Antony* 49.7-51.2 and Tim Vivian, 'A Journey to the Interior' in Vivian, *Words to Live By,* 59–98.

183. Dahlman notes, 240 (l. 2), that many manuscripts have an additional sentence: 'He had his cell about eighteen miles from that same Sketis'.

184. See n. 15 above.

185. This is required for the sense. Clugnet's version has it.

186. Syr 3 makes Daniel prophetic: 'One day the blessed one said to his disciple, "Go look, my son, near the cave of the old man. When you find a clay tablet with something written on it, bring it with you"'.

187. On this theme see chapter III of the Systematic Apophthegmata; Guy, ed., *Les apophtegmes.*

188. On the symbolic meaning of fruit, see Mt 3:10, 7:17-20, and Lk 13:6. On the theme of the monastic descendants of Abraham, see the coptic *Life of Macarius of Scetis* 3, 8, and 15 in Vivian, trans., *Saint Macarius the Spiritbearer,* and Vivian, 'Saint Antony the Great and the Monastery of Saint Antony by the Red Sea' in Elizabeth S. Bolman, ed., *Monastic Visions* (New Haven: Yale University Press: 2002), Chapter One, for how Macarius the Great and Antony were seen as second Abrahams. The abrahamic theme also figures in the *Life of Bishoy;* see Vivian, '"A Man Holy and Perfect"'.

189. See Gen 21:1-7.

190. 2 Kgs 2:1-18.

191. See Ex 34:29-35 (Moses descends from Mount Sinai) and Mt 17:2 (the transfiguration of Jesus).

192. Ps 31:5, Lk 23:46.

193. Daniel strips down to his loincloth and thus trades places with the deceased *abba*.

194. Dahlman notes, 242 (l. 52) that many redactions are more explicit: 'his breasts were those of a woman, like two dried-out, withered leaves'.

195. For a circumspect and unadorned account of the post-mortem discovery of one transvestite, see AP Bessarion 4. For the 'recognition scene', see *Life of Pelagia* 49 (Petitmengin, 93; Brock and Harvey, 61). Hilaria/Hilarion was also recognized at death by her withered breasts, which 'were not those of a woman'; see *Vita Sanctae Hilariae*, in Drescher: 6 (Coptic), 75 (English translation). Dahlman, 242 (l. 52) disagrees that this scene where the brother finds the 'eunuch' is a recognition scene. Maybe we're both right: it is for the disciple but not for Daniel. Teresa Shaw has commented, *The Burden of the Flesh,* 235–236, 'Descriptions of the physical changes brought on by food deprivation emphasize reduction in sexual humors through drying and cooling, drying or shriveling of the breasts, and general destruction of the female characteristics or "nature" of the body . . . . But there is more. The virgin's physical regimen not only alters the internal processes of nutrition and sexuality; it is part of an overall effort to alter the external presentation of her body.'

196. Apparently a liturgical meal with Communion (see the next sentence).

197. The empress.

198. Gk: *to Pempton;* see n. 35 above.

199. The group of lavras, cenobias, and hermitages at the fifth milestone west of Alexandria, known collectively as *To Pempton.* The Fifth (Milestone) was apparently on the same route heading west out of Alexandria as such other monastic settlements as Enaton, at the ninth milestone, Oktokaidekaton, at the eighteenth milestone, and Eikoston, at the twentieth. On these monasteries, see Paul van Cauwenbergh, *Étude sur les moines d'Égypte depuis le concile de Chalcédoine (451) jusqu'à l'invasion arabe (640)* 64–78. The syriac version of this story says that Anastasia founded her monastery at the Enaton; see Brock and Harvey, eds., 148, and Arm 3 (Chapter Five).

200. *Agōnizetai* is a technical monastic term, borrowed from athletics, used to designate fighting or contending against Satan or demons. This monastic term clearly signals a recurrent monastic theme: that those who are not monks (often those living in cities) are also able to 'contend' and, indeed, attain holiness (or 'salvation', as it is often put). In fact, they are often models for the monks, rather than the other way around.

201. 2 Tim 4:7.

202. Syr 3 (Chapter Four) continues: 'When the blessed one arrived at his cell, he sat down and wrote what he had seen and heard. This Anastasia, the patrician lady, is the deaconess who lived in the days of the patriarch Severus, holy to God. He wrote many letters to her in answer to the questions she asked him when she was in the monastery with the sisters before she went to the desert of Scetis.

'Here ends the story of a sister who was thought to be insane and [the story] of Anastasia, the patrician lady and deaconess.'

203. Gen 18. Slav W (Chapter Seven) makes this connection explicit: 'who welcomes Christ and strangers'.

204. Gen 21:1-7.

205. 2 Kgs 2:1-18.

206. Ps 31:5, Lk 23:46.

207. For a similar discovery, see I.10 below.

208. See n. 196 above.

209. The following at first seems to be spoken by Abba Daniel, but the petition *to* Daniel later on shows that the author—the disciple?—is speaking.

210. 2 Tim 4:7.

211. From the greek Synaxary, 10 March.

212. Justinian I (483–565) became emperor in 527.

213. Mt 13:25.

214. 1 Tim 6:12, 2 Tim 4:7, Acts 9:15.

215. 2 Kgs 2:1-18.

216. Communion.

217. Ps 31:5, Lk 23:46.

218. This last sentence alludes to what Daniel tells his disciple in I.8 A and B.

219. Coptic (Chap. 2): 'Our holy father Abba Daniel was in Egypt [outside of Scetis, usually in Alexandria or towards Babylon (Cairo)] another time with his disciple on their way back to Scetis, for they were sailing down the Nile'; Eth (Chap. 3): 'Once, when Abba Daniel, together with his disciple, was in the City of Egypt, he wanted to return home'. Goldschmidt-Esteves Pereira, 39, note 1, followed by Dahlman, 220 (l. 2), tentatively identify the 'City of Egypt' as the Upper Egyptian town of Kift (known in Greek as Koptos, in Arabic as Qift), twenty-five miles northeast of Hermopolis Magna (Luxor), presumably on the basis of the phonetic similarity between this name and Giʿiz *hagärä Gibs* (= 'the City of Egypt'; Gibs. meaning 'Egypt' in Giʿiz). According to Michael Kleiner, however, this identification is doubtful on linguistic as well as historic grounds; see his note, Chapter Three, n. 44.

220. As Dahlman notes, 220 (l. 4), the original meaning of κτῆμα (*ktēma*), used here, was 'piece of property', 'possession' but later the word came to designate large estates with tenant farmers. By the 6th c., it 'refers to large farms,

including fields and the buildings and workshops'. Since the term *chōrion,* 'village', is used immediately below (see the next note), I have chosen to combine here the ideas of 'farming' and 'village'.

221. See n. 15 above.

222. Marie Drew-Bear, *Le nome Hermopolite*, 42, says that a χωρίον (*chōrion*) could designate vaguely 'a place' (*topos*) or, more precisely, a fortress, estate, or village. This last was current in the byzantine period and replaced *kōmē*; thus *chōrion* evolved into modern greek *chōrio*, 'village, hamlet'. Two of my favorite modern place names in Greece are Elaiochōrion (from *elaia*, 'olive tree') and Astrochōrion (from *astēr*, 'star'). For a list of sites in the hermopolite nome designated as *choria*, see Drew-Bear, 388.

223. Dahlman points out, 221 (l. 15), that such a description as this has parallels with personal descriptions 'found in papyri and official documents. Their purpose was identification, and they often included descriptions of the person's age, height, hair, facial and other special features'. Latin, following a different greek MS, has 'While they were talking together, an old hunchbacked layman, many days into his long old age, appeared'. Dahlman, 221 (l. 15), accepts 'hunchback' and offers good support; see Chapter Six, p. 243, however, for opposing reasons.

224. A sign of hospitality, but see also Jn 13:5 and Lk 7:36-50.

225. See Mt 6:19-21.

226. See n. 59 above. In I.2 Daniel feeds a leper at noon.

227. Dahlman, 80, astutely connects the 'repenting secret saint' Eulogius with the theme of 'secret holiness'. One should adduce further, moreover, the parallels that Daniel's order to his disciple to be silent has in the Gospels, esp. Mk 1:32-34, 1:44, 3:12, 4:12, and 4:33.

228. Eulogia, 'blessing, benediction', is an important theme in the dossier; for references, see the Index. 'Eulogios' is the masculine form of 'eulogia'. The word is apparently unattested except as a name.

229. See n.26 above.

230. *Lausiac History* 17 reports that Macarius the Great becomes a monk as a young man at the age of thirty. Clugnet: forty years old; 232, 283, 914, 378: about forty years old or less. Copt: When I was a young man, forty years ago; Syr: When I was young, forty years ago; Lat: When I was a young man forty years ago.

231. See n. 120 and the Index for further references.

232. *Enguan* (ἐγγυάω) means to pledge oneself as surety for a loan or something, to act as a guarantor or co-pledge. As Dahlman observes, 223 (l. 83), 'the theme of a holy person standing guarantor and taking upon himself the sins of someone else is known from other hagiographical texts'. See her note for references.

233. *Hagian Anastasin.* The pilgrim Egeria in Late Antiquity mentions many times in her diary the Anastasis, which was part of Constantine's Basilica of the Holy Sepulcher in Jerusalem. As one of her modern editors notes, 'Moving from west to east, we find first the Anastasis, or sanctuary of the Resurrection, a church in the round, in the center of which was the grotto of the Holy Sepulchre' where, in Daniel's vision, the young man is sitting on the stone. See Gingra, trans., 24.

234. See Mt 28:2 and parallels.

235. Justin I became emperor in 518 and ruled until 527, when he was succeeded by Justinian I.

236. See n. 128 above. See *Life of Antony* 6.1 for, apparently, the first appearance of a black boy in monastic literature; the image may have its origins in Eph 6:12 ('the prince of darkness'), a text cited in *Life of Antony* 21.3. The armenian text has 'black demons'. For references on this subject, see David Brakke, *Athanasius and the Politics of Asceticism* (Oxford: Clarendon Press, 1995), 229, esp. n. 97. The belief that the Devil and demons took the form of Ethiopians was common in early monastic literature; as Lucien Regnault points out, *La vie quotidienne*, 'the form that they seem to have especially affected was that of male or female Ethiopians, whose swarthy color evoked the blackness of malice'. For his catalogue of Ethiopians in monastic literature, see 201–202, and on the Devil and demons in general, 189–207. For a general study, see F. M. Snowden, *Blacks in Antiquity: Ethiopians in the Greco-Roman Experience* (Cambridge, Massachusetts: Harvard University Press, 1970). For studies on christian attitudes, see Peter Frost, 'Attitudes toward Blacks in the Early Christian Era', *The Second Century* 8 (1991) 1–11; and Andrew Nugent, 'Black Demons in the Desert', *American Benedictine Review* 49.2 (June 1998) 209–221. For further references, see Ramsey, trans., *John Cassian: The Conferences* 73–74; Cassian, *Conferences* 1.21.1 and 2.13.7.

237. *Amma* usually, but not always, designates a female monastic; see Lampe 89b (3).

238. *Paxamatia* or *paxamadia* was bread baked and dried in small loaves that could be stored and soaked in water for later consumption. See AP Agathon 20, Macarius the Great 33, Achilles 3; *Lausiac History* 22.

239. 'Contemplative quiet': *hēsychia*. Probably also here is a warning—given by a non-monastic, and a woman at that!—against wandering monks. On this topic see especially Daniel Caner, *Wandering, Begging Monks: Spiritual Authority and the Promotion of Monasticism in Late Antiquity*, The Transformation of the Classical Heritage XXXV (Berkeley: University of California Press, 2002). Caner draws attention to the canons of the Council of Chalcedon; famous (or infamous) for its christological decisions, the council is less well known for its canon that once and for all subordinated monks to bishops: 'Let those who pursue a monastic life in each city and village be subordinate to their bishop'.

240. That is, he would abandon his monastic profession for 'the world'.

241. The title/name 'Augustus' was first used by Octavian Caesar in 27 BCE; he gave the title 'Augusta' to his wife Livia. From the time of Domitian (lived 51–96 CE) the Roman Senate conferred the title 'Augusta' on the wife of the emperor.

242. Emperor Anastasius died on 9 July 518, without grooming a successor, although each of his nephews, Hypatius, Pompeius, and Probus, had hopes of succeeding him. While Hypatius, who was commander-in-chief in the East, was out of the city, Justin, the leader of the bodyguard, managed to buy his way into power and became emperor. Justin adopted his nephew and on 1 April 527 made Justinian co-emperor. Justin died on 1 August of that year. Early in 532 Hypatius rebelled against Justinian, was defeated, and on 19 January he and Pompeius were executed and their bodies were cast into the sea: 'Their property, and that of those senators who had supported them, was confiscated. The patricians who had been with them, people whose identity we unfortunately do not know, fled'. See John Moorhead, *Justinian* (London—New York: Longman, 1994) 14, 21–22, 46–47.

243. The armenian is more explicit: When I saw him covered with dust and dirt and worn out from stonecutting; Copt: and I saw that a large crowd of people was boasting about him.

244. Ps 104:24. Dahlman notes, 227 (ll. 212-213), that one manuscript has 'who lifts up the poor from the earth and raises the needy from the dunghill', Ps 112 (113):7.

245. Ps 75:7.

246. Ps 89:6.

247. Ps 94:7.

248. Dahlman notes that one manuscript, adding, 'Thus I have told you where I know him from, and also why you may not repeat this to anyone', repeats the theme of 'secret holiness' from the beginning of the story.

249. BN MS Coislin 283, f 163–163v.

250. See above, note 58.

251. On tombs and their association with demons, see *Life of Antony* 8–10.

252. *Synaxis*, the weekly community meeting for semi-anchorites, those who lived alone or in groups of two or three outside the monastery and who joined the community on Saturday and Sunday for Communion, worship, and meals.

253. BN Gk 1605 (12th c.), ff. 264v-267. This is Clugnet's apt title; the MS, vaguely and inappropriately, has 'Concerning Abba Doulas', although the latin version does make Doulas the subject of the story.

254. The Devil.

255. Again, the Devil.

256. The sacred vessels (as they are called below) used for the Eucharist.

257. On this official, who had important duties in the monastery, see Cyril of Scythopolis, *Life of Sabas* 43, and Moschus, *Spiritual Meadow* 50.

258. The day of judgement.

259. For a similar occurrence, see I.4 above.

260. That is, the day of judgement.

261. *Metanoia*. See n. 100 above and the Index.

262. John Wortley suggests that *eulogia* here, 'blessing', means that the monks wanted to take a 'relic' from the deceased brother: hair, clothing. This is certainly possible, and is how Lat 5 understands matters: 'one of them wanted to take a relic from his remains'. See the *Life of Saint Daniel the Stylite* 98–100. For further references to eulogia, see n. 120 and the Index.

263. Apparently this is the superior or archimandrite of the monastery. Arabic suggests that there are two leaders: the 'superior of the cenobium' and 'the teacher of the lavra'.

264. See Lk 24:12, of Jesus' clothes in the tomb.

265. This story is attributed to 'Abba Daniel' in a significantly different and longer syriac version (see Syr 5). MS Coislin 126 does not connect this story with Abba Daniel, places the unnamed brother in 'Egypt', that is, outside Scetis, and does not identify the city as Alexandria. Three greek MSS., however, BHG 2102e, make the unnamed monk Daniel, while the syriac version leaves the monk anonymous but makes Daniel the narrator of the story; see Sebastian P. Brock, AB113 (1995) 269–280; 269. Given the fact that BHG 2102e names Daniel as the monk and since the locales of the syriac story narrated by Daniel, like many of those in the Daniel Dossier, are Scetis and Alexandria, it seems reasonable to include it here.

266. Translated by John Wortley from BHG 2102e from an unpublished critical text prepared by Evangeli Sakkas.

267. Scetis. Compare the monk's behavior with Antony's scrupulous care for his sister, *Life of Antony* 3.1.

268. Gen 44:29.

269. Presumably he then buries the corpse.

270. See n. 128 above.

271. Early monastic literature commonly associates evil, evil deeds, evil persons, and the Evil One (Satan) with stench.

272. *Philanthrōpia*.

273. Translated from the text edited by Nau, 'Histoires', 174–175, based on Paris BN Coislin 126 (10th/11th c.) [BHG 1438h].

274. The monastic elders.

275. 'Brothel' is literally 'workshop of lawlessness'. In the syriac version the brother tells her to go back and get a covering for her head.

276. In the syriac he follows her bloody footprints until he finds her. The syriac then follows with a long account of a dream that the brother has.

277. John Moschus, *Spiritual Meadow* 114; PG 87:2977-2980. The title in PG, not very appropriate, is 'The Life of Abba Daniel the Egyptian'. For another

translation, see John Moschus, *Spiritual Meadow*, 94–95. Derwas Chitty, *The Desert a City*, 145–147, believes that this Daniel is the same Daniel of Scetis.

278. See n. 15 above.

279. Terenuthis is not far from Scetis, and Daniel certainly could have traveled there. After the first devastation of Scetis in 407–408, Poemen and others went to Terenuthis (AP Anoub 1); Abba Macarius the Great travels to Terenuthis (Macarius 13), as does Abba Xanthias (Xanthias 2). Evelyn White, 242, believes that 'Abba Daniel the Egyptian' is the same person as Abba Daniel of Scetis, but rightly says that there is really no way to be sure.

280. A not uncommon theme in early monastic literature; see AP Macarius the Great 1.

281. Translated from the text edited by Mioni, 61–94; 92–93 (XI [151]). Numbers in brackets refer to the pages of Mioni's text. Another translation of this story may be found in *The Spiritual Meadow*, 226–227. There is also a version in the ethiopic Patericon; see Chapter Three, Appendix I.

282. Possibly either at or near the present-day monasteries of Deir al-Baramus or Deir Anba Maqar in the Wadi al-Natrun (Scetis), both places associated with Macarius the Great.

283. See above, n. 129.

284. See I.1, note 27, above.

285. See Mt 16:19.

286. Translated from Evergetinos, *Synagōgē* 3.16.7, 211-212. I wish to thank John Wortley for supplying this text, translation, and notes. Numbers in brackets indicate paragraph numbers in Evergetinos' text.

287. Many monks bathed rarely or not at all. They particularly associated public baths with pagan licentiousness. Below, Daniel says, 'Our holy fathers Antony and Pachomius, Amoun, Serapion, and the rest of the God-bearing fathers inspired by God decree that no monk should ever strip naked other than for reasons of severe illness and necessity'.

288. John Moschus tells the story of a miraculous spring that refused to supply a bath installed in a monastery (*Spiritual Meadow* 80). In AP Poemen 11 (Ward, 168), 'a priest of Pelusia heard it said of some brethren that they often went to the city, took baths and were careless in their behavior', so he took away their habits from them. The moral of this saying, however, is about not judging others and the priest 'repents' and returns the brothers their habits.

289. Gal 1:10.

290. Mt 7:1.

291. That is, he is sick, and therefore his bathing is justified. In *The Spiritual Meadow* 158b a monk is saved from dying of dehydration by bathing.

292. *Aithiopissa*, usually associated with deeds of sexual license; see notes 128 and 236.

293. Goats were considered especially licentious, as the phrase 'he's an old goat' still testifies.

294. See *Life of Antony* 60.5-10 where Amoun crosses the Nile this way.

295. Calderini, *Dizionario*, 1935–1987, does not mention a church in Alexandria dedicated to Saint Isidore. This must, however, be a reference to Isidore of Antioch, who was martyred in the persecution of Diocletian and whose feast day in the Coptic Church is 19 Bashans (14 May, Julian, 27 May Gregorian).

296. Κωσταντίνου, which is a short form for Κωσταντινοπόλεως, as occurs with a number of other greek cities in Egypt (e.g. Panos, for Panopolis).

297. The *silentiarius* was a court attendant at Constantinople whose responsibility was to maintain order and silence in the Sacred Palace.

298. *Paideusis huperēphanō ptōmati*, literally, 'the chastening of an arrogant "corpse"' (for 'body'), suggesting that sinful behavior had already 'killed' this monk.

299. Scetis, the Wadi al-Natrun.

300. Or 'standard-bearing', *sēmeiophoroi*, fathers (see n. 304 below), the miracles being the *indicators* of sanctity.

301. Translated by John Wortley from Codex Sinaïticus 448; from Regnault's translation in *Les sentences des Pères du désert*, item 1762, J762.

302. The 'passions' for early monastics were the disordered desires that pull humans away (literally 'distract') from God.

303. Translated by John Wortley from BN Coislin 283 ff 130v-132, No. 296 (BHG 2102f), slightly modified, and Cod. Athen. 257 ff 219-20; it has the title 'Longinus the monk and that people in the world should not lightly condemn monks'. See also Regnault, *Les sentences: Série des Anonymes* 171-173 (#K296, 1490/2).

304. 'Wonder-worker' (*sēmeiophoros*) is used of an anonymous *abba* in Alphabetical Apophthegmata Daniel 8 (*PG* 65:160A). See n. 300 above.

305. Timothy III, pope from 519–537.

306. A *syncellus* was an associate of a patriarch, a clergyman of high rank who, nominated by the emperor, often succeeded a patriarch, especially in Constantinople.

307. See above, n.129.

308. Possibly a 'fool' like Abba Mark in I.1 above.

309. That is, human beings can literally be anti-Christs.

310. 1 Tim 5:20.

311. A not uncommon occurrence in Late Antiquity.

Chapter 2: The Coptic Life

1. We wish to thank Mark Moussa for his assistance with this chapter.

2. For two few examples, see 'A Discourse on Saint Onnophrius' by Pisentius in Vivian, *Paphnutius* 167–188; and 'An Encomium on Saint Antony' by John of Shmun in Vivian-Athanassakis, *The Life of Antony* 1–35.

3. See Chapter One, pp. 43–44 and 77–83.

4. Although vague, such a location is accurate: many, if not most, ancient monasteries were situated on the edge of civilization, on land between arable farmland and the desert.

5. Evelyn White, 247; Leslie S. B. MacCoull, '"When Justinian Was Upsetting the World": A Note on Soldiers and Religious Coercion in Sixth-Century Egypt', *Peace and War in Byzantium: Essays in Honor of George T. Dennis, S.J.*, ed. Timothy S. Miller and John Nesbitt (Washington DC: Catholic University of America Press, 1995) 107 n. 1.

6. For a fifth-century example, see Tim Vivian, 'Humility and Resistance in Late Antique Egypt: *The Life of Longinus*', *Coptic Church Review* 20.1 (Spring 1999) 2–30, rpt. in Vivian, *Words to Live By*, 239–281.

7. Evelyn White, 246 and 247, although he acknowledges that John of Nikiu (*Chronicle* XCIV.18) says that Justinian 'stirred up a severe persecution in the land of Egypt'. He concludes, 247, that the story 'has been inserted in the Coptic version rather than deleted from the Greek . . . . The probability is that it is a mere reflection from its almost exact counterpart in the history of Samuel of Kalamûn'. There are, however, considerable differences between Daniel and Samuel: Daniel belongs to the sixth century while Samuel lived in the seventh. Despite Evelyn White's assertion, the anti-chalcedonian passage in the *Life of Samuel* is far from being an 'almost exact counterpart' of that in the coptic *Life of Daniel*. It is longer, more florid, and more violent, although in both accounts the anti-chalcedonian heroes—Daniel and Samuel—are forced to flee Scetis. See Anthony Alcock, ed. and trans., *The Life of Samuel of Kalamun* (Warminster: Aris & Phillips, 1983) 6–7 (Coptic), and 79–81 (English). Manuscript considerations are not decisive: the chief MS of the *Life of Samuel* probably dates to the ninth century (Alcock, vii) while the MS of the coptic *Life of Daniel* belongs to the tenth century.

8. Charles A. Frazee, 'Late Roman and Byzantine Legislation on the Monastic Life from the Fourth to the Eighth Centuries', *Church History* 51/3 (September 1982) 263–279; at 271.

9. See Edward R. Hardy, 'The Egyptian Policy of Justinian', *Dumbarton Oaks Papers* 22 (1968) 21–41, and Frazee, 271-272.

10. John of Nikiu, *Chronicle* 90.84; R.H. Charles, trans., *John of Nikiu, Chronicle* (London—Oxford: Williams & Norgate, 1916) 143. According to John, *Chronicle* 90.81-83, 'a great earthquake' devastated Egypt 'and the remembrance

of this calamity has been preserved for us by our fathers, the divinely-influenced Egyptian monks. For these earthquakes were due to the change in the orthodox faith brought about by the emperor Justinian, who had hardened his heart more than his father's brother [Justin], who had preceded him.'

11. John of Ephesus, *Lives of the Eastern Saints*, ed. E. W. Brooks, Patrologia orientalis 17 (Turnhout: Brepols, 1923) 20–21.

12. See Susan Ashbrook Harvey, *Asceticism and Society in Crisis,* Transformation of the Classical Heritage 18 (Berkeley: University of California Press, 1990) 79.

13. See K. H. Kuhn, ed. and trans., *A Panegyric on Apollo, Archimandrite of the Monastery of Isaac, by Stephen, Bishop of Heracleopolis Magna* 10, CSCO 394, Scriptores Coptici 39 [Coptic], 395 and 40 [English] (Louvain: Secrétariat du CorpusSCO, 1978).

14. Hardy, 33–34. Theodosius' 'successor' (who is not recognized by the Coptic Orthodox Church) was a monk, Paul the Tabbenisiote. Given what was to follow (see below), the irony was that Paul was a pachomian monk, probably from Canopus. He did not hold office long and apparently had little or no power outside Alexandria. Paul was the last pro-chalcedonian patriarch who was Egyptian; after him they were all foreigners and were all consecrated abroad and sent to Egypt (see Hardy, 34). As Hardy wryly concludes, 41, 'So the separate existence of the Coptic Church, something which the Emperor never intended, is the one permanent result of the Egyptian policy followed by Justinian, or indeed, as one should rather say, of the policies followed by Justinian and Theodora.'

15. See James E. Goehring, *Ascetics, Society, and the Desert: Studies in Early Egyptian Monasticism* (Harrisburg Trinity Press, 1999) 241–261. Another anti-chalcedonian monastery, that of Moses of Abydos, apparently continued to flourish after Moses' death (by 550); see Mark R. Moussa, 'Abba Moses of Abydos', Unpublished M.A. Thesis (Washington DC: The Catholic University of America, 1998) 55.

16. Goehring, 243, who collates the various materials and implicitly accepts the basic historicity of the accounts; for the fragmentary coptic text, see Emile Amélineau, *Monuments pour servir à l'histoire de l'Egypte chrétienne aux IV, V, VI et VII siècles,* Mémoire de la Mission archéologique Française au Caire, IV, fasc. 1–2 (Paris: 1888–1895) 744–745, supplemented by Paris MS (Bibliothèque Nationale) 12913, fol. 14(r), edited by Tito Orlandi (codice GC, foglio 5 recto). I wish to thank Mark Moussa for supplying me with this material.

17. See Kuhn, ed., *Panegyric on Apollo* 10.

18. Goehring, 244 n. 17.

19. Goehring, 244–247.

20. As the *Panegyric on Apollo* puts it (Kuhn, ed., 395 [40]:13–14 describing not Abraham's but Apollo's departure: 'And thus he departed from Pbow at that

time, having kept as apostolic the Constitution of the Apostles which says: If the ungodly seize a monastery [*topos*, 'place', which, however, in Coptic also came to mean 'monastery'], flee far away'.

21. I. Forget, ed., *Synaxarium Alexandrinum,* Corpus Scriptorum Christianorum Orientalium 47-49, 67, 78, 90, Scriptores Arabici, ser. 3, 18-19 (Rome, K. De Luigi, 1905–1926) 401–405.

22. See Kuhn, ed., *Panegyric on Apollo* 10 (395 [40]:13: 'They who came together at Chalcedon mixed the cup of the Jews' religion, and he who shall drink it, his reward is the office of archimandrite of Pbow'.

23. Goehring, 249; see also W. H. C. Frend, *The Rise of the Monophysite Movement* (Cambridge: Cambridge University Press, 1972) 273–275.

24. Goehring, 251.

25. See the *Bohairic Life of Pachomius* (SBo) 71; *Pachomian Koinonia, 1, The Life of Saint Pachomius*, trans. and ed. Armand Veilleux (Kalamazoo: Cistercian Publications, 1980) 93.

26. Another source, the *Life of Macrobius*, appears to show that Justinian's 'persecution' was neither systematic nor systemic; see Clara ten Hacken, 'Coptic and Arabic Texts on Macrobius, an Egyptian Monk of the Sixth Century', in Stephen Emmel, *et al.*, edd., *Ägypten und Nubien in spätantiker und christlicher Zeit* (Wiesbaden: Reichert, 1999) 2:123. Macrobius' community, the *Life* says, suffered no persecution during Macrobius' abbacy in the sixth century. Macrobius' community was at Sarga, twenty-five km. south of Assiut, and was probably too unimportant and too distant to merit imperial attention. There is also no record of a confrontation at this time between imperial troops and the monks of Abba Moses of Abydos; see Moussa, 54.

27. MacCoull, 108.

28. MacCoull, 107 n. 5.

29. MacCoull, 109. In the *Life of Samuel of Kalamun* 7 (Alcock, 7–8 [Coptic], 79–80 [English]), 'Cyrus the criminal' sends a *magistrianus* and 200 soldiers to Scetis to force compliance to the Tome of Leo.

30. MacCoull, 111, 108; see her article for a discussion of the make-up and use of such troops.

31. MacCoull, 113.

32. MacCoull, 110 [emphasis added].

33. MacCoull, 108.

34. The sources about Abraham share the same uncertainty about the abbot's departure; see Goehring, 241–261.

35. See *Samuel of Kalamun* 6–7 (Coptic) and 80–81 (English). The *Life of Samuel of Kalamun* and the anti-chalcedonian section of the *Life of Daniel* in fact have close parallels with one another. One of them, therefore, is dependent on the other, or else they share a common tradition. It seems to me that the *Life of Samuel*, with its much lengthier anti-chlacedonian polemic, incorporates material

from the *Life of Daniel*. Samuel's dates are roughly 597–695; the *Life* as composed by Isaac, however, may be as late as the early ninth century (Alcock, ix). In the beginning of the *Life*, Isaac mentions that he is guided by the oral tradition of four generations: 'Moreover, they also, our holy fathers, heard from their fathers who were before them, and they heard from their fathers, who were the disciples of that great one, Apa Samuel' (Alcock, 74.) The *Life of Samuel* is definitely a patchwork and is relatively late so the presence of material from the *Life of Daniel* in it would not be difficult to account for.

36. See also the *Panegyric on Apollo* 13–19.

37. Moussa, 'Abba Moses of Abydos' 1.

38. D.W. Johnson, ed. and trans., *A Panegyric on Macarius, Bishop of Tkōw, Attributed to Dioscorus of Alexandria*, CSCO 415–16 [Scriptores Coptici 41–42] (Louvain: Secrétariat du CorpusSCO, 1980) 221.

39. For a possible example, see Johnson, *A Panegyric,* 221.

40. Johnson, 223. The four figures of this period are Daniel of Scetis, Abraham of Farshut (formerly of Pbow), Abba Apollo from the Monastery of Isaac, and Abba Moses of Abydos.

41. Johnson, 224.

42. Van Cauwenbergh, 26–27.

43. Tambōk is little-known in the ancient sources. See Wolfgang Kosack, *Historisches Kartenwerk Ägyptens* (Bonn: Rudolf Habelt, 1971), 'Karte des koptischen Ägypten, Blatt 1, Delta', 5C. Kosack gives Tambōk's location as 'certain', but Stefan Timm, *Das christlich-koptische Ägypten in arabischer Zeit: eine Sammlung christlicher Stätten in Ägypten in arabischer Zeit, unter Ausschluss von Alexandria, Kairo, des Apa-Mena-Klosters (Der Abu Mina), der Sketis (Wadi n-Natrun) und der Sinai-Region* (Wiesbaden: L. Reichert, 1984–1992) 2481, concludes, 'Whether the similarity of the Coptic and Arabic place names alone is sufficient argument for the identification of the Coptic Tambok with the Arabic at-Tambuq cannot be determined. Up to now the sources have not offered a more precise designation of the place where Daniel died. Nothing is known of ruins of a Christian monastery near at-Tambuq'. But there was not necessarily a monastery at Tambōk.

44. As the armenian version (Arm 7) of the story about Anastasia confirms: 'She lived twenty-eight years in Scetis and no one knew about her except me and, today, you, except for one other person and his disciple. They knew because when I had to go somewhere I would order them to take water to her, and no one knew about her, who she was or what sort of person she was except you and me alone. The emperor sent numerous magistrates looking for her, but they could not find her'. See also Evelyn White, 246–247.

45. The account of Daniel's death has numerous very close, even word-for-word, parallels with the account of the death of Isidoros the Anchorite in the homily *On Cana of Galilee* by Patriarch Benjamin I; see C. Detlef G. Müller, *Die*

Homilie über die Hochzeit zu Kana und weitere Schriften des Patriarchen Benjamin I. von Alexandrien (Heidelberg: C. Winter, 1968) 32r-33r. Internal evidence suggests that this second encounter between Benjamin and Isidoros should be dated to 644.

46. See Evelyn White, 154–155, 161, and 166.

47. Evelyn White, 250, accepts the historicity of the attack.

48. *History of the Patriarchs* 226.

49. Evelyn White, 249.

50. Eth also has this story.

51. Eth has this material.

52. Eth has this material.

53. Eth has this material.

54. Eth has this material.

55. The eighth of Pashons, or Bashans—May 3 (Julian), May 16 (Gregorian)—is still the feast day of Daniel in the Coptic Orthodox Church.

56. Translated from Vat. Copt. LXII (10th c.), f. 38-55v., ed. Ignazio Guidi, 'Texte Copte', *Revue de l'Orient Chrétien* 5 (1900) 535–552. On the text, see Guidi, ROC 6 (1901) 51-52. Numbers in brackets within the translation indicate the pages of Guidi's article. Section titles are our own. The numbers in brackets following the section titles indicate the order of the story in the greek dossier in Chapter 1.

57. Ps 67:36 LXX. Numbers between backstrokes within the translation indicate pages in Guidi's text.

58. On the virtues in early monastic thought, see Tim Vivian, 'Ama Sibylla of Saqqara: Prioress or Prophet, Monastic or Mythological Being?' *Bulletin of the Saint Shenouda the Archimandrite Coptic Society* 5 (1998-1999) 1–17, rpt. in Vivian, *Words to Live By,* 379–393.

59. In Arabic, apparently following coptic (and greek) usage, 'the Great Feast', without further qualifying words, designates Easter and 'the Minor Feast' designates Christmas.

60. Following Guidi's suggestion that ⲛⲁϥⲗⲉⲁⲉⲃⲟⲗ equals ⲛⲁϥⲗⲉⲁⲉ ⲉⲃⲟⲗ, which corresponds with περιῆγεν (Clugnet: p. 60 line 11; Dahlman: #2, line 12, p. 120). See Crum 141a s.v. ⲗⲉⲗⲉ.

61. See Chapter One, n. 25.

62. The Gk has 100 *noumia* (Dahlman) or *folleis* (Clugnet); *arkiōn*, which Guidi merely transliterates, appears to be unattested. On these coins, see Chapter One, n. 26.

63. The Gk suggests that this obeisance is being done in a mocking manner.

64. Coptic: ⲁϥⲟⲩⲱϣ ⲉϥⲱⲧⲕⲉⲛⲁ ϥⲱⲧ = ⲡⲱⲧ; Gk: The imbecile came to himself and confessed.

65. Gk has Mark spending eight years at the Pempton Monastery and eight years in Alexandria.

66. The coptic text switches back and forth from 'Abba' to 'Apa'.

67. That is, he had died.

68. Gk has the disciple going to Scetis and monks from Scetis going up to Alexandria. The Enaton was the collection of monastic communities at the ninth milestone west of Alexandria.

69. The greek account has them in the Thebaid. 'Egypt' as elsewhere means outside Scetis, usually in Alexandria or towards Babylon (Cairo).

70. The coptic switches to first person plural here.

71. Gk is clearer: It was his custom to do this, and from evening until morning he would not allow a single crumb to remain in the house.

72. A folio is missing; the lacuna corresponds to lines 165–181 of the ethiopic text. I have supplied the missing text, set in a different font, from the greek translation.

73. See Chapter One, nn. 59 and 226.

74. A *kas* was 1/24 of a *solidus* and was a day's pay for a laborer, equaling a *keration*; cp. Chapter One, n. 228.

75. The Gk MSS have 'a holy man' or 'a person dressed in a holy manner'. For other accounts of 'a man of light', see Tim Vivian, *Paphnutius,* pp. 54, 158, 163.

76. Reading ⲭⲉ ⲋⲁⲛϯ ϥⲛⲁⲛⲟⲅⲉⲙ in order to correspond with Gk ἐγγύησαι περὶ τῆς ψυχῆς αὐτοῦ ὅτι σώζεται ἐν τοῖς πλείοσι (Dahlman, 152, ll. 83-84).

77. See Chapter One, n. 233.

78. Literally: dry. See Crum 602a, who cites this passage; Gk: he struck rock, heard a hollow-sounding thunk, so he struck again and found a small hole.

79. Gk: Israelites. Ishmaelites = Muslims, an anachronism perhaps introduced by the translator in the tenth century.

80. Gk: Justin. Justinian's uncle, Justin ruled 518–527 and was succeeded by Justinian I.

81. Translating ϥⲅⲥⲓ ⲉⲣⲟ (Ὄντως σύ) as 'please'. Gk: Surely you, mother, will give me three dried loaves of bread so I may eat; I haven't eaten today.

82. ϥⲅⲥⲓ ⲉⲣⲟ.

83. Part of a folio is missing here, corresponding to lines 242–265 of the ethiopic text. I have supplied the lacuna from the greek translation.

84. He would abandon his monastic profession for 'the world'.

85. Reading ⲁϥⲉⲣⲱⲛⲓ ⲅⲁⲣ ⲉⲣⲟⲓ ⲛⲭⲉ ⲡⲁⲅⲏⲧ, which corresponds with some Gk MSS, instead of the text's ⲁϥⲉⲣⲟⲩⲱⲓⲛⲓ ⲅⲁⲣ ⲉⲣⲟⲓ ⲛⲭⲉ ⲡⲁⲅⲏⲧ.

86. The coptic has an intriguing word play that the greek lacks. 'Up' and 'high' translate coptic *shōi*, and 'beyond your abilities' renders *sapshōi ntekjom*,

literally, 'higher than your strength or power'. Thus, in Coptic, Daniel's dreamt punishment, hanging high in the air, fittingly matches his 'crime' of committing himself to more than he could do.

87. In the Gk text it is Justin who dies and Justinian becomes emperor.

88. See Chapter One, n. 242.

89. Ps 113:7.

90. Taking ⲉⲡϫⲓⲛⲧⲉ as ⲉⲡϫⲓⲛ.

91. Hell.

92. Gk lacks this story, which Copt and Eth have. Gk lacks the rest of the *Life* but Eth has it.

93. Text: ⲉⲩϭⲟϩ ⲉⲃⲟⲗ ⲛϩⲏⲧⲥ; See Crum, 797a.

94. Monasteries were often attacked by outlaws who probably considered them easy pickings; see *Historia Monachorum* 10.3 for the example of Patermuthius, who attacks the hermitage of a female anchorite, and AP Macarius the Great 40 for the example of a thief pillaging Macarius' cell.

95. Coptic: *ballin*. Karel C. Innemée, *Ecclesiastical Dress in the Medieval Near East* (Leiden: Brill, 1992), notes, 24, that the *ballin* was 'an Episcopal insignium', 'a silk band of 4-5 meters long that is draped around the head', and 55, that *ballin* and *pallin* 'are used for both omophrion and ballin'. Eth: Bring me a monk's garments and a black cloak that is fully covered with crosses, in the image of the one worn by Abba Daniel.

96. Villagers in the Middle East and Greece still sleep on the roofs in summer because it is cooler there.

97. When Abba Daniel visits the monastery of Apa Jeremiah near Hermopolis in I.4 (Chapter One), the sisters perform the same rituals.

98. Ps 2:11; Phil 2:12. The bohairic coptic NT, following the Gk, has 'fear and trembling' at Phil 2:12.

99. Text: ⲁϥⲉⲣⲁⲡⲟⲗⲁⲍⲉⲥⲑⲉ, which is not attested; the simplest suggestion seems to be that ⲁϥⲉⲣⲁⲡⲟⲗⲁⲍⲉⲥⲑⲉ comes from Gk ἀποτάσσεσθαι.

100. For another account of monastic opposition to the Tome of Leo in Egypt, see Vivian, 'Humility and Resistance', 2–30, esp. 24–29; rpt. in Vivian, *Words to Live By*, 267–273.

101. Justinian is not thus vilified above in the story about Eulogius, showing that the account of Daniel and the Tome of Leo is a later addition or at least has a different provenance.

102. In the *Life of Samuel of Kalamun*, 'holy Apa Samuel', like Daniel, 'leaped up' in defiance against the Tome; see *Samuel of Kalamun*, ed. Alcock, 6 (Coptic) and 80 (English).

103. These anathemas, which may have been formulaic, are very similar to those uttered by Samuel of Kalamun; see the *Life of Samuel of Kalamun*, ed. Alcock, 7 (Coptic) and 81 (English): '*Anathema* to this *Tome. Anathema* to the *Council of*

Chalcedon. *Anathema* to the *impious* Leo. *Anathema* to everyone who *believes according* to it' (the italics are Alcock's). See also Johnson, ed. and trans., *A Panegyric on Macarius* IX.5–6.

104. See Chapter One, n. 58.

105. Wolfgang Kosack designates Tambōk's 'certain position' north north-east of Babylon (Cairo), in the eastern Delta, close to 31° longitude and 31°30' latitude; see Kosack, *Historisches Kartenwerk Ägyptens* (Bonn: Rudolf Habelt, 1971), 'Karte des koptischen Ägypten, Blatt 1, Delta', 5C. On p. 33 he cites MS Vat. Copt. 68.

106. *Homologia* means confession or profession of faith, that is, the true—non-chalcedonian—faith.

107. April 26 (Julian), May 9 (Gregorian).

108. Text: † ⲭⲉⲣⲁ, which may be taken as † ⲭⲉⲣⲉ, that is, 'give greeting' (χαῖρε), but may also mean 'offer one's hand' (χεῖρα), that is, the disciple extended his hand, waiting for the elder to extend *his* hand so the disciple could kiss it in the traditional monastic way of greeting. The superior, however, normally extends his hand first, so the person of lower rank may take it in his hand and kiss it.

109. From the second half of this sentence to the end (that is, up to the Doxology), this section has parallels with the homily *On Cana of Galilee* by Patriarch Benjamin I; see Müller, 32r–33r.

110. Si 12:7.

111. Coptic art, as at the Syrian Monastery in the Wadi al-Natrun and at the Monastery of Saint Antony by the Red Sea, commonly represents Abraham, Isaac, and Jacob holding in their laps the saved in paradise.

112. The story of Moses speaking with God five-hundred seventy times was apparently common in the coptic tradition. It is found in the coptic Synaxary entry for Moses the prophet (Toute 8) and also occurs in a ninth-century acrostic hymn for Saint Shenoute; for the latter see K. H. Kuhn and W. J. Tait, *Thirteen Coptic Acrostic Hymns* (Oxford: Oxford University Press, 1996) 137.

113. 1 Cor 3:2, 1 Pet 2:2.

114. There is a lacuna in the text; these lines are supplied by conjecture from *On Cana of Galilee* by Patriarch Benjamin I, ed. Müller, 32r-32v.

115. Another lacuna; the lines are again supplied from *On Cana of Galilee*, 32v.

116. The text does not say who the first prophet is.

117. Cp. Chapter One, I.8 (p. 76): just before her death, the 'eunuch' Anastasia does the same.

118. Lk 23:46. Anastasia (see n. 117) says the same.

119. May 3 (Julian), May 16 (Gregorian), the feast day of Abba Daniel on the Coptic Orthodox Church calendar.

120. Text: he.

121. Text: him.

122. 'Deacon' in both instances translates the abbreviation ⲡⲓⲁⲓ.

123. Text: ⲓⲥⲁⲁ. It is possible, however, that Isaa represents the arabic form of 'Esau', ('Isa), written in a corrupted coptic form. Since the manuscript was copied in the tenth century, this remains a possibility.

124. Text: ⲟ̄ⲟ̄. Some coptic texts end with ⲫⲟ̄, 99, which represents the sum of the numerical values of the letters in 'Amen' (1 + 40 + 8 + 50). Here it appears that the scribe has attempted to write ⲫⲟ̄, but either did not know how to count in Coptic or was perhaps thinking in Arabic and writing in Coptic.

125. Text: ⲥⲉⲩ2ⲣⲡⲓⲥ, which may indicate Serapis.

126. See Chapter Three, Appendix IV.

127. I. Forget, *Corpus scriptorum christianorum orientalium* 47–49 [Arabic 3–5] (Paris, 1905) 292–93 (text); CSCO 78 [Arabic 12] (Rome, 1921) 112–114 (trans.).

128. Markiyya.

129. Satan, the Devil.

130. Anba = Abba or Apa, 'Father'.

131. It is uncertain what 'Dimas' refers to. The greek text (Chapter One, I.1) has 'His name was 'Mark of the Horse'.

132. Plural in the text.

133. The Arabic *sīrah* is very similar to *vita* and can have a number of different nuances: 'way of life', 'life/biography', 'reputation', 'mention (of a certain individual)'.

134. Or: the diseased.

135. Lit.: makes them rulers of.

136. 1 Cor 2:9.

137. Forget, *Corpus scriptorum christianorum orientalium* 67 [Arabic 11] (Paris, 1912), 165–166 (text); CSCO 90 [Arabic 13] (Louvain, 1926), 250 (trans.).

138. Wolfgang Kosack, *Historisches Kartenwerk Ägyptens* (Bonn: Rudolf Habelt, 1971), 49, does not list a city or town with this name but does list el-Burlus and el-Burlus el-Ramla, both in the north-central Delta. From the greco-coptic names for el-Burlus—Parallou, Parhalos—it seems likely that el-Borollos can be identified with el-Burlus. See Randall Stewart, 'Burullus, al-', CE 2.427A: 'Town in Egypt located somewhere between present-day Baltim and al-Burj on the eastern shore of Lake Burullus in the northern Delta.'

139. Forget, *Corpus scriptorum christianorum orientalium* 47–49 [Arabic 3–5] (Paris, 1905) 236–237 (text); CSCO 78 [Arabic 12] (Rome, 1921), 414–415 (trans.).

140. Gk accounts: Justinian. The coptic-arabic account gives a positive role to Empress Theodora, who in the greek accounts wants to exile Anastasia.

141. Forget, *Corpus scriptorum christianorum orientalium* 67 [Arabic 11] (Paris, 1912), 109–110 (text); CSCO 90 [Arabic 13] (Louvain, 1926), 108–109 (trans.).

142. Forget, CSCO 67 [Arabic 11] (Paris, 1912), 200–201 (text); CSCO 90 [Arabic 13] (Louvain, 1926), 197 (trans.).

143. Kosack, 24, lists a Tuna and a Tuna el-Gabal and, 23, a Tanta in the central Delta. The ethiopic version (Chapter Three, Appendix, #4) locates Tunah (or Tuna) in 'the region of Qida in Upper Egypt'.

Chapter 3: The Ethiopic Life

1. Most of the notes are by Michael Kleiner; a few are by the editor. Unless otherwise indicated, cross-referenced notes refer to notes in this chapter.

2. Gi'iz ('Ethiopic' or 'Classical Ethiopic'), the indigenous name for the language of the Aksumite state (1st–7th/8th c. CE), later became the virtually exclusive language of ethiopian literature (including the Synaxary) up to the nineteenth century, long after its demise as a spoken language. Gi'iz, and more particularly its vowels, have been, and still are, transcribed in various ways. Until recently what we might call the Orientalist tradition was dominant in ethiopian philology and preferred *shwa* (ə), a symbol which stems from Hebraistics, in transcribing the vowels (which technically could be described as short, central, and lax). The resulting transcription was *Gə'əz*, which is quite acceptable and probably in scholarly publications still the most frequently used latin rendering. For a number of reasons, *Gə'əz* then sometimes became *Ge'ez*, which, however, is phonetically and systemically unsatisfactory and should be avoided. *Gi'iz*, the transcription used here, has two main advantages over more traditional and more Orientalist *Gə'əz*. First, it contains no 'strange' *shwa* symbol and so does not erect an unnecessary barrier to accessibility. Second and more importantly, the normal english *i* (as in *bit*) is a phonetically more adequate transcription for the underlying Gi'iz vowel than *shwa*, as this Gi'iz vowel is, in linguistic terminology, articulated 'higher' than what 'central' *shwa* normally denotes. This is also the reason why ethiopian scholars as well as educated laypersons today mostly use *i* when transcribing the name of their classical literary language.

3. A manuscript at Saint John's University in Collegeville, Minnesota (EMML 1-7636: 2796, ff.80a–81b and 88a–94a [fourteenth century]), gives a homily about Abba Daniel of the Monastery of Scete for the seventh of Takhsas (Taḫśaś): 'In the name of the Father and of the Son and of the Holy Spirit. Acts of the holy Abba Daniel of the Desert of Scetis, at the Monastery of Saint Macarios, which Priest Mecari wrote' (fol 80a). We wish to thank Getatchew Haile for this information.

4. For these stories, see Chapter One; the numbering of the pieces is that of Chapter One.

5. The ethiopic version we have was undoubtedly translated from Arabic. For the arabic Daniel dossier, see Chapter Eight.

6. The present coptic pope, Shenouda III, for example, lives part of the year in the papal compound at the Monastery of Saint Bishoy in the Wādī an-Naṭrūn (Scetis).

7. Guidi, 435–38 [419–22].

8. Guidi, 209–212 [193–196].

9. Colin, PO 44.3: 318–21 [86–89].

10. Colin, PO 47.3: 226–29 [34–37]. See Appendix III for a translation.

11. In the introduction to his edition of the ethiopic Synaxary (PO 15.5), Sylvain Grébaut distinguishes three groups of manuscripts which do not all share the same Synaxary entries. The group that he believes contains original entries he designates 'Recension primitive', while he calls a secondary group 'Revision ou Vulgate'. A third group with a few local saints he terms 'Propre'.

12. *Däbr* originally means 'mountain' or 'mount' (arabic *jabal*). The 'ä' at the end is 'of' (*däbr-ä* = 'mountain of'). Its secondary meaning, which has now become dominant, is 'monastery' and 'desert'. So *Däbrä Sihat* is 'the monastic settlement of Scetis'.

13. Grébaut, PO 15.5: 633–38 [91–96].

14. A similar confusion appears in BN MS fonds éthiopien 126 (eighteenth century), excerpts from the Ethiopic Synaxary. There, 'Abba Daniel of the Monastery of Saint Macarius in Scetis' is associated with Anastasia (Gk I.8) and Andronicus and Athanasia (I.5). See Clugnet, ROC 6: 87, and Goldschmidt—Esteves Pereira, viii.

15. Translation of the Gi'iz (Classical Ethiopic) *Treatise on Abba Daniel of Scetis*, as published by Goldschmidt and Esteves Pereira, *Vida do Abba Daniel do Mosteiro de Sceté*, Lisbon, 1897). The Goldschmidt/Esteves Pereira edition was based on the MS orient. fol. 117 of the then Royal Library of Berlin (today the Staatsbibliothek zu Berlin—Preussischer Kulturbesitz). At the time this manuscript was the only known Gi'iz copy of this text, and to the best of my knowledge this is still true today. Together with the ethiopic version, Goldschmidt and Esteves Pereira submitted a portuguese translation of the text with some annotations. In 1901 Ignazio Guidi published a short article, 'Corrections de quelques passages du texte éthiopien', ROC 6: 54–56, with corrections of the Goldschmidt/Esteves Pereira edition. Guidi suggests thirty or so alternative readings for the Gi'iz text and corrections of printing errors.

16. Goldschmidt/Esteves Pereira translate the title as 'Homily of Abba Daniel of the Monastery of Scetis' (*Homilia do abba Daniel do mosteiro do Sceté*, 29). While the Gi'iz text (*Dirsan zä-Abba Dani'ēl . . .*) lexically and grammatically permits such a rendering, the context for two reasons precludes it: 1) The present text

is not a homily, but a treatise. Therefore polysemic *dirsan*, which comprises both meanings, must here be translated accordingly. 2) The text reports on Abba Daniel, but nowhere claims to have been composed (or, for that matter, preached) by him. Therefore the genitive particle *zä-* here must denote a *genitivus obiectivus* and not a *subiectivus*.

17. The ethiopic transformation of 'the Monastery of Scetis'. According to Goldschmidt/Esteves Pereira (30, note 1), Gi'iz *Sännayt* (*Šännayt* in scholarly transcription) is derived from Coptic *Šiēt* (Greek *Skētis*) via Arabic *Šihāt*. In the ethiopic translation, which was made from Arabic, the translator presumably read arabic *ī* as an *n* , a mistake easily committed since the basic shape of the arabic letters for *ī* and *n* is identical; the two are distinguished only by two small dots below the basic shape (for *ī*) versus one dot above it (for *n*). Moreover, in medieval arabic MSS such diacritical dots are occasionally omitted, the mother-tongue reader being expected from the context to interpret the letter correctly without them. For a non-Arab, however—such as an ethiopian translator—this task is obviously much more difficult. By replacing arabic *ī* with *n*, we arrive at an ethiopic form **Šänhat* (the *ä* functioning as a sort of default vowel in Gi'iz, having been filled in due to the change from vocalic *ī* to consonantic *n* and the ensuing need for a new vowel to complete the syllable), which then easily could have been further modified to **Sänhat*. (An asterisk before an ethiopic word indicates a philologically hypothesized form.) A very similar form, *Sinhat*, occurs once in the Goldschmidt/Esteves Pereira edition; cf. n. 83 below. The next transformational step would have been the substitution of the Gi'iz symbol for *ha* (in ethiopic script, this sequence of two sounds is represented by a single sign) by the one for *ya*, which looks rather similar, leading to **Sänyat* as the interim result. The transformation of *Šihāt* into *Šännayt* was then completed through metathesis of *y* and *a*. This last step at least may have been helped along by a latent desire to arrive precisely at *šännayt*, as in Gi'iz this also is the feminine form of the adjective 'beautiful'. Consequently, there may have been such a laudatory designation for a revered monastery.

18. Scholarly transcription: Taḫśaś; fourth month of the ethiopian calendar, extending from December 10–January 8. Takhsas 7 therefore corresponds to December 16.

19. Takhsas 7 / December 16.

20. Section titles follow those of the coptic version (Chapter Two) and are the editor's.

21. Goldschmidt/Esteves Pereira (29, note 2) suggest an allusion to Ps 92:6a.

22. References in brackets are to stories in the greek dossier, Chapter One. Numerals between backstrokes within the translation (e.g. /4/) refer to page numbers in the edition of Goldschmidt/Esteves Pereira.

23. In scholarly transcription: Bäsṭasiyos; the dot below the *t* indicates its ejective pronunciation. The name results from the ethiopic translator's misreading

of greek Anastasios, presumably in its arabic transcription, and mistaking its *n* for a *b*. Such a mistake can easily occur, as in Arabic the two letters are differentiated only by a diacritical dot above (for *n*) or below (for *b*) the same basic shape. Cf. also notes 17, 36, 61, and 99.

24. The Giʿiz text does not indicate unambiguously who comes to see whom every week. Is it the castrate who regularly visits Abba Daniel, or does the latter regularly venture out to the desert cave? Contextually the second option makes more sense, especially in view of how the narrative subsequently unfolds.

25. The Giʿiz text of Goldschmidt/Esteves Pereira in this passage appears to be slightly ungrammatical. They give *Wä-yi'ēzziz lotu Abba Dani'ēl räd'o kämä yisäd* (3f.), while one would expect *Wä-yi'ēzziz lotu Abba Dani'ēl lä-räd'u kämä yisäd . . . .* Guidi, 'Corrections', does not comment on this phrase.

26. That is, Abba Daniel.

27. Literally: heard (*sämĭ'o*).

28. In the Giʿiz original, the preceding exchange between the castrate and Abba Daniel contains a play with the multiple meanings of the verb *fäṣṣämä* which is not easily transposed into English. The basic meaning of *fäṣṣämä* is 'to complete, fulfill, consummate', like greek *teleō*. The castrate uses the word with this sense when he says that through Daniel's teachings many have attained fulfillment. In his reply, however, Daniel employs *fäṣṣämä* in the sense of 'to fulfill / complete *one's life*', hence 'to die'. The skillful and linguistically conscious use of *fäṣṣämä* continues into the next sentence, where it underlies 'to give fulfillment'.

29. Abba Daniel.

30. 2 Kgs 2:1-18.

31. The Giʿiz suffix equivalent of the sentence-closing pronoun 'you' is in the singular (*-kä*). This is inconsistent with the Giʿiz plurals otherwise found in this phrase, be it in the introduction to the direct speech (*yibēlomu* = he said to *them*) or in the verbs of the direct speech themselves, which are marked as 2nd ps. masc. pl. (*ī-tiklĭ'u, fänniwu*). However, since English 'you' is number-neutral, the inconsistency of the Giʿiz text is automatically leveled in the translation.

32. Ps 31:5, Lk 23:46.

33. Scholarly transcription: Ṭirr, with an ejective *t*. Ejectives are a class of consonants—more precisely stops—peculiar to the Ethio-Semitic languages. In transcription ejectives are indicated either by an added dot under the simple consonant (e.g. *ṭ*; this is the system here employed) or by an apostrophe following it (e.g. *t'*). An exception is often the ejective variant of /k/, which frequently, here included, is transcribed as *q* (instead of *ḳ* or *k'*). Ṭirr is the fifth month of the Ethiopian calendar, extending from January 9-February 7. Ṭirr 26 therefore corresponds to February 3.

34. Goldschmidt/Esteves Pereira here have the imperative *a'imir* = 'Know!' or 'Understand!' (5, line 66/67). In the context, however, it makes much more sense to read instead the first person singular *a'ammir* =' I know'. The difference between the two verb forms is minimal in the ethiopic script, especially since the doubling of the *m* would not be expressed in it. Even Goldschmidt/Esteves Pereira, contrary to their own Giʿiz text, in their portuguese translation here have *sei* = 'I know' (33).

35. Literally 'Everything that there is about her' (*kʷillo zä-konä iminnēha*).

36. Scholarly transcription: Bäsṭiyanos, with an ejective *ṭ*. The reference probably is to the byzantine emperor Justinian(os), who ruled 527–565. Word-initial *b* of the Giʿiz name form can convincingly be explained as a misreading of word-initial *y* in the name's arabic transcription. In arabic script, *b* and *y* have the same basic shape and are differentiated only by the number of diacritical dots below: one for *b*, two for *y*. Cf. also nn. 17 and 23 above as well as nn. 61 and 99 below.

37. Särgīs in proper Giʿiz transcription; ultimately a transformation of greek Sergios (latin Sergius).

38. Goldschmidt/Esteves Pereira have 'brother' in the nominative case (*iḫʷ*; 6, line 99), while its syntactical position clearly requires it to be in the accusative (*iḫʷä*). Guidi, 'Corrections', already pointed this out.

39. A derivation from / corruption of Greek Markos (Mark).

40. Goldschmidt/Esteves Pereira have the plural, 'patriarchs' (*līqanä pappasat*; 7, line 108), which could alternatively also be translated as 'archbishops'—as indeed Goldschmidt/Esteves Pereira do (*arcebispos*, p. 36). In view of the context, however, a reading in the singular (*līqä pappasat*) and the corresponding translation clearly appear preferable. Cp. Guidi, 'Corrections', 54.

41. The term *giʿz*, which here rather freely (but context-sensitively) is rendered as 'story', has a broad range of meanings. At its semantic core lie such concepts as 'nature, character, essence; temperament, conduct, manner, mode of life'. Goldschmidt/Esteves Pereira, 36, translate *giʿz* as *vida passada,* 'past life'. See also the next note.

42. 'Story' here renders Giʿiz *nägär*, which quite literally means 'speech, discourse, story'. The fact that *nägär* here is used more or less synonymously with *giʿz* vindicates the latter's translation as 'story' a few words earlier (cp. the previous note).

43. In Goldschmidt/Esteves Pereira, Giʿiz *ḥimam*, 'illness', appears in the nominative (7, line 125f.), whereas the context clearly requires it to be a genitive (as already pointed out by Guidi, 'Corrections', 54). In the Giʿiz, a reading in the genitive would entail an emendation of *ḥimam* to *ḥimamä*. The above translation (unlike that of Goldschmidt/Esteves Pereira, cp. their 36) presupposes such an emendation.

44. Goldschmidt/Esteves Pereira, 39, n. 1, tentatively identify the 'City of Egypt' as the upper egyptian town of Kift (known in Greek as Koptos, in Arabic as Qifṭ), presumably on the basis of the phonetic similarity between this name and Giʿiz *hagärä Gibṣ* (= the City of Egypt, *Gibṣ* meaning 'Egypt' in Giʿiz). This identification, however, remains doubtful on linguistic as well as historic grounds. Linguistically, the sound changes necessary to arrive from coptic Kift via arabic Qifṭ at Giʿiz *Gibṣ* are many and do not, on aggregate, appear plausible. Moreover, since Giʿiz *Gibṣ* also simply means 'Egypt' (regardless of whether or not it can refer to Kift as well), it appears historically as well as linguistically compelling to see it as a reflex of greek 'Aigyptos'. This greek name for the country was itself derived from Het-Ka-Ptakh (House of the Soul of [the God] Ptakh), the indigenous egyptian name for its ancient capital Memphis, located on the left bank of the Nile some miles southwest of present-day Cairo. Against this backdrop, it appears more convincing to identify Abba Daniel's 'City of Egypt' with Memphis rather than Kift. Greek: across from the Thebaid.

45. Or: town; Giʿiz *hagär* comprises both meanings.

46. Or 'saluted, greeted', or even 'kissed'; Giʿiz *ammiḥa* comprises all these meanings. Note, however, that the text uses a different (and semantically unambiguous) verb, *sä'amä* when, a few words earlier, it speaks of the old man kissing Abba Daniel's feet.

47. Goldschmidt/Esteves Pereira have: they held a lamp in their hands (*wäwista idäwïhomu maḫtot*; 9, line 158f.), but the plurals clearly do not fit into the context and hence need emendation. See also Guidi, 'Corrections', 54.

48. As the counting of the hours began at six o'clock in the morning, the eleventh hour refers to 5:00 p.m.

49. Scholarly transcription: Awlogïyos; derived from greek 'Eulogios'.

50. Goldschmidt/Esteves Pereira here have a misprint: instead of *ya'attiwänï* ('he took me') they give *ya'attäwänï* (10, line 187)—a non-existent and indeed even impossible verb form. See Guidi, 'Corrections', 54.

51. Guidi, 'Corrections', 54, convincingly argues that the Giʿiz consecutive or final conjunction *kämä*, here rendered as 'so that', is itself probably the result of a contextually inappropriate translation of arabic *ḥattā*. This *ḥattā* is also a temporal conjunction (or preposition) with the meaning of 'until'. From the context it appears clear that in the arabic *Vorlage* of the Giʿiz version presumed *ḥattā* was employed in this latter sense. The appropriate Giʿiz translation hence would have been *iskä* (= until) instead of *kämä*.

52. Literally: into Awlogiyos's gown (*wistä libsu lä-Awlogïyos*).

53. Nomadic Arabs, who by the sixth century had already been roaming the desert areas of Egypt and the Sinai for many centuries.

54. In Greek: Anastasios. Emperor Anastasios I ruled Byzantium 491-518. (The scholarly transcription of the ethiopic name form would be Basṭasiyos, with an ejective *ṭ*.) See also notes 23, 36, 61, and 99.

55. With this translation I follow Guidi's conjecture ('Corrections', 55) regarding a likely corruption of the Gi'iz text in Goldschmidt/Esteves Pereira. As the last words of the sentence under discussion they have (p.11, line 236f.): *gibär mäfqidäkä, wi'itu däbrikä* = 'do what you need to do; that is your monastery!' This makes little sense. Guidi proposed reading *wä-'itu* instead of *wi'itu*, which would be translated as 'and then return to' instead of 'that is'. This makes much better sense, and the orthographic change required to produce this text is minimal—even more so in ethiopic script than in latin. Reading *wä-'itu*, however, necessitates a second emendation: the nominative *däbrikä* ('your monastery') would have to be changed to the accusative of direction *däbräkä* ('*to* your monastery').

Goldschmidt/Esteves Pereira render this passage as *De dia trabalha; o teu monte é a tua necessidade.* ('Work by day; your mountain [monastery] is what is necessary for you'; 43). This translation solves the problem inherent in this phrase by reading it with a different syntactic division, namely as: *gibär* (work), *mäfqidäkä wi'itu däbrikä* (what is necessary for you is your monastery). Ingenious as this may seem, it would require that *mäfqid* ('necessity; intention, desire'—here supplemented with the possessive suffix second person singular masculine-*kä*), as the phrase's subject, be in the nominative case = **mäfqidikä*. The text, however, clearly has it in the accusative, as *mäfqidäkä*.

56. Literally: does them good (*yašännī lomu*).

57. Or 'sat'; *näbärä* means both.

58. Goldschmidt/Esteves Pereira have *näfs* ('soul'; 13, line 273) instead of the orthographically very similar *näfas* (wind). See Guidi, 'Corrections', 55.

59. Or 'hang me up, suspend me'; Gi'iz *säqälä* comprises all these meanings. However, as the scene takes place in Jerusalem and as the infant clad in light is reminiscent of the Christ child, 'to crucify' here (and in the following phrase) appears to be the preferable translation.

60. Goldschmidt/Esteves Pereira have *tänäz(z)äzku* for 'I felt comforted' (13, line 279). Such a verb form would have to go back to a verbal stem **tänäz(z) äzä* = 'to be / feel comforted'. According to Leslau, *Comparative Dictionary of Ge'ez* (Wiesbaden 1987), 412, however, such a verbal stem does not exist. The verb form under question therefore needs to be emended to *tänazäzku* (from the stem *tänazäzä*), which exists and provides the desired meaning.

61. Scholarly transcription: Bisṭīyanos, presumably for the greek 'Justinianos'. This Bistiyanos is no longer the same emperor Bastasiyos / Anastasios (491–518) under whom Eulogius first came to Constantinople. Gi'iz Bistiyanos rather suggests that the reference here is to Anastasios' second successor Justinian I (527–565). Yet it appears possible, even likely, that the hagiographer, on account of the similarity of their names, confused Justinian with his predecessor—and Anastasios's immediate successor—Justin I (518-527). See also the next footnote, as well as nn. 23, 36, 54, and 99.

62. If the conjecture of the last footnote is correct and Bistiyanos is Justin I (518–27), his successor, who here remains unnamed, would be Justinian I (527–565). This would place the events subsequently narrated at around 527—a much more plausible time frame than 567, at which date we would arrive if we identified the Bistiyanos of our text with Justinian instead of Justin.

63. Three of the former emperor's (= Justin's) high officials.

64. In the greek text there are four conspirators: Hypatius, Dexikratius, Pompeius, and Eulogius.

65. 'Unfairness' renders Gi'iz *adliwo*, literally: 'making weigh' (one side of a balance at the expense of the other). Goldschmidt/Esteves Pereira inadequately render *adliwo* as 'adulation' (*adulação*, p.45).

66. Ps 113:7; Ps 75:7.

67. Goldschmidt/Esteves Pereira have 'they said to me' (*yibēlunī*: 15, line 325). In the context this makes no sense; it needs to be emended to 'he said to me' (*yibēlänī*), as already Guidi indicated, 'Corrections', 55.

68. Goldschmidt/Esteves Pereira translate as if the last phrase were still sub-ordinate to the main verb 'to pray': 'and that I may not do evil again' (*e eu não torne a fazer o mal*; 46). The Gi'iz verb *dägämä* ('to repeat something, to do something again'), which here is crucial, belongs however, to the verbal stem I, 1. Therefore its conjugated form *idäggim* which we here encounter cannot be interpreted as a subjunctive (as would be the case if *dägämä* belonged to stem I, 2), but only as an indicative. This in turn implies that *idäggim* is not subordinate to 'to pray', but the main verb of a new and independent clause.

69. The words in brackets have no Gi'iz equivalent in Goldschmidt/Esteves Pereira, where it therefore appears as if Abba Daniel is still addressing the following sentences, like the preceding one, to Awlogiyos/Eulogius. From the content, however, it is clear that what he says can be directed only at his curious disciple to whom he relates Eulogius's story. Guidi, 'Corrections', 55, noted this deficiency in the Gi'iz text of Goldschmidt/Esteves Pereira, and indicated that in the coptic version of Abba Daniel's life it is indeed the disciple to whom the following admonitions are addressed. Hence either the ethiopian translator here misunder-stood his arabic *Vorlage*, or already it had corrupted the coptic version.

70. Goldschmidt/Esteves Pereira have (15, line 330) '. . . until you have died' (*iskä yiḥēwwäṣäkä* [*sic*], literally: 'until he [God] comes to visit you'). The second person singular in the object pronoun (or, in the Gi'iz, the object suffix), how-ever, is obviously out of place in this context and needs to be replaced by the first person. Moreover, the Gi'iz verb-stem orthography is faulty in Goldschmidt/Esteves Pereira: from a nonsensical *yiḥēwwäṣ* it needs to be altered to *yiḥēwwiṣ*. The correct Gi'iz verb form, complete with object suffix, would therefore be *yiḥēwwiṣänī* ('he comes to visit me'). Guidi, 'Corrections', 55, very briefly indi-cated these problems.

71. She is unnamed here but below is called Dontiris; in the greek text her name is Thomaïs.

72. Literally: 'and he had a son' (*wä-botu wiludä*). As to the translation of this phrase, Goldschmidt/Esteves Pereira interpret *wilud* (word-final *-ä* is only a case ending) as the plural of *wäld* (son, child) and therefore render: '. . . and he had sons' (. . . *e tinha filhos*: 46). While formally possible, the following sentences make it clear that a plural understanding of *wilud* is not appropriate in the present context. Here, *wilud* rather has to be seen as the lexicalized masculine passive participle to the verb *wälädä* ('to give birth; to beget'), with the fixed meaning of 'male child, begotten son' (Leslau, *Comparative Dictionary of Ge'ez*, 159).

73. From the Gi'iz text it is not entirely clear whether it was the father or the son who worked in the vineyard. The natural assumption would seem to be that it was the young man (and so indeed translate Goldschmidt/Esteves Pereira: *e o filho trabalhava na vinha*, 46). However, a little further on the text relates that the father, as part of a wicked stratagem, one night called on the son to guard 'his' (whose?) vineyard. As this seems to have been something out of the ordinary, it could suggest that, if anybody, it was the father who normally guarded the vineyard, and that it hence also was his property and place of labor.

74. This story and the preceding (Gk I.6) were originally one story.

75. In the ethiopian tradition, the name of the virtuous and steadfast young woman killed by her father-in-law (scholarly transcription of her Gi'iz name form: Donṭiris, with ejective *ṭ*.). In Greek, Thomaïs. Beyond the general context, this identification finds corroboration in the fact that in the Gi'iz text the adjective 'holy' next to Dontiris stands in the feminine (*qiddist*). On a different note, Goldschmidt/Esteves Pereira point out (47, note 2) that the ethiopian Synaxary on 7 Takhsas (December 16) commemorates, among others, a female saint Diyontiros / Donṭiris (from Greek Diontyras?), though without relating her story. The Synaxary of the copts (compiled in arabic) on the other hand, which served as the basis for the ethiopian one, does not mention this female saint. Note that the 7th of Takhsas also is the day of the commemoration of Abba Daniel.

76. Literally: 'a child' (*ḥiṣan*). Since it is clear from the context that the reference must be to the virtuous young woman killed by her father-in-law, the less gender-neutral translation as 'girl' seems more appropriate. Morever, already in the paragraph relating her burial, the young woman had been termed *ḥiṣan*, which on that occasion too was rendered 'girl'. Perhaps *ḥiṣan* (instead of *bi'isīt*, 'woman') is used in these contexts to highlight Dontiris's child-like innocence and chastity.

77. Goldschmidt/Esteves Pereira (48, n. 2) identify upper egyptian Armon with modern-day Armant, about ten miles south of Luxor. Known in antiquity as Hermonthis (to the Greeks) or Ermont (to the Copts), it was a provincial capital during the early christian centuries.

78. Literally: 'and said to him' (*wä-tibēlo*).

79. The nuns thus receive Abba Daniel in Christ-like fashion. The spreading of their garments on the ground is reminiscent of Jesus' entry into Jerusalem (cf. Mt 21:8; Mk 11:8; Lk 19:36), the washing of his feet evokes the episode recounted in Luke 7:37ff.

80. Literally: 'the widow / the old, unmarried woman' (*ibēr*).

81. The text here seems to imply (a) that despite all the agitation which followed the uncovering of the allegedly insane nun's secret, the whole monastery thereafter had gone back to sleep again, and (b) that the 'foolish' nun, despite the changed circumstances, was not approached by anybody, nor did she approach the community, but was left to spend the night on her own, as if nothing had happened. Both implications run counter to common sense; the text here appears to be lacking in narrative logic. See the greek version.

82. See 1 Cor 1:20.

83. 'Scetis' in the Gi'iz text here is written *Sinhat* (Goldschmidt/Esteves Pereira, 20). By contrast, in the title of our text the Gi'iz reflex of Scetis is *Šännayt*. *Sinhat*, however, closely resembles *Sänhat* which was reconstructed as an intermediary stage in the transformation of Coptic *Šiēt* into Gi'iz *Šännayt* (see nn. 17 and 134).

84. Literally: 'poured' (*soṭät*).

85. By way of hendiadys, 'confusion and embarrassment' here render the single Gi'iz term *ḥafrät* which comprises both (Leslau, *Comparative Dictionary of Ge'ez,* 259) Goldschmidt/Esteves Pereira [52] inadequately render *ḥafrät* as *affronta*, 'insult, affront').

86. Goldschmidt/Esteves Pereira have 'man' in the nominative case (= *bi'isī*; 21, line 506), while grammatically it must be in the accusative (= *bi'isē*).

87. The phrase is surprising, as the preceding text suggests that Abba Daniel had clearly identified the sitting figure as human before.

88. In Goldschmidt/Esteves Pereira, 'his sin' appears in the nominative (= *ḥaṭī'atu*; 22, line 522), while it clearly must be in the accusative (= *ḥaṭī'ato*).

89. Literally: baskets (*asfarīdatä*). As the narrative further on consistently speaks of only one basket, however, it makes sense to regard this initial plural as a corruption and to replace it with the singular. This appears all the more appropriate in view of the parallelism with the one jug.

90. In Goldschmidt/Esteves Pereira the verb form 'you (who) listen' is misspelled *tisämmä'omu* (22, line 530). This needs to be corrected to *tisämmi'omu*.

91. Goldschmidt/Esteves Pereira have: '. . . so that you save us' (*kämä tadḥinnä*, contracted from **tadḥinä-nä*), which in the context makes no sense. A reading of the Gi'iz verb with the object suffix of the first person singular *-nī* (= *kämä tadḥin-nī*, from underlying **tadḥinä-nī*) instead of first person plural *-nä* not only leads to a much better meaning, but is also plausible as the original version of

the text, as the difference in orthography between the two forms is as minimal in ethiopic script as in the latin transcription. The parallelism with the first person singular 'look after *me*' (emphasis added) a little further on in the text also militates for an original first person singular suffix in the form here under discussion.

92. The winter of the egyptian desert of course must not be equated with the winter of more northerly parts. In an ethiopian (con)text a further complication arises from the differences in climate and seasons between Highland Ethiopia and Egypt. Highland Ethiopia has no real equivalent of winter. Instead it has a rainy season, known as *kirämt,* lasting from July till September. This term is commonly— and also in this instance—translated into european languages as 'winter'. The average ethiopian reader of (or listener to) this passage, on the other hand, will probably spontaneously have imagined that Egypt likewise enjoyed a rainy season or *kirämt.*

93. In Goldschmidt/Esteves Pereira (23, line 550) the verb appears in the singular (*ī-nätgä*), but a reference to both the basket and the jug makes much better sense here than to the jug only. Therefore I suggest that the Giʿiz text here should be emended to have the plural verb form *ī-nätgu* (which might very well be a restitution of the original Giʿiz text), and translate accordingly.

94. Mt 5:40.

95. The phrase is puzzling: Who exactly gave the new tunic to whom? Contextually, one would expect that Abba Daniel here receives a new tunic from the abbot and then sets out into the desert to deliver it to the female hermit; this is also what the continuation of the text suggests. Yet third person 'him' (*lotu*) seems to exclude a reference to Abba Daniel, who otherwise relates the story in the first person (cp. the preceding 'I went', 'I told the story'). Should we therefore understand that it was the abbot who took the new tunic out into the desert to the female hermit (about whose sex, one would then have to assume, he had not previously been informed by Abba Daniel, as the text says that he brought it to 'him')? While grammatically the most natural understanding of these few words, this interpretation makes little sense contextually. A way out of the dilemma would be to assume textual corruption, a change from an original first person phrase (*He brought *me* what I had wanted / *amṣiʾa līta zä-fäqädku) to one in the third person (*amṣiʾa lotu zä-fäqädä*).

96. Goldschmidt/Esteves Pereira (54, note 1) tentatively identify Ṭanewos with Greek *Thennēsos,* Coptic *Thennesi,* Arabic *Tinnīs,* a city on an island of Lake Manzala (between Damietta and Port Said, northeastern Delta coast).

97. 'She had died' appears as *aʿräft* in Goldschmidt/Esteves Pereira (23, line 566). This Giʿiz spelling is faulty and needs to be corrected to *aʿräfät.*

98. This verb form appears as *yimoʾo* in Goldschmidt/Esteves Pereira (24, line 573), while *yimaʾo* would be correct.

99. Or: became emperor; *nägśä* comprises both meanings. Basṭīyanos likely refers to the byzantine emperor Justinian(os) (527–565), who is often given the

epithet of 'the Great'. See also nn. 36, and 61. Not only linguistically but also historically, the identification of 'Bastiyanos' with Justinian makes sense, as this emperor was very much engaged in religious politics, actively trying to bridge the ever-widening gap between the Greek and the Oriental Churches. In order to achieve this goal, he did not, contrary to the impression conveyed by our text, rely exclusively on authoritarian and repressive measures, but also launched a number of theological initiatives aimed at bringing about a compromise. Ultimately, however, he failed; the atmosphere palpable in the present episode of our text may help to understand why.

100. The Council of Chalcedon (near Constantinople) took place in 451. It defined the christological dogma of the Church, maintaining the so-called 'dyophysite' doctrine that there are two natures in Christ: a truly human and a truly divine one. This ran counter to the prevailing theological thinking (and feeling) in Egypt and much of the rest of the Orient, where traditionally the divine aspect of Christ had been highlighted, and which more generally was little prepared to come to terms with the greek theological vocabulary and concepts that to a large extent shaped the theology of the times. Over time and partly as a consequence of Chalcedon, many of the Oriental Churches broke away from Byzantium theologically—and soon afterwards, under arab domination, also politically—and adhered to the so-called 'monophysite' doctrine which maintains that there is only one divine-human nature in Christ.

101. In the south of Scetis.

102. Or 'is'; *näbärä* comprises both meanings.

103. Or 'profess' (*nä'ammin*).

104. Contrary to the allegations imputed to Abba Daniel, the Council of Chalcedon neither denied the sufferings of Christ nor strayed from the belief in the triune God. Daniel's invective, however, is a telling example of the passions often aroused by dogmatic conflicts in Late Antiquity, especially if they were coupled with political and cultural antagonisms.

105. Or 'flogged him'; *qäśäfa* comprises both meanings.

106. See Chapter Two, n. 111.

107. See Chapter Two, n. 112.

108. Or 'each of its own color' (*zä-zä zī'ahu ḥibromu*).

109. See Ps 31:5, Lk 23:46.

110. Corresponding to December 16 (cp. n. 18 above). In Goldschmidt/Esteves Pereira the month's name is misspelled as 'Täkhsas'.

111. On the day of his death, 7 Takhsas.

112. Scholarly transcription Ḥidar. Third month of the ethiopian calendar, extending from November 10 to December 9.

113. Translated from the text edited by Colin, PO 44.3 (no. 199): 318-321 [86–88]. Numerals marked with backstrokes within the translation refer to page numbers in Colin's text.

114. Honorius in the Giʿiz text appears as Anorēwos. The roman emperor Honorius (395–423) shared the reign with his brother Arcadius. While the latter ruled over the eastern half of the empire (which was to evolve into Byzantium), Honorius was the monarch of the west. In reality, however, he was largely powerless and depended on his germanic generals. Yet this lack of real power may have helped him eventually to acquire saintly status in Christianity. The noun translated here as emperor is *niguś*. While literally it means 'king' (emperor would be *niguśä nägäśt*, literally 'king of kings'), its rendition as emperor appears appropriate in all those contexts where—as here—the reference is to the roman or byzantine monarch.

115. Contender in spiritual struggles' renders *mästägadil*, formed from the root *g-d-l*. The religious language-lexemes derived from this root regularly are semantically very charged and complex, comprising, *inter alia*, the notions of spiritual struggle, a pious life, devotion, and asceticism. In translation, the semantic complexity of these lexemes often makes it necessary to resort to circumlocutions (see nn. 150, 156, 169, 178, 183, 188, 190, 191, and 262).

116. 'Abba Mäqaris' in the Giʿiz text. The monastery of Abba Macarius (Greek: Makarios) is named after the coptic saint Macarius the Great (300–390) who spent most of his life as an ascetic in Scetis (the Wādī an-Naṭrūn). Over time Macarius, who is reported to have been in close contact with Saint Antony, attracted a large number of followers who lived nearby. See n. 135 below. On Macarius, see Vivian, *Saint Macarius the Spiritbearer*.

117. 'Monasteries of Scetis' renders *gädamatä Asqēṭis*. While *gädam* (pl. *gädamat*) by way of metonymy can also indicate a monastery, its core meaning is 'wilderness, desert' (see, for example, the first sentence of this paragraph, where it underlies the english 'desert'). But since it appears a little contrived—though not impossible—meaningfully to speak of a plurality of deserts / wildernesses of Scetis, the translation of *gädamat* as 'monasteries' has been preferred in this context. Because 'desert, wilderness' is the semantic core of *gädam*, part of the ethiopian tradition also appears to have felt uneasy with the plural *gädamat* here: Colin's edition shows (note 34, p.[86]/318) that MS **E** here has the singular variant *gädam* (in the genitive form *gädamä*). In his translation, however ([87]/319), Colin uses 'the deserts [*les déserts*] of Scetis'.

118. Standing in prayer.

119. Honorius was emperor of the western half of the Roman Empire (see n. 114 above), so the ethiopian tradition is obviously wrong to locate him in Constantinople. However, this mistake is almost certainly not an ethiopian innovation, but can be presumed to have been already present in the arabic exemplar from which the Giʿiz version was translated. It may even go back to the coptic text and times. In any case, this misplacement of Honorius is an indication that for substantial parts of the christian Orient, Rome, from a certain time onwards, was synonymous with the Byzantine Empire, that memories of the

Western Empire had faded, and that therefore the conditions of the Byzantine era could in good faith be projected back in time.

120. Or 'ashes'; Giʻiz *ḥamäd* means both.

121. MS **E** here has the interesting variant 'to the city of Rome' ([86]/318, n. 37 of Colin's edition), which would contradict the previous identification of Rome with Constantinople in this text (n. 119 above).

122. Literally: 'When the servant saw Abba Daniel, he was blessed by him' (*täbaräkä*); Colin translates accordingly (*Quand le serviteur vit abba Dān'ēl, il en reçut une bénédiction*). But in the context this makes little sense. Should we assume that Abba Daniel, immediately after his arrival in a strange and bewildering place, went around randomly blessing passers-by? Obviously the context requires us to assume that the emperor's servant asked for the egyptian monk's blessing before he received it.

123. Or 'God will bless you'. In the Giʻiz verb stem employed here, the forms for the optative and the indicative are indistinguishable in ethiopic script.

124. There is no equivalent for the direct object pronoun 'him' in Colin's Giʻiz text. However, the context here clearly requires a complement for the transitive verb. Moreover, in ethiopic script the forms for 'he took' (*wäsädä*) and 'he took him' (*wäsädo*) look extremely similar and can easily be confused by scribes copying manuscripts. Therefore there is the very real possibility that originally the Giʻiz text had 'he took him' (*wäsädo*), which was only later leveled to 'he took' (*wäsädä*).

125. Awlogīs in the Giʻiz text (see nn. 49 and 167). See also the story of Eulogius the Stonecutter in Abba Daniel's long hagiography. In that narrative, however, Eulogius is not a pious monk despite the luxurious setting, but conversely an originally decent craftsman whose character has been corrupted by his sudden career at the imperial court. The story of the latter Eulogius also takes place two hundred years later (cp. the introduction).

126. Three p.m., or the ninth hour (as the Giʻiz text literally says), was the customary monastic mealtime.

127. The idea that bread presents a particular health hazard may seem somewhat bizarre to moderns, especially when the present text has Abba Daniel over many years subjecting himself to many other strenuous ascetic practices which, from a modern perspective, would appear to jeopardize one's physical well-being much more than the consumption of bread. Yet the following lines make it clear that Abba Daniel here is motivated not by any kind of spiritual reservations, but by straightforward concerns about his health.

128. That is, after the emperor has finished settling civil and/or criminal cases.

129. Thereby producing wickerwork such as baskets or mats.

130. Scholarly transcription: Īyasu (Ethiopic for Joshua). Four ethiopian emperors bore that name: Iyasu I, the Great (ruled 1682–1706), Iyasu II (1730–1755), Iyasu III (1784–1788), and Iyasu IV (1830–1832). As to which Iyasu is

intended here—which would indicate when the manuscripts used by Colin for his edition were written—see the next note. There is also a reference to an emperor Iyasu at the end of the Synaxary extract for Takhsas 7, again without specifying which one is meant. Presumably it will be the same as the Iyasu in this extract. See n. 157 below.

131. The name means 'Of/Belonging to the Holy Spirit'. One would normally think that a person referred to as the emperor's Beloved One would be his wife. However, I could not identify any wife of the four Iyasus who bore the name of Zä-Mänfas Qiddus. Or should the 'Beloved One' refer to someone other than the emperor's consort? This possibility cannot categorically be ruled out, and since the name of Zä-Mänfäs Qiddus is essentially gender-neutral, also men—friends, favorites, particularly loyal and trusted officials of the emperor—have to be considered as candidates. Against this background, it is worth mentioning that one of the highest officials of Iyasu I bore the name of Zä-Mänfäs Qiddus.

132. Translated from Grébaut, PO 15.5: 633-638 [91–96]. Numbers within backstrokes in the translation refer to pages of Grébaut's text.

133. Scholarly transcription: Taḫśas. See n. 18 above.

134. For 7 Takhsas as the day of Abba Daniel's death, see above, page 149. For the designation of his monastery as Sihat (scholarly transcription *Sīḥat*), as opposed to Sännayt in the Life, see nn. 17 and 83 above.

135. For Abba Macarius, see n. 116 above.

136. Scholarly transcription: Paṭrīqa. This refers to Gk I.1, the story of Anastasia, the patrician lady from Constantinople. The text above misinterprets Anastasia's status / title of patrician lady (*paṭrīqa*) as her proper name, and also wrongly ascribes royal status to her. See also the extract from the Synaxary for 8 Ginbot (May 16) below, which equally gives a very condensed—and again slightly different—account of Abba Daniel's involvement with Anastasia.

137. Anisṭiyos in the Giʿiz text.

138. In the Life, Anastasia does not have a husband. That she is ascribed a husband here could be due to a conflation with the figure of Athanasia (similar but different name) from the Synaxary for Hamle 28. In that narrative, however, it is not *only* Athanasia's husband who knows her true identity; rather nobody, *not even* her husband, is aware of who she really is.

139. See the story about Mark (in the Giʿiz text: *Märka*) in the Life above.

140. Or 'virtuous deeds'; *tirufat* has both meanings.

141. See the story about Eulogius (Giʿiz here: Awlogīs) in the Life above.

142. Or 'it', that is, Eulogius' newly gained wealth. The text here is ambiguous and can be interpreted both ways.

143. That is, to the emperor of Byzantium in Constantinople.

144. To Constantinople.

145. Presumably the soldiers now under Eulogios' command and guarding him. See the Synaxary for 8 Ginbot below: Daniel 'saw how Eulogius had

become an important military commander, riding on a horse and surrounded by many soldiers'. However, the possessive 'his' (Gi'iz: *-hu*) could also be interpreted as referring to the emperor.

146. Or 'crucify him'. See nn. 59, 170, 173, and 343.

147. Literally: him (*-hu*). The reference could therefore also be to Abba Daniel.

148. Or 'town / village'. See n. 45 above.

149. See the story of The Female Hermit in the Life above, pp. 145–147.

150. 'To live a life of spiritual struggle' renders Gi'iz *tägadälä* (the concrete verb form here is *titgaddäl*). For a brief discussion of the semantic complexity of the underlying Gi'iz root *g-d-l*, see n. 115; see also nn. 156, 169, 178, 183, 188, 190, 191, and 262.

151. See 'Abba Daniel Refuses to Accept the Tome of Leo' in the Life above. On the Tome and its theological and ecclesiastical implications, see nn. 100, 104, and 175.

152. See the story of The Woman Who Pretended to Be Mad in the Life above, pp. 141–143.

153. See the story of The Thief Who Repented in the Life above, pp. 143–144.

154. Here and at its next occurrence in this paragraph, 'nuns' is not, as was customary, expressed metaphorically through the term 'virgins' (*dänagil*), but instead through *mänäkosayiyat* (literally: 'she-monks'), a loanword derived, like english 'monk', from Gk *monachos*.

155. That is, with the water with which the others before had washed the feet of the thief posing as Abba Daniel.

156. Or 'a life of spiritual struggle'; *tägadilo* (in context: *näbärä Abba Dani'ēl bä-tägadilo*) is a semantically complex and charged religious term, comprising, *inter alia*, the ideas of spiritual struggle, a pious life, devotion, and asceticism. This semantic complexity—and at the same time vagueness—normally requires that this term (as well as other derivatives of the same root) be rendered through circumlocution rather than one single lexeme. See nn. 115, 150, 169, 178, 183, 188, 190, 191, and 262.

157. Ethiopic for Joshua. See also n. 130 above.

158. Gi'iz: *Sīhat*. See nn. 17, 83, and 134.

159. In Gi'iz, the object pronouns (or rather, more precisely, object suffixes) of the second persons singular and plural are differentiated according to gender: separate suffixes indicate whether the objects are masculine or feminine. Through the form of the object suffix for 'you', the ethiopian reader, unlike the english-speaking one, is already here made aware that the addressee of this second stanza is a female, namely the Virgin Mary, as is made explicit in the final verse.

160. That is, for the benefit of Daniel, not Eulogius, as would also seem possible from this poem's context. Compare, however, the episode of Abba

Daniel's reckless vouching for the integrity of Eulogius' character in the Life above, and particularly in the much more detailed account of the same story in Gk I.9 (Chapter One).

161. In Gi'iz, the poem has end rhymes. The rhyme pattern for stanza 1 (with some minor licenses taken by the poet) is a-a-a-b-a, the pattern for stanza 2 is c-c-d-c-d. Poems like this one, saluting the celebrated saint and recapitulating the central episode(s) of his or her spiritual contendings, are often found at the end of ethiopian hagiographic narratives. They constitute a poetic genre of their own, called *sälam* (Greetings of Peace) after the word with which they normally begin. See n. 192 below.

162. Translated from Colin, PO 47.3 (no. 211): 226–229 [34–37]. Numbers within backstrokes in the translation refer to pages of Colin's text.

163. Ginbot 8 / May 16. Ginbot is the ninth month of the ethiopian calendar, extending from May 9 to June 7.

164. Gi'iz: Anistasiya.

165. See the first episode in Abba Daniel's hagiography above (Gk I.8, Chapter One). The short account here gives no particular reason why Anastasia took up the monastic life, and at the same time conveys the impression that she was a native of Egypt. Abba Daniel's greek hagiography, by contrast, makes it clear that Anastasia fled to Egypt from Constantinople because she wanted to escape from the improper approaches of Emperor Justinian. See also the extremely condensed account of this same story at the beginning of the extract from the Synaxary for Takhsas 7. The Gi'iz term underlying 'patrician lady' here is *śiyimt*, literally 'an appointed woman': a lady holding high public office. From Abba Daniel's hagiography, however, it is clear that Anastasia did not herself hold high office—which at any rate would have been all but impossible for any woman in sixth-century Byzantium—but rather came from a family of notables and / or aristocrats. Moreover, in the hagiography Anastasia is explicitly described as a *bäṭrīqa* or patrician lady (which the 7 Takhsas extract misinterprets as her proper name). For these reasons, *śiyimt* in the present context has, somewhat freely, also been rendered as 'patrician lady'.

166. Or 'cave'. Underlying Gi'iz *bä'at* has both meanings.

167. Gi'iz here: *Awlägīs*. See nn. 49 and 125 above, as well as the Synaxary extract for Takhsas 7 (where the Gi'iz text has *Awlogīs*).

168. Cp. Mt 6:19-21, a very literal understanding of which explains why Eulogius' conduct could be considered as pious and exemplary.

169. For Gi'iz *gädl*; see nn. 115, 150, 156, 178, 183, 188, 190, 191, and 262.

170. Or 'crucified'. Gi'iz *säqälä* has both meanings. Gk: 'they hung me up with my arms tied behind my back'. See nn. 59, 146, 173, and 343.

171. Grammatically, the Virgin's entreaty could be on behalf of either Eulogius or Abba Daniel. Comparison with Abba Daniel's long hagiography as well as with the Synaxary episode for Takhsas 7, however, shows that Abba Daniel here is the object—or at least the primary object—of the Virgin's intercession.

172. Or 'city' or 'village'. See n. 45 above.

173. Or 'crucified' (see nn. 59, 146, 170 and 343).

174. 'Orthodox' here should be taken in its literal sense of 'true, right-worshipping', not as a reference to the Orthodox Church. This is made clear by the use of *riti't* for orthodox, as opposed to *ortodoksawīt*, which would indicate the Orthodox Church. Ultimately, of course, the Orthodox Church calls itself by this name because it is convinced of the truth (*rit'*) of its doctrine.

175. This is again, as in the Synaxary episode for Takhsas 7, a very condensed account of Abba Daniel's rejection of the so-called Tome of Leo, the written document (*mäṣḥaf*) in question. For a fuller version of the same story, see the Life above; for historical background, see nn. 100 and 104 above.

176. Translated from the text edited by Guidi, PO 7.3: 209–212 [193–196]. Numerals within backstrokes refer to the pagination of Guidi's text. This entry also occurs in the Coptic / Arabic Synaxary; see Chapter Two, Appendix 5.

177. On 1 Ḥamlē (as is the scholarly transcription). Ḥamlē is the eleventh month of the ethiopian calendar, extending from July 8 to August 6.

178. 'Spiritual contenders' renders *mästägadilan,* the plural of *mästägadil*; see n. 115 above for further comment on this term, as well as nn. 150, 156, 183, 188, 190, 191, and 262.

179. In the Gi'iz text Benjamin appears as *Binyamīn*.

180. Or 'town'. See nn. 45 and 172 above.

181. In the coptic version (Chapter Two, Appendix, #5), the brothers come from Tunah in the diocese of Tanda. Wolfgang Kosack, *Historisches Kartenwerk Ägyptens* (Bonn: Rudolf Habelt, 1971) 24, lists a Tuna and a Tuna el-Gabal as well as (23) a Tanta in the central Delta—far to the north of Upper Egypt.

182. The church.

183. 'Virtuous and perfect mortification' renders *gädl śannay wä-fiṣṣum*. The term *gädl* is, like *mästägadil*, derived from the root *g-d-l*; see nn. 115, 150, 156, 169, 178, 188, 190, 191, and 262. Polysemic *gädl*, which in other contexts could also be translated as 'spiritual struggle' or 'pious life' (cp. note 188), in this instance has been rendered as 'mortification', mainly on account of the verb *täṣämdä* ('devoted himself') with which it occurs here. This verb literally means 'to yoke oneself, to subjugate oneself (to pious exercises)', thus clearly indicating deeds of self-mortification.

184. The eucharistic bread.

185. In Ethiopic, the last half of the sentence is in the singular ('for a sick man, if he were about to die, they would then give him some of it'). However, since the sick man of the text certainly is not a specific individual but represents any sick person, a translation in the plural seems appropriate here.

186. That is, because the snake had devoured and defiled the eucharistic bread.

187. Presumably because the snake's flesh was not considered fit for consumption.

188. 'Pious lives' here renders *gädl*. See see nn. 115, 150, 156, 178, 183, 190, 191, and 262.

189. 'Virgin' (*dingil*) often metaphorically refers to a nun, and should probably be understood to do so here too.

190. 'Everything' here and in the preceding line has no direct equivalent in the Giʿiz text. The general context, however, and particularly the use of the term *gädl* (see n. 115) which normally implies the religious assessment of a whole life and not just of a single incident, here twice seems to require its insertion: It appears sensible to assume that the virgin relates the entire story of Biyoka and Benjamin to the faithful, and not only the episode with the snake.

191. 'Written hagiography' here translates *gädl*, thereby demonstrating yet another, this time rather technical, shade of meaning of this complex term in Giʿiz religious language (see nn. 115, 150, 156, 178, 183, 188, 190, and 262).

192. The rhyme pattern of this *sälam*-poem (see n. 161) in the original is a-a-b-a-b. See n. 161 above.

193. Translated from the text edited by Guidi, PO 7.3: 435–438 [419–422]. Numerals within backstrokes in the translation refer to pages of Guidi's text.

194. In Ethiopic: Andranīqos, Atinasya.

195. Meaning, presumably, a short while after they had been married.

196. In Ethiopic: Yoḥannis, Maryam.

197. Or 'with dysentery'; *fäṣänt* is polysemic and means both (See Leslau, *Comparative Dictionary of Geʿez*, 156; Gk: 'burning up with fever').

198. Job 1:21 (LXX), Ps 112:2 (LXX).

199. Literally: the 'temple / shrine / sanctuary' (*bētä mäqdäs*).

200. Nuns.

201. The Giʿiz text in all the manuscripts used by Guidi has *bi'isītu*, 'his woman / wife' (emphasis added). This would seem to imply one or both of two things: a) that everybody was at least aware that she was a woman, but not that she was Andronicus' wife; b) that Andronicus for one was aware of her true identity, and that it was only the other monks who were left in the dark. But the following lines make it clear that neither of these implications of the reading *bi'isītu* is tenable. Therefore it seems advisable to here emend the Giʿiz text to read *bi'isīt*, 'a woman', without the possessive suffix -*u*. Guidi, however, appears not to have had any problem with the form *bi'isītu*, since he did not comment on it and straightforwardly translated it as *sa femme* ([421]/437).

202. Guidi ([421]/437) translates this sentence *Il arrivait qu'Abbā Daniel les visitait en même temps et leur parlait du prix de leurs âmes* ('It occasionally happened that Abba Daniel visited them at the same time and spoke to them about the value of their souls'). At three points this translation appears not to do justice to the original. First, the regularity of Abba Daniel's visits, which is indicated by Giʿiz *kona . . . yiḥēwwiṣomu* ('he used to visit them'), is not adequately rendered by *Il arrivait qu'Abbā Daniel les visitait* ('It occasionally happened that Abba

Daniel visited them'). Second, Guidi's *en même temps* ('at [one and] the same time') does not reflect the distributive character of Gi'iz *bä-bä-aḥatti gīzē*, which I try to capture with 'every once in a while'. Third, it appears that *prix de leurs âmes* ('the price / value of their souls'), though a more or less literal rendition of Gi'iz *räbaḥa näfsomu* ('gain of / for their souls'), does not properly reflect the contextual meaning of this expression. I here interprete *räbaḥa näfsomu* to mean 'gain *for* their souls' and have therefore rendered it, somewhat freely, as their spiritual progress.

203. The main text of Guidi's edition has the plural, *misṭīratä qiddisat* ('Holy Sacraments', literally 'Holy Mysteries'), which in the context appears problematic. However, the apparatus to the edition shows that one of Guidi's manuscripts (**P**) has the singular *misṭīrä qiddisat*, which in the context makes more sense and on which Guidi also based his french translation (*le Saint Mystère* 421/437). Against this background it is surprising that Guidi did not put the singular form in the main text and relegated the plural to the apparatus.

204. Gi'iz *täsäwwärä libbunnahu*, literally 'his reason vanished'; see Leslau, *Comparative Dictionary of Ge'ez,* 306, 520.

205. His fellow monks.

206. Literally 'her bones' (*a'ṣimtīha*).

207. In the Gi'iz original, all five lines of the poem rhyme in *-a*.

208. Translated from Arras, *Patericon Aethiopice*, CSCO 277, Scriptores Aethiopici 53:191 (No. 268); Arras' latin translation may be found in CSCO 278:141 (No. 268). For a list of the seven sayings, see the Index Personarum, CSCO 278:179, s.v. 'Daniel (mon[achos])'. The numeral in parentheses after the titles refers to the numbering of the greek dossier (Chapter One).

209. The following episode actually is the 268th in the *Patericon.* The manuscripts, however, with considerable variation between them, often lump together two or more distinct apophthegmata under one number. In the manuscript used by Arras as the basis for his edition, this episode appears as no.196, which number Arras includes in his text. Therefore it is also reproduced here.

210. Literally: 'when your wife gives birth' (*sobä tiwällid bi'isītikä*), in the present tense (= the so-called Gi'iz imperfect). From what follows, however, it becomes clear that it is not Abba Daniel's wish to be present at the time of the birth itself, but only to be informed immediately thereafter.

211. This time the Gi'iz verb is in the perfect (*wälädät*), which, depending on the context, may be translated as an english imperfect, perfect, or pluperfect.

212. Arras, *Geronticon.*

213. Arras, *Geronticon.* CSCO 476:68-69; CSCO 477:46-47. Numerals in parentheses following the titles refer to the numbering of the greek dossier (Chapter One).

214. In the immediate context it remains unclear what exactly the 'many things' (*gibr bizuḫ*) attained by the blind mendicant are. As the narrative continues, it first becomes clear that he is not quite as destitute as it initially appears (though he certainly is not rich, either). Later on it even turns out that the mendicant's attainments are not so much material as spiritual. Against this backdrop it seems appropriate to point out that Giꜥiz *gibr* is an extremely polysemic term which, in addition to 'thing(s)', can also be translated 'deed', 'service', or 'power' (see Leslau, *Comparative Dictionary of Geꜥez*, 178). The phrase therefore might also be rendered as 'He has acquired many (spiritual) powers' or 'He has performed many (extraordinary) deeds'. The underlying arabic original here could well be more precise. In the Giꜥiz, however, the meaning of the phrase under discussion cannot be determined with certainty. See nn. 237, 326, and 348 below.

215. Literally: 'stand' (Giꜥiz: *qum*). See n. 218 below.

216. Giꜥiz *mik*ʷ*rab*. This term is ambiguous; it can refer to any building erected for purposes of worship and devotion. Its reference in this context is difficult to determine with certainty. Most likely it is to the Church of Saint Mark (even though *bētä kristīyan* and not *mik*ʷ*rab* is the standard Giꜥiz term for 'church'), but a reference to a shrine (a mausoleum?) devoted to Saint Mark, the patron saint of the Church of Egypt, cannot be excluded. Gk I.3 with greater precision refers to 'Saint Mark's Outside-the-City'. Arras, CSCO 477:47, translates *mik*ʷ*rab* as 'temple' (*templum*). See n. 222 below.

217. Literally 'passed by it' (*ḫaläfä*).

218. Literally 'stand' (*qum*). See n. 215 above.

219. The shekel, mostly known as a unit of currency from the Hebrew Bible and then as the revived currency of modern-day Israel, was originally a unit of weight.

220. Literally 'was heard' (*täsämꜥa*).

221. 'High official' renders Giꜥiz *mäggabī*, a rather unspecific term which can refer to a multitude of public and church offices. Its precise reference in the given context cannot be established, which is why the unspecific 'high official' has been chosen as a translation. Arras here renders *mäggabī* as 'prefect' (*praefectus*; CSCO 477:47), the greek dossier has 'the Great Steward'.

222. Again for Giꜥiz *mik*ʷ*rab*; see n. 216 above. Arras also in this instance translates *mik*ʷ*rab* as 'temple' (*templum*; see CSCO 477:47).

223. Saint Mark.

224. To the blind mendicant.

225. Giꜥiz: Matēwos. Judging by the pattern known from countless other Giꜥiz manuscripts, this Matēwos / Matthew was not a contemporary or associate of the wonder-working blind mendicant, but simply a scribe who here inserted his name in order to win the saintly man's blessings. The name appears again at the end of *Geronticon* episode 71 (cp. n. 312).

226. Arras, *Geronticon*. CSCO 476:70-73; CSCO 477:47-49.

227. Literally 'who was called' (*intä täsämyät*).

228. Gi'iz here is Qisṭasiyos: This is the most far-reaching distortion the saint's original name Anastasia (or Anastasios, in its masculine form) has undergone in the ethiopian tradition. In the parallel account about her in Abba Daniel's long Gi'iz hagiography, she appears as Bäsṭasiyos, whereas in the short reference to her in the Synaxary account for Ginbot 8 / May 16 she is Anisṭasya.

229. A *mi'raf* is a traditional ethiopian measure of length; the distance it denotes is uncertain and has perhaps been historically variable. In principle, since *mi'raf* is derived from the root *'-r-f* ('to rest'), it makes sense to construe it, in an ethiopian context, as a day's march. In the present setting, however, this is not helpful a) because a distance of eighteen days' march would be far too long, and b) because here we find ourselves in a greco-egyptian context in which *mi'raf* therefore can only render a greco-egyptian measurement term (perhaps already distorted through translation into Arabic). The greek account, though, does not specify the distance. Arras here translates *mi'raf* as *stadium* (*c.* 200 m; CSCO 477:47). In terms of history as well as distance, this appears contextually plausible.

230. An allusion to Gen 18.

231. The Gi'iz text here uses *näfs* ('soul') in combination with the direct object suffix of the third person singular masculine to express the reflexive nature of the verb (*anśi'a . . . näfso*, literally, 'he raised his soul up', meaning 'he raised himself up'). This is patently modeled on the arabic manner of expressing reflexiveness, in which *nafs* (which in Arabic also means 'soul') serves this very purpose. The indigenous functional Gi'iz equivalent of arabic *nafs*, however, is *ri's* ('head'). Normally one would therefore expect the text to here have *anśi'a . . . ri'so*. The appearance of *näfso* instead is clear evidence that this episode—and likely the whole Gi'iz *Geronticon*—was translated from Arabic. See nn. 58, 251, 285, 288, and 338.

232. Or 'kissed him'. The ambiguity arises from the fact that Gi'iz has no neuter in the third person singular. The masculine object suffix of this person and number (*-o*, here in *sä'amo*) can therefore refer to either Abba Daniel or to his head.

233. Literally: at all times (*bä-kʷillu gīzē*).

234. The Gi'iz has this plural (*abäwīhu*), whereas contextually a singular (*abuhu*) would seem more appropriate. It is therefore tempting to conjecture that extant *abäwīhu* arose through the corruption of an original *abuhu*. The Greek though too has 'fathers'.

235. 2 Kgs 2.

236. While English 'you' can refer to the singular or the plural, Gi'iz distinguishes its second (and third) person direct object pronominal suffixes according

to number and gender. The Giʿiz object suffix underlying this 'you' is -*kä*, which refers to the masculine singular. Thus Anastasia here appears to be addressing herself to Abba Daniel only. However, this apparent attempt on her part to keep the secret about her sex exclusively between the two of them contrasts with her use of the plural 'except you [two]' (*zä'inbälē-kimu*) at the end of this phrase, which seems to signal her willingness to let the disciple also in on it. Should we therefore assume that this initial sg. -*kä* is a corruption of an original pl. -*kimu*?

237. For Giʿiz *gibr*, see n. 214 above as well as nn. 326 and 348 below.

238. The kiss of peace, part of the eucharistic ritual.

239. While it must be considered highly extraordinary and hardly in keeping with traditional piety that someone should bless himself, Giʿiz *baräkä riʾso* seems to be saying exactly this, apparently leaving little room for interpretation. (Arras too has *benedixit sibi*; see CSCO 477:48). Should we, faced with this dilemma, assume a corruption of the extant Giʿiz text? Or is it permissible to here interpret *baräkä riʾiso*, with some freedom, as 'he took his farewell', given that Leslau, *Comparative Dictionary of Geʿez*, 105, notes 'bid farewell' as one of the rarer meanings of *baräkä*? Greek lacks 'blessed himself'.

240. The 'he' must be assumed to refer to Abba Daniel's disciple a) because it appears natural that he rather than his master would do this physically demanding work, and b) because Abba Daniel is explicitly re-introduced as the grammatical subject in the next sentence ('the Elder'), for which there would have been no need if the author had assumed him to be the one doing the grave-digging. Yet the text easily lends itself to the idea that Abba Daniel dug the hermit's grave because normally—that is, if the context does not clearly require otherwise—the Elder, and not his disciple, would be taken as the default reference of an unspecific 'he'. The greek text has them both digging the grave.

241. Without the insertion of 'upper' and 'under', which are not found in the Giʿiz text, the passage would make little sense. First, if Abba Daniel after her demise took off all of Anastasia's clothes, he would be disregarding her last wish. Second, if he had already undressed her completely, it would be absurd for him to tell his disciple to now shroud her 'on top of his clothes'. Surprisingly, Arras keeps his translation of this passage strictly literal (see CSCO 477:48). Gk: the old man stripped off the clothes he [the alleged eunuch] was wearing and said to his disciple, 'Clothe him with more than what he is wearing'.

242. For Giʿiz *habt*. In rendering this as 'palm-leaves', I follow Arras who translates *e palmis erat* (CSCO 477:48). However, I cannot find *habt* (or any plausible orthographic variant thereof) in any of the Giʿiz dictionaries at my disposal with the meaning of 'palm-leaves', or indeed referring to any other imaginable clothing material. I am familiar with *habt* only with the meaning of 'gift, donation'. In addition, Leslau, *Comparative Dictionary of Geʿez*, 720, lists only *ṣäbär*, *śor* and *dägʷäʿalē* as Giʿiz terms for 'palm, palm tree'. While I do not

understand how Arras arrived at his translation, I follow it a) because it makes sense in the context, b) because I have nothing better to offer, and c) because it seems to find confirmation as the text continues (see n. 244 below). Greek: The eunuch was wearing a patched cloak and a loincloth made from palm fiber.

243. Literally 'moist, wet, humid' (*riḥist*).

244. For 'palm-leaves' the Giʿiz text this time employs the clear and unambiguous term *dägʷäʿilē* (a variant of *dägʷäʿalī*), which suggests that earlier *habt* likely also has this meaning (see n. 242 above for context).

245. Arras' Giʿiz text has *liḥwat*, a form which I cannot identify or analyze. In my translation I assume that it is a corruption of, or misprint for, *liḥqät*, 'she grew up, she had grown up'. Such a corruption or misprint appears likely because the characters for *wa* and *qä* resemble each other closely in ethiopic script. Arras also translates 'she grew up' (*adolevit*; CSCO 477:49), thus implying a reading of the Giʿiz verb as *liḥqät*.

246. Theodora (who in the Giʿiz text appears as Ta'odira or Tawdira) was the wife of Emperor Justinian I (527–565) and herself a highly controversial figure.

247. Literally 'the place' (*mäkan*).

248. Literally 'wanted to send forth for her' (*yafäqqir yifännu bä'intī'aha*).

249. Literally 'another' (*kali'*).

250. Giʿiz *nägäda*. Arras incorrectly translates this as 'her travels / pilgrimage' (*eius . . . peregrinatio*; CSCO 477:49) because he fails to distinguish between two homonymous Giʿiz roots *n-g-d*. One of these—the one Arras opts for—produces lexemes from the sphere of 'travel, trade', while the other, pertinent here, is attested only with the lexeme *nägäd* ('tribe, clan, kin, stock, family, lineage'). Arras' translation is clearly incorrect because the *n-g-d* root referring to the semantic field of travel / trade does not produce a lexeme *nägäd*, only forms approximating it (like *nigd, nägd, nigdät;* see Leslau, 390ff.). Additionally, in the context in which Abba Daniel in chronological order recapitulates the stations of Anastasia's life, it makes sense to assume that he begins with her noble origins, not with her flight to Egypt.

251. Or 'for our souls'; Giʿiz *laʿlä näfsatīnä* can be understood in either sense. See nn. 231 and 338.

252. Arras, *Geronticon*, CSCO 476:73-80; CSCO 477:49-54.

253. See the parallel narrative in the ethiopic Synaxary for Ḥamlē 28 above. The name Andronicus here appears as Indränīfos (Ḥamlē 28: Andranīqos), Athanasia as Atinasya (as Ḥamlē 28). The name form Indränīfos is further evidence that this *Geronticon* episode (and likely the whole *Geronticon*) was translated from Arabic, as the most conspicuous divergence between Indränīfos and Andronicus (or greek Andrōnikos)—the *f* instead of a *k* at the beginning of the last syllable—can convincingly be explained through the assumption of an underlying arabic Andraniqūs. In arabic script the letters *f* and *q* differ only in the number

of diacritical dots on top of the same basic shape (one for *f*, two for *q*). In manuscripts a *q* can therefore easily be mistaken for an *f* by an inattentive translator or scribe, especially if the two dots on top of the *q* have not been neatly executed, but rather merged into a single larger one. See also nn. 231, 285, 288, 322, and 338.

254. One of the metropolises of Late Antiquity, located about twelve miles inland from the shore of the Mediterranean near its northeastern corner. Antioch today lies in Turkey and bears the name Hatay.

255. Giʿiz *mängid wistä birur*, literally 'a trader in money / silver'.

256. Literally 'was a lover of' (*mäfqirītä*).

257. This translation in the plural is based on the Giʿiz textual variant *bomu*, which Arras relegates to the apparatus (CSCO 476:73). In my judgement, however, *bomu* here makes much better sense than *latī* = 'she possessed,' which appears in Arras' main text. Greek: They were very wealthy.

258. Literally 'for the order / class of the monks' (*bäʾintä śirʿatä mänäkosat*).

259. In Giʿiz: Yoḥannis, Maryam.

260. Literally 'gave' (*wähabu*).

261. See 1 Cor 7:29—which is the testimony only of Saint Paul, not of all the apostles. Note the change in subject / number in the Giʿiz text, from the husband ('he') to the married couple as a whole ('they').

262. For *mästägadilan*, singular *mästägadil*, a rather unspecific term which can denote anyone engaged in a strenuous, but normally voluntary, spiritual struggle or exercise. See n. 115 and nn. 150, 156, 178, 183, 188, 190, and 191. However, the text here otherwise speaks only of those who, quite without their choosing, are afflicted with various grave illnesses. It therefore appears possible that *mästägadilan* here mistranslates an unknown arabic term which might have referred to still another class of physically ill people. Gk: 'Every Sunday, Monday, Wednesday, and Friday, from evening until dawn Andronicus would devote himself to washing the men while his wife, because of her love of the poor, would devote herself to washing the women'. See Gk I.5.

263. Or 'from scabies' (or a similar skin disease), or generally 'from sores / open wounds'. The underlying Giʿiz *zälgäsä* (here present in the form of its passive participle *zilgusan*) is a rather unspecific verb applied to a whole range of grave and outwardly visible afflictions which comprises all the listed illnesses (see Leslau, *Comparative Dictionary of Geʿez*, 637). Greek omits.

264. On this saint, see Chapter One (Gk), n. 114.

265. Since hours were counted from six AM, the sixth hour would be about noon. Time is still reckoned this way in Ethiopia.

266. See Job 1:21.

267. The Giʿiz text actually says 'the patriarchs' (*liqanä pappasat*), but this plural obviously makes little sense in the given context. Moreover, since the text in the next sentence speaks of only one patriarch, initial 'patriarchs' must be considered a corruption.

268. This translation follows a textual variant (*Wä-sobä bäṣḥat ḫabä mita*), which Arras relegates to the apparatus (see CSCO 476:75, n. 4-1). His main text reads: 'When her husband came / arrived' (*Wä-sobä bäṣḥa mita*).

269. Literally 'order me' (*azzizänï*).

270. Arras' main text has 'among the monks' (*ma'ikälä mänäkosawïyan*), whereas 'among the nuns' (*ma'ikälä mänäkosawïyat*) appears as a variant in the apparatus (see CSCO 476:75).

271. Arras regards 'blessed' (*buruk*) not as a qualifier of the wife's speech but as a term applied to the husband, and translates accordingly: *Dixit ei benedictus: Bonus sermo tuus*: 'The blessed one [the husband] said to her, "What you say is good"' (CSCO 476:51). There is no reason, however, why the text should suddenly start referring to the husband as a 'blessed one'.

272. Literally 'and' (*wä-*).

273. The translation is doubtful. It renders *qädamï wä-dagimä*, literally 'the first / the beginning and the second'. The element *dagimä* ('the second') in this phrase is strange and smacks of a mistranslation from arabic. Arras syntactically divides the phrase differently, separating *qädamï* from *wä-dagimä*, and letting a new semantic unit begin with the latter. He thus translates: 'what had happened to them first, and secondly they said to him' (*quae advenerant sibi antea, et iterum dixerunt ei*; see CSCO 477:51. The full phrase in Gi'iz is: *qädamï wä-dagimä wä-yibēliwwo*). Arras' translation, however, ignores the second 'and' (*wä-*) between *dagimä* (his 'secondly') and *yibēliwwo* ('they said / wrote to him') which makes his syntactical analysis of the phrase impossible.

274. Literally 'said' (*yibēliwwo*).

275. Literally 'this' (*zäntä*).

276. Or 'advantageous / beneficial / gratifying'; Gi'iz *bäqᵘᵉēt* comprises all these meanings. However, as any envisaged reward for the benefactors should probably be understood to be mainly or even exclusively spiritual, the chosen translation seemed preferable because it relegates notions of monetary profit to the background.

277. Gi'iz *nägid*. At its most basic level, this term simply means 'travelers'. It later acquired the meanings of 'traders' and 'pilgrims'. The translation 'pilgrims' was chosen here because the text next speaks of traveling monks, while ordinary worldly travelers—including merchants, presumably—are mentioned last. This sequence suggests that initial *nägid* refers to a class of spiritual travelers. Arras' translation of *nägid* as *infirm[i]* ('patients, sick ones'; see CSCO 477:51) is inadequate.

278. Literally 'that you receive it' (*kämä titwäkäf wïtä*).

279. The verb employed here, *täsänabbätä*, is not part of the traditional Gi'iz vocabulary, but is a loanword from Amharic, one of the modern ethio-semitic successor tongues of Gi'iz. Amharic is currently one of the two most widely spoken languages of Ethiopia (the other is cushitic Oromo).

280. See Gen 12:1. The scene is also reminiscent of the exodus from Sodom of Lot and his family (Gen 19:24ff.) in which Lot's wife cannot refrain from looking back at her devastated home and as a consequence is turned into a pillar of salt. Athanasia is spared that fate—perhaps because, despite a nostalgic last glance, she ultimately accepts her departure (or so contemporary theologians might have argued).

281. The Holy Land or, more specifically, sites in Jerusalem.

282. Actually the shrine of Saint Menas outside Alexandria; see Chapter One, n. 122.

283. That is, three PM. See nn. 126 and 265 above.

284. Presumably a donkey.

285. Literally 'until I go now to Scetis, and I will return' (*iskä aḥawwir yi'izē ḫabä il-Asqēṭis wä-igäbbi'*). The extant Giʿiz text is stylistically infelicitous and smacks of a flawed translation from Arabic. In this context, one notes that the *il-* in *il-Asqēṭis* transcribes the Arabic article *al-*. This is further evidence that at least this *Geronticon* episode, but likely the whole work, was translated from Arabic. See also nn. 231, 253, 288, 322, and 338.

286. The Giʿiz text furnished by Arras here seems to be corrupt. It has *bä-kämä qalu ṣidq*: 'as his word is justice / righteousness', which makes only limited sense. Through the emendation of only one ethiopic character, however, we arrive at *bä-kämä qalu ṣadiq*; this has been translated above and fits the context much better. Moreover, God's *qal ṣadiq*, his 'righteous / true / just word', is a fixed formula of piety. Finally, it may be pointed out that Arras too translates this phrase as God's 'true word' (*verbum . . . verum*; see CSCO 477:52) and thus does not follow the Giʿiz text he provides in CSCO 476.

287. The reference surprisingly is only to the husband, as Giʿiz *lä-kä* makes clear. In Giʿiz, as in Arabic, all references to a second person are specific with regard to number and gender.

288. Giʿiz *ṣiʿīd* for 'Upper Egypt' transcribes only that region's arabic appellation *aṣ-ṣaʿīd* ('the Upstream Country'), but does not attempt to translate, let alone explain, it. Ordinary ethiopian hearers / readers of this passage therefore likely did not form a correct idea about what this toponym *ṣiʿīd* actually referred to. See the beginning of *Geronticon* No. 72 below (with note 316) for a parallel. See also nn. 231, 253, 285, 322, and 338.

289. The reference probably is to the (second) pachomian monastery located at Fāw al-Qiblī ('Fāw of Upper Egypt') near Qinā, about two hundred fifty miles south of Cairo. Next to its predecessor at nearby Tabennisi proper—which soon had to be evacuated—this monastery was the earliest foundation by Saint Pachomius (fourth century), the 'father' of egyptian cenobitic monasticism. Consequently it remained for centuries the spiritual center of the pachomian tradition. Greek 'the Thebaid to the monastery of the Tabennisiotes'; see Chapter One, n. 125.

290. The Gi'iz text is *wä-wï̈tu albäso lä-Indränīfos askēma*, literally 'He [Abba Daniel] then dressed Indränifos in the *askēma*', that is, he made him a monk. The *askēma* is the traditional monastic cloak; the term ultimately is derived from Greek *schēma*, 'garment'.

291. The Holy Land and in particular Jerusalem.

292. Literally 'made / performed' (*gäbrä*).

293. Or 'kissed'—in a purely social, non-erotic manner. Gi'iz *ammiẖa*, here rendered by way of a hendiadys as 'greeted and embraced', essentially refers to a greeting which involves some close physical contact, be it in the form of a kiss (on the cheek), an embrace, or both. See n. 302 below.

294. Literally 'over their eyes' (*dība a'yintīhomu*).

295. The translation attempts to render Gi'iz *zä-ī-taläwwäṭa iminnēha ar'ayahu*, literally 'because his appearance had not changed from her'. A literal translation here makes little sense. I therefore propose to regard the whole phrase as condensed from two originally distinct but overlapping ideas and formulations. As a consequence—in order to de-condense—I have chosen to translate *zä-ī-taläwwäṭa . . . ar'ayahu* twice: once literally as 'because his appearance had not changed'; and once more freely and by integrating the otherwise erratic *iminnēha* ('from her') into it, as 'because she had not forgotten his appearance' ('his appearance had not changed from her'). I am aware that this solution is tentative at best. Should one perhaps just ignore *iminnēha*, which would immediately lead to a straightforward sentence?

296. Greek: 'she looked like an Ethiopian'; see Chapter One, nn. 128 and 236.

297. For *wä-nikun kämä ī-bädawiyan*, literally 'and let us be like non-Bedouins'. In view of the lines that follow in the Gi'iz text (esp. 'The saintly woman spoke to him all along the way'), the intended meaning of this somewhat enigmatic phrase perhaps is 'let us therefore behave civilly, let us entertain each other with conversation instead of just marching on in brooding silence, as uncouth Bedouins might do'. If this were the case, it would be the exact opposite of what the greek version has, which here says: 'Let us travel in silence as though we were traveling alone'. Arras though in his edition also notes the variant *ī-täbaṣaḥiyan* ('people not associated with one another'; see Leslau, 111) for *ī-bädawiyan* ('non-Bedouins'). This might reflect an older layer of the Gi'iz text trying to capture the sense of the Greek (which presumably was accessible to the ethiopian translator only in the guise of a more or less accurate arabic version). If so, readers / copyists in Ethiopia apparently soon found this passage obscure and re-interpreted it, perhaps not very felicitously, by changing it to *ī-bädawiyan*. Concomitantly, the phrase cited above about Athanasia conversing with Andronicus all along their joint march, which would run counter to the thrust of the greek text, would have to be presumed to be a Gi'iz (or perhaps already arabic) accretion.

298. Matthew (Gi'iz: Matēwos) presumably is the abbot of the monastery where she lived in the guise of a monk. Greek: she said to him, 'The prayers of the old man will travel with us'.

299. Greek lacks this sentence.

300. The masculine variant of Athanasia.

301. Greek: 'Go, and I will wait for you at the Oktokaidekaton', the monastic community at the eighteenth milestone west of Alexandria. The Gi'iz, however, here has a date rather than a location. Perhaps the Gi'iz also once had the correct text (possibly *wistä minēt zä-18* = in the monastery of the 18th [mile]), but later copyists, without a sound knowledge of Egypt's monastic landscape, no longer understood the phrase. They therefore tinkered with the wording in various ways in order to improve the passage, which then backfired.

302. Both english verbs together render *ammiḫa* (+ *lotu*: him). For further explanations regarding the semantics of *ammiḫa*, see n. 293 above.

303. Greek lacks this sentence.

304. Literally 'wants' (*yifäqqid*); see also the next note.

305. Literally 'you want' (*tifäqqid*); see the previous note.

306. Literally 'the flesh of Christ' (*śigahu lä-Kristos*).

307. 'Her life's struggle' renders *gädla*. *Gädl* (literally: struggle; word-final -*a* of *gädla* is the possessive suffix third person feminine singular) always carries a strong connotation of spiritual endeavor. See nn. 115, 150, 156, 169, 178, 183, 188, 190, 191, and 262.

308. The Gi'iz text has the plural *ti' imirtatä*, but as there is only one written document that makes little sense.

309. Literally 'he was concealed from his mind' (*täsäwwärä im-ḫillunnahu*).

310. Arras' Gi'iz text has *yastärkib* = '(began to) devote himself to, busy himself with'. However, this makes little sense in the context and must be viewed as metathesized from an original *yastäbrik*, 'he fell on his knees, he knelt'. Arras' translation of *anxie reputare* ('[began] to fearfully reflect on'; see CSCO 477:54) does not do justice even to the *yastärkib* that he himself provides.

311. That is, the Eucharist, as earlier.

312. Gi'iz: Matēwos. The same scribe's name appears at the end of *Geronticon* episode 68 (see there, with n. 225).

313. Arras, *Geronticon*, CSCO 476:80-87; CSCO 477:54-59. For parallel Gi'iz versions of this story, see Abba Daniel's long hagiography as well as the Synaxary extract for 8 Ginbot (16 May) above.

314. Gi'iz: Awlogīyos.

315. If the Gi'iz text of this sentence so far (*yibē Abba Dani'ēl*) is read with a different syntactic division, it yields the translation 'Abba Daniel says' (thus indeed Arras: *Dixit pater Daniel*; CSCO 477:54). Linguistically, this possibility is rooted in two facts: a) in Gi'iz subjects regularly follow the sentence-initial verbs; b) in the third person singular Gi'iz distinguishes only between feminine and

masculine, but does not have a neuter. Therefore the reference of the masculine verb form *yibē* can either be to the narrated episode itself ('it says') or to a masculine narrator, Abba Daniel. However, this latter interpretation then runs into the difficulty that the following story is told in the third person, which would be odd if Abba Daniel himself were the narrator. The same problem is encountered again at the beginning of *Geronticon* No. 472 (see n. 362 below).

316. The Giʿiz text has *ṣiʿīd* for 'Upper Egypt'. See n. 288 above for a parallel.

317. 'Unsheltered travelers' renders Giʿiz *gidufan*, literally 'repudiated / despised / lost ones, outcasts' (see Leslau, *Comparative Dictionary of Geʿez*, 181). These translations, however, seemed too harsh for the present context. Arras translates *gidufan* as *perditi* ('lost ones'), a latin term with strong religious overtones; see CSCO 477:54.

318. That is, let us leave it to God whether or not we will find some shelter.

319. 'Like strangers' renders Giʿiz *kämä zä-nägd*. As *nägd* denotes little more than 'people traveling to foreign places', this same phrase could also be rendered as 'like travelers', 'like merchants', or 'like pilgrims' (thus Arras: *ut peregrini*; see CSCO 477:54). Yet in the present context 'strangers' seems preferable a) because it is functionally unspecific (unlike 'merchant' or 'pilgrim'), and expresses b) the dimension of being lost in a foreign environment (unlike the neutral 'traveler').

320. Literally 'who would console / comfort him' (*zä-yinazzizo*), which in this context must mean that he was living alone, without a wife, children, or other relatives.

321. The ethiopic version omits here the ongoing argument in Gk I.2 (Chapter One) between Abba Daniel and his disciple.

322. From arabic *dirham*, a currency unit in much of the medieval Islamic Orient. Ultimately the term is derived from Greek *drachma*. The greek dossier, though, has *keration* here, which again demonstrates (see also nn. 231, 253, 285, 288, and 338) that this Giʿiz text was not translated directly from Greek, but from a christian arabic version that itself was written only in islamic times, when with Islam the *dirham* had become Egypt's currency.

323. Literally 'did to me likewise'.

324. Standing up for extended periods of time was a common ascetic practice in many branches of oriental monasticism.

325. Literally 'like a dead person' (*kämä zä-miwwit*).

326. For Giʿiz *wi'itu śannay gibr*. However, because *gibr* is highly polysemic (see Leslau, *Comparative Dictionary of Geʿez*, 178; see also nn. 214 and 237 above as well as n. 348 below) this phrase could also be rendered as 'he has good work'; greek dossier: 'No, he's doing fine.' For whichever translation one opts, the quoted Giʿiz phrase appears unidiomatic, even ungrammatical. I would suggest that it be emended to *wi'itu bä-śannay gibr*, the added *bä-* meaning 'in', which the Giʿiz text otherwise lacks. The translation 'he has good work' is reached from the literal 'he is in good work'. Arras translates this phrase as *Nunc sane*

bonum est ('Currently things are indeed fine'; CSCO 477:55), which transforms *wi'itu* ('he / it') into *nunc sane* ('currently indeed') and leaves *gibr* untranslated.

327. Arras' Gi'iz text has 'he said' (*yibē*), but the context here clearly requires 'I said' (*ibē*). Arras himself translates *dixi*, 'I said' (CSCO 477:55), but neither emends the Gi'iz text accordingly nor comments on his translation.

328. In purely grammatical terms, the reference of *wi'itu* ('he') here is unclear: the saint in priests' clothes, or the youth (Christ)? Presumably the latter, as the context suggests. Theoretically, however, it could even refer to the last-mentioned Eulogius.

329. Literally 'listened to' (*säm'a*).

330. Literally 'said' (*yibē*).

331. 'Children of Israel' follows a textual variant in Arras' Gi'iz edition, whose main text has 'Children of Ishmael' (*däqīqä Isma'ēl*). The Ishmaelites also appear in this same context in the parallel narrative of Abba Daniel's long Gi'iz hagiography. Yet there they figure as contemporaries of Eulogius and Abba Daniel, nomadic Arabs who in Late Antiquity were roaming the desert areas of the Near East, including Egypt—and as such they make sense. Here, however, the reference is to a distant past ('the days of . . .'), and in such a context 'the days of the Children of Israel'—the time before Moses even led Israel out of Egypt—clearly is the superior variant. The greek dossier also has 'Israelites'.

332. Or Justinian? Gi'iz has 'Däsusyanos', which bears a stronger resemblance to Justinian[os] (r. 527–565) than it does to Justin[os] (r. 518–527). Yet it is by no means obvious that Däsusyanos is a reflex of Justinian[os], and generally the Gi'iz version can hardly be regarded as historically authoritative. Later on in this episode, for instance (n. 346), the emperor—presumably the very same one—appears as Yosyos; and in Abba Daniel's long Gi'iz hagiography Eulogius comes to Constantinople under emperor Anastasios (r. 491-518; of his name, Däsusyanos, cannot possibly be a reflex). In view of all this, it makes sense here to follow the greek dossier and identify the emperor in question as Justin, which seems the best compromise solution between history and philology.

333. For Gi'iz *yazihhinomu* (literally 'he provided them leisure / rest / tranquility'), a textual variant which Arras relegates to the apparatus (see CSCO 476:83); in his main text he has *yizzaḥanomu*. This conjugated verb form, which might tentatively be translated as 'he was at ease with them, he associated with them without inhibitions', has the same root *z-ḥ-n* as *yazihhinomu*. It would, however, have to be derived from *täzaḥanä*, a different verbal base, while *yazihhinomu* is derived from the base *azḥanä*. Yet such a verbal base *täzaḥanä* is not attested in Leslau, *Comparative Dictionary of Ge'ez*, 634. While this does not absolutely preclude its existence and legitimate use in works of Gi'iz literature, it, in addition to the semantics of the phrase, strongly militates in favor of reading here *yazihhinomu*.

334. Or 'about him'. Since Gi'iz in the third person singular does not distinguish between animate and inanimate, the reference of *botu* cannot be determined with certainty.

335. Or was it the other way around, and Eulogius gave a beautiful palace or park (Giʿiz *ʿaṣäd* has both meanings) as a gift to the emperor? (Greek:ʿEulogius also bought a large house'.) The extant Giʿiz text (see next paragraph) can be construed in both ways because it is philologically inconsistent in some small details; the reader therefore is left only with the choice of where precisely to regard it as corrupt and in need of emendation. Depending on this choice, one or the other meaning is produced. To this translator it makes more sense to opt for Eulogius as the gift's recipient rather than its giver, not least because the essence of the story is about Eulogius' moral corruption. In addition, the text just a few words later informs us that the gift was commonly known as 'the Egyptian's palace'. Such a designation was likely coined after its resident / owner, not its donor. Still further down we then learn that Eulogius indeed lived in a magnificent residence. This cumulative evidence in my judgement convincingly rules out the possibility that Eulogius gave the *ʿaṣäd* to the emperor instead of receiving it from him.

But there remains a philological problem. The Giʿiz text of the past two sentences runs: *wä-fäqädä ammiḫa ḫabä niguś gibrä kiburä bizuḫa. Wä-qärbä niguś wä-wähabo ʿaṣädä ʿabbayä śännaytä*, which would literally translate: 'He wanted [to give] as a gift to the emperor something expensive and big. Thus the emperor approached [him] and gave him a big and beautiful palace.' This is obviously self-contradictory. In order to make sense of the passage, one has to delete *ḫabä* ('to') in the first sentence, which leads to the translation I have provided above. The alternative is to change the nominative *niguś* ('the emperor') at the beginning of the second sentence into accusative *niguśä*, which would allow this second sentence to be rendered as:'He [Eulogius] thus approached the emperor.' Such a translation would then tally with the previous sentence left unchanged, its *ḫabä* not discarded. Arras avoids dealing with the problem posed by this passage. He does not touch the letter of the text—and thus undermines, or at least considerably diminishes, the narrative's coherence. He first translates *voluit [dare] donum ad regem* ('he wanted [to give] a gift to the king'), a translation which, it has to be said to his credit, he at least marks as 'uncertain' (*interpretatio incerta*: CSCO 477:56). Then, however, he proceeds as if the following were not intended as a specification of the gift given by Eulogius—in Arras' reading we never find out what that allegedly was—but rather a completely new statement about how the emperor reciprocated by granting Eulogius his splendid residence (or, rather,'garden', as he chooses to translate *ʿaṣäd: et appropinquavit rex et dedit ei hortum magnum pulchrum:* 'then the emperor approached [him] and gave him a big and beautiful garden'; CSCO 477:56).

336. Literally 'do you not know?' (*ī-ya'märkä-nu*).

337. Literally 'they [beat me up]' (*zäbäṭunī*).

338. Literally 'my soul [was / became] small'. The copula is only implied in *ni'ist näfsiya,* in accordance with the rules of Giʿiz grammar. While certainly not

ungrammatical, the phrase appears unidiomatic. This could be attributed to the text having been translated from Arabic and not being an original composition (see also nn. 231, 253, 285, 288, and 322). However, there is also the possibility that the extant Gi'iz text has been corrupted, through metathesis, from an original *si'nät näfsiyä* ('my soul was incapacitated / lost its strength'), which would make for much more idiomatic Gi'iz.

339. Literally 'Suddenly sleep covered me' (*wä-kädänänī niwam gibtä*).

340. Literally 'to speak on it' (*kämä itnaggär wistētu*).

341. Literally 'Now my soul was compressed / narrowed' (*wä-ṣäbäbät näfsiyä*).

342. For Gi'iz *täfäṣṣämku*; the translation is uncertain. Literally, *täfäṣṣämku* means 'I was completed, I was finished', and from the latter there is perhaps a semantic bridge to the meaning I here propose as contextually adequate. Arras renders *täfäṣṣämku* as *obmutui* ('I fell silent'; CSCO 477:57). It is unclear how he arrived at this translation.

343. Or 'crucified'; Gi'iz *säqälä* has both meanings; see nn. 59, 146, 170, and 173 above. While the setting of the scene at Golgotha suggests 'to crucify' as preferable, the following 'by my arms' makes much more sense if one here assumes a suspension, not a crucifixion. Also, the preceding binding of Daniel points in this direction. The Greek is unambiguous: 'they hung me up with my arms tied behind my back' (see Gk I.9).

344. Arras' Gi'iz text has *siräy*, which would be the *masculine* singular of the imperative. Theoretically this masculine form could be explained through the assumption that Daniel here addresses himself to Christ instead of to Mary, but contextually that makes little sense. Textual corruption appears as the more likely explanation for masculine *siräy* instead of the required feminine *siräyī*. Verbs with stems ending in *y* are particularly prone to this type of corruption as in casual pronunciation the feminine ending *-ī* can easily merge with the almost homophonous stem-final *-y*.

345. The Gi'iz text of Arras' edition has 'I then went to the sea constantly praising him [God], (*wä-ḥorku ḥabä baḥir inzä a'akkʷito*). However, this makes little sense as the text states earlier that Daniel had already boarded a ship. Indeed he had seen the whole previously recounted dream vision while asleep on that ship. One would therefore expect the Gi'iz text to say *wä-ḥorku ma'dotä* [not: *ḥabä*] *baḥir inzä a'akkʷito*, literally 'I went *across* the sea constantly praising him [God].' This is precisely the substance of the above translation, which for stylistic reasons is non-literal.

346. Gi'iz: Yosyos; see n. 332. The greek dossier again is unambiguous: 'Three months later, I heard that Justin had died and Justinian was now emperor in his place.'

347. Literally 'with his soul alone' (*bä-näfsu baḥtītu*).

348. My translation of Gi'iz *täsäwwärä bä-gibrä miskīnan*, literally 'he hid / screened himself through the act of (*gibrä*) paupers / wretched ones /beggars'.

In addition to its basic meaning—'act, action'—*gibr* can take on a host of other meanings, e.g., 'affair, matter, thing; manner, mode; condition, situation; office, charge, function, duty; service, business' (Leslau, *Comparative Dictionary of Ge'ez*, 178; see also nn. 214, 237, and 326 above). In the translation of this phrase some amount of interpretation is thus inevitable. One manuscript here has the variant *bä-gibrä mink^wisinna*, which, adhering to my contextual interpretation of *gibr*, I would translate as 'by posing as a monk'. The existence of a variant at this very spot indicates that even within the ethiopian textual tradition *bä-gibrä miskīnan* was felt to be not without its problems. Greek: 'Then he fled and went to his own village and exchanged his clothing for that of the country folk who lived there' (see Gk I.9).

349. Literally 'returned to himself' (*gäb'a habä ri'su*).

350. This translation follows the variant *hiqqä kimmä wä-hata'kä wistētu dihrä*, which Arras relegates to the apparatus. His main text, *hiqqä kimmä zä-im-tikat hati'a bä-wistētu dihrä*, would have to be translated, to my understanding, as 'in it you later almost became a sinner as of old', which would make little sense. Arras himself translates as *paulum abfuit quin caput tuum olim perdidisses in eo postea* ('once you later just barely escaped losing your head in it'; CSCO 477:58), which philologically I find rather puzzling. Greek has only: 'Eulogius, you wretch, get up, take your stonecutting tools and you too go, before you also lose your head. There is no royal court here!' It thus lacks an equivalent of the problematic last phrase of the Gi'iz text.

351. Presumably the reference is to the specific rock formation where the opening to the treasure cave was.

352. Literally 'on them' (*wistēta*).

353. Literally 'in it' (*wistētu*); the reference to the cave is inferred from the context.

354. Literally 'his earlier labor / effort' (*dikamo zä-haläfä*).

355. Or 'face'; Gi'iz *gäṣṣ* has both meanings.

356. Ps 104:24.

357. Ps 75:7.

358. Come with Abba Daniel and Eulogius to the latter's house, that is. There is a leap in time here in the narrative: Abba Daniel skips telling us how, after Eulogius' appearance at nightfall, they recognized each other again and how Eulogius, following his usual practice, went around gathering and taking in unsheltered travelers for the night. By now the reader / listener is expected to fill this part in.

359. Greek: 'I wish that you had not even had what you had!'

360. For more information on this currency unit, see n. 322 above.

361. Arras, *Geronticon*, CSCO 476:304-306; CSCO 477:207-209. For parallel ethiopic versions see Abba Daniel's long hagiography as well as the Synaxary excerpt for 7 Takhsas above.

362. The Giʿiz text so far runs: *Yibē Abba Dani'ēl inzä* . . . . Read with a different syntactic division, this could also be translated as 'Abba Daniel says: While . . .' (as indeed Arras does: *Dixit abbas Daniel: Dum* . . . . CSCO 477:207). The linguistic basis for this ambiguity in the Giʿiz text has been explained in the discussion of the analogous situation at the beginning of *Geronticon* No. 72 (see n. 315 above). Here, as there, however, it makes better sense to regard the third person singular masculine verb *yibē* as referring to the narrative itself (and therefore translate 'it says') rather than to Abba Daniel as narrator (resulting in 'Abba Daniel says'). Otherwise one would have to assume that Abba Daniel tells the following story about himself in the third instead of the first person, which would be odd.

363. In the parallel narrative of Abba Daniel's long hagiography, the city's name is given as Armon. This city can with some confidence be identified with modern-day Armant, about twelve miles south of Luxor. During the early christian centuries Hermonthis (its greek name, though the greek dossier has Hermopolis) was a provincial capital and hence a town of a certain importance.

364. Literally 'a monastery in which there were virgins' (*minēt zä-wistētu dänagil*).

365. The abbess.

366. A 'Monastery of Jeremiah' existed near Saqqāra, about fifteen miles southwest of Cairo. This location would make it a possible, indeed a plausible, way station *en route* from Scetis to Ar[mi]mon / Armant / Hermonthis (see n. 363 above). Whether a nunnery ever existed there alongside the monks' monastery, however, is unclear. Yet even if it did, it would have to be considered strange if Abba Daniel sought shelter for the night there rather than among fellow monks in the immediate vicinity. Or was the monks' monastery purposefully left out of the narrative for didactic reasons? Or are we rather to assume that the reference is to another 'Monastery / Nunnery of Jeremiah' rather than the institution near Saqqāra? See Chapter One, n. 88.

367. Giʿiz, unlike English, distinguishes between genders in the second person. Both imperative verb forms in this sentence, as well as the equivalent of the english pronominal 'you', appear in Giʿiz in their masculine singular forms, even though they clearly refer to the abbess. The repeated occurrence of these masculine forms makes it unlikely that they are simply mistakes. They probably should instead be seen as stylistic devices: they express the idea of the desexualization of the abbess in the eyes of the speaker, the fact that she, in her ascetic life, is regarded as 'male'. Moreover, they may be markers of respect in recognition of her quasi-masculine position of authority. See n. 371 below.

368. Scetis was not—and is not—a monastery but rather a wadi (modern Wādī an-Naṭrūn), a strip of land with water in mostly arid Egypt, with a number of monastic communities.

369. Literally 'at the place of the Elder' (*ḫabä mäkanä Arägawī*). The scene is reminiscent of Christ's triumphal entry into Jerusalem (Mk 11 and parallels).

370. Giʿiz: *nuḫa wälīt*. Taken at face value, this phrase has no discernible meaning: *wälīt* is not in the Giʿiz lexicon, and while *nuḫa* by itself can either mean 'her length' or 'the length of ', this is not enough to salvage the phrase as a whole. How, then, can one make sense of it, and more specifically the sense 'The Ridiculous One'? A starting point is provided by the occurrence of a similar *aḥawlīt* below (n. 375), in a context which makes unequivocally clear that it must be a highly derogatory term, virtually synonymous with 'idiot'. Against this backdrop it makes sense to interpret *aḥawlīt* as an orthographic variant (as they often occur in Giʿiz) of *ahawlīt*, which then can be linked with the root *h-w-l-y*. This root denotes the semantic field of ridicule, mockery, and jeering (see Leslau, *Comparative Dictionary of Geʿez*, 220). While the proper philological analysis and interpretation of the form *ahawlīt* is not without problems of its own (see again n. 375 below), we are here primarily concerned with *nuḫa wälīt*, for the understanding of which *ahawlīt* can perhaps serve as a key. In *ahawlīt* the element *-ḫa / -ha* of *nuḫa* has already been integrated with *wälīt*. I further propose to regard *nu-* as an orthographic corruption of original *tä-*: In ethiopic script (in which each character normally denotes a sequence consonant-vowel) the two characters look quite similar. On the basis of this proposal we arrive at **tähawälīt*, which may be derived—even though imperfectly—from the verbal base *tähawläyä*, 'to be mocked, to be riciduled, to be jeered at'; therefore 'the Ridiculous One'. Specifically, the desired form from the verbal base *tähawläyä* would have to be its feminine active participle, *tähawlayīt*. The difference between this form and the reconstructed **tähawälīt* is small enough to allow us to regard the latter as a corruption of required *tähawlayīt*. Interestingly, Arras here also translates 'the very ridiculous one' (*perridicula*; CSCO 477:208)—without, however, commenting on how he arrived at this rendition.

371. Interestingly, the underlying Giʿiz imperative this time appears in the feminine singular, unlike the imperatives the disciple earlier used with the abbess (see n. 367 above). What accounts for the difference? The fact that here it is not the abbess, but an ordinary nun who is addressed, and that she, because of her status or her younger age, is considered less desexualized or less an authority figure? Or the fact that it is the other nuns—and not Abba Daniel's male disciple—who speak here, and that they can be more frank in their language because they are of the same sex as the addressee?

372. Ethiopic omits here a paragraph about eating and humility; see above, p. 49. Perhaps the ethiopic (or antecedent arabic) translator considered the episode unworthy of Abba Daniel.

373. 'Gently' renders Giʿiz *bä-bä-ḥiqq*, literally 'little by little, gradually'. Surprisingly, Arras here translates *bä-bä-ḥiqq* as 'time and again, repeatedly' (*etiam atque etiam*; CSCO 477:208).

374. Greek lacks this sentence.

375. The context clearly requires this or a similar translation for Giʿiz *aḫawlīt*; see n. 370 above). Leslau, *Comparative Dictionary of Geʿez,* 220, however, notes no lexeme *ahawlī* (*ahawlīt* would be the feminine), nor even a verb *ahawläyä* from which such a form could be derived. Moreover, a hypothetical verb *ahawläyä* would, under normal circumstances, have to be construed as a causative to the attested base *hawläyä* ('to mock, ridicule, make fun of, jeer at'), i.e., 'to incite, to mock', etc. While it appears contextually mandatory to interpret *aḫawlīt* as 'fool', the concrete form remains a bit enigmatic and is suspect of being the result of textual corruption (perhaps of *tähawalīt* again? See again n. 370 above.)

376. 'As far as I am concerned' renders Giʿiz *im-riʾsiyä*. While the meaning of the element *riʾsiyä* is clear ('my head, my self, myself'), the translation of the whole remains somewhat doubtful on account of the wide variety of meanings that the preposition *im-* can take. These range from 'out of, from' (spatial) to 'since' (temporal) to 'on account of, because of, out of' to 'from the perspective of'.

377. Literally 'respond' (*awäśśi*'). Furthermore, *bä-qidmēkin* ('before you') in *anä bä-qidmēkin qidmä mänbärä liʿul awäśśi' bäʾintīʾakin*) has been left untranslated. It makes little sense in the context since semantically it effectively duplicates the simple *qidmä* ('before'). In its form—with initial *bä-* and the final suffix *–kin* of the second person feminine plural—it appears to have been influenced by neighboring *bäʾintīʾakin* ('in your [second person feminine plural] favor'). On account of these two reasons I consider *bä-qidmēkin* to be a later accretion to the text.

378. See Gen 1:26. This reference and the use of 'Torah' do not appear in the version of this story in Abba Daniel's long Giʿiz hagiography above. The greek version makes no reference to Scripture here either, but the armenian ('because God has chosen fools such as this woman and loves them') ties what Daniel says explicitly to 1 Cor 1:27. An arabic version also includes this scriptural reference and cites the Torah; see Chapter Eight, n. 42.

Chapter 4: Syriac Accounts

1. There are fifteen sayings attributed to Daniel in the syriac *Paradise of the Holy Fathers,* but this Daniel is the fifth-century disciple of Arsenius; see Ernest A. Wallis Budge, *The Paradise or Garden of the Holy Fathers* (London: Chatto & Windus, 1907), Index, 2. 343, s.v. 'Daniel'.

2. See the General Introduction, pp. 13–15. Syr 3 ad Syr 4 are, in fact, in a different Aramaic dialect—Christian Palestinian Aramaic. I am indebted to Sebastian Brock for this information.

3. Brock, 'A Syriac *Narratio*', 269.

4. Translated by Rowan A. Greer from the text edited by F. Nau, *Revue de l'Orient Chrétien* 5 (1900) 391–396, using Paris MS BN 234, fol. 339–341 (thirteenth century). Numbers in parentheses before the title of the pieces indicate the numbers of the corresponding greek texts in Chapter One. Numbers in brackets within the translation are those of Nau's text. The title of the syriac text is 'A story concerning a blessed sister who lived in a monastery with other sisters who thought her insane and simple-minded. Also a story of a blessed patrician lady [see Syr 3 below]'. A previous translation of this story, based on Nau's text plus British Library MS Add 14649, may be found in Sebastian P. Brock and Susan A. Harvey, *Holy Women of the Syrian Orient* (Berkeley: University of California Press, 1987) 143-145.

5. Tabennisi was the site of Pachomius' first monastic settlement. Gk I.4 says these women lived in 'a monastery for women . . . called the Monastery of Abba Jeremiah'. 'Tabennesian' probably means 'pachomian'; see Chapter One, n. 125. Ewa Wipszycka, 'Le monachisme égyptien et les villes', 321, reasonably argues that the translator or editor of the syriac version probably had little or no knowledge of the monasteries in Egypt and believed that all monasteries there were pachomian.

6. The sister is a drunk in Gk I.4.

7. The one supposed insane.

8. Translated by Rowan A. Greer from the text edited by Bedjan, 6:405-417, apparently an eclectic text based on two nearly identical MSS: British Museum Add. 14.649 (eleventh century), fols. 96–99, and BN fonds syriaque 235 (thirteenth century), fols. 204–209.

9. On this saint and his shrine, see Chapter One, n. 113.

10. Approximately three in the afternoon. Nau notes, 402, n. 1, that the London MS has 'the sixth hour' (twelve noon), while the Paris MS has 'the ninth hour'. Gr I.5B has noon.

11. Gr I.5A: before the altar.

12. Job 1:21.

13. Gk I.5 is clearer: She came back and said the same thing.

14. Gen 12:1.

15. The pilgrimage shrine of Saint Menas is not in Alexandria, although two greek MSS also say it is. On this shrine, see Chapter One, n. 121.

16. See Chapter One, n. 124.

17. See Chapter One, n. 127.

18. See Chapter One, n. 128 and Index.

19. Translated by Rowan A. Greer from the text edited by F. Nau, *Revue de l'Orient Chrétien* 5 (1900) 396–401, using Paris MS BN 234 (thirteenth century), fols. 342–344. The title of the syriac text is 'A story concerning a blessed sister who lived in a monastery with other sisters who thought her insane and simple-minded [see Syr 1 above]. Also a story of a blessed patrician lady'. Numbers in

brackets within the translation are those of Nau's text. A previous translation of this story, based on Nau's text plus British Library Add 14649, may be found in Brock and Harvey, 145–149.

20. Gen 21:1-7.

21. See 2 Kgs 2:1-18.

22. Gk I.8: the old man stripped off the clothes he was wearing and said to his disciple, 'Clothe him with more than what he is wearing'.

23. The eunuch.

24. The image of the breasts like withered leaves occurs in only some Gk MSS.

25. See Chapter One, n. 41.

26. The Gk account ends here.

27. Severus of Antioch (465–538); General Introduction, p. 14.

28. See Syr 1 above.

29. Translated by Sebastian P. Brock from Müller-Kessler and Sokoloff, 3:97-98, under the title 'What Abba Daniel related to his disciple concerning a patrician lady'.

30. Translated by Sebastian P. Brock from Müller-Kessler and Sokoloff, 3:69-97, 'The Life of Eulogios the Egyptian, who was a Stonecutter.'

31. The Gk account begins in the third person.

32. Daniel's foreknowledge is lacking in the greek accounts.

33. Five PM.

34. See Chapter One, n. 226.

35. Gk I.9: He's been a stonecutter by trade since he was a young man up to today; today makes it more than a hundred years.

36. See Chapter One, n. 233.

37. Text: son. In Palestinian Aramaic, 'son' is an easy corruption of 'uncle'.

38. See Chapter One, n. 128.

39. A sweet crisp golden-brown bread, often given to children and babies and made from bread that is baked, sliced, left to dry out, and then baked again.

40. Gk I.9: the doorkeeper attacked me and beat me with rods until he had broken every bone in my body. 'Lacerated' is uncertain.

41. See Chapter One, n. 242.

42. Ps 104:24; Ps 75:7.

43. Translated by Brock, 277–280, based on a single surviving MS, British Library Add. 14645, ff. 154r-155v, which was copied at the Syrian Monastery in the Wadi al-Natrun (Scetis) in 935–936 (Brock, 270). For the significantly different and shorter greek version, see III.1 in Chapter One.

44. 'Mountain' in Coptic can denote a monastic community, and this use was likely borrowed in the Syriac.

45. 1 Tim 1:15.

46. Mt 9:13; Mk 2:17; Lk 5:32.

47. Lk 7:48. The 'woman . . . who was a sinner' is often described in later texts as a prostitute.

48. Gk III.1 lacks the remainder of the syriac version, but ends positively.

49. See Dan 7:10 and 14.

50. Or 'Indian': *hendwâyâ*. The belief that the Devil and demons took the form of Ethiopians was common in early monastic literature; see Chapter One, n. 128 and 236.

51. See 1 Sam 2:30. The wording does not agree with the Peshitta (syriac Bible), but agrees with the LXX.

Chapter 5: Armenian Accounts

1. On Clugnet and Dahlman's texts, see 'The Daniel Dossier' in the General Introduction to this volume, pp. 4–11, and 'A Note on the Greek Texts' in Chapter One, pp. 41–42. All references to notes (n., nn.) refer to notes in this chapter unless otherwise indicated.

2. References are to Leloir: volume number (with the tractates of that volume in parentheses), tractate number (with its title), and the number of the piece. Titles (and numbers in parentheses) in the left column refer to the greek dossier (Chapter One).

3. For the sake of completeness I have supplied a translation of Leloir's latin text, but Leloir does not supply the Armenian and I was unable to obtain the text. See the relevant greek accounts in Chapter One for notes.

4. Leloir, II (*Tractatus* V-IX) 119-121:V (*De fornicatione*) 47 R. References are to Leloir (see n. 2 above), with the addition of page numbers after the volume number. I have placed the accounts in the order followed in Chapter One and have supplied for each piece the information for Leloir's volume. In Armenian the title of each piece is the same: Daniel of Scetis.

5. Gk: Sergius.

6. Satan.

7. Armenian: *Enetaçik*.

8. Leloir, IV (*Tractatus* XVI-XIX) 70–72: XVIII (*De thaumaturgis patribus*) 43.

9. Gk: disciple. In the next paragraph, the Armenian switches to singular.

10. Plural.

11. See 1 Cor 4:10. Gk: Abba Mark the fool for God; var.: Abba Mark the fool.

12. See Arm 1 above.

13. Leloir, II (*Tractatus* V-IX) 201–207:VIII (*Contra ostentationem*), 3.

14. Daniel says this at the end of the greek account.

15. Gk lacks the final two sentences.

16. See 1 Cor 1:27, a reference that the armenian makes more explicit than the Gk ('for God loves drunkards such as these').

17. Leloir, II (*Tractatus* V–IX) 193–199:VII (*De sustinentia*) 49 R.

18. Sunday.

19. See Is 61:1, Lk 4:18.

20. Job 1:21 (LXX).

21. In the greek version, John is Andronicus' father-in-law.

22. See Gen 12:1.

23. Gk: the Oktokaidekaton. *Duodecim* would indicate a monastic community at the twelfth milestone, but such a community is unknown.

24. The Eucharist.

25. The armenian now follows the longer conclusion of the greek text (see Chapter One for both versions).

26. Leloir, II (*Tractatus* V–IX) 35–37:V (*De fornicatione*) 30A & B.

27. See Mt 27:24, Acts 20:26.

28. This paragraph seems to summarize Gk I.7; see Arm 6 below.

29. Gk: the Oktokaidekaton; see n. 23 above.

30. Gk: eighteen. The armenian translator apparently misread 'eighteen' as 'twelve' twice.

31. Satan.

32. Leloir, II (*Tractatus* V–IX) 111–112:V (*De fornicatione*) 36 R.

33. Greek: the Oktokaidekaton; see nn. 23 and 29 above.

34. Leloir II (*Tractatus* V–IX) 163–168:VII (*De sustinentia*) 40A and 40B.

35. Gk: 'Bring your tools and come alone with the brother'.

36. See Col 3:16.

37. See Gen 18:1-15.

38. See Lk 23:46.

39. See 2 Kings 2:1-18.

40. See Gen 3:19.

41. Lk 23:46.

42. The monastery at the fifth milestone west of Alexandria, though, according to the greek sources, it was not a monastery or monastic settlement for women.

43. Leloir III (*Tractatus* X–XV) 172–179: XIII (*De hospitalite et misericordia*) 10.

44. Arm here essentially excises the Nika riots, the reason for the emperor Justinian wanting Eulogius' death; see Chapter One, n. 242.

45. Ps 92:5.

46. Five PM in the greek sources; the usual time for eating was the ninth hour, about 3 PM.

47. Jn 20:28.

48. Ps 104:24.

49. Pss 77:14-15, 86:10.

50. Ps 113:7.

51. Ps 94:7.

52. Literally: we. Greek lacks the first person singular testimony.

53. Judgement day.

54. Leloir III (*Tractatus* X–XV) 152–153: XII (*De oratione*) 11A & B.

55. That is, outside the monastic communities of Scetis, Kellia, and Nitria.

56. See the previous note.

Chapter 6: Latin Accounts

1. Translated from Huber. The numerals in parentheses refer to the numbers of the stories in Huber's edition; numerals in brackets indicate the numbering of the greek text.

2. This shows confusion on the latin translator's part; the Thebaid is far south of Scetis. The confusion arises because at the beginning of the greek account (I.9), Daniel 'was across from the Thebaid, having with him also his disciple'. Towards the end of the story, Daniel is called 'Abba Daniel of the Thebaid'. See the map for the location of the Thebaid.

3. *Confratres.*

4. See above, p. 243. See Dahlman, 221 (l. 15), for a discussion of 'hunch-backed'.

5. About 5 PM.

6. In Gk I.9, Daniel finds himself in the Church of the Resurrection in Jerusalem, part of Constantine's Basilica of the Holy Sepulcher in Jerusalem.

7. The text shifts from singular to plural.

8. I.e. a demon; see Chapter One, nn. 128 and 236.

9. In the greek version, this takes place in the Church of the Holy Resurrection.

10. About noon.

11. Ps 113:7.

12. Ps 75:7.

13. Ps 89:6.

14. 2 Kings 2:1-18.

15. Ps 31:5, Lk 23:46.

16. See Jn 11:35.

17. Gk: at the fifth milestone outside of Alexandria, that is, at the monastic community called To Pempton.

18. Gk: the Oktokaidekaton outside Alexandria, the monastic community at the eighteenth milestone west of Alexandria.

19. Gk lacks this final sentence.

20. In the greek account (Gk II.2), Doulas tells the story of the despised monk.

21. Satan.

22. In Gk II.2, an unnamed monk, not Doulas, is the object of the community's vitriol.

23. Latin: *me.*

24. Latin: *secretarium.*

25. Three PM.

26. See Lk 24:12.

27. Gk: Abba Apollo; see Chapter One, n. 81.

28. Gk: it is better for you to be devoured by wild beasts outside rather than by those inside; see Chapter One, n. 92.

29. Gk: licking the soles of his feet.

30. There is a problem with the greek text here (there is no reason for Abba Daniel to say what he says; see, however, the disciple's behavior in Gk I.9, the story of Eulogius), which has continued in the latin account.

31. Gk: when all the sisters had gone to sleep.

32. Latin: *vicaria.*

Chapter 7: Old Church Slovanic Accounts

1. Van Wijk, 337–339. Numbers in parentheses refer to the stories in the greek dossier (Chapter One of this volume).

2. Van Wijk, 348–351, also publishes two other, very fragmentary, versions. Because they are so incomplete, they are not translated here. He notes, 347–348, '[t]hat what we actually have here are two independent translations is clear not only from the rather large number of duplicate translations, but also from the fact that the two Slavic texts have their origins in two different Greek editions'.

3. Translated from van Wijk, 340–347, from Wiener Codex slavicus 42 (**W**) and Berliner Alphabetikon (Wuk 40) (**B**). Numerals within backstrokes refer to pages of van Wijk's text. Van Wijk presents the texts in parallel columns but we have presented them here consecutively.

4. Version **B** lacks 'and strangers'. See Gen 18.

5. See Gen 21:1-7.

6. See 2 Kings 2:1-18.

7. Ps 31:5, Lk 23:46.

8. See Gen 12:2, 7.

9. Gen 21:1-7.

10. 2 Kings 2:1-18.

11. Ps 31:5, Lk 23:46.

Chapter 8: Arabic Accounts

1. For a preliminary idea of the scope of this literature, see Georg Graf, *Geschichte der christlichen arabischen Literatur*, I, *Die Übersetzungen*, Studi e Testi 118 (Vatican City: Biblioteca Apostolica Vaticana, 1944).

2. See the work in this field by Sidney H. Griffith, for example, his *Arabic Christianity in the Monasteries of Ninth-Century Palestine* (Aldershot, Hants and Brookfield, Vermont: Variorum, 1992).

3. See Samuel Rubenson, 'Translating the Tradition: Some Remarks on the Arabization of the Patristic Heritage in Egypt', *Medieval Encounters* 2 (1996) 4–14.

4. See Mikael Tarchnisvili, *Geschichte der kirchlichen georgischen Literatur: auf Grund des ersten Bandes der georgischen Literaturgeschichte von K. Kekelidze*, Studi e Testi 185 (Vatican City: Biblioteca Apostolica Vaticana, 1955); and Gérard Garitte, *Catalogue des manuscrits géorgiens littéraires du Mont Sinaï*, CSCO 165/subs. 9 (Louvain: L. Durbecq, 1956).

5. See the remarks and bibliography of Ugo Zanetti, 'Les chrétientés du Nil: Basse et Haute Égypte, Nubie, Éthiopie', in Robert F. Taft, ed., *The Christian East, Its Institutions and Its Thought: A Critical Reflection*, OCA 251 (Rome: Pontificio Istituto Orientale, 1996) 181–216, especially 209–211.

6. Graf, *GCAL* I, pp. 403–404. For translations from Greek and Coptic, see below. Graf lists a syrian orthodox manuscript that is a translation from Syriac to Arabic: Jerusalem, St. Mark Bishāra lit. 38 (1732/3), a collection of one hundred twenty-five saints' lives including 'Andronicus and Athanasia' (no. 16) and 'Eulogius the Stonecutter' (no. 17).

7. *Bustān al-ruhbān: 'an ābā' al-kanīsah al-qibṭūiyyah al-urthīdhuksiyyah ṭibqan li-l-nuskhah al-khaṭṭiyyah al-aṣliyyah* [*The Garden of the Monks: From the fathers of the Coptic Orthodox Church, according to the original manuscript*], 2nd edition (Cairo, 1956).

8. Georg Graf, *Geschichte der christlichen arabischen Literatur*, II, *Die Schriftsteller bis zur Mitte des 15. Jahrhunderts*, Studi e Testi 133 (Vatican City: Biblioteca Apostolica Vaticana, 1947) 41–45.

9. Ibid., 42.

10. Ibid., pp. 43–44 (the *Philosophical Chapters* and *On the Orthodox Faith*).

11. Joseph-Marie Sauget, 'Le paterikon du manuscrit arabe 276 de la Bibliothèque Nationale de Paris', *Muséon* 82 (1969) 363–404.

12. The manuscript in its present state is out of order. Sauget (see previous note) gives a detailed reconstruction.

13. See the General Introduction to this volume, 7–17, and Gk I.1–I.9 in Chapter One, above. [Professor Swanson completed this chapter before knowing of Dahlman's work, discussed in the two earlier references in this note—ed.]

14. Sauget, 'Paterikon', 401–404. Sauget added Vatican Sbath 90 (1688) and Vatican Sbath 182 (1695) to Graf's list (*GCAL* I, p. 42) of Vatican ar. 77 (1684, same copyist as Sbath 90); Vatican ar. 944; Oxford, Bodl. ar. christ. Uri 88; Beirut, Bibliothèque Orientale 491 (1690); and Jerusalem, St. Anne 61.

15. Aziz Suryal Atiya, *The Arabic Manuscripts of Mount Sinai: A Hand-List of the Arabic Manuscripts and Scrolls Microfilmed at the Library of the Monastery of St. Catherine, Mount Sinai* (Baltimore: The Johns Hopkins Press, 1955).

16. ff. 358v-370r.

17. ff. 55r-59r. The arabic recension of 'Eulogius' represented in these two Sinai manuscripts, like the syriac version, begins in the first person. See Chapter Four.

18. ff. 106r-111v. Atiya also indicates a copy of 'Andronicus and Athanasia' in Sinai ar. 456 (13th c.), but here we find only the very beginning of the story— the title and five lines of text—on f. 175r.

19. Yūsuf Ḥabīb, *al-Qiddīs al-Anbā Dāniyāl, qummuṣ barriyyat Shīhīt: 'an aqdam al-makhṭūṭāt bi-l-lughah al-qibṭiyyah* (Cairo: Maktabat Markaz al-dirāsāt al-qibtiyyah, 1964). I am grateful to Wadi Abullif OFM, for alerting me to the existence of this book and making a copy available to me.

20. Yūsuf Ḥabīb, *Dāniyāl*, 11. Three manuscripts of the monastery library are mentioned in the bibliography (p. 116) and sometimes mentioned in the footnotes: MS 280; MS 318; and MS 175 *nusukiyyāt*.

21. There are a number of indications that Yūsuf Ḥabīb transcribed his sources with care, for example:

- In his version of 'Mark the Fool' he draws attention to a correction that needs to be made in the arabic text: *al-Bamṭun* (= 'the Pempton') for *al-Mīṭun* (*Dāniyāl*, 59, note 1).
- His text of 'The Monk and the Demons' (*Dāniyāl*, p. 70) is very close to the greek text, although with the addition of a 'happy ending': 'The Lord opened the ears of the brother, and when he heard that [conversation] he marveled, regretted his deeds, repented, and became a successful monk'. This ending is also found in the armenian version: see Chapter Five.
- His text of 'The Thief Who Repented' (*Dāniyāl*, 70–73) is very similar— but not copied from—the text published in *Bustān al-ruhbān* (and translated below).

22. See below, 277–279.

23. Graf mentions that there is an arabic 'Life of Abba Daniel' in Paris, B.N. syr. 197 (sixteenth century), ff. 35v-37r; *GCAL* I, p. 404.

24. *Qiṣṣat ḥayāt al-Qiddīsah Anāsīmūn al-Sā'iḥah* [*The Story of the Life of Saint Anasimun the Wanderer*], written by Sa'īd Yūsuf and produced by Mājid Tawfīq (Cairo: The Church of Saint George and Saint Abraham in Heliopolis, 2000).

25. al-Qummuṣ Sim'ān al-Suryānī, *al-Ābā' al-Sawāḥ* [*The Wandering Fathers*] (Metropolitanate of Banī–Suwayf and al-Bahnasah, 1986) 96-104. Fr Sim'ān

gives two manuscripts of the Syrian Monastery, 298 mayāmir and 280 mayāmir, as his sources for the story.

26. The earliest witness I can find to the expanded story is al-Qummuṣ Anastāsī al-Ṣamū'ī–lī, *Firdaws al-Aṭhār* [*The Paradise of the Pure Ones*], 2nd printing (The Monastery of Saint Samuel the Confessor, n.d.) 85–96. A copy of this printing entered the Franciscan Library in Cairo in June 1983. In the summer of 2003 I found, in addition to the film, three published retellings of the (expanded) story of Saint Anāsīmūn published in 2001-2002, one in a collection on *The Virgin Mary and the History of the Generations of Virgins* by the Convent of Abū l-Sayfayn in Old Cairo, and two small pamphlets.

27. *Bustān al-ruhbān* 356–358. A very similar text is found in Yūsuf Ḥabīb, *Dāniyāl*, 78–80. Numerals within backstrokes refer to pages in *Bustān al-ruhbān*.

28. Or 'Ārmūn the City'. This awkward rendering of Hermopolis (as found in the greek story) was passed on to the ethiopic version; see Chapter Three, n. 77.

29. In Arabic simply *al-umm*, 'the Mother'.

30. Presumably Jeremiah, as the greek text indicates.

31. *'alā lisān*, 'upon the tongue of'.

32. *Balālīn*, the plural of *ballīn*.

33. *Habīlah* in *Bustān al-ruhbān*; *balhā'* in Yūsuf Ḥabīb, *Dāniyāl*, 79.

34. The arabic here, like the ethiopic, omits details about Daniel taking offense about the food served him.

35. *Maṭāniyāt*.

36. 'Burning of the heart': *ḥurqat qalbiha*. An inattentive scribe could quite easily transform the word *ḥurqah* into *ḥuzn*, 'sadness', which may explain the reading in the ethiopic text.

37. *Nāqūs*.

38. Yūsuf Ḥabīb's copy (*Dāniyāl*, p. 80) has simply: 'Wretched woman that I am! The Enemy has expelled me . . . .'

39. Yūsuf Ḥabīb's copy (*Dāniyāl*, p. 80) has *quwwah*, 'power'. This may well be the better reading.

40. *Minbar*.

41. *Ḥanjarah*, lit. "larynx."

42. See Chapter Three, n. 374, where 'Torah' passes into the ethiopic text. References to the Torah (Arabic: *al-Tawrāt*) are common in christian arabic literature because of the use of the term in the Qur'an. Muslims recognize the revelation of a scripture called al-Tawrāt to Moses, and so christian writers would frequently appeal to al-Tawrāt in their apologetics (along with appeals to *al-Zabūr*, or the Psalms revealed to David, and *al-Injīl*, or the Gospel revealed to Jesus).

43. *Bustān al-ruhbān*, 358–360.

44. Satan.

45. *Ballīn*.

46. Reading *qulansuwah* for *qulūniyyah*.

47. As in the previous story, Arabic has *al-umm*, 'the Mother'.

48. *Lammā aradna an yafrushna lahu fī 'uluww al-dayr*. This expression, which corresponds closely to the Coptic, may have been distorted in some copies to give something like what is found in the ethiopic text. Perhaps *yafrushna*, 'they spread out', was deformed into *yarfa'na*, 'they raised'.

49. This parenthetical aside is lacking in all other languages.

50. The rest of the arabic version is much longer than, and differs radically from, the coptic.

51. *Ba'd*, which could also be translated 'one'.

Index

Since Greek is the primary language of the Daniel Dossier, the Index does not list references repeated in other languages. For example, the Index does list important words and topics for the main greek version of Mark the Fool (I.1), but does not index words and topics in the coptic and other versions. Exceptions have been made for material not found in Greek, e.g. the extra anti-chalcedonian material in Coptic and the Synaxary readings in Greek, Coptic, and Ethiopic.

Each story is listed thus:
Mark the Fool
    Greek, 43–44
    Coptic, 105–107
    Etc.

And also, indented, under Abba Daniel